Brief and practical study helps and comments for each day's reading.

The Reader's Companion *to the* Five Day Bible Reading Schedule

Five Day Bible Reading Schedule included —
read both Old and New Testaments!

Introduction

Would you like to regularly read God's word and understand it? Could meaningful study of the Scriptures become an important part of your spiritual growth this year? Would you like to take the Bible deeply into your heart so you know God better than ever?

Welcome to The Readers' Companion to the Old and New Testaments! The goal of The Reader's Companion is to assist you in regularly studying the Bible. The Companion does this by making the Scriptures more understandable. Being able to "get it," to comprehend the Scriptures, is of enormous value to every disciple. First, reading with understanding is essential if we are to live out what we read. The Bible's goal is not simply to give us knowledge but instead to transform how we live (James 1:22). This is not possible if we do not first understand what is going on in the text, what it means, or what is being said. Secondly, when we understand the Scriptures, we are reading we are changed by them and that gives us incentive to continue and read more. All of us need self-discipline when it comes to Bible reading. Much vies for our time and attention today. With The Five Day Bible Reading Schedule you only need to read one chapter a day to complete the entire New Testament this year. If you add to that reading about four to five chapters a day in the Old Testament you can complete the entire Bible in a year. Reading all those chapters will require the self-discipline to put aside other matters and read God's word. Yet when we see in our own lives the work of God through His word we are encouraged to keep it up and to do even more. In short, nothing succeeds like success, and when you have had success reading the Bible because you are understanding it you will want to read more.

Always do the readings in the order given on the Schedule. Thus, if it lists Chronicles before Kings then the reading in Chronicles should be done first. Harmonizing all the Bible says during some eras - prophets, history, psalms - can be complicated but we have done the best we can to put material together that goes together. This too enhances understanding.

This can be a significant year of spiritual growth for you if you will dedicate yourself to the reading of the Bible. Of course, the Companion will help, but you must do the work. That means you have to persevere and even overcome discouragement. Don't quit if you fall behind or even miss a week or two. Just pick right back up where the schedule is and begin anew. The most important decision you can make about Bible study is the one you can make right now: I will do this. I will not quit, I will not give up. I'm in it for the duration. This year will be the year I set the habit of regularly reading the Bible. Make that determination, set your heart, and let's go forward to a great year of reading and understanding the Bible!

May the Lord bless all our efforts to read, understand, and live His word.

Mark Roberts

Table of Contents

Weekly Reading Schedule

Readers Companion for the Old and New Testaments

Week 1 OT January 1 - 5
Week 1 NT January 1 – 5
Week 2 OT January 6-12
Week 2 NT January 6-12
Week 3 OT January 13-19
Week 3 NT January 13-19
Week 4 OT January 20-26
Week 4 NT January 20-26
Week 5 OT January 27-February 2
Week 5 NT January 27-February 2
Week 6 OT February 3-9
Week 6 NT February 3-9
Week 7 OT February 10-16
Week 7 NT February 10-16
Week 8 OT February 17-23
Week 8 NT February 17-23
Week 9 OT February 24-March 2
Week 9 NT February 24-March 2
Week 10 OT March 3-9
Week10 NT March 3-9
Week 11 OT March 10-16
Week 11 NT March 10-16
Week 12 OT March 17-23
Week 12 NT March 17-23
Week 13 OT March 24-30
Week 13 NT March 24-30
Week 14 OT March 31 - April 6
Week 14 NT March 31 - April 6
Week 15 OT April 7-13
Week 15 NT April 7-13
Week 16 OT April 14-20
Week 16 NT April 14-20
Week 17 OT April 21-27

Week 17 NT April 21-27

Week 18 OT April 28-May 4

Week 18 NT April 28-May 4

Week 19 OT May 5-11

Week 19 NT May 5-11

Week 20 OT May 12-18

Week 20 NT May 12-18

Week 21 OT May 19-25

Week 21 NT May 19-25

Week 22 OT May 26-June 1

Week 22 NT May 26-June 1

Week 23 OT June 2-8

Week 23 NT June 2-8

Week 24 OT June 9-15

Week 24 NT June 9-15

Week 25 OT June 16-22

Week 25 NT June 16-22

Week 26 OT June 23-29

Week 26 NT June 23-29

Week 27 OT June 30 - July 6

Week 27 NT June 30 - July 6

Week 28 OT July 7-13

Week 28 NT July 7-13

Week 29 OT July 14-20

Week 29 NT July 14-20

Week 30 OT July 21-27

Week 30 NT July 21-27

Week 31 OT July 28-August 3

Week 31 NT July 28-August 3

Week 32 OT August 4-10

Week 32 NT August 4-10

Week 33 OT August 11-17

Week 33 NT August 11-17

Week 34 OT August 18-24

Week 34 NT August 18-24

Week 35 OT August 25-31

Week 35 NT August 25-31

Week 36 OT September 1-7

Week 36 NT September 1-7

Week 37 OT September 8-14

Week 37 NT September 8-14

Week 38 OT September 15-21

Week 38 NT September 15-21

Week 39 OT September 22-28

Week 39 NT September 22-28

Week 40 OT Sept 29 - October 5

Week 40 NT Sept 29 - October 5

Week 41 OT October 6-12

Week 41 NT October 6-12

Week 42 OT October 13-19

Week 42 NT October 13-19

Week 43 OT October 20-26

Week 43 NT October 20-26

Week 44 OT October 27-November 2

Week 44 NT October 27-November 2

Week 45 OT November 3-9

Week 45 NT November 3-9

Week 46 OT November 10-16

Week 46 NT November 10-16

Week 47 OT November 17-23

Week 47 NT November 17-23

Week 48 OT November 24-30

Week 48 NT November 24-30

Week 49 OT December 1-7

Week 49 NT December 1-7

Week 50 OT December 8-14

Week 50 NT December 8-14

Week 51 OT December 15-21

Week 51 NT December 15-21

Week 52 OT December 22-28

Week 52 NT December 22-28

Week 1 – Jan 1 – Jan 5

Genesis 1-2; Mark 1; Psalm 19

Gen 3-5; Mark 2;

Gen 6-8; Mark 3; Psalm 104

Gen 9-11; Mark 4

Gen 12-15; Mark 5; Psalm 148

Week 2 – January 6-12

Genesis 16-18; Mark 6;

Gen 19-20; Mark 7; Psalm 1

Gen 21-23; Mark 8; Psalm 107

Gen 24-25; Mark 9; Psalm 4

Gen 26-27; Mark 10

Week 3 – January 13-19

Genesis 28-29; Mark 11

Gen 30-31; Mark 12; Psalm 11

Gen 32-34; Mark 13; Psalm 145

Gen 35-37; Mark 14; Psalm 12

Gen 38-40; Mark 15

Week 4 – January 20-26

Genesis 41-42; Mark 16;

Gen 43-44; Galatians 1; Psalm 24

Gen 45-46; Gal 2; Psalm 108

Gen 47-48; Gal 3; Psalm 25

Gen 49-50; Gal 4

Week 5 – January 27-February 2

Exodus 1-3; Gal 5;

Exodus 4-6; Gal 6

Exodus 7-9; Ephesians 1; Psalm 105

Exodus 10-12; Eph 2;

Exodus 13-15; Eph 3; Psalm 114

Week 6 – February 3-9

Exodus 16-18; Eph 4;

Exodus 19-21; Eph 5; Psalm 33
Exodus 22-24; Eph 6; Psalm 109
Exodus 25-27; Philippians 1; Psalm 90
Exodus 28-31; Phil 2

Week 7 – February 10-16

Exodus 32-34; Philippians 3
Exodus 35-37; Phil 4; Psalm 26
Exodus 38-40; Hebrews 1;
Leviticus 1-3; Heb 2; Psalm 27
Lev 4-7; Heb 3

Week 8 – February 17-23

Leviticus 8-11; Hebrews 4; Psalm 110
Lev 12-14; Heb 5; Psalm 111
Lev 15-18; Heb 6; Psalm 31
Lev 19-20; Heb 7
Lev 21-23; Heb 8

Week 9 – February 24 – March 2

Leviticus 24-25; Hebrews 9; Psalm 81
Lev 26-27; Heb 10; Psalm 112
Numbers 1-2; Heb 11; Psalm 64
Num 3-5; Heb 12
Num 6-7; Heb 13

Week 10 – March 3-9

Numbers 8-11; Colossians 1
Num 12-14; Col 2; Psalm 28
Num 15-18; Col 3; Psalm 113
Num 19-21; Col 4
Num 22-25; Luke 1

Week 11 – March 10-16

Numbers 26-29; Luke 2
Num 30-33; Luke 3; Psalm 35
Num 34-36; Luke 4
Deuteronomy 1-3; Luke 5; Psalm 36
Deut 4-5; Luke 6

Week 12 – March 17-23

Deuteronomy 6-9; Luke 7
Deut 10-14; Luke 8; Psalm 5
Deut 15-18; Luke 9; Psalm 115
Deut 19-22; Luke 10; Psalm 6
Deut 23-26; Luke 11

Week 13 – March 24-30

Deut 27-31; Luke 12
Deut 32-34; Luke 13; Psalm 13
Joshua 1-4; Luke 14; Psalm 143
Joshua 5-8; Luke 15; Psalm 14
Joshua 9-13; Luke 16

Week 14 – March 31 - April 6

Joshua 14-17; Luke 17
Joshua 18-21; Luke 18; Psalm 15
Joshua 22-24; Luke 19; Psalm 116
Judges 1-3; Luke 20; Psalm 16
Judges 4-6; Luke 21

Week 15 – April 7-13

Judges 7-8; Luke 22
Judges 9-11; Luke 23; Psalm 17
Judges 12-16; Luke 24; Psalm 146
Judges 17-18; Acts 1; Psalm 21
Judges 19-21; Acts 2

Week 16 – April 14-20

Ruth 1-2; Acts 3;
Ruth 3-4; Acts 4; Psalm 37
1 Samuel 1-2; Acts 5; Psalm 120
1 Sam 3-5; Acts 6; Psalm 23
1 Sam 6-8; Acts 7

Week 17 – April 21-27

1 Samuel 9-10; Acts 8
1 Sam 11-13; Acts 9; Psalm 38
1 Sam 14; Acts 10; Psalm 124

1 Sam 15-16; 1 Chr 1; Acts 11; Ps 39
1 Sam 17; 1 Chr 2; Acts 12

Week 18 – April 28-May 4

1 Sam 18-19; 1 Chr 3; Acts 13; Ps 59
1 Sa 20; 1 Chr 4; Acts 14; Ps 56, 57, 142
1 Sam 21-22; 1 Chr 5; Acts 15; Ps 52
1 Sam 23-24; 1 Chr 6; Acts 16; Ps 54
1 Sam 25; 1 Chr 7; Acts 17

Week 19 – May 5-11

1 Sam 26-27; 1 Chr 8; Acts 18
1 Sam 28-29; 1 Chr 9; Acts 19
1 Sam 30-31; 1 Chr 10; Acts 20
2 Sam 1-2; 1 Chr 11; Acts 21; Ps 96, 106
2 Sam 3-5; 1 Chr 12; Acts 22; Ps 122

Week 20 – May 12-18

2 Sam 6; 1 Chr 13; Acts 23; Psalm 60
1 Chron 14-16; Acts 24
2 Sam 7-8; 1 Chr 17; Acts 25; Ps 132
2 Sam 9-10; 1 Chr 18-19; Act 26; Ps 89
2 Sam 11-12; 1 Chr 20; Acts 27; Ps 51, 32

Week 21 – May 19-25

2 Sam 13-14; Acts 28
2 Sam 15-17; Romans 1; Psalms 3, 63
2 Sam 18-20; Romans 2; Psalm 34
2 Sam 21-23; Romans 3; Psalm 18
2 Sam 24; 1 Chr 21; Romans 4

Week 22 – May 26-June 1

1 Chr 22-25; Romans 5; Psalm 78
1 Kings 1; 1 Chr 26-28; Romans 6
1 Kings 2; 1 Chr 29; Romans 7
1 Kings 3; 2 Chr 1; Romans 8; Ps 42
1 Kings 4; Prov 1-2; Rom 9; Psalm 43

Week 23 – June 2-8

Proverbs 3-5; Romans 10;

Proverbs 6-7; Romans 11; Psalm 7
Proverbs 8-10; Romans 12; Ps 144
Proverbs 11-13; Romans 13; Ps 8
Proverbs 14-15; Romans 14

Week 24 – June 9-15

Proverbs 16-18; Romans 15
Proverbs 19-21; Romans 16; Ps 40
Proverbs 22-23; 1 Thess 1; Ps 117
Proverbs 24-25; 1 Thess 2; Ps 41
Proverbs 26-28; 1 Thess 3

Week 25 – June 16-22

Proverbs 29-31; 1 Thess 4
Song of Sol 1-3; 1 Thess 5; Ps 72
Song of Sol 4-6; 2 Thess 1
Song of Sol 7-8; 2 Thess 2; Psalm 127
1 Kings 5; 2 Chr 2; 2 Thess 3

Week 26 – June 23-29

1 Kings 6; 2 Chr 3; 1 Timothy 1
1 Kings 7; 2 Chr 4; 1 Tim 2; Psalm 44
1 Kings 8; 1 Tim 3; Psalm 30
2 Chr 5-7; 1 Tim 4; Psalm 121
1 Kings 9; 2 Chr 8; 1 Tim 5

Week 27 – June 30= July 6

1 Kings 10-11; 2 Chr 9; 1 Tim 6
Ecclesiastes 1-3; 2 Tim 1; Psalm 45
Eccl 4-6; 2 Tim 2; Psalm 125
Eccl 7-9; 2 Tim 3; Psalm 46
Eccl 10-12; 2 Tim 4

Week 28 – July 7-13

1 Kings 12; 2 Chr 10-11; Titus 1
1 Kings 13-14; 2 Chr 12; Titus 2; Ps 47
1 Kings 15; 2 Chr 13-14; Titus 3
2 Chr 15-16; 1 Kings 16; Philemon
1 Kings 17-18; Jude; Psalm 119

Week 29 – July 14-20

1 Kin 19-21; 2 Chr 17; Matt 1; Ps 129

1 Kings 22; 2 Chr 18; Matt 2

2 Chr 19-20; 2 Kings 1; Matt 3; Ps 20

2 Kings 2-3; Matt 4; Psalm 48

2 Kings 4-6; Matt 5

Week 30 July 21-27

2 Kings 7-8; 2 Chr 21; Matt 6

2 Kings 9-10; Matt 7; Psalm 49

2 Chr 22-23; 2 Kin 11; Matt 8; Ps 131

2 Chr 24; 2 Kings 12; Matt 9; Psalm 50

Joel; Matt 10

Week 31 – July 28-August 3

Jonah; Matt 11

2 Kings 13-14; 2 Chr 25; Mat 12; Ps 53

Amos 1-3; Matt 13

Amos 4-6; Matt 14; Psalm 55

Amos 7-9; Matt 15

Week 32 – August 4-10

Hosea 1-3; Matt 16

Hosea 4-6; Matt 17; Psalm 58

Hosea 7-10; Matt 18;

Hosea 11-13; Matt 19;

Hosea 14; 2 Chr 26-27; Matt 20; Ps 61

Week 33 – August 11-17

2 Kings 15-16; Matt 21

Isaiah 1-3; Matt 22; Psalm 9

Isaiah 4-6; Matt 23;

Micah 1-4; Matt 24; Psalm 10

Micah 5-7; Matt 25

Week 34 – August 18-24

Isaiah 7-10; Matt 26; Psalm 22

Isa 11-13; Matt 27; Psalm 118

Isa 14-16; Matt 28

Isa 17-19; 1 Cor 1; Psalm 62

Isa 20-22; 1 Cor 2

Week 35 – August 25-31

Isaiah 23-25; 1 Cor 3

Isa 26-29; 1 Cor 4; Psalm 65

Isa 30-32; 1 Cor 5

Isa 33-35; 1 Cor 6

2 Chr 28; 2 Kings 17; 1 Cor 7; Psalm 66

Week 36 – September 1-7

2 Chr 29-31; 1 Cor 8

2 Kings 18-19; 2 Chr 32; 1 Cor 9; Ps 67

Isa 36-37; 1 Cor 10; Psalm 123

2 Kings 20; Isa 38-40; 1 Cor 11; Ps 68

Isa 41-44; 1 Cor 12

Week 37 – September 8-14

Isa 45-48; 1 Cor 13

Isa 49-52; 1 Cor 14; Psalm 69

Isa 53-55; 1 Cor 15; Psalm 128

Isa 56-59; 1 Cor 16; Psalm 70

Is 60-63; 2 Cor 1

Week 38 – September 15-21

Isa 64-66; 2 Cor 2

2 Kings 21; 2 Chr 33; 2 Cor 3; Ps 71

Nahum; 2 Cor 4; Psalm 149

2 Kings 22-23; 2 Cor 5; Psalm 73

2 Chr 34-35; 2 Cor 6

Week 39 – September 22-28

Habakkuk; 2 Cor 7

Zephaniah; 2 Cor 8; Psalm 74

Jeremiah 1-4; 2 Cor 9; Psalm 130

Jer 5-7; 2 Cor 10; Psalm 75

Jer 8-10; 2 Cor 11

Week 40 – Sept 29 - October 5

Jer 11-13; 2 Cor 12

Jer 14-16; 2 Cor 13; Psalm 76

Jer 17-20; James 1

Jer 22, 23, 26; James 2; Psalm 77

Jer 25, 35, 36, 45; James 3; Ps 133

Week 41 – October 6-12

Jer 27, 28, 29, 24; James 4

Jer 37, 21, 34; James 5; Psalm 79

Jer 30-33; 1 Peter 1

Jer 38, 39, 52; 1 Pet 2

2 Kin 24-25; 2 Chr 36; 1 Pt 3; Ps 126

Week 42 – October 13-19

Lamentations; 1 Peter 4; Psalm 137

Obadiah; Jer 40-42; 1 Pet 5; Ps 147

Jer 43, 44, 46; 2 Pet 1;

Jer 47, 48, 49; 2 Pet 2; Ps 80

Jer 50-51; 2 Pet 3

Week 43 – October 20-26

Ezekiel 1-3; John 1

Ezek 4-6; John 2; Psalm 82

Ezek 7-9; John 3

Ezek 10-12; John 4; Psalm 83

Ezek 13-15; John 5; Psalm 136

Week 44 – October 27-November 2

Ezek 16-18; John 6

Ezek 19-21; John 7; Psalm 84;

Ezek 22-24; John 8; Psalm 134

Ezek 25-27; John 9; Psalm 85

Ezek 28-30; John 10

Week 45 – November 3-9

Ezek 31-33; John 11

Ezek 34-36; John 12; Psalm 86

Ezek 37-39; John 13; Psalm 87

Ezek 40-42; John 14

Ezek 43-45; John 15; Psalm 135

Week 46 – November 10-16

Ezek 46-48; John 16

Daniel 1-3; John 17; Psalm 88

Dan 4-6; John 18

Dan 7-9; John 19; Psalm 91

Dan 10-12; John 20

Week 47 – November 17-23

Ezra 1-2; John 21

Ezra 3-4; 1 John 1; Psalm 92

Haggai; Zechariah 1; 1 John 2; Ps 138

Zech 2-5; 1 John 3; Psalm 93

Zech 6-8; 1 John 4

Week 48 – November 24-30

Zech 9-11; 1 John 5

Zech 12-14; 2 John; Psalm 94

Ezra 5-6; 3 John; Psalm 95

Esther 1-3; Rev 1; Psalm 139

Esther 4-6; Rev 2

Week 49 – December 1-7

Esther 7-10; Rev 3

Ezra 7-10; Rev 4; Psalm 97

Nehemiah 1-3; Rev 5;

Neh 4-6; Rev 6; Ps 98

Neh 7-9; Rev 7; Ps 140

Week 50 – December 8-14

Neh 10-13; Rev 8

Malachi 1-4; Rev 9; Ps 2

Job 1-3; Rev 10; Psalm 29

Job 4-7; Rev 11; Ps 99

Job 8-11; Rev 12

Week 51 – December 15-21

Job 12-14; Rev 13; Ps 100

Job 15-17; Rev 14

Job 18-20; Rev 15; Ps 141

Job 21-23; Rev 16; Ps 101

Job 24-27; Rev 17;

Week 52 – December 22-28

Job 28-30; Rev 18

Job 31-33; Rev 19; Ps 102

Job 34-36; Rev 20
Job 37-39; Rev 21; Ps 103
Job 40-42; Rev 22; Psalm 150

Back to Table of Contents.

The Reader's Companion for the Old Testament

Week 1 Genesis 1-15

Reading 1 - Genesis 1-2

Introduction to Genesis - Welcome to the book of origins. Genesis shows us the origins of our world (chs. 1-2), the origins of the nations (chs. 2-11) and the origins of Israel (chs. 12-50). This helps focus us on Genesis' importance. It spans two thousand years in its text while other books at most span a few hundred. Genesis becomes the essential background for understanding the events which make the nation of Israel the people of God and make God the one true God that must be worshiped by all. Genesis develops several key themes: that God is the Creator, sin's consequences are disastrous, that God's ultimate purpose is to restore man to fellowship and relationship with Him, and that this purpose will be worked out through Abraham's children, the nation of Israel.

1 - These chapters brim with some of the most important material in all of Scripture. The key issues today in Genesis 1 is how does this square with evolution's portrayal of origins and are these days literal 24-hour periods? The answer to the first question is that Genesis 1 and 2 do not and cannot be fit into the evolutionary model. The Bible reader must decide if he/she will believe what inspired writers (and Jesus, see Matthew 19:4-5) said about our world's origins or stand on the shifting sands of scientific theory. Biblical creationism is absolutely indispensable to the Bible's integrity (see Jno 1:3; Acts 17:23; 1 Cor 11:8-9; Heb 11:3). The days in chapter 1 are certainly 24-hour periods of time. That is the natural reading of the text, the word "day" is never used figuratively when attached to a number, Exodus 20:11 uses this as 24-hour days, and Adam is made on Day Six but is only 130 years old when Seth is born (Gen 5:3). Make certain you allow this chapter to speak to you of God's unimaginable power and the authority that comes to Him as our Creator.

2 - Note how these verses are beautifully arranged to echo the opening verse (1:1) and add information to them. These accounts are complementary, not contradictory. Chapter 2 also adds to the "special-ness" of man that began in 1:26. Man there is made in God's image, but here we learn that man is subservient to God. Verse 9 is a source of much discussion. What is the "knowledge of good and evil?" It may mean the consequences of what would happen if Adam disobeyed God's commands. Man would have known good if he obeyed; he knew evil because he disobeyed. The chapter closes with the founding of the first home. Notice how everything is now good. This changes dramatically in chapter 3.

Reading 2 - Genesis 3-5

3 - In chapter 3 the devil arrives (verse 1) to test man (note John 8:44; Rev. 20:2; 2 Tim. 2:12). The text wants us to see the folly and foolishness of sin. Man had so much and threw it all away stupidly. Notice the test wasn't intelligence but man's trust of God. Is God good or is He holding out on us, keeping us from what we really need? Eve paints God too harshly (verse 2), adding prohibitions God did not make, and sin enters the world. A key issue here is the woman leading the man, a reversal of God's plan that has disastrous consequences (verse 6). As bitter as this chapter is it does contain hope: the first Messianic prophecy (verse 15).

4 - Watch the spread of sin, and it's not just a repeat of chapter 3. Sin gets worse (murder!), and man becomes embittered against God. This chapter also introduces the theme of the oldest son

not always getting the blessing or being the one through whom God works. There is much speculation about Cain's failure (verses 4-6), but in truth all we know is that he sinned. God did accept grain offerings later (Lev 2:1ff) so his lack of a blood sacrifice may not be the problem. He certainly failed to "offer by faith" (Heb 11:4) but faith means more than just positive instruction. Faith involves a heart that longs to serve God. Cain never seems to possess such a heart. The chapter concludes with two genealogies (verses 17-26). Cain's descendants invent various technologies and seem to specialize in sin (verses 23-24). Seth's line worships God (verse 26). The story of those two families continues in chapter 5.

5 - Chapter 5 looks dull and dry to the modern reader, but it certainly confirms the effects of sin as spoken by God. Man does die! Indeed, the exception to this unfailing rule in chapter 5 points out some interesting points on how to live and not die (verse 22).

Reading 3 - Genesis 6-8

6 - The interesting note about marriage between the "sons of God" and "the daughters of men" that begins the chapter attracts much speculation (verses 1-2). Some see angels marrying women here, but this seems doubtful. Why are men punished for what angels do (verse 3)? How would angelic marriages relate to the increase of sin we find in verse 5? Instead what we should see is that the line of Seth, known for worshiping God, intermarried with the line of Cain, known for worldliness and sin. The result was the dilution of godliness and the spread of evil everywhere. verse 9 uses the language of Enoch's deliverance from death to speak now of Noah: he walked with God. The point is clear: God delivers those who walk with Him. The chapter ends with an emphasis on Noah's obedience (verse 22). That is how one walks with God.

7 - Chapter 7 tells of a worldwide cataclysm of unprecedented dimension. Remember, if this was simply a local flood Noah could have walked to safety. Notice again Noah's obedience (verses 9, 16).

8 - The chapter begins with "God remembering," (verse 1) a phrase that means God acts decisively (Exo. 2:24). Noah patiently waits and is rewarded for his obedience.

Reading 4 - Genesis 9-11

9 - Chapter 9 shows us a fresh start for creation. The earth had been filled with violence, but now begins anew with the same command given to Adam and Eve. This is the third time God blesses man (1:28; 5:2) and the third time man is told to multiply (1:28; 8:17). Unfortunately, sin reappears as well (9:18-27). Many look for hints of a more sinister deed by Ham than what the text simply reports but in a society that values honoring parents as the Old Testament world did this is more than enough. The Bible is stressing that the Flood did not cure the problem of sin. Sin marches on.

10 - This table of nations shows how the world was repopulated. The focus is shifted squarely to Shem (verses 21-31), showing him to be the most important.

11 - How did the nations become so divided? The tower of Babel shows how man's pride ruins everything, as sin continues. Man is deliberately violating God's command to "go forth," choosing instead to cluster (verse 4). The chapter ends with a man named Abram (verses 27-32), one of the most significant characters in human history.

Reading 5 - Genesis 12-15

12 - God calls Abram (verses 1-3), a call Abram will gradually fully accept (notice Abram does

not leave his family at first). Abram is made three great promises: his descendants will be a great nation, they will inherit Canaan, and the Messiah (the remedy to the sin problem begun in chapter 3) will come through his lineage to bless the world. These promises will be refined and further explained as we journey with Abram but they form the basis of the Old Testament. Why is the Bible about the Israelites? Because they are Abraham's descendants and God wants us to see how He fulfilled His promises to them. Notice how Abram doesn't trust God's promise of care, so he tries to protect himself with lies (verses 11-13). Yet God still bears with Abram and cares for him! We want to keep our eye on Abram's growing faith. He's not the astonishingly obedient and faithful man we think of him as being quite yet, is he?

13 - Chapter 13 shows just how God did keep His word: Abram became exceedingly rich. Riches can cause problems (verses 5-8), leading Abram to finally pull away from family, as God had always wanted. One of the key themes we want to observe is how Abram's faith develops. People think of Abram as a giant of faith from the very beginning but this is not so. Abram isn't even in complete obedience to God here!

14 - Lot is the Bible's version of that crazy family member who is always getting into trouble. Lot's interest in financial prosperity over spiritual things (13:11, 13) pays off badly when the city is attacked and he is taken in the raid. Abram rescues him (what riches - Abram owns 318 slaves!, verse 14). On the way home Abram meets Melchizedek, one of the most mysterious figures in the Bible. We know little of him but Hebrews 7 makes it clear he is a unique and significant Bible figure as he is both king and priest. Even one as great as Abram pays a tithe to him!

15 - Abram is afraid (verse 1), perhaps that the raiders will return, or that the lands he got in the division with Lot can't sustain him, or because he has no son. God reassures Abram, spelling out the promises in even greater detail. The covenant ceremony (verses 9-21) is strange to us but it means "let this happen to me (i.e. be cut in half) if I fail to honor the covenant." God uses the local customs Abram was familiar with to swear a great oath to Him and reassure Him. Romans 4:1-5 and James 2:21-23 both use verse 6 as a model of how we are saved by faith today, but that faith does not exclude obedience. Back to Table of Contents.

Week 2 - Genesis 16-40

Reading 1 - Genesis 16-18

16 - Read verses 3-4 carefully and you'll hear Genesis 3 all over again. It sounds just like what Eve did! We need to learn from this account the foolishness of trying to "help God!" Abram's lack of leadership here causes strife in his home and will cause further troubles down the road. Where is Abram's faith in God's promises? Notice again that Abram struggles in his walk with God just as people do today. It will be thirteen years before God speaks to Abram again (compare 16:16 and 17:1).

17 - Chapter 17 is a watershed in the Abraham story. It marks a most significant turning point, and the Bible does all it can to alert us to how crucial these events are. Notice it is very precisely dated. A cluster of dates (16:16; 17:1, 17, 24) mark this section out as special, just as the flood story is marked. Also striking here is the change of name for Abram and Sarai to the more familiar Abraham and Sarah. Further, there are five long speeches from God. This culminates in the sign of circumcision. Abraham's immediate obedience is striking (verse 26).

18 - Abraham's amazing relationship with God is demonstrated here, especially in God's patience with Abraham's attempts to intercede for Sodom and Gomorrah (verses 22-33). Why does God tell Abraham His plans? Because that is what friends do (verse 17), and Abraham can use it as a teaching opportunity (see 19:27-28).

Reading 2 - Genesis 19-20

19 - This is an incredible story of wickedness and disbelief, wrapped up in God's unbelievable patience with Lot. Finding Lot smack in the middle of city life in Sodom (the city gate was the center of town life, verse 1) is disappointing. It will cost him his family. The depravity of the men of Sodom is frightening (verse 5). We wonder that Lot would offer his daughters - perhaps he was grasping at straws and trying to say anything that would stop these wicked men (verses 8). Notice that even when struck blind they don't go home but keep trying to sin (verse 11)! Lot's story ends miserably in incest and shame. 2 Peter 2:7-8 commends him but sometimes it hard to see why!

20 - Chapter 20 finds Abraham lying again. He still doesn't fully trust God to care for him, does he? Verse 3 shows that God does respect sincere hearts and good intentions. Verse 11 reveals Abraham's wrong assumption about these people! Assumptions like this get us in trouble.

Reading 3 - Genesis 21-23

21 - The weaning of verse 8 could take place as late as three years old. Ishmael is 13 years old here. Sarah's unhappiness (verse 10) is that Ishamel might inherit along with Isaac. This was very hard on Abraham, showing again that we reap what we sow. Abraham's mistake in chapter 16 just keeps bringing a harvest of strife! The chapter ends with God once again making good on His promise to care for Abraham (verses 22-34).

22 - This is one of the most famous, and most difficult to read, chapters in the Bible. It represents Abraham at his highest point, displaying a trust in God that is dazzling. What Abraham is told to do appears to violate God's very nature (verse 2). His immediate obedience is awe-inspiring to see (verse 3a). Hebrews 11:17-19 tells us the affirmation of verse 5 was based on faith. "Know" in verse 12 has troubled meaning. It just means knowledge confirmed by action. God knows everything (Psalms 147:5). This is merely God speaking in a way we can understand, i.e. "You

have demonstrated your trust with your deeds." We need to take this chapter to heart. Here is how faith acts when human thinking contradicts God's word! Note the use of this story in Rom. 8:31-32; Hebrews 11:17-19 and especially James 2:21-23.

23 - The death of Sarah must have been hard for Abraham. Along with that, Abraham realizes that for all his journeying in Canaan _ the so-called Promised Land _ he doesn't own a square inch of it! The chapter shows the respect with which Abraham was held by the Canaanites, and reminds us again that God's time is often not ours.

Reading 4 - Genesis 24-25

24 - Chapter 24 highlights again God keeping His promises (verses 1, 35). We're encouraged to see Abraham's faith as well (verse 7). He trusts that God will help the servant find the right woman. That woman is Rebekah (verse 15) who unfortunately has a greedy brother, Laban (verse 30a). We will see much more of Laban's greed in years to come.

25 - Abraham's death gives the author of Genesis the opportunity to "tidy" up several loose ends. One of the big keys is verse 18 where we learn that Ishmael's family (verses 12-18) settled outside the land of Canaan. Ishmael is not the child of promise and he and his descendants do not live in the promised land. Verses 29-34 contain a huge event, as Esau sells off his birthright. The birthright is not the same as the blessing that Esau loses in ch. 27 (27:36). What was the birthright? The birthright was the double portion given to the firstborn and the special privileges that go with being first (cf. Gen. 43:33). Esau cares little for this honor and foolishly sells it for a plate of stew (verse 33).

Reading 5 - Genesis 26-27

26 - Isaac doesn't make the mistake Abraham made of going to Egypt. God tells him to stay in Canaan (verse 3) and he does so (verse 6). However, Isaac shows the same lack of faith in God's protection his father had (verse 7). These Philistines (verse 8) are not the Philistines of Saul and David's day. We are unsure who they are. "Laughing with" (ESV) (verse 8) is a euphemism for physical intimacy. Note that like with Abraham God blesses and cares for Isaac (verses 12, 29b). Verse 34 raises further issues about Esau's character as he marries not one but two Canaanite women!

27 - Chapter 27 is full of questions. Doesn't Isaac know the oracle of 25:23? Why doesn't Isaac bless the whole family (as Jacob does in ch. 49)? Interestingly, what looks like a deathbed scene in verse 1 is hardly that. Jacob will be gone for 20 years (31:38) and return to see his father's face (35:27). The over-riding theme is that God's purposes cannot be over-turned. For whatever reason Isaac seeks to make Esau the one whom God

will use in bringing about the fulfillment of the great promises to Abraham but it is not to be. God has announced His intent (25:23) and that is what will happen. You cannot fight against God successfully! In this chapter we also have profound insight into Jacob's character. He is a schemer and trickster par excellence, even willing to use God's name in his deception (verse 20)! God will have to remold a man like this for him to be useful to the Lord! Back to Table of Contents.

Week 3 - Genesis 28-40

Reading 1 - Gen 28-29

28 - The remodeling of Jacob's character begins straightway. Rebekah's deception costs her the son she loves. This chapter is marked off by vows (see verse 13 and then the closing vow in verse 20). All of this material is built on the idea that Jacob will come home someday. Jacob must have been confused and afraid. He would need encouragement, and fortunately, God provides it. Note the repetition of the promises to Abraham in verses 13-15. Those promises go forward in the person of Jacob now, and they are the basis of a ladder up to heaven. The way to God is found in the promise of the Messiah to come.

29 - Chapter 29 shows the trickster getting "schooled" by Laban, the master trickster. Jacob arrives in Haran and is relieved to find relatives (verse 11). Shortly he finds himself being fooled by Laban into marrying an extra wife (verses 24-25)! This leads to the Great Baby Race (29:30-30:24).

Reading 2 - Gen 30-31

30 - While some might think the prospect of having four women vie over you enticing this verses actually reveals the sadness and depravity of polygamy. Jacob really only loves Rachel, yet often he cannot be the wife he loves and when he is she is unhappy! Further, we should see that sex does not equal love, as Jacob is with Leah sexually several times but she knows she is unloved (29:32). Verse 14's mandrakes may be a plant that was thought to make one fertile. The chapter ends with Jacob ready to leave Haran, having received God's blessings in an abundant way as God promised (verse 43).

31 - The emphasis here is on God's care (note verses 5, 7, 13, 24, 29, 42 that all explicitly give God the credit for Jacob's prosperity). Jacob is a changed man. He no longer relies on his wits but trusts instead in God! Interestingly, the covenant of Mizpah (verses 46-49) is often cited in a very warm and fuzzy context, but here it was anything but that. Jacob says "You stay on this side of the boundary and may God get you if you come after me!" He has had it with his troublesome father-in-law hasn't he?

Reading 3 - Genesis 32-34

32 - Chapter 32 is filled with tension. Jacob has wanted to go home for so long, but what of Esau and his desire to kill Jacob? In the moment of crisis Jacob prays (verses 9-12). In his prayer Jacob asserts his obedience (verse 9), shows humility (verse 10), uses God's past actions to bolster present faith (verse 10b), asks God specifically for help (verse 11) by claiming the promises God made (verse 12). What a model of prayer! The episode of Jacob wrestling with God (verses 22-32) is shrouded in mystery. Why does God attack Jacob? How can Jacob hold God? When does Jacob realize he is wrestling with God? The key here seems to be Jacob's name change. "Jacob" means "trickster" but that is changed to "Israel" (verse 28). "Israel" means "God fights" - the idea may be that God will fight for Jacob and so he doesn't have to live by trickery any more. God will see him through the confrontation with Esau in the morning. Some are confused by verse 30 because the Bible affirms no man can see God and live (Exodus 33:20). This simply means Jacob saw a manifestation of God. No one can see God in His pure unaltered, unshielded form and live.

33 - Verse 2 doesn't make Jacob look very brave does it? In verses 12-15 Jacob doesn't seem

very interested in hanging around with Esau. Is he afraid this good mood will pass? Perhaps a better reason is that he has been told to go home and this isn't it so he needs to press on (31:3, 13, 32:10).

34 - This material seems almost out of place, but it provides key insight into Jacob's fathering style. After reading this chapter we can easily believe brothers like this would sell Joseph into slavery. In verse 2 the language is very violent. The term "lay" is used in Scripture for the sexual relationship, but is not the same as the term "to know" which is better for the marital relationship. This is nothing but a sexual assault. Count the personal pronouns in verse 30. This is very bad fathering. Jacob seems unconcerned about sin or about innocents who were murdered. His main issue is his own personal safety! Such poor fathering can only reap a harvest of misery, as we will see.

Reading 4 - Genesis 35-37

35 - Chapter 35 seems a little disjointed. But much of this relates to how Moses has been telling the stories of the patriarchs in a set order: divine call, obedience, promises reaffirmed, journey, birth of sons, death of wife, genealogies, etc. Verse 1 tells that it is time for Jacob to pay the vow he made so long ago (note verse 7). Verse 4 is very disturbing. Why did Jacob's household have idols in it? Some think this might have been spoils taken from Shechem (ch. 34). Verse 5 explicitly points to God's care once again, as God keeps His word to Jacob. Verse 20 describes a kind of a tombstone. The site was known as late as Jeremiah's time (Jer. 31:15). Reuben's conduct in verse 22 is very serious because it shows how Reuben was trying to seize first place in the family. The man who possesses his father's harem stands to be first when the father dies (see 2 Samuel 12:8). Jacob won't forget it (see Gen 49:4).

36 - This material looks totally useless . Why do we care about Esau's genealogy? First, genealogy and relationship were important to Israel. This text establishes who the Edomites are and their relationship to Israel. Second, this fits the pattern of Genesis as it deals with the patriarchs, always giving the line of the non-promise family first. Thus we are learning who really matters in the story. Finally, the chapter establishes that Esau's descendants move out of the land of promise and live in the south (see 37:1).

37 - Verse 1 sets up right away that Jacob is living in the promised land as he should. Verse 2 designates a new section in Genesis with the familiar "these are the generations of ——" marker. One of the dominant themes in the Jacob-Joseph story that follows is God's providence. Joseph is not the hero here - God is! The Bible never says anything negative about Joseph, but the conduct of verses 2-11 seems, at least, to be very unwise. Verse 3's coat is famous but many don't realize what it meant. Jacob gave a "royal robe" to Joseph, clearly signaling to all that Joseph was the firstborn and would be treated as such. Leah's children are "out" and Rachel's boy is "in." Jacob's blindness at the strife such would surely cause is simply amazing. Note how in verse 12 Jacob would have reasons to be concerned about his family's safety in the area of Shechem (see Gen 34) wouldn't he? The convoluted reasoning of "murder is wrong but selling him is okay" is astonishing (verse 27). Jacob is deceived in verses 32-33, giving a good example of lying without words.

Reading 5 - Genesis 38- 40

38 - This material appears to be out of place and little more than an interruption to the Joseph narrative. It does establish that Joseph is gone a long time. It also furthers the theme of

deception. Jacob deceived Isaac, his boys deceived him, later Joseph tricks the brothers and here Judah is fooled. Probably most importantly, we get to see some changes in Judah. Jacob mourns for Joseph but Judah doesn't seem to mourn at all for his sons. He appears to be a hard man. Yet later, in 44:18ff he tenderly appeals for Benjamin with great warmth. What happened? The confession of 38:26 fits right in here - he is a changed man. Character change is a chief concern of Genesis, enough that the story stops off here to let us see it. Verse 17's reference to a pledge means he must give her security that he will pay for her services later. This figures also in how Judah is exposed (verse 25).

39 - Verses 2-3 sound exactly like how God had been with Abraham when he went to Egypt (see also verse 21). Verse 9 is just as stellar as it gets. Joseph is far from home, has every reason to justify/rationalize sin and yet refuses because he keeps his sights clearly on what God wants. Stunningly faithfulness results in worse circumstances for Joseph - at least for the immediate future. But God was still with Joseph (verse 23). We need to learn not to use bad situations to decide if God is with us!

40 - Lots of time probably passed here (verse 1). From 37:2 and 41:46 we can calculate the total time of slavery and imprisonment for Joseph was 13 years . Did Joseph wonder if God had forgotten him? Yet in verse 8 he shows a clear understanding of how God holds the future in His hands. In verse 20 we get a great lesson on real prophecy: it is specific and it comes to pass. Of course the cupbearer didn't bring Joseph's name up (verse 23). Who would want to remind the king of that time when he suspected his cupbearer of bad things and threw him in jail?

Back to Table of Contents.

Week 4 - Genesis 41-50

Reading 1 - Gen 41-42

41 - Underline in your Bible all the places where God is mentioned/credited to here and you will quickly see the Scripture's emphasis in this story. A double dream was for double emphasis (verse 32), meaning Pharaoh must pay attention to the dreams and act decisively. Verse 51 is ironic, for the very name shows Joseph has not really forgotten home.

42 - Joseph's brothers arrive in Egypt (verse 3) and our story takes an incredible turn. Three main points will be made here: (1) God's providence in caring for the promise He made to Abraham, (2) the change in Joseph's brothers, and (3) the importance of forgiveness. Verse 9 connects to those dreams so long ago. Look at the guilty consciences these men have lived with for so long (verses 21, 28)! Sin imprisons, doesn't it? Joseph is careful here (verse 23) because he needs to learn what kind of men his brothers are now. Are they sorry for what they did to him? Verse 38 reveals that Jacob didn't trust his boys, did he? He could remember when his son Joseph disappeared and there seems to be lingering suspicions, doesn't there?

Reading 2 - Gen 43-44

43 -This may be the greatest story of forgiveness and a lack of seeking revenge ever recorded. Joseph has totally trusted in God and has no need of such. Reuben is not in good standing, Levi was part of the Shechem mess and Simeon is in Egypt. That leaves Judah (verses 3-5). In verse 34 Joseph sets it up so that Benjamin is favored. He wants to see how the brothers will react to such favored treatment. Will they abandon the favorite again?

44 - Chapter 44 shows Joseph putting huge pressure on the brothers (verse 12). Will they give up Benjamin like they did him? Verse 16 holds the key: real confession of guilt and sin. Verse 18 begins the longest and most impassioned speech in Genesis. At first reading it may appear to be little more than a recapitulation of what has happened, but if you look closer it reveals real repentance.

Reading 3 - Gen 45-46

45 - Joseph's remarkable willingness to look on the "bright side" and give all credit to God (verses 5-9) shows his remarkable character. Remember, what the brothers did was wrong and the fact that God brought good from it doesn't excuse them. It just points to how great God is!

46 - God reassures Jacob that it is alright to go to Egypt (verse 3). The promises are reaffirmed and there is the added information that Egypt is where they will become a great nation. Verse 26 tells us of the small band that came to Egypt. Num 1:46 tells us over 600,000 fighting men came out. How God blessed Israel!

Reading 4 - Gen 47-48

47 - Jacob's summary of his life (verse 9) is fairly accurate. Life has been difficult, but many of the difficulties came because of what he did! We are so steeped in liberty and democracy that verse 20 sounds like cruel exploitation. The people of Egypt certainly don't see it that way (verse 25).

48 - Chapter 48 has Jacob adopting Joseph's sons as his own (verses 5-6), ensuring that Joseph will receive a double portion. This is why there is no tribe of Joseph in Israel - he is represented by Ephraim and Mannaseh. Again we have a reversal, with the younger getting the "goodies"

instead of the older (verse 14).

Reading 5 - Genesis 49-50

49 - This is the Bible's first long poem, mixing prophecy and blessing. Jacob looks ahead and speaks to the future of each tribe as they go to Canaan. As we expect, verse 4 has Jacob transferring the "first born-ness" from Reuben. Verse 5 references the destruction of Shechem (Gen 34). Verse 10 is the key here. The scepter and "Shiloh" refer to the power and authority of the Davidic kings, ultimately fulfilled in the Messiah, Jesus the Christ.

50 - Verse 5 emphasizes where Jacob's people really belong: Canaan. Verse 15 is a classic example of people expecting the worst of others because, as the brothers reveal, this is how they would act if the situation was reversed! Verses 24-25 conclude Genesis on a note of great certainty that the promises made to Abraham will be fulfilled. Back to Table of Contents.

Week 5 - Exodus 1-15

Reading 1 - Exodus 1-3

Introduction to Exodus - Exodus is a clear and obvious sequel to Genesis. In the Hebrew it begins with the word "and" showing connection to what went before. Biblically speaking the exodus is the most significant event in the Old Testament. It is the event that makes Israel the people of God and moves them forward as the tool God will use to bring the greatest promise to Abraham, the Messiah, to fruition. Time and time again the Bible refers to the Exodus as the definitive proof of God's power, greatness and love for Israel.

1 - One of the key ideas in the chapter is the multiplication of Israel's population (note verses 7, 10, 12, 20). The promise to Abraham to make his descendants a great nation is coming to pass! Verses 1-4 virtually repeated Gen 35:22-26, showing the close tie of Exodus to Genesis. Verse 8 opens 400 years after Genesis 50. What happened? Why doesn't the Bible cover that long silent period? Because that material doesn't advance the story of God fulfilling the promises to Abraham in His quest to save sinful humanity. The story resumes when something important happens. That "something" will actually be a somebody: Moses. Verses 13-14 show how God providentially makes Egypt a place Israel will be glad to leave. The chapter concludes with Pharaoh and God locked in a struggle. God wants to multiply Israel and Pharaoh wants to limit their population growth. Some get lost in verses 19-21 thinking God blessed lying. No, God blessed their courage. They should not have lied and we should know lying is always wrong without the Bible having to stop the story to tell us.

2 - Chapter 2 introduces us to Moses. His life divides neatly into three periods: first forty years he lived in Egypt, the next forty years he was a shepherd in Midian, and the final forty years he was the Deliverer (see Exo 7:7; Acts 7:23, 25, 30; Deut 34:7). Verse 12 shows a Moses ready to act but one that has not learned patience and submission to God. Verse 15 makes it clear that Israel isn't much interested in leaving Egypt. Moses' father-in-law, Reuel (verse 18), is later referred to as "Jethro" (3:1) which may be a title.

3 - Do we realize what an improbable choice Moses is? He failed in chapter 2 and ran away! But forty years of shepherding have prepared him to be God's man ... if he will just agree to go! The exact location of

Horeb or Sinai (verse 1) is much debated but not important to us. Remember, it has been 430 years since God has spoken (verse 4). God last spoke in Genesis 46:2-4 to Jacob. Verse 8 emphasizes the Promised Land heavily. Verse 11 doesn't sound like the proud man of 2:11 does it? Moses has learned humility and been emptied of himself! What does God's name, "I Am who I Am" mean (verse 14)? The idea here is the "One who always is" and emphasizes God's eternal nature and power. He has the power to deliver Israel! Some object to verse 22 claiming it is stealing, but the term should be "ask" not "borrow." The Israelites do not begin their journey violating the command not to steal!

Reading 2 - Exodus 4-6

4 - The only excuse God gives any credence to is this one because people should not be asked to believe a message from God without proof. So God provides Moses the means to back up the incredible claims he makes (verses 2-9). Verse 10 is not true (see Acts 7:22). Verse 13 is the truth: Moses just doesn't want to do it. God never lies to Moses, telling him clearly that Pharaoh won't listen (verse 21). This is the first we hear of "hardening his heart," a major theme in what is

to come. Verses 24-26 are puzzling. It seems Moses had failed to circumcise his children. He cannot be God's messenger if he won't submit to the message (see Gen 17:9-14).

5 -Remember the question of verse 2. It is exactly what the plagues are designed to answer. Pharaoh will learn who God is! Note the reasonableness of the request in verse 3, and that Moses isn't requesting liberation of Israel at this point. Pharaoh's harsh reaction (verses 6-9) seems brilliant. By verses 20-23 the people's spirit is broken and Moses and Aaron seem to have lost faith in God. Did they not expect any opposition to God's word?

6 - Moses and Aaron need a better understanding of God's plan. God affirms the promises to Abraham again (verses 2-3). God also tells Moses and Aaron his purposes in why He is doing as He is: to teach Israel who God is (verse 7). God could have "vanished" Israel from Egypt and "popped" them into the Promised Land at once but that wouldn't build faith. The chapter ends with a genealogy (verses 14-30) that shows what nobodies Moses and Aaron really were. If God hadn't been with them (repeated in verses 10-13 and verses 26-30) they would have failed completely.

Reading 3 - Exodus 7-9

7 - The war between God and Pharaoh begins in earnest. Verse 5 is a huge key. The plagues are not random events but carefully chosen actions that directly target Egypt's false deities (Egypt had a frog god, for example), reveal them to be frauds, and teach all (including Israel) who really is God. If the student will underline every occurrence "you will know that I am God" as he/she reads in the text the crucial importance of this idea will be seen. We do not know if the magicians did a trick or were enabled by demonic power to duplicate Moses' wonders (verses 11-13). They provide those who don't want to believe a reason to do so (verse 13).

8 - The magicians would have been more impressive if they got rid of the frogs, not made more (verse 7)! Note the emphasis in verse 10. This is what the plagues are about. The fourth plague seems to have been a biting fly, which would be particularly unpleasant.

9 - 9:16 reveals God's agenda: Pharaoh is nothing but an instrument to reveal God's greatness. This explains verse 12's statement that God hardened Pharaoh's heart. The hardening of the heart can happen because of how a person reacts to God's message. Often the illustration of butter and cement is used. The same sun melts one and hardens the other. But more is working here than just that. God has given Pharaoh plenty of chances to obey and he refused. Now God, in His sovereignty, determines to use Pharaoh to teach His people who God is and humble Pharaoh (note verse 17). We should learn from this that a person who doesn't want to do right, who sets himself against God as Pharaoh did, may well be used by God as an example to others so that they may come to know God. Verses 20-21 provides a great example of how real faith always works.

Reading 4 - Exodus 10-12

10 - Verses 1-2 further explain the hardening of Pharaoh's heart exactly as explained above. Verse 3 reveals that what sounded so good from Pharaoh in chapter 9:27-28 was fake repentance.

11 - One final plague will come. Notice how Pharaoh's stubbornness hurts many innocent people. Sin always affects more than the sinner!

12 - As the Passover is used by Jesus to explain His death and the new covenant in the Lord's Supper (see Mt. 26:17; Mk. 14:12; Lk. 22:7-8) is extremely important material. What can be

more important than an event that resets the calendar (verse 2)? This event marks the Israelites becoming God's people, as they are redeemed from horrible judgment and death by the grace and mercy of God. Note the importance of their faithful obedience so they can receive God's grace (verse 28). Verse 29 has a punishment-fits-the-crime feel. Egypt had killed so many Israelite first-borns and now that comes back to haunt them.

Reading Five - Exodus 13-15

13 - Verse 1links Israel's redemption from slavery with the redemption of the firstborn. God "owns" the people now, an important idea for Christians today (see 1 Cor 6:20; 1 Peter 1:18-19). "Sanctify" means to consecrate, set apart for God's use.

14 - We are uncertain of the exact site of the Red Sea crossing (verse 2). Incidentally, the widely circulated Internet story that Egyptian chariot wheels have been found at the bottom of the Red Sea is a hoax. Verse 11 reveals a stunning lack of faith on the part of Israel. Did they not see the Plagues? Verse 31 tells us God's actions finally seem to have had the desired effect. As we see that scene again by the eye of faith may it have the same result on us today!

15 - contains one of three songs composed by Moses (Deut 31:22; Ps 90). The overwhelming emphasis is on Jehovah God, who is mentioned by name ten times. Notice there is no emphasis or mention of Moses. He has learned a lot from the time when he would deliver the people on his own! Verses 6-10 well summarize the song: God's righteous anger unleashed on those who resist and fight against Him. Both Egypt and Israel now know who is God! Sadly, Israel doesn't let the Plagues and Red Sea deliverance transform their faith as they grumble against God (verses 22-27). One of the big themes in this part of Exodus is grumbling. Except for two references (Josh 9:18; Ps 59:15) every other occurrence of "grumbling" in the O.T. is found in Exodus 15,16, 17 and Numbers 15, 16, and 17! Back to Table of Contents.

Week 6 - Exodus 16-31

Reading 1 - Exodus 16-18

16 - It has been exactly one month since leaving Egypt (verse 1). All the newness the adventure, the joy of being free, even the death of the Egyptians at the Red Sea, would be behind them now. Now there is nothing but boring, wearisome traveling. That may contribute to the grumbling we see here. It shows us how we need to be ready to persevere with the Lord and serve without complaining over the "long haul." Note verse 4: God was testing and training Israel already! Manna comes from the Hebrew word "what?" and we are still asking exactly what it is (verse 14). We do not know except that it was the miraculous provision of the Lord. Verse 15 shows us that part of manna's purpose was to teach day to day dependence (see Deut 8:3). The stubbornness of these people is truly amazing (verse 27)!

17 - This episode is referred to in Deut 6:16 and Matthew 4:7. Don't confuse it with what happens in Numbers 20. That is a completely separate event. The people are being tested by God but unfortunately they grumble and test God instead (verse 3). Moses' outstretched arms represent an appeal to God for help (verse 11).

18 - The point here may be the contrast between Amalek and Jethro. Two Gentile groups encounter Israel - one is destroyed while the other helps. We do know when Zipporah and family left Egypt (verse 2). Perhaps they went on ahead after the Exodus. We wonder if verse 9 indicates conversion? Moses lived with him 40 years - did he teach Jethro? It is important to see that Moses can take advice from others - even from a non-Israelite!

Reading 2 - Exodus 19-21

19 - Chapter 19 is a watershed chapter. In this chapter the people arrive at Sinai (verse 2) and spend the rest of Exodus here. For a year Israel will be at Sinai, learning and building. No less than fifty-eight chapters of Scripture happen here (Exo 19-40; Lev 1-27; Num 1-10). That means some of the most crucial events in the Bible occur here, framed by the covenant between God and Israel. In many ways the rest of the O.T. is simply the story of how Israel kept (and didn't keep) this covenant. As if that isn't important enough, for the first time the people of God receive law. God will now work with a whole nation, not just the heads of families. This law will serve as the basis for the covenant relationship with God and His people, and was an extension of the Abrahamic promise. What is it like to live with God? How must a people act who dwell with the Lord? What does holiness mean and look like? The Law of Moses answered those questions. Verses 5-6 spotlight how the Israelites were the chosen people of God, giving them three special ties. They were a "treasured possession" (God's valued property set aside for His purposes (see also Deut. 7:6; Titus 2:14), a "kingdom of priests" (everyone in the nation, initially, would be a priest), and a "holy nation," a nation of people that would show the world the right way to live. Verse 15 provides a dramatic contrast to idol worship and its perverse orgies. Sexual relations within marriage were not wrong (see 1 Cor 7) but this was not the time for that.

20 - The giving of the Ten Commandments stands as a monumental moment in history. It has been observed that the 10 Commandments are not like any other law. They are very simple, contain no penalties, could not be enforced by human courts (how can a court detect coveting?), and emphasize individual responsibility, not group salvation. The first command (verse 3) deals with the object of worship: God and God only. The second command (verses 4-6) prohibits idolatry in any and every form. Any attempt to "make God" necessarily

leaves something out and thus distorts who God really is. Verse 5 confuses some but we must not let human ideas about jealousy color our view of God. This doesn't mean God is suspicious of others, it means He deserves our sole devotion and expects it. "Visiting the iniquity of the father on their children" doesn't impugn the justice of God but refers to how God's judgments have far reaching affects. Verse 13 says life is sacred. Some translations have "thou shalt not kill" which leads to every kind of misunderstanding. The term is "murder," not "kill." Verse 17's prohibition of coveting forever puts to rest the idea that the Old Testament didn't care about the heart. Coveting is a desire for something so strong a person will do anything to get it. The chapter closes with information about building altars, essential for the covenant ceremony in chapter 24.

21 - Various laws to keep order and peace in the nation of Israel begin here. Slavery, while allowed, is tempered (verses 1-11), and life is seen as absolutely sacred (even unborn life, verses 22-23). There is a symmetry in these laws as the punishment must fit the crime.

Reading 3 - Exodus 22-24

22 - Emphasis on integrity is seen in verses 8 and 11. Note the change to the first person as God expresses concern for oppressing foreigners (verses 21-24).

23 - This section emphasizes justice. There is also an emphasis on worship with a forward look to the time when they will be in Canaan (verses 20-33). Verse 33 is one of the key verses for Israel's history.

24 - Verse 1 resumed the story from 20:21. Note verse 8 - it is the blood that seals and ratifies the covenant (see Hebrews 9:15-23). Many miss the significance of verses 9-11. Look carefully: people eat in God's presence! The Bible is the story of humanity being restored to a right relationship with God where we can be with Him and live in His presence. This is what Adam and Eve had and forfeited. Now we see a little bit of that regained via the Law of Moses. It isn't a perfect situation and it's not all we would want but it is a start.

Reading 4 - Exodus 25-27

This material can make for tedious reading but it is important. The Tabernacle was an extremely important building in Israelite history. A couple of points worth remembering are that it was very small (the tent itself would be about 45 feet by 15 feet), it was tremendously beautiful (with bronze, silver and gold used in graduated steps as one moved closer to the Holy of Holies), and it was very, very separate. There was a linen fence around the Tabernacle, meaning few Israelites ever saw inside the Tabernacle, and only one Israelite ever saw inside the Holy of Holies. It is also important to note that scripturally there is no basis for allegorizing the Tabernacle's details (i.e. the two staves of the ark of the covenant represent the Old and New Testaments, etc.). As you read these instructions keep your eye on several key points. First, God has His reasons and we must obey. Obedience to the pattern as revealed is heavily stressed in Exodus. Second, God's inapproachability. The Tabernacle was better than nothing, but it was, in effect a very pretty barrier between God and His people. The Law did not completely open up the way to God. Much can be learned here about reverence as well. People did not drop in on God for a quick visit! Finally, the details of worship matter to God. If you tire of reading this material let this point sink in again and again. Let no one say "We can worship as we please - God doesn't care." The enormous amount of material dedicated to describing a worship structure shows otherwise!

Reading 5 - Exodus 28-31

28 - The ephod mentioned repeatedly here is a special garment a priest wore as a sign of his

office. Verse 30's reference to Urim and Thummin shows how they knew all about these stones but we certainly do not. Urim and Thummin were the means by which decisions were made (see Numbers 27:21; Exo 22:8-9) but we are not sure how.

29 - Note verses 45-46. The purpose of the Exodus was so God could live among His people and that is exactly what happened. The Tabernacle was placed in the center of the camp with the Tribes arranged around it. God and His people once again were dwelling together.

30 - We are not entirely certain of the purpose of the census tax in verses 11-16.

31 - When God wants a task done He will raise up those who can do it and invest them with the skills necessary (see verses 1-5). The chapter ends with an explanation of how the Sabbath is a sign of the covenant between Israel and God (verses 12-18). Back to Table of Contents.

Week 7 - Exodus 32 - Leviticus 7

Reading 1 - Exodus 32-34 -

32 - This chapter records one of the most stunning sins ever. While Moses is gone receiving the Law the people grow impatient so they build an idol and worship it! The calf is probably the bull Apis from Egypt. Notice that the idol is identified with Jehovah (verse 5). Verse 6's "rose up to play" is a euphemism for sexual activity (see Gen 26:8). Thus this was nothing but copying Egyptian and Canaanite idol worship complete with perverse activity in the name of "worship!" The people were idle, impatient, ungrateful (note verse 1's "this

Moses") and lacked good leadership. Sin followed. Moses prays about God's reputation (verse 12) a powerful way to pray. Look at his character growth here - in chapter 3 he didn't even want to go and now is interceding for the people! Verse 20 contains a summary of Moses' actions, with specific details then to follow. Evidently all sinful activity didn't cease just because Moses appeared (verse 27), so stronger measures were needed. Notice that in verses 30-33 Moses tries to make atonement for the people by offering himself! At the end of the chapter we are left wondering where God and Israel stand. Will He still be their God? Will they go forward? The whole project is at a crisis point!

33 - the key issue in the chapter is verse 2: God is not going with the Israelites any more. Instead an angel will lead them. Verses 7-11 are a parenthesis that detail Moses and God's usual procedures. The action resumes in verse 12. In verses 12-23 Moses' pleads with God for the divine presence (note verses 15-17) and that intercession works. God will continue with the people of Israel.

34 - The covenant is renewed as God will again go with them. In verses 1-9 Moses is treated to a special manifestation of God. It is an awesome and incredible self-disclosure by the Lord. From it we learn of God's commitment to love (mercy) and justice. Don't get lost in verse 7. God is not unfair and this doesn't mean God punishes the innocent. "Visiting" is always related to idolatry (note Exodus 20:5; Hosea 8:13; 9:7,9; Jeremiah 14:10; Lamentations 4:22). These passages help us understand that God is a jealous God and will not tolerate the substitution of non-gods for Him. On a national level this means God will judge the nation that worships idols (see 2 Kings 23:26). On an individual level it simply means the consequences of sin may be forced upon children and grandchildren (especially the sin of idolatry). The wickedness of idolatry changes a culture and community - a sad consequence all must bear. Note the request of verse 9: it is Moses' chief concern. The rest of the chapter (verses 10-28) renews the covenant between Israel and God. Moses' shining face (verses 29-35) is made much of in 2 Corinthians 3:17-18.

Reading 2 - Exodus 35-37

35 - Huge lessons on giving are learned here. Note verse 5, 21, 22, 26 and 39. Giving is not a percentage matter. It is a heart matter! Hearts that are 100% given to God never have trouble finding the right percentage. In verses 30-36:1 Bezaleel and Oholiab are chosen to lead the Tabernacle project. God's wisdom in this is evident. They had a pattern to work from but trouble could still arise over who would do what, or matters of judgement like what to make first, or what tool to use, etc.

36-37 - These detailed instructions present the reader some difficulty because they appear tedious and tiresome, but there is value in reading through them all. By so doing we will see the worth of the Tabernacle (it must have been truly splendid) as well as see God's determination to have His worship done as He desires down to the last detail. God sweats the details and so do His people!

Reading 3 - Exodus 38-40

38-39 - This material completes the Tabernacle construction. Catch the emphasis in chapter 39 on "as the Lord commanded Moses." We must do what God says and that is especially true in worship!

40 - Verse 1 tells us that Israel has been at Sinai one year. The emphasis remains on "as the Lord commanded Moses" as this phrase occurs seven more times. God then approves of the Tabernacle and visibly moves into His new home (verses 34-38). The fellowship and relationship between God and His people is restored, at least in some measure, as God lives among His people! What a moment.

Reading 4-5 - Leviticus 1-7

Introduction to Leviticus - Since Exodus 19:1 the Israelites have been at Sinai. They have entered into a covenant relationship with God and God is dwelling in their midst. Israel was, without doubt, God's special people. But how do they maintain that relationship? They aren't going to be at Sinai forever. They are headed to the pagan land of Canaan. What then? Leviticus describes how to live as holy people before a holy God. They need to know how to function in that Tabernacle, how to worship their God, how to live in the presence of God as His holy people. Leviticus is the blueprint for the covenant, for the working relationship between God and His people. The book has an easy breakdown:

Regulations for sacrifices, chs. 1-7

Ordination of Aaron and sons, chs. 8-10

Laws regulating purity, chs. 11-15

The day of the atonement, ch. 16

Laws pertaining to holy living, chs. 17-26 - "the holiness code"

Laws on tithes and offerings, ch. 27

Leviticus is not easy reading for today's reading. It can be repetitive and a bit wearisome. "What value is all of this for today's Christian?" the reader wonders. If we watch for several keys as we read we can gain much from Leviticus. Keep your eye on the idea of God's holiness, that sin is serious business, and that God is concerned with all parts of life. There is much here that informs our worship. We cannot worship as we want and expect to please God. Just ask Nadab and Abihu!

Readings 4 and 5 - Leviticus 1-7

Chs. 1-7 - Without getting lost in the details we want to pay attention to this important section of Leviticus. The regulations for sacrifices occupies one fourth of the book. The reader will note that the sin offering (ch. 1) and guilt offering (Lev. 4:1-5:13; 6:24-30) seem nearly the same. It is hard for us to be certain about all the differences. The peace offering (Lev 3; 7:11-36) is also difficult, though the emphasis there may be on the simple and profound joy of being in relationship with God. Guilt offerings (5:14-6:7) differ from sin offerings in that they require restitution. Application comes easily here. This is where we learn about sacrifices, what they mean, what that is all about. Since everything in Christianity is based on Jesus' sacrifice we would be very poor without this material. How would we ever understand the price of sin or blood atonement without Leviticus? Other key truths should be seen again and again as we read these chapters. For example, we learn what sin is. It is a violation of God's law (see 4:2 and 5:1). Note the repeated emphasis on "commandments." We also learn here that sin is serious business. God does not wave away sin, telling people it doesn't matter and it is no big deal. Sin costs. It requires the death of a fine, unblemished animal. That death was a sign of what happens to man when he sins (Gen. 2:16-17; Isaiah 59:1-2). Chapter 4 details how ignorance is no excuse. Perhaps most of all, Leviticus 1-7 teaches that sinners need grace. Did the Israelites want to pay the real price for sin, their own lives? By God's grace He allowed an animal to stand in for them. Grace operated even in O.T. times! In summary: Israel must have been a people aware of sin, what it means, what it costs, and what to do about it. How God's people need this now. Finally, if you have time read Hebrews 9:23-10:1; 10:14. The sacrifices of Leviticus were only shadows until Jesus came. They pointed to the "Lamb of God that takes away the sin of the world." We just cannot appreciate Jesus without this sacrifice section in Leviticus! Back to Table of Contents.

Week 8 - Leviticus 8-23

Reading 1 - Lev 8-11

8 - Chapter 8 tells of ordaining Aaron's sons. One of the key ideas here is "as Jehovah commanded" (8:5,9,13,17, 21, 29, 34, 36). That refers to the instructions of Exodus 29 which means this chapter is the execution of that pattern. Consecration (verse 10) means to be set apart, to be made holy. Verse 23 looks weird to us but it just show that hearing, hands, and feet are consecrated (devoted) to God.

9 - Chapter 9 has Aaron and sons entering the priestly office. The key here is divine approval and acceptance (verses 22-24). There has been fire before, but now great fire comes from God to show approval of all that has been done. God is manifesting His approval and acceptance of Aaron's installment and more specifically, his first sacrificing. We would do well to remember that Aaron failed miserably in the incident with the Golden Calf at Sinai. God gives sinners a second chance, doesn't He?

10 - Chapter 10 is famous for the sin of Nadab and Abihu (verses 1-3). The contrast here is between Aaron doing as he was commanded (9:11, 16, 21) and Nadab and Abihu failing to do the same. This sad story stands for all time to remind us of the folly of doing as we want, rather than obeying God. Verse 9 makes us wonder if Nadab and Abihu were drunk? The chapter closes with another problem (verses 16-20) where they didn't eat as they were supposed to. Aaron argues it is not appropriate to feast when your sons and brothers have been killed (verse 19).

11 - This section (laws regulating purity, chs. 11-15) repeatedly uses the terms "clean" or "unclean." We must understand what that meant in Israel to understand today's reading. To Israel everything was either clean or unclean. Clean or cleanness basically means "pure" or "purity." Uncleanness was the opposite of holiness, and seen as incompatible with it. Uncleanness was represented by all that was repugnant, ugly or distasteful. Some of this is, however, hard to exactly figure. How can some animals be "pure" and others not? Various ideas for the dietary, hygiene and sanitation laws have been proposed. Some have argue that some of these legislated what was not done in that society (similar to Americans not eating dog - we just don't do it). Others have seen hygiene and separation from what would cause disease or illness (which seems very good but doesn't explain everything). There is a heavy emphasis in Leviticus on separating from Canaanite ways of doing. That may be in play here - if Canaanites ate certain foods in the worship of idols we would understand God's prohibitions. In the end we have to admit that we cannot provide an explanation as to why some things are clean or unclean, but understanding everything that is behind God's law is not and was not necessary to obedience. All of this clean/unclean business revolves around the issue of a people living in the presence of God and what it takes to maintain holiness in His presence. Just as we would not expect one to come into a king's presence all filthy and dirty, so God did not wish a dirty people before Him. Jehovah dwelt among these people and expected physical cleanliness to be maintained. Chapter 11 deals with the animal kingdom. I believe there is much to be made of this list being given to prevent sickness. The clean animals were exclusively vegetarian. In a warm climate their flesh would not decay as rapidly as meat-eaters' would. We can also see the rationale for not eating crustaceans because they are sea-scavengers, and carry disease. Of course contact with the dead is an excellent way to transmit disease.

Reading 2 - Lev 12-14

12 - Chapter 12 deals with laws concerning childbirth. We have no idea why the time of impurity was different for having boys over having girls (verses 4-5).

13 - Chapter 13 begins the section on leprosy, covering how to examine for leprosy. The world here for leprosy is a generic word, that is not specific to "classic" leprosy. The same word is used of body swellings, inflamed spots, mold or mildew in clothes, fungus on the wall of the house, and even dry rot. The point here is that a person who was unclean could infect others so he had to identify himself as being unclean (verse 45).

14 - Chapter 14 deals with how to restore the unclean. There is a very unusual ceremony that took place outside the camp to show that cleansing had occurred. Notice that Jesus always urged healed lepers to obey these laws (see Matthew 8:4; Mark 1:44; Luke 17:14).

Reading 3 - Lev 15-18

15 - Chapter 15 deals with the law concerning discharges. One of the questions here is always "Why did sexual activity within marriage make one unclean" (verse 18)? Understanding clean and unclean help us understand this law. A person who was unclean could not go to worship _ they could not enter the Tabernacle grounds. Sexual activity within marriage certainly wasn't sinful but these laws made it clear that such activity did not belong in the Tabernacle. Why? Because in Canaan the people worshiped through perverse sexual activity and temple prostitution. All of this was tied up in fertility rites that would (hopefully) bless the land. God made a careful distinction here so that no one would think that was how to worship! Banning sexual activity from Israel's worship must have marked it as distinct and very different from all other religions.

This may be a good time to pause and make application of all this reading. Reading Leviticus is tough because it seems repetitious and to be disconnected from our lives. However, God still demands purity and holiness today (see James 1:27). The question of obedience that faced Nadab and Abihu faces us now. Further, these chapters show God's concern for all of life. People want to divide God out of life, as they compartmentalize life. They have work, home, fun and then religion. That won't work. God legislated how all of life was to be lived. Finally, we note that God's laws are for our good. The hygienic nature of the dietary restrictions, and the quarantine of the lepers all point to God's wisdom and our need to trust Him.

16 - Chapter 16 is crucially important because it discusses the single most important event in Israel's calendar, the Day of Atonement. Now known as Yom Kippur it is kept to this day by observant Jews. Most importantly for us, it relates directly to Jesus' sacrifice for our sins. The directions are fairly clear. The ESV uses the term "Azazel" in verse 8 onward, which may cause confusion. The term just means the "sent away goat" or the "escape goat." Atonement was made for the priest (verses 11-14), the Tabernacle (verses 15-19), and the people (verses 20-28). The atonement sacrifice is unique, requiring two goats. One provided blood for the cleansing of the people, and the other was the scapegoat, symbolically carrying sins away. The symbolism is clear: sin was removed and exterminated from the camp and the presence of God. In great contrast to the rejoicing accompanying the other feast days the people afflicted themselves (verses 29-33), probably meaning they confessed sin, mourned sin and fasted. Much is made in the NT of Christ and the Day of Atonement. It was prophesied He would be the atoning sacrifice (Isaiah 53:10), and Paul makes much use of this imagery (Rom 3:25; 4:25; 5:12; 8:3; 2 Cor 5:21). Hebrews also makes much of this (see 9:12-10:10 - the reader may find that reading this material immediately after reading Lev 16 provides insights into Hebrews previously unseen). 1

Peter 2:24 cites Isaiah 53 and 1 John 2:1 uses the term "propitiation" meaning covering, like the word "mercy seat." Jesus is our great High Priest making atonement for our sins!

17 - Chapter 17 begins the Holiness Code. The material here is primarily concerned with protecting the right relationship with God that Israel enjoyed as they lived in His presence. It details how holiness must be reflected in every part of life, even sexuality, faithfulness to covenants, justice and fairness, and worship. Every aspect of human behavior is touched on here. The key to it all is the expression, "I am the Lord." That expression occurs 32 times in these 6 chapters. I encourage you to underline each of those as we see that God is the Creator and we see the Lord exercising His right as the Creator to tell His people the shoulds and oughts of everyday life. Verses 1-9 forbid the setting up of other altars to compete with the Tabernacle. Since life is in the blood (verse 11) blood was not to be eaten as a common thing.

18 - Chapter 18 details laws of sexual sin. These laws preclude conforming to Canaanite practices (note verses 3, 24-30), and protect the sanctity of the marriage relationship. The sexual relationship in marriage is not dirty or immoral, but a wondrous blessing given by God that He protects from being misused and abused (see Heb 13:4).

Reading 4 - Lev 19-20

19 - Chapter 19 emphasizes our fellow man. There are 28 negatives here, prohibiting things that God knew would cause social disorder. Note the emphasis on the poor in verses 9-10 and how God's "welfare program" was work! We may wonder about the prohibition against mixing animals, seeds and even cloth

(verse 19), but again God's people were to understand separate-ness from the peoples around them. When they got dressed or harnessed animals they would be reminded of this spiritual truth.

20 - Chapter 20 has laws setting people as having value. Many laws from other cultures set property as having more worth than people!

Reading Five - Lev 21-23

21 - Chapter 21 gives special laws for the priesthood. They were subject to special regulations on attending funerals (verses 1-4) and marriage (verses 6-9, 13-15). Notice that just as sacrifices were to be unblemished so were the priests (verses 16-24). Some might object to this as being "politically incorrect" but God has the right to determine who serves, and the example before the people of giving God the best was important.

22 - tells of what priests could not do. The purpose of these laws is given in verses 31-33.

23 - Chapter 23 begins the great discussion of religious feasts. The Feast of Weeks or Pentecost (verses 15-22) is also called the Feast of Harvest (Ex. 23:16) because it marked the end of grain harvest. The Feast of Tabernacles (verses 23-44) marked the end of the religious year with an eight day celebration. Note the emphasis on joy associated with this feast (verse 40). In worshiping God there is a time for solemnity (verse 27) and for joy (verse 40). Back to Table of Contents.

Week 9 - Leviticus 24-Num 7

Reading 1 - Lev 24-25

24 - Chapter 24 begins with more details about caring for the Tabernacle (verses 1-9) but then tells the story of a blasphemer (verses 10-23). The story helps us see how important God's law really is. This man, part of the "mixed multitude," cursed the personal name of God, Jehovah (verse 11). Since respect for God undergirds all obedience to God's law this was a very serious matter. The legal case brought against him gives opportunity to discuss the principle of law known commonly as the lex talionis, the law of retribution. Many have thought the idea of "life for life" and "eye for eye, tooth for tooth" (verses 17-21) to be hopelessly barbaric. Of course it is nothing of the sort. Instead it forbade unlimited personal revenge for even the slightest offenses and guaranteed that capital crimes were punished accordingly. Who wants to live in a society where murderers get off lightly but if a man steals a five dollar item he is executed? The punishment should and must fit the crime. Further this law guaranteed justice for all, Israelite and stranger (verse 22).

25 - Chapter 25 sets forth Sabbath laws, including the idea of a Sabbath for the land every seven years (verses 1-7). It would take considerable faith in God to let your land lay fallow once every seven years (verses 20-21)! Take notice of verse 23's statement that God holds title to the land. The close relationship between God and the land and His people is very important in later prophetic books. As you read through the laws of redemption (verses 23-55), related to the Year of Jubilee described in verses 8-19, watch for the compassion and care that was to be extended to fellow Israelites. How we treat others matters to God!

Reading 2 - Chapter 26-27

26 - Chapter 26 deals with consequences to choices. Notice the heavy use of the "if .. then" sequence (verses 3-4, 14-16, 18, 23-24, 27-28, 34, 40-42). Many ancient treaties concluded with a section to discuss the blessings of upholding the treaty and the terrible consequences of failing to do so. This material echoes this practice. Much of the "curses" or bad consequences here are simply the result of God withdrawing His divine favor and protection from Israel. Note the special provisions of repentance in verses 40-45. God is good and ready to forgive isn't He?

27 - Chapter 27 covers special vows. These vows were beyond the regular requirements of the Law, and were not mandatory. They seem to have been made to seek the Lord's blessings. The chapter details vowing and people (verses 1-8), animals (verses 9-13), property (verses 14-29), and produce (verses 30_34). You could not vow first-born animals because they already belonged to God and anything irrevocably vowed to God ("things under the ban" verse 28), perhaps looking ahead to things taken in the battles at Canaan, or that were unholy due to use in idol worship. These verses emphasize that what one says to God is to be taken seriously.

Reading 3 - Numbers 1-2

Intro to Numbers - This book receives its name because there are two censuses taken in it. The first census was taken of the generation that left Sinai for Canaan (ch. 1), and the second is of those who resume the journey (ch. 26). Perhaps a better title might be "in the wilderness" because this book concerns mostly about the journey from Sinai to the edge of Canaan, the critical mistake made there and then the wilderness wandering.

1 - Note the date in verse 1. The Israelites have been gone from Egypt for 13 months. This means

they were camped at Sinai approximately one year. The counting here has to do with preparing for war (verse 3)

which is why the Levites are not counted. The tribe of Levi will not be used as soldiers. Verse 46's total of over 600,000 fighting men makes us estimate there would be more than 2 million Israelites in all.

2 - Numbers 2 gives us the camping and marching order. Note verse 9 saying "these shall break camp first."

Reading 4 - Num 3-5

3 - counts the Levites in verses 1-39. There is a difference in being a Levite and being a priest (verses 6-7). Priests were from the family of Aaron, worked inside the Tabernacle doing the actual offerings and services. Levites were a whole tribe who were dedicated to assisting the priests, working the physical things of the Tabernacle, etc. Remember the Levites were chosen by God based partially on their faithful service in the Golden Calf incident (Exodus 32:25-29; Deut. 10:8-9). The chapter concludes (verses 40-51) by discussing how the Levites were taken to redeem all the firstborns of Israel. God owned the first borns based on the deliverance of Israel's first borns in Egypt (Exodus 12-13). Apparently there had been 22, 273 first born children since they left Egypt, but there were only 22,000 Levites so 273 had to be ransomed with money.

4 - gives the straightforward "work orders" for each clan in the tribe of Levi. The family of Kohath covered everything and carried the Tabernacle furniture (verses 1-20). No one was to see anything at any time (verses 5, 15, 18-20), reminding us that the average Israelite never saw inside the Tabernacle or saw the furniture that was in there! The family of Gershon carried the actual Tabernacle itself _ all the veils, screens, and coverings (verses 21-28). The family of Merari carried the boards, pillars and sockets necessary to set up the Tabernacle (verses 29-33).

5 - begins by repeating some of the material on uncleanness from Leviticus (verses 1-4). The powerful lesson is clear: if God is in your midst then uncleanness must be put out. We may weary of repetition but God is teaching us through repetition. Perhaps the worldliness in the church shows how we have failed to learn it! The test for adultery (verses 11-31) must have been an awesome deterrent to what is now a common place sexual sin. We are not certain if the "wasting away" (verses 21-22, 27) meant the woman died or became barren. It does show that jealousy, while not being wrong, must be dealt with. Unresolved jealousy has no place in marriage.

Reading Five - Num 6-7

6 - Numbers 6 discusses the law for Nazirite vows. People took Nazirite vows because they wanted to dedicate themselves in a special way to the Lord. It involved a separation from (fruit of the vine, cutting hair and funerals), and a separation to (they were separated to the Lord, evidently for special service, prayer, meditation, etc.). Samson is the most famous Nazirite in the Bible (Judges 13). Aaron's blessing (verses 22-27) is well worth much study and thought. It is a beautiful and powerful statement of God's blessings upon Israel.

7 - records the donations of Israel to support the Tabernacle. While this seems repetitive we learn that everyone doesn't have to have the same _ some things should be distributed based on need. Merari's family gets the most wagons because they had the largest and heaviest burdens and no one complained about it. The reader wonders why all twelve gifts are carefully listed instead of just one summary statement? The answer is simple: no gift goes unrecorded in God's list! God

sees each gift and each giver individually. Isn't that encouraging?Back to Table of Contents.

Week 10 - Num 8-25

Reading 1 - Num 8-11

8 - Chapter 8 shows the consecration of the Levites. The Israelites lay hands on the Levites (verse 10) to present them as the people's representatives. Then the Levites lay hands on the bulls (verse 12) to show their desire to serve as a living sacrifice and be pure from sin.

9 - Chapter 9 begins with the Passover (verses 1-14). Once completed the people can "move out" for Canaan. As the journey begins we wonder how the people will know how to go, and verses 15-23 answer that question. God would guide them with the Divine cloud.

10 - In chapter 10 the journey finally begins. How thrilling it must have been to set out for the Promised Land!

11 - Here we get the pattern for what will become a common occurrence: the people complain, the Lord punishes them and Moses intercedes for the people. Notice that the "rabble" (probably people of mixed descent) start everyone complaining in verse 4. God's people can be influenced by others, can't they? How can anyone long for the days of slavery? (Verse 5). See how irrational murmuring can be? All this complaining finally does Moses in, as he bitterly asks God for relief (verses 10-15). His real problem seems to have been taking his eyes off of God and putting too much on himself, as he says "where am I" and "I am not able" (verses 13-14). God responds to this by "deputizing" the seventy elders (we met them in Exo 24:9-11) so that leadership is shared (verse 16-30). No one person, not even a Moses, can do it all!

Reading 2 - Num 12-14

12 - Chapter 12 records more problems for Moses. The charge against Moses (verse 1) that he married a Cushite woman had nothing to do with what was upsetting Miriam and Aaron. The real issue here is jealousy (verse 2). We do not know why only Miriam was punished (verse 10). Perhaps she was the stronger personality and the leader in this sin. Moses makes intercession even for those who criticize him (verse 13). He is a remarkable man!

13 - Chapter 13 is a sad chapter. The ten spies bring back a two-fold report: the land is very good, but we cannot possibly take it (verses 27-29). Their faithlessness is highlighted by Caleb and Joshua's faith (verse 30). Notice how rapidly the spirit of defeat-ism catches on. Caleb has to still the crowd! All that happened in Egypt, at Sinai and in the wilderness does not seem to have built Israel's faith. We do well to realize that even the miraculous work of God won't build faith in stubborn hard-hearted folks!

14 - Chapter 14 continues the failure of chapter 13. The people pay Moses a back handed compliment when they seek a new leader to take them back to Egypt (verse 4). That means they know Moses wouldn't take them back. The key to the whole incident is verse 8: "if the Lord delights in us He will bring us into this land." Israel should have trusted in God to do as He said! Often in Scripture the punishment that God brings perfectly fits the crime, and that is the case in verse 31. Moses' sad question in verse 41 rings true today: disobeying God never leads to success.

Reading 3 - Num 15-18

15 - Chapter 15 contains the laws of the covenant (again), showing the covenant is still in effect despite the sin of chapters 13-14. There is a strong emphasis on one law for all (verse 15). The execution in verses 32-36 illustrates the law against highhanded sin explained in verses 30-31.

God takes obedience seriously.

16 - Chapter 16 shows the problems of grumbling and disobedience will continue during the Wilderness Wandering. Once again we meet people who are jealous of Moses' position (verse 3). Korah and company are unhappy to do the tasks God gave them, even though they were needed and very important works (verse 9). Verse 11 makes clear their complaint is against God, not Moses. Some may be unhappy that God would direct the Israelites to wander in the wilderness until an entire generation died but verse 41 reveals how hard-hearted these people really are.

17 - Chapter 17 continues the story of Korah's rebellion. Aaron's rod is used as a visual aid to confirm his place and role (verse 8). The breakthrough here is that the people finally realize they need a priest (verses 12-13).

18 - Chapter 18 finishes the story of Korah's rebellion, as support for the (needed) priesthood is outlined. Verse 5 makes clear the tie back to 17:12-13. There would be most holy things (verses 9-10), to be eaten only by priests and not anyone else. Verses 11-19 discuss other holy things to be eaten by anyone who was clean. Finally the Levitical tithe is set up in verses 21-24.

Reading 4 - Num 19-21

19 - Chapter 19 gives the regulations for being purified if you touched the dead. There would be lots and lots of bodies during the Wilderness Wanderings, as more than a million people would die over the next forty years. Hebrews 9:13-14 alludes to these rituals because Jesus purges us from dead works and cleanses the conscience.

20 - Chapter 20 tells of the death of Miriam and Aaron (verses 1, 22-29). This clues us that we have moved forward to the fortieth year of Wilderness Wandering (see Num 33:38-39 to confirm this chronology). In between these deaths is Moses's great sin (verses 2-13). We are struck by what may seem as an overly harsh punishment (verse 12), however Moses' sin is just like the sin at Kadesh that doomed an entire generation: not granting God His proper place (at Kadesh they didn't trust God while here Moses didn't honor God) and, of course, being disobedient. In effect, Moses joined that group. If they couldn't come into Canaan then neither can he. It is a hard lesson but one not lost on the new generation of Israelites. When they get to the edge of Canaan they will go in without hesitation!

21 - Chapter 21 moves the people closer to Canaan. The journeying in verses 10-20 make very clear that the people now have direction. No more circling aimlessly in the wilderness. They are headed for the Promised Land now (see 33:41-47 for more detail here)! The story of the brass serpent (verses 4-9) shows that sin brings judgment. Note Jesus' use of this story in John 13:15. The two victories on the east side of the Jordan gives Israel control of the Trans-Jordan (verses 21-35). Moses will preach the sermons of Deuteronomy from here.

Reading 5 - Num 22-25

22 - Today's reading is devoted to Balaam. The reader naturally wonders who this Balaam is. Some other references seem to say he was a pagan soothsayer who did not care about God (see 22:7; 24:1; Joshua 13:22). Even if he was a true prophet, which seems doubtful, it is clear that his heart was not right with God. He wants to curse Israel because he longs for money, even if it means opposing the people of God. What a miserable story this is. In chapter 22 we quickly learn that Balaam will do anything for money, even when God tries to stop him. Moab wasn't attacked when Israel came into the Transjordan area but now the Moabites are concerned Israel could turn south and destroy them (verse 3). Remember the acts of cursing and blessing are much more

powerful at this time then just saying bad or good things about someone. In Genesis 27:37 Isaac could not change what he had pronounced when Jacob tricked him. Blessings and cursing were taken very seriously!

23-24 - Chapters 23-24 shows Balaam's frustrations. Despite his carnal desires he cannot curse Israel, though he tries four different times. Note the clear connection with Abraham's promises in 23:10 and 24:9. 24:17 speaks of the star and scepter. The star is a symbol of a ruler, meaning this is probably Christ. The New Testament will use Balaam as an example of those who love money more than God (2 Pet 2:15; Jude 1:11; Rev 2:14)

25 - Chapter 25 finishes the Balaam story with the account of Moab taking Balaam's advice. His name doesn't appear until 31:16 because the sin of the people is the focus in this account, but he is the instigator of this massive defection to the enemy camp. Verse 6 reminds us that weeping over sin is not enough. Action is required! Back to Table of Contents.

Week 11 - Num 26-36; Deut 1-5

Reading 1 - Num 26-29

26 - Chapter 26 records a census. Several truths emerge as we read through these numbers. First, this numbering is necessary to determine who will get what land in Canaan (verse 54). Second, this chapter makes clear God did as He said He would (verses 63-65). We always want to notice when the Scripture points out how God is faithful to do as He said He would.

27 - Chapter 27 grants remarkable rights to women (verses 1-11).

28-29 - Chapters 28 and 29 contain laws for various offerings. Why is this here? First, Leviticus details how to do the sacrificing, but does not cover the when or how often. The time element is dealt with here very carefully. Secondly, this would remind the new generation they must continue to serve the Lord even when reaching the land of prosperity. Finally, we should take note that these offerings were not instituted by man but by God. He and He alone can regulate worship.

Reading 2 - Num 30-33

30 - Numbers 30 deals with vows. The children of Israel are headed to Canaan, where they will be very prosperous. What if a woman rashly vowed some of this prosperity to the Lord? In some circumstances a woman's vow could be nullified (verses 5, 8, 12). It is interesting to note the rights accorded women in Israelite society, something far different from what most women enjoyed at this time. The clear emphasis in the chapter is verse 2. Vows must be kept. God keeps His word and so must His people!

31 - Chapter 31 describes God's holy war against Midian. The war is described as "vengeance" (verses 2-3), and as retribution for enticing Israel to sin (verses 15-16). Phinehas' leadership (verse 6) must have been very encouraging to the soldiers. We meet Balaam again in verse 8, and his role in the sin of Numbers 25 is now told (verse 16). Some are offended by God's wrath expressed in the destruction of women and children (verse 17). Much about this is beyond the scope of this Companion but we should never imagine God's wrath to be out of control, capricious or irrational. In other words, God's anger is not like human anger. God's wrath is expressed against sin (Romans 1:18). The Canaanite tribes we meet here and in Judges were guilty of terrible, perverse sin (such as human sacrifice) in their idolatry. They turned away from God and refused His longsuffering patience to repent (Genesis 15:16). We do well to remember that God is good, loving and kind. These are extreme measures that God resorted to only when other measures failed, and to protect the Messianic promises to Abraham. No one today has enough information, or wisdom, to question God and how He runs this world (see Romans 9)!

32 - Chapter 32 shows an unexpected windfall for Israel. The tribes of Reuben and Gad and one clan of Manasseh ask for territory on the east side of the Jordan. Initially Moses is angered at this request, imagining that the people will wonder if Reuben and Gad think Canaan can't be taken and so are quitting. Such discouragement could provoke a re-enactment of the miserable mess at Kadesh Barnea forty years ago (verses 7-8). However, God graciously grants this land to them providing they are willing to supply men for the conquest of Canaan (verses 20-22).

33 - Chapter 33 gives the record of the wilderness wandering, showing that while Israel appeared to be wandering aimlessly God knew exactly where they were at all times. It also transitions the story forward to Canaan. The wilderness wandering is over.

Reading 3 - Numbers 34-36

34 - This chapter gives the specific boundaries for Canaan (verses 1-15) and designates the officials who will participate in the division of the land (verses 16-29).

35 - Chapter 35 establishes the Cities of Refuge. If a person accidentally killed someone he fled to the nearest City of Refuge. There would be a trial (verse 12), and if the killing was determined to be an accident the manslayer would be spared, but he would have to live in the City of Refuge until the high priest died (verse 25) and could not leave the city without risking death (verses 26-27). This would be a punishment, even if not as severe as capital punishment. This chapter shows how sacred life is and how serious God expected His people to take murder (note verse 31). Murder was expected to be avenged less the land be polluted with innocent blood which defiles it (verses 33-34; note Genesis 4:10). Even an accidental killing had serious consequences.

36 - Chapter 36 deals with a special inheritance problem. If women married outside their tribe their land would then pass to another tribe when they died, resulting in another tribe taking possession of a plot of land in the midst of another tribe's lands.

Reading 4 - Deut 1-3

Introduction to Deuteronomy - A good argument can be made that Deuteronomy ought to be thought of the as the most important book in the Old Testament. It is heavily quoted in the N.T., appearing in 21 books, quoted 83 times. Jesus answers all three temptations from Deuteronomy, and kings were commanded to read it (17:18-20). Interestingly, it is actually four sermons from Moses that are framed in the vassal treaty format that was commonly used in Moses' day. These treaties were used when a greater country or empire conquered a smaller and weaker nation (the vassal nation). Those treaties had six parts: a preamble, the mutual history of the two nations, general stipulations (obligations) provisions for reading the treaty, witnesses to it, and finally the blesses and curses of keeping the treaty/violating it. Deuteronomy follows this pattern carefully and very deliberately. As it does so it spells out the covenant between God and Israel, and fully explains that it was a relationship based on love. God had done so much for Israel, He expected Israel to respond with wholehearted devotion and love.

1-2 - Moses' first speech could well be titled "Trust and Obey." Think of Moses' audience: none of them are older than sixty (except Joshua and Caleb). So Moses carefully does a historical review from Sinai to the present moment (chapters 1-3). Moses wants to show the importance of this moment. He wants them to realize the crossroads they now stand at. His message is clear: "remember what happened to your parents when they stood where you stand now." They failed (1:26-32, 43). You must do better! Believe in God, trust in Him and obey Him! 2:14 lists the wandering as 38 years, probably giving credit for the two years spent at Sinai. The total time spent in the wilderness was 40 years.

3 - Chapter 3 finishes the story of Israel's history . That leads to tomorrow's reading in chapter 4 about God's law.

Reading 5 - Deut 4-5

4 - chapter 4 drives home the need for obedience by extolling the value of God's Law. The Law is not given to burden people or ruin their lives but to guide life because God loves us (verses 1-8). God has specifically not revealed Himself in a form that could be made into an idol or statue because He wants His people to focus on His Word (verses 15-21). Moses urges love for God by telling of God's unique actions for Israel (verses 32-40). 4:44-49 begins Moses' second sermon,

"This is God's Law."

5 - Chapter 5 states the basic principles of the "treaty" or covenant, the Ten Commandments. Note the emphasis on God liberating them from Egypt (verses 6, 15). God's love caused Him to deliver these people. This should cause the only proper response from the people: heart-felt devotion. God is appealing to Israel's heart to love Him and serve Him out of love. This is always the basis for our obedience to God! Back to Table of Contents.

Week 12 - Deuteronomy 6-26

Reading 1- Deut 6-9

6 - Chapter 6 links closely to the prior section because God wants a response to His love. He wants His people to love Him with all their heart (verse 6). Moses understands this and wants Israel to realize it as well, and to pass this along to successive generations (verses 6-9, 20-25).

7 - Chapter 7 reveals the chief obstacle to Israel keeping covenant with God and loving Him as described in chapter 6: Canaanite idolatry. The ungodly people of Canaan would have to be removed, and God would do the fighting for Israel necessary to see this done (verses 18-24).

8 - Chapter 8 contains Moses' appeal to the lessons of the wilderness wandering. Remember to trust in God (verse 3, cited by Jesus in Matt 4:4). Battle against pride that might cause you to forget God (verses 11-20). Notice that disobedience is defined as "forgetting God" (verse 11).

9 - In chapter 9 Moses mounts a strong warning against self-righteousness. He reminds Israel their foes are greater than they are and so without God they couldn't possibly conquer Canaan (verses 1-3), and that God is not doing this because Israel is so righteous (verses 4-5). The facts are, Moses then says, that Israel is not very righteous at all. He then recounts Israel's failure at Sinai (verses 6-29). This history lesson continues into chapter 10.

Reading 2 - Deut 10-14

10 - Chapter 10 accents God's grace in renewing the covenant with a stubborn people, even selecting priests from a family famous for failing (verses 1-11). Israel must therefore serve the Lord with all their heart (verses 12, 16). Obedience to God, as always, is in their own best interest (verse 13).

11 - In chapter 11 Moses reminds the people what God can do, and that they have seen Him at work (verses 2-7). They must therefore choose the way of life and serve God and He will bless and protect them.

12-13 - Chapters 12-13 set forth laws concerning purity of worship. There was to be a central sanctuary to worship God, not many worship sites like the Canaanites used (Chapter 12). False prophets (13:1-5), friends deciding to do evil (13:6-11) and even whole cities (13:12-18) might challenge right worship with temptations to idolatry. All such evil must be stamped out.

14 - Chapter 14 separates Israelite ways from Canaanite ways. Israel would not mourn like pagans did (verses 1-2), and their diet would be different as well (verses 3-20). The boiling of a goat in its mother's milk is believed to be a pagan fertility rite (verse 21). The chapter ends with provisions made for the support of the Levites scattered throughout Israel in their respective cities. They would be cared for with the tithe (verse 27).

Reading 3 - Deut 15-18

15 - Chapter 15 gives us more of the regulation of day to day life in Israel. Note the strong emphasis on brotherhood in Israel, with the stronger helping the weaker. Verse 9 is key. God knows the intent of our hearts! There simply would be no need to be tight-fisted (note verse 11) for the Lord would bless them beyond their imagination.

16 - Chapter 16 sets out the regulations of the major festivals and feasts (verses 1-17) and then follows it with material on Israel's justice system that will extend into the next chapter.

17 - Chapter 17 continues the discussion of justice in Israel by detailing what to do with apostates (verses 1-7) and how to set up central tribunals (verses 8-13). Observe carefully the respect due these courts. The chapter then makes provision for a king (verses 14-20). Some have argued that Israel sinned by asking for a king in 1 Samuel 8 but these laws show how Israel was not wrong in requesting a king. The trouble in Samuel is the kind of king wanted. If the requirements given here are followed the real king would be Jehovah. The earthly king would simply be a man depending on God, not wealth or his large army.

18 - Chapter 18 gives important information about revelations from God (verses 9-22). A word from God would not come through fortune tellers or magic (verses 9-14), and all such practices are thoroughly forbidden. God will speak through prophets (verses 15-22). Jesus is final expression of verse 18 (see Acts 3:22). The test of a prophet is given in verses 20-22, but we do well to remember the other test given in chapter 13:1-5. Even if the word of a prophet comes to pass (meeting the test of chapter 18) he is not to be believed if he teaches something contrary to the already revealed will of God.

Reading 4 - Deut 19-22

19 - Chapter 19 repeats the laws of the cities of refuge, adding three cities (verse 2) to the three on the east-side of Jordan (4:41-43). These cities made sure someone accused of murder received a fair trial. Verses 18-19 provide insight into the way God's law punished people: the punishment needs to fit the crime.

20 - Chapter 20 discusses the conduct of war. Verse 4 is the key idea here. God will fight with Israel. The battle is His. In light of this, those who don't trust in God aren't needed or wanted (verse 8). Too often God's people act as if numbers matter most, placating and dragging along the faithless and unwilling. What a mistake!

21 - Chapter 21 reinforces the sacredness of human life, with its "unsolved murder" ceremony (verses 1-9). We may be surprised to find the harsh punishment to be meted out to a rebellious child (verses 18-21) but the reader should be reminded that if this was done occasionally it probably would not need to be done again, and even more importantly, God was determined for the family to be the bedrock of the nation. That cannot happen when parental authority isn't respected. Galatians 3:13 uses verse 23 to say that Christ's death not only was horribly painful but shameful in the worst way. Crucifixion said to Jews "this one is accursed of God." Jesus bears that curse for us!

22 - Chapter 22 provides for some curious reading in verses 1-12. Why couldn't men wear women's garments (verse 5) or sow mixed seed in a field (verse 9) or mix animals in the yoke (verse 10) or mix kinds of cloth in clothing choices (verse 11)? The answer is found by remembering that Israel was to be separated and holy, completely different from the pagan nations around them. They wouldn't act like them, or dress like them. They would give no place to sexual perversion or homosexual perversion. Even when it came time to sow a field or get dressed they would be reminded of their unique identity as God's people (note verse 12). The chapter concludes with laws on sexual immorality, showing how seriously God takes the sexual relationship.

Reading 5 - Deut 23-26

23 - Chapter 23 begins with those who are excluded from the worships assembly. Verse 1 doesn't sound very politically correct today, but may reflect those who had mutilated or cut themselves

in the worship of idols. The "forbidden union" of verse 2 may be with a temple prostitute. The other laws in this chapter again stress the need for God's people to be holy and pure as they were living before God on God's land.

24 - Chapter 24 does not encourage or sanction divorce, but instead regulates the practice so that it would not grow worse. The "indecency" of verse 1 is uncertain (it is not sexual immorality - a person was stoned for such). The aim of the law is to make divorce so serious and irreversible that it was not done lightly or frivolously. Jesus tells us this law was made because Israel's hearts were hard (Matthew 19:8). Divorce doesn't please the Lord. Note the law of gleaning given in verses 19-22. These laws form the basis for some of the key action in the book of Ruth.

25 - Chapter 25 regulates several parts of day to day life in Israel. Beating someone would be a severe punishment that was regulated carefully (verses 1-3). Animals could be used to farm with, but not exploited (verse 4). If land was to stay in the family then an heir to a dead man must be produced, and so the laws of Levirate marriage ensured (verses 5-10). Verse 11's stunning law may relate to this - a man's ability to bear children was very important.

26 - Chapter 26 contains the moving ceremonies and worship relating to the bringing in the first fruits of the harvest. This feast would normally happen at the Feast of Weeks (Lev 23:15, 20; Num 28:26) but here the emphasis is on depending on God, being thankful and being obedient to Him. Back to Table of Contents.

Week 13 - Deut 27-34; Joshua 1-13

Reading 1 - Deut 27-31

27 - Chapter 27 discusses an important annual ceremony in Canaan, where the Law would be read and responded to. The curses are not direct quotations of the Ten Commandments, but all are close in nature to the basic concerns of the Covenant. Verses 15 and 24 add the dimension of secrecy - God would know and punish evildoers even if everyone else didn't know!

28 - Chapter 28 is one of the pivotal chapters in the Old Testament. It maps out the history of the Israelite nation in advance because, unfortunately, they choose the curses instead of the blessings. Over and over the prophets will refer to this part of Deuteronomy as they warn of impending judgment due to idolatry (verse 23 is fulfilled in Elijah's time, 1 Kings 17:1) and God punishes His people just as He warned He would. The reader should note that more time is spent on the curses than blessings because a full description of the horror of disobedience should urge Israel to obedience. This chapter also sets before Israel the truth that life is not arbitrary, but governed by God and their response to Him.

29 - Chapter 29 begins a new sermon that runs through chapter 31. Much of this chapter can be summarized as a failure to perceive (verses 2-4) and a tendency to forget (verses 5-9). Moses recite these facts to strongly urge full obedience to God as the people enter into covenant relationship with Him (verses 10-15). The final verse (29) is often quoted but here it means that the future is unknown, but what is known is God's Word. They can and must obey it.

30 - Chapter 30 continues these ideas, making three key points. First, the cause of dispersion would be a lack of love for God as evidenced by not obeying the Law (verses 1-10). Note the heavy emphasis on the heart and loving God here (see verse 6 and verse 16, for example). However, obedience is not impossible (verses 11-14). Verses 15-20 then conclude by calling the people to decision and commitment.

31 - Chapter 31 settles the important matter of succession, as Joshua is chosen to succeed Moses. Moses sounds a somber note of warning in verse 16, a verse that summarizes much of the Old Testament we will read.

Reading 2 - Deut 32-34

32 - Chapter 32 is the song of "The Rock" (verses 4, 15, 18, 30, 31). The song makes it clear that God is good and kind, that He loves Israel and that He has fully kept His side of the bargain.

33-34 - Chapters 33-34 closes Deuteronomy. Moses blesses each tribe (in this order: sons of Leah, sons of Rachel, and then the sons of handmaids) and then dies. Notice that Moses does not die of old age but simply because God took him (verses 7). It is time for Israel to move forward into the Promised Land and time for new leadership for God's people. It is time for Joshua!

Reading 3 - Joshua 1-4

Introduction to Joshua - Joshua is an exciting and easy to read book. However, as we read it we must remember that the main purpose of such history is not our entertainment or chronology, but showing God's work. The Old Testament rotates around the Abrahamic promises of Genesis 12. Exodus shows part of those problems coming to pass as his seed becomes a great nation, but progress on the promises is temporarily blocked as the Israelites fail to have the faith needed to enter the Promised Land. The promise thread is now rejoined in Joshua as they take the Promised Land. This book will also show us much of the dangers of apostasy, while teaching us much about God (such as His faithfulness to keep His word, His holiness and graciousness). Let's read Joshua!

1 - Chapter 1 begins with the preamble to the whole book (verses 1-9). The theme of covenant obedience is repeated again and again (verses 3, 7-8, 13, 17-18). Verse 15 makes clear that rest cannot be enjoyed by anyone till enjoyed by all.

2 - Chapter 2 starts with spies, but a very different result is obtained from a spy report this time than the last time Israel sent out spies (Numbers 13). Verse 15 is a summary of how the discussion at Rahab's house ended. Then more details follow (verses 16-21). This is a very common way of reporting Israelite history in the Bible. A summary statement is then followed by the details, but readers can be confused because it appears Rahab let the spies out and then talked to them. Watch for this kind of "summary first, details to follow" pattern. The spies fool their pursuers by going west into the hills instead of directly east to where Israel was waiting on the other side of the Jordan (verse 16).

3 - Chapter 3 centers on the ark of the covenant. It is literally the center of the story, mentioned here and at Jericho. The ark serves as the reminder of the visible presence of God. God is going with His people - leading them into the Promised Land (verse 3)! Verse 7 gives the purpose for the miraculous crossing of the Jordan: accredit Joshua as the leader of Israel as Moses was. The people could've built boats, or waded across at a shallow crossing. Instead God duplicates the Red Sea miracle so the people will trust Joshua and trust in God (verse 10). What a sight to see, especially since it was springtime and the Jordan was at flood stage (verse 15)!

4 - Chapter 4 is devoted to remembering the great Jordan river crossing. Joshua constructs two memorials - one in the center of the Jordan (probably visible at low water times) as described in verse 9, and one at Gilgal (verses 8, 20). The purposes for these memorials were two-fold: God wanted Israel's children taught of His great power (verses 4-7, 22-23) and God wants to be known by all people (verses 21-24).

Reading 4 - Joshua 5-8

5 - Chapter 5 begins preparations for the conquest of Canaan. First the people of God need to complete the covenant of circumcision. Verse 2 is puzzling. What is the "second time?" It may be that the older generation's circumcision in Egypt is reckoned as the first circumcision, and since those under forty were not circumcised in the desert this is deemed the second. That brings up the question of why they weren't circumcising in the desert (verse 5)? v. 5 - why hadn't they participated in these ceremonies during the wilderness wanderings? We are not certain. It may have been suspended during the time of disobedience and unbelief that marked the wilderness wandering. It may have been spiritual neglect. Verse 9 references that God had removed the stigma of being slaves. No longer could they be taunted as slave people, nor could God be charged with failing to deliver the people (Num. 14:13-16; Deut. 9:28). Compare 6:1 and verse 13 and it is apparent this is the Lord talking with Joshua.

6 - Chapter 6 details the fall of Jericho. The city is given to Israel (verse 2) but still requires faithful obedience to receive God's gift _ a marvelous lesson today.

7 - Chapter 7 is full of terrible errors. Aachan's sin (verse 1) demonstrates how the actions of one man does affect the whole. Verse 3 reflects trust in soldiers and numbers, rather than in God. Where is the consultation with God for this operation? Joshua should have prayed first, as the Lord would surely have told him of the sin in the camp (verse 10). Verse 24 confuses some but

Aachan's family must have known what he did (how would you hide something under your tent floor without your family knowing about it?). Note the law on this point in Deuteronomy 24:16.

8 - Chapter 8 can be a bit difficult due to some summary statements inserted along the way, but the basic plan is clear: a force is put in hiding (verse 3, 12), then a pseudo-attack force under Joshua engages Ai and then flees (verse 15). When the men of Ai are drawn from the city the hidden attackers destroy it, leaving the men of Ai no escape and no chance, as Joshua turns his force back on them (verses 20-22).

Reading 5 - Joshua 9-13

9 - Chapter 9 records the miserable trick of the Gibeonites. Again Joshua fails to pray to receive God's guidance before acting (verse 14).

10 - Chapter 10 records the southern campaign, featuring the famous "long day battle" (verses 12-13). There is an urban legend circulating that NASA computers have "discovered" this long day but that report is fallacious. The "book of Jasher" mentioned in verses 14 seems to be an early Israelite history book full of stories of heroes and battles. It is mentioned again in 2 Sam 1:18. Note the heavy emphasis on God fighting for Israel (verses 8, 10, 14, 42).

11 - Chapter 11 records the campaign against northern kingdoms. Again, God fights for Israel (verses 6, 8, 20).

12 - Chapter 12 lists all the kings God defeated for Israel.

13 - Chapter 13 begins the division of the land, setting boundaries on the east side of the Jordan. Failure here is specifically mentioned (verse 13) and does not bode well for Israel's future. Back to Table of Contents.

Week 14 - Joshua 14-24; Judges 1-6

Reading 1 - Joshua 14-17

14-17 - The remaining chapters of Joshua in this week's reading (chapters 14-21) discuss the division of the land at great length and detail. Why is all of this tedious detail in Scripture? The answer is simple. The Old Testament is not given to entertain but to show God's faithfulness. God promised the land to Israel and these records show they received all that God promised. The Scriptures emphatically state again and again that God did exactly as He promised. They got the land! Highlights in this section include Caleb receiving his inheritance (14:6-15), and Caleb and Othniel doing the same (15:13-19). Both stories seem to make the point that if you wanted your land you could certainly go and take it. The failure to clear out all the Canaanites (stated at least three times: 14:13; 16:10; 17:12-13) was a faith and obedience failure, not a matter of a lack of ability or strength (note this particularly at 17:16).

Reading 2 - Joshua 18-21

18-21 - Chapters 18-21 continues the division of the land, including Joshua's land (19:49-51), the cities of refuge (chapter 20) and the cities for the Levites (chapter 21). The key to all of this material is the summary in 21:43-45. God cannot fail and He did not fail. Israel received the land promised to Abraham so long ago!

Reading 3 - Joshua 22-24

22 - Joshua 22 tells a story of misunderstanding that nearly goes disastrously wrong. The eastern tribes return to their homes across the Jordan (verse 4) and promptly built an altar (verse 10). Since there was to be but one central site for worship (see Deut 12:4-14) the other tribes viewed this as a serious breach of the covenant (verses 12-20). Fortunately, before attacking their brethren they listened to the explanation of the tribes (verses 22-29). The altar was there to remind all Israel that the tribes on the east side of Jordan were part of Israel and part of Israel's worship. Having learned what the altar was for, all was well again (verse 30).

23 - Chapter 23 contains Joshua's farewell address. Verse 1 says "a long time afterward" but what this is a "long time afterward" is not clear. Most take it to mean "a long time after God gave Israel rest." Chapters 23-24 occur shortly before Joshua dies at the age of 110 (24:29). If he was roughly the same age as Caleb at the time of the conquest (85) then approximately 25-30 years have passed. Joshua's admonition here draws heavily on the language of Deuteronomy, encouraging Israel to finish the conquest (verse 5) and be faithful to the Lord (verses 6-8). Joshua solemnly warns the people that if they don't want the people of Canaan out of the land the punishment will fit the crime: God will leave those people in place (verses 12-13).

24 - Chapter 24 is Joshua's famous last word at the renewal of the covenant ceremony. This speech is in the form of treaties from Joshua's day. The treaty used here is called a vassal treaty. It was employed when a superpower conquered a smaller nation (called a vassal nation). These treaties generally had six parts: a preamble identifying the Great King, a history of the situation, stipulations, curses and blessings, witnesses cited and provision for depositing the treaty document. Watch for these pieces of the treaty as you read the chapter, outlining the relationship between God and the vassal nation, Israel. Verses 14-15 seem to suggest Israel worshiped idols in Egypt (note Ezekiel 20:7), and Leviticus 17:7 seems to suggest that this also went on during the wilderness wanderings. Israel needed to choose who they would serve! Notice the emphasis on heart (verse 23). The book concludes with three funerals (verses 29-33). These are key men:

Joshua helped them gain the land, Joseph looked forward in faith to the land and Eleazar helped them divide the land. These passages also help provide a link between Judges and Joshua. Joshua 24:29-31 parallels Judges 2:6-10, just as Joshua 1:1 links with Deut. 34.

Reading 4 - Judges 1-3

Introduction to Judges - The book of Judges covers the "wild wild west" period of Israel's history. The key verse is Judges 21:25, showing how the book is designed to explain why Israel needed a king. The emphasis in Judges is twofold: (1) the wickedness of humans (as the book details a continual cycle of apostasy, repentance, rest and then apostasy again) and (2) the long-suffering, patience and goodness of God. Over and over again He delivers and saves a people who do not deserve His grace and mercy. Many think of the hero stories in Judges, like Samson or Jael, but the real hero of the book is God!

1 - Today we begin the story of Judges. The story unfolds as we would expect: Judah and Simeon seeking God's help to drive out their enemies (verses 1-8). Verse 8 seems to be a temporary capture (note verse 21). While God had given Israel rest from the large powerful nations and tribes that inhabited Canaan there was still "mop up" work to be done. Verse 13 introduces Othniel who becomes a judge in 3:9. But all is not well. The chapter continues by saying there were many groups Israel "did not drive out" (verses 19, 21, 27, 31, 33). What happened here, especially in verse 19?

2 - Chapter 2 answers our questions in verses 1-5. Israel's trouble is unfaithfulness, not iron chariots (verse 2)! If they had been faithful God would have given them a complete victory. Joshua's death provides an opportunity to note further failure on the part of parents (verse 10). Already we can sense that Judges will be a book of disobedience and destruction. Verse 11 summarizes the rest of the book, kicking off the cycle of the judges that we will read again and again for the first time. Verse 16 speaks of judges but these men were largely military leaders, not judges in the judicial sense. Note the emphasis on God's pity and compassion (verse 21).

3 - Chapter 3 records three of these leaders, Othniel (verses 7-11), Ehud (verses 12-30) and Shamgar (verse 31). Ehud is famous for being left handed (verse 15), which enabled him to hide his sword where people didn't expect a sword to be (verse 16)! Shamgar's "oxgoad" is a long stick or staff sharpened on one end (to keep the oxen in line) and filed to a blade on the other end to clean mud and dirt off the plow.

Reading 5 - Judges 4-6

4 - Chapter 4 tells the amazing story of Deborah. The battle account is fairly straightforward, featuring the courage of two women (Deborah and Jael) set against the cowardice of Barak. Notice that Deborah was a judge in the more conventional sense of the term (verse 5). When one considers military tactics of the day - the two armies lined up across from each other and then the two lines charged headlong into each other - the thought of what 900 iron chariots could do is truly frightening (verse 13). But God overcomes Sisera's superior forces (verse 15) leading to total victory.

5 - Chapter 5 focuses on the Song of Deborah celebrating and detailing the victory. The theme here is God's great power contrasted with the cowardice of some peoples who did not answer the call to battle (verses 16-17, 23).

6 - Chapter 6 begins the saga of Gideon. It turns out that he is not much of a hero, at least at first (he perpetually needs propping up by God, note verses 36-40). The usual pattern varies in verses

7-10 where God sends a prophet instead of a judge. It is clear only the people don't deserve to be delivered. God's grace leaps to the front of the story again as Gideon is selected (verses 11-24). The common sense of verse 31 is certainly needed today! Back to Table of Contents.

Week 15 - Judges 7-21

Reading 1 - Judges 7-8

7 - Chapter 7 records the defeat of the Midianite army. God takes great pains to make certain He is credited with the victory (verse 2). The people need a spiritual lesson more than just a military triumph! Once again Gideon's faith wavers and God encourages him (verses 9-15). Verse 22 makes certain we recognize that it was God who gave the victory, not brilliant military tactics.

8 - Chapter 8 finishes up the Gideon story. In verse 2 he uses a soft answer to turn away wrath and avoid a civil war. The towns of Succoth and Penuel refuse to cooperate with Gideon, lest they be implicated if Midian regrouped and defeated Gideon. The crazy nature of these times is indicated in verses 22-27 when Gideon sins. Gideon is to be commended in verse 23 because he knew that he was not Israel's real king. However, in verse 27 he made an ephod, an apron like garment used to seek God's will. Even if this was done with good intentions it became an idol and Gideon and his family participated in wrongful worship.

Reading 2 - Judges 9-11

9 - Today's reading opens with Abimelech's wild tale (chapter 9). He is the son of a concubine (8:31), kind of a "secondary" wife whose children would not inherit. Abimelech becomes little more than a thug who hires more thugs (verse 4) and then tries to usurp his way into being king. Jotham challenges Abimelech, using the allegory of the thorn bush to say Abimelech is a worthless no good man who will end up destroying himself and all around him (verses 7-21). Jotham's curse or prophecy comes to pass (verses 22-57) because God is determined that Abimelech pay for his crimes (verses 23-24). Abimelech has to deal with mistrust in his own ranks (verse 31), and finally dies an ignominious death (verses 53-54), something ultimately done by God (verses 56-57).

10 - Chapter 10 fires up the cycle of the judges again, highlighting God's increasing impatience with the people's unwillingness to be faithful and committed to Him (verses 11-14). But He will save them again, this time using an unlikely hero named Jephthah.

11 - Chapter 11 tells the story of Jephthah. He is not born to the right family (verse 1) but his military skill causes such niceties to be forgotten (verse 8). Jepthah negotiates to secure peace from the Ammonites (verses 12-28) but when that fails war breaks out. What exactly happened to his daughter, the subject of his foolish vow in verses 30-31, remains controversial. Some think she simply did not marry, a disaster for a Jewish woman. However the text certainly seems to say he did sacrifice her. Such would be wrong but the time of the Judges was not a time when there was a high level of spirituality in Israel!

Reading 3 - Judges 12-16

12 - Judges 12 finishes the Jephthah story with a sad tale of a civil war. An important point to consider is how Ephraim is already pushing for the lead in Israel, accounting themselves to be the most important tribe (verse 1). Verse 4 reveals real arrogance on Ephraim's part toward the tribes on the other side of the river. Note as well there is no appeal to God or prayer. Instead this is civil war showing how divided Israel had become. The chapter concludes with a list of judges we know little about. It is possible all of these judges were serving at the same time, but judged different tribes in different parts of the land.

13 - Chapter 13 begins the story of a very different kind of judge, Samson. He leads no army, nor

does he rally troops. Instead he performs heroic acts single-handedly. In all of this he may well be the most troubling character in the book. He is a wild man, governed by wild passions, and completely lacking in spirituality or self-discipline. Yet he is the perfect man for the times because it appears that God's people are completely content to be assimilated into Philistia. They aren't crying out in repentance and in 15:9-13 they won't even fight! So God uses a man with personal vengeance and personal grievances to create friction between southern Israel and Philistines. Verse 2 begins the story in the foothills, about 15 miles west of Jerusalem. Samson is to be a Nazirite (verse 5), which were people who took a vow to be specially set apart to God. Their main restrictions were abstinence from the fruit of the vine, no cutting of the hair and no touching corpses (see Num 6). They were to be models of holiness (cf. Amos 2:11-12). Note Manoah's immediate belief in his wife and wonderful prayer not to see the angel himself but to know how to raise this special child (verse 8). Verse 18 reveals this Angel had a divine name too wonderful for man to pronounce. Manoah's wife has uncommon sense in verse 23!

14 - Chapter 14 continues the Samson showing, with his fatal weakness for foreign women being revealed in verse 1. Notice that life seems to be going on rather well, as there is the giving and receiving of sons/daughters in marriage (a violation of the Law, Deut 7:1-3). We are impressed with the feat of strength in verse 6 but should not be surprised he told no one because touching a corpse violated his Nazirite vows. "Feasting" in verse 10 would usually involve drinking. Is Samson violating his vows again?

15 - Chapter 15 is a chapter of revenge and bloodshed. The wheat harvest (verse 1) would be in June. Verse 8's "hip and thigh" seems to be an obscure proverbial statement, perhaps like our expression like "cleaned his clock." Note the complete acceptance of Philistine domination in verse 11, and the refusal to help Samson as he fights alone (verses 15-17). In verse 18 Samson credits God for the victory but then seems to nearly blaspheme. He is truly a man out of control.

16 - Chapter 16 brings Samson' tragic tale to an end. Once again we see his lack of self-control as he visits a prostitute in verse 1, and continues to be mesmerized by foreign women (verse 4). The amount spoken of in verse 5 would be a great deal of money, perhaps over 100 pounds of silver. No wonder she is so persistent! Why Samson can't see that Deliah is trying to do him in (verses 6-21) is stunning. Samson's abilities have led him to be ridiculously overconfident. The great irony in the Philistine's claim that their god had given them Samson (verses 23-24) is that it is the Lord who gave Samson to the Philistines (verse 20).

Reading 4 - Judges 17-18

17 - Judges concludes with two appendices that are chronologically out of order (compare 18:12 and 13:25) but serve to underline Judges' key theme: the people lack the leadership necessary to "hold them" to God's Law and righteousness. The appendices also illustrate the moral decay that occurred in the period of the judges. These people lack the heart to obey God, and must be made to obey. Judges 17 tells the miserable story of Micah and his idols. He is a thief who took 1100 shekels (verse 2). As a yearly wage was 10 shekels (verse 10) this was a huge sum of money. The curse causes Micah to confess and return the money, and so his mother blesses him to reverse the threat of the curse (verse 2b). What happens next is syncretism, the combining of religions. The money is dedicated to Jehovah but made into an idol! They are worshiping Jehovah, but using an idol to do so. Verse 8 shows the Levites are not being well supported, a consistent problem for them. What a mess we have here. Note the departures from the Law: idols were not to be made to symbolize God, only Aaron's sons to be priests (not Levites), and the

Tabernacle was the center of worship, not every home. Everything is in confusion (verse 6).

18 - Chapter 18 finds the Danites having trouble taking their allotted territory, so they scout far in the north, as Laish is some 100 miles from their original territory (verse 7). The Danites steal Micah's idols, priestly garment (the ephod), and his priest as they go by (verse 17)! They conquer Laish in verses 27-29, founding the most northern city in Israel. This gives rise to the common expression "from Dan to Beersheba."

Reading 5 - Judges 19-21

19 - Our reading closes this week with the second appendix, the story of another civil war. These chapters recount one tribe's terrible immorality and the aftermath. Judges 19 starts the story with a man losing his concubine (a kind of secondary wife) and finding her again (verses 1-3). All seems well until they end up in a city that doesn't extend hospitality to strangers (verse 13), a terrible violation of the custom of hospitality. In a day without hotels this simply was not done. Verses 22-30 show how this town is the second coming of Genesis 19 and Sodom and Gomorrah! The man's callousness in verse 28 is sickening.

20 - Chapter 20 shows things going from bad to worse. Benjamin defends the evil men instead of giving them up (verse 13) and full-fledged civil war erupts. As we read the accounts of the three battles (verses 19-35) the obvious question is why didn't they immediately prevail over Benjamin since their cause was just? But notice the presumption in what they are doing. First, they only ask "who will go?" not "should we go" (verse 18). They do ask counsel in verse 23 but only after already setting the battle line again (verse 22). Finally they ask if they should go (verse 28) and it is clear the defeats have driven them to humility and the Lord.

21 - Chapter 21 ends the story and the book with Israel realizing they have gone further in the slaughter then perhaps they intended (verse 3). What follows is some chicanery to get around a rash oath and save the tribe of Benjamin that looks like an Old Testament version of Sadie Hawkins day (verses 16-24)! Verse 25 is the last word in Judges and it leaves the reader hungering for some leadership that can bring these people back to the Lord. Back to Table of Contents.

Week 16 - Ruth; 1 Samuel 1-8

Reading 1 - Ruth 1-2

Introduction to Ruth - Everyone loves a good story, and Ruth is a classic. This little book is not difficult to read, understand or appreciate. It is the only book in the Bible devoted entirely to the domestic history of a woman. Immediately we notice that while this book occurs during the "time of the judges" (1:1) it is a stark contrast to the darkness and wickedness of the time of the Judges. This is a book full of hope and faith, reminding us of good people trying to do right. To get the full value of Ruth we need to watch God at work. This is a book about providence, and we don't want to get so lost in the story that we fail to notice the God who is behind all that happens.

1 - Chapter 1 opens with a scene of bitterness. Verse 1's famine tells us the people are in sin (see Deut 28:28). Was leaving Bethlehem to live in Moab a sin? Some think so. It at least was not wise, as Elimelech and Naomi's sons marry foreign women. In verse 12 Naomi says she can't get married and if she did it would take too long for her to rear sons for her widowed daughter-in-laws to be able to exercise the rights of Levirate marriage. Ruth's famous pledge (verses 16-17) includes loyalty to Naomi, but is really more about her willingness to take Naomi's God as hers. What will God do with a Moabite who shows such faith?

2 - Chapter 2 begins with gleaning (verse 2). This is a practice specifically provided for in the law (Lev. 19:9-10; 23:22; Deut. 24:19-21) in which poor people were allowed to harvest the corners of the fields and even go through the fields to get what the harvesters miss on the first pass. It would be very difficult and hard work. The rest of the chapter sets up the budding relationship between Boaz and Ruth as he shows her unusual kindness and protection (verses 8-23). Verse 23's "end of the barley and wheat harvests" would be from late April to early June.

Reading 2 - Ruth 3-4

3 - Chapter 3 doesn't give us a time element, so we don't know how much time has elapsed between chapters 2 and 3. Notice how divine providence does not eliminate human activity (verse 5). The whole scene of Ruth uncovering Boaz's feet (verses 7-14) is very strange to us our own engagement customs probably seem odd to other cultures. Regrettably some have tried to make this into some sort of sexual encounter, but such would be a violation of the Law, goes completely against the character of both Ruth and Boaz, and defies how the Bible holds them up as examples. The customs are different than ours but that doesn't mean they are sinful! Boaz goes to great lengths to compliment Ruth's character (verse 11) and protect her reputation (verse 14).

4 - Chapter 4 finishes the story with the happiest of endings. The near kinsmen is challenged by Boaz to buy Naomi's field (verse 4) but decides not to when he realizes he also must take Ruth as a wife if he buys the field (verse 5). It would cost to buy the land and then it would not be his or his children's _ it would belong to any children he had with Ruth. His unwillingness to marry Ruth clears the way for Boaz to marry her (verses 9-10). Naomi had begun with a bitter word (1:13, 20) but now finds God has provided more than she could ever have imagined (verses 14). She is now in the line of David and even Jesus Christ (verse 22). This book stands as a marvelous testimony that it is possible to live right in bad times, and how God blesses those who will trust Him!

Reading 3 - 1 Samuel 1-2

Introduction to 1 Samuel - 1 & 2 Samuel were originally one book. The Septuagint (LXX) was the first to separate them, as the scroll was probably too difficult to handle as one. This book speaks of difficult and desperate times. The judgeship did not end with Samson. Eli and Samuel both serve as judges (1 Sam. 4:18; 7:6, 15, 17). The wild times we saw in Judges continue as well. The nation is in spiritual apostasy, in which all are doing exactly as they please. Oppression, violence and brutality are the norm. Something must be done, and this book introduces what the people believe to be the solution: a king. 1 Samuel is easily divided into 3 parts: chs. 1-7 - Samuel, chs. 8-15 - Saul up to his rejection, chs. 16-31 - decline of Saul, rise of David. The book teaches God's control in all events, as He accomplishes His will despite every obstacle, including disobedience. It also helps us see that God does not view or value as men do. Reversal of fortune and God unexpectedly blessing or using the most unexpected person is a key element in Samuel.

1 - Chapter 1 begins with a barren woman (verse 2). Barrenness was practically the worst thing that could happen to a woman, as her husband's hopes of an heir depended upon her. Often it was interpreted as a sign of divine disfavor. Verse 6 helps us realize that while the Bible does not specifically condemn polygamy in the Old Testament it shows us again and again the evils that accrue from this departure from God's original plan for marriage. As a sign of how wild things were at the Tabernacle Eli doesn't seem to find it out of the ordinary to find a drunk woman at the Tabernacle (verse 13)! Notice how God answers Hannah's prayers through entirely natural means (verses 19-20). Jesus' birth is a miracle, while Samuel's birth is entirely natural. God can work through natural means! Samuel would be weaned around two to three years, making him quite small to leave at the Tabernacle (verse 22).

2 - Chapter 2 well illustrates the theme of reversal. Hannah's song (verses 1-10) makes strong contrasts: weak and strong, full and hungry, barren and fertile, dead and alive, sick and well, poor and rich, humble and exalted. The reader is now given more information about the degradation at the Tabernacle. Verse 16's technical details about sacrifices may be lost on us but the fat would be God's part. Hophni and Phinehas are stealing from God! That is the idea in verse 25. Who is the "faithful priest" of verse 35? Some think Samuel, others Zadok, while some see this as Messianic prophecy of Christ.

Reading 4 - 1 Samuel 3-5

3 - Chapter 3 records the call of Samuel. Verse 1 explains Israel's dire situation and why Eli doesn't realize God is talking to Samuel at first. The prophecy Samuel receives is a strong one, as the penalty for despising the priesthood was death (Deut 17:12). Eli's unemotional acceptance of what Samuel says (verse 18) is incredible. Why doesn't Eli repent and cry out to the Lord for mercy?

4 - The prophecy Samuel delivered comes to pass (chapter 4). While the Philistines were a terrible foe we read nothing of Israel consulting God (note verse 3). Instead they elect to treat the ark like a lucky rabbit's foot or pagan idol - as if there was some sort of power in the box (verse 4). It didn't work, did it? We can understand Eli's shock (verse 18) when we begin to think of what the ark meant for Israel. It was the sign of God's presence with them, it held the Law of Moses (the Ten Commandments) and was the emblem of God's covenant with Israel. Had God abandoned His people? Other passages may indicate that Shiloh was overrun by Philistines, because after the battle the Tabernacle is not in Shiloh, and the Ark is not returned there (see Psalms 78:57-66; Jeremiah 7:12-15; 26:1-9).

5 - Chapter 5 is a humorous chapter. While the Philistines celebrate their gods who gave them victory over Israel those gods cannot even control the images representing them! Personal suffering confirmed that Israel's ark needed to go back to Israel (verses 11-12)!

Reading 5 - 1 Samuel 6-8

6 - Chapter 6 combines common sense on the Philistines' part with divine activity. Why do the Philistines make golden tumors to return with the ark (verse 4)? Some see sympathetic magic - sending away what had struck at them, while others argue that at this time the custom was to make a model of the healed part of the body. The appearance here of mice cause some to see bubonic plague here, as the tumors, rats and plague are all linked here. Verse 9 shows wonderful common sense - something Israel seems too often lack. The number of men struck in verse 19 varies in different translations because the Hebrew is uncertain.

7 - Chapter 7 looks like a return to the book of Judges. Some 20 years pass (verse 2) before the people of God, oppressed by the Philistines, finally ask God for help and God provides them a deliverer in Samuel after their repentance. Note the conviction and confession that Samuel draws from the people in verse 3. Why they poured out water in verse 6 is unknown. It may have been an offering or symbolic of repentance. Just as in Judges, God fights for them (verse 10). He demonstrates that He is the real God of the storm, not Baal. Verse 12 is where the well-known hymn "Here I Raise My Ebenezer" comes from. We all need a place where we mark out and remember God's great deliverance and help, don't we?

8 - Chapter 8 shows the hard fought lesson at Ebenezer is soon forgotten. The people lapse back into the cycle of the Judges and this time their solution is not repentance but a new kind of leader. They want a king (verse 5). It is important to remember that having a king was not out of the question for God's people. The blessings of Jacob hint at a king (Gen. 49:10), Balaam prophesied it (Num. 24:17-19), and Moses positively says it will happen (Deut. 17:14-20). How would we understand Jesus as King if Israel had never had a king. The trouble here is the kind of king that Israel wants: a military leader (note verse 20) who can win them victories in battle (12:12 shows the imminent threat of Ammon figures into this). It is clear they have lost faith in God to give them victory, and are attempting to mimic the pagan nations around them. Thus they reject God (verse 7). Samuel warns them about kings (verses 10-18 - underline the repetitive term "take" in your Bible) but the people are determined to have a king. Verse 22 shows that sometimes God gives us what we want even when it's not good for us because we are just too stubborn to listen to Him! Back to Table of Contents.

Week 17 - 1 Samuel 9-17; 1 Chron 2

Reading 1 - 1 Samuel 9-10

9 - Chapter 9 finds exactly the kind of man Israel was looking for in a king, by describing him physically (verse 2) while his spiritual qualifications are completely lacking. Through a long train of events God's controlling hand is seen in bringing Saul to Samuel. While Saul is never spoken of as possessing the kind of spirituality that we meet at once in David he at least is humble (verse 21). Unfortunately, this humility won't last.

10 - The anointing of Saul begins the chapter (verse 1) though it is a secret anointing. Saul will be publicly proclaimed king later. There is a heavy emphasis here on God's Spirit empowering Saul to be king (verses 6, 9). Verse 8 summarizes what may have been more detailed instructions about assembling Israel at Gilgal once Saul had settled in as king and awaiting Samuel (see 13:13). While some do not understand the signs Samuel gives Saul whereby he can know he is God's choice (verses 11-12) Saul would know and be certain that he would be king. Once again we find humility, if not reluctance, on Saul's part (verse 22). How this will change as power goes to his head!

Reading 2 - 1 Sam 11-13

11 - Chapter 11 shows how terrible conditions had become in Israel. Nahash allows the men of Jabesh-Gilead to make an appeal for help, clearly believing none will come (verse 3). Saul is found plowing (verse 5), showing that no one was treating him like a royal dignitary. His proclamation as king in chapter 10 seems to have meant little. He will have to show the people he can be a leader. This is exactly what happens (verse 11). Note how Saul gives God the credit for the victory, and even shows mercy (verse 13). Sadly, that will change too.

12 - Chapter 12 contains Samuel's farewell address. Samuel acknowledges the transfer of power from himself to Saul (verse 2), while reminding the people that a king will "take" (remember chapter 8) much from them. Verses 6-12 defend God's actions, showing God as the real leader of the Israelites. He has constantly delivered them, but they want a king instead. Verse 13 is the hinge verse: everything has changed now, but Samuel makes it clear that even with a king the issue is still faithfulness. If Israel is not faithful to God a king won't help them. Verse 17's sign is time dependent. Wheat harvest is in June, a time when it is very dry and there is no rain. Rain and thunder during the dry season would be very unusual, and perhaps even a threat to their crops. Verses 24-25 are keenly prophetic of the rest of Israel's history under kings.

13 - Chapter 13 begins Saul's reign in earnest. Though the next several chapters will detail some military victories it becomes quickly apparent that Saul is not the right man for the job (note 15:35). His basic problem is illustrated in this chapter: Saul will not submit to God's instructions as given through Samuel the prophet (note 1 Chron 10:14). Verse 1 reads differently in different translations because the Hebrew here is very difficult and uncertain. Acts 13:21 gives his reign as forty years. What begins as a small victory suddenly leads to full-scale war with Philistia, something Israel seems ill-prepared for (verses 6-7). This is Saul's first real crisis. What will he do? Unfortunately, he blows it - recklessly charging ahead and violating Samuel's instructions (verses 8-12). What exactly was Saul's sin? It is not the offering of the sacrifice. The text may mean Saul had a priest to do it (one was there, 14:3). Samuel was not a priest and he offered (7:9); other kings did so also (David, 2 Sam. 24:25, Solomon, 1 Kings 3:15). His sin was his failure to obey the prophet, a sin he commits again in ch. 15. Saul proves that he doesn't consider

himself bound by God's instruction, or subservient to the prophet who speaks for God. David isn't any less sinless than Saul, but he always obeys prophetic instructions. The chapter concludes by noting how poorly equipped the Israelite army is (verses 19-23). What will happen to Saul's outnumbered and empty handed forces? Chapter 14 holds the answer!

Reading 3 - 1 Samuel 14

14 - Who would expect a great victory after 13:19-22's pitiful description of the state of Israel's armament? Chapter 14 shows that one man's courage and faith (Jonathan) combined with God's willingness to give Israel the victory radically changed the situation. Jonathan's great faith in verse 6 is truly inspiring. It isn't surprising the garrison ran in verses 14-15. They surely thought there must be more of these great warriors coming. They couldn't imagine a one man attack. Note that Israelites are part of the Philistine army (verse 21), showing that again Israel is in danger of assimilating into Philistia. Saul's rash command (verse 24) results in the Philistines escaping to fight again (verse 52).

Reading 4 - 1 Sam 15-16; 1 Chron 1

15 - Chapter 15 records the beginning of the end for Saul's reign. Verse 2's history is found in Exodus 17:8-16. Verse 12 is very disturbing. Where is the credit to God for the victory? In this entire episode Saul seems overly concerned with his image (note verse 30). Samuel makes plain that worship not based on obedience means nothing to God (verse 22), a valuable lesson for today. After watching Saul shift the blame, reluctantly admit wrong and worry over his image it is clear he is not the man to lead God's people (verse 35). God gave Israel what they wanted but their desire for the wrong kind of king will cost them dearly.

16 - Chapter 16 shifts the story firmly to David. Does God instruct Samuel to lie in verse 2? No, there are two purposes for this trip, sacrificing and anointing, and both will be fulfilled. But a public disclosure of a private mission could have led to a civil war. Verse 13 is a crucial verse in 1 Samuel. The passage on the anointing of David ends with the Spirit, the next set of verses begin with Saul's loss of the Spirit. Truly this is a "hinge" verse. Saul is no longer the focus of the story, and even Samuel has now completed his career and becomes a fairly minor character from this point on. What of the evil spirit in verse 14? Some see this as only depression (as Saul realizes he is rejected by God) because it can be helped by music. Others see this as demonic possession. There are chronology issues with verses 17-23 because Saul appears not to know David in chapter 17. This may be out of order or could be a summary statement, with chapter 17 filling in more of the details of how David came to be in the court permanently.

1 Chronicles 1 - Chronicles begins with nine chapters of genealogy. This is hard for today's modern reader, but the key here is to note this isn't just a collection of names, but a list showing connection in names. Watch for those links. The connection in these first three chapters is a continuous line from Adam through Noah through Abraham to David. The long list of names here reminds us of God's faithfulness to His promises.

Reading 5 - 1 Samuel 17; 1 Chronicles 2

17 - Chapter 17 is one of the most famous chapters in the Bible. The story of David and Goliath sets before us a man cut from different fabric than Saul. The chief aim of the chapter is to contrast Saul and David. Make sure you note the huge differences in Saul and David (for example verses 11, 33 contrasting with verses 26, 32). The other emphasis is David's great faith (note verses 26, 45-47). David isn't a fool. He uses the past (verses 34-37) to bolster his

confidence in God, gathers his weapon and meets an enemy who terribly underestimates him (verse 43). The result is a huge victory (verses 52-53). How often God's people just need one person to demonstrate faith and then everyone will!

2 - 1 Chronicles 2 puts special focus on the tribe of Judah because this is David's tribe. Back to Table of Contents.

Week 18 - 1 Sam 18-25; 1 Chron 3-7

Reading 1 - 1 Sam 18-19; 1 Chron 3

18 - Chapter 18 continues the theme of David's continued success, with particular emphasis on God giving that success (verses 12, 14). Saul knows that God is with David (verse 28) but will fight against him anyway, thus in effect fighting against God!

19 - 1 Samuel 19 records the final break between Saul and David. Saul's paranoia becomes increasingly evident, and David becomes a full-fledged refugee in fear of his life. We wonder why Michal has an idol in her house (verse 13). It might be a captured souvenir, or may reflect pagan inclinations. Often Saul does not seem to be a very spiritual man. The power of the Spirit in verses 20-24 is seen in a very unusual way. Usually the Spirit fills a person to do great deeds and gives strength and power to accomplish those deeds (as in Samson's case). Here the Spirit incapacitates, and in Saul's case, humiliates him as he takes off his royal robes (verse 24). Saul is fighting against God and cannot win.

3 - 1 Chronicles 3 narrows the focus to David. Notice verses 10-16 give a summary of southern kings in just a few verses. Their stories are not important here, just their connection to David.

Reading 2 - 1 Sam 20; 1 Chron 4

20 - Chapter 20 shows that even Jonathan can see the futility of his father's actions. Verse 15 speaks of "cutting off," an expression not familiar to modern readers. Jonathan is asking David not to exterminate him and his family when he becomes king. It was customary for a new king to put to death the former king's extended family so there could be no rival claimants. Jonathan knows what God is doing with his own father and with David and sides with David. David's generosity is not surprising to us. He is not the kind of man who needs to kill the innocent to hold onto power _ the very opposite of Saul. Verse 30 contains vulgar, coarse language, showing more of Saul's (lack of) character. The signal that Jonathan set up was in case it wasn't safe to speak with David. Apparently it was safe so Jonathan wants to personally say good-bye to David (verse 40).

4 - 1 Chronicles 4 - today we read the genealogy of Judah (4:1-23), of Simeon (vv. 24-43), of the Transjordan tribes (ch. 5). Note the prayer of Jabez in 4:9-10. It is singled out as a remarkable example of prayer for us.

Reading 3 - 1 Sam 21-22; 1 Chron 5

21 - Chapter 21 is not a good chapter for David. David lies to Ahimelech (verse 2) and eats what is not lawful for him to eat (violating express law - Exodus 29:32-33; Leviticus 22:10-16; 24:5-9) in verse 6. Psalm 34 and 56 may come from this episode, as David flees (verse 10). Why he goes to Philistia is a mystery. Did he think he would not be recognized? He is, and nearly dies as a result!

22 - Chapter 22 is a terrible chapter. David is collecting to himself all kinds of troubled people (verse 2). We probably do well to think of this group as thugs and ruffians. This becomes the nucleus of his band of "toughs" that are not to be trifled with. Note that David listens to God (verse 5), something Saul refuses to do. The contrasts in the two men become ever clearer. Saul's delusional paranoia (verse 8) seems to rage out of control, and Saul directly attacks God by having the priests murdered (verses 16-18). The massacre of the priests at Nob stands as the low point in Saul's reign. It is incredibly wicked, and leaves Saul with no one to consult with God for

him (as if the Lord would speak to him anyway). Meanwhile, David takes responsibility for what he has done (verse 22). Remember how Saul refused to take responsibility for failure in chapter 15. David is nothing like this morally bankrupt man who will wear the crown for only a little while longer!

5 - 1 Chronicles 5 gives the genealogy of the tribes that settled on the east side of Jordan. Note God's faithfulness to His people when they call to Him (verse 20).

Reading 4 - 1 Sam 23-24; 1 Chron 6

23 - As we follow the thrilling story of David being chased by Saul it is critical for the reader to observe the differences in Saul and David. Saul continues to show himself unfit to lead God's power while more and more we realize that David is cut from "different cloth." 1 Samuel 23 emphasizes these differences. Verses 1-5 highlight David's growing faith. Even his own men were afraid to go and save Keilah (verse 2) but David obeys God anyway. The ephod of verse 6 becomes very important. It is a priestly garment that played a role in the priest consulting God (verse 9). This time David only asks God once and obeys. Note the emphasis (again) on how Saul is actually fighting against God (verse 14). Verse 27 reveals that Saul has left the land unprotected pursuing his personal vendetta against David! Make certain you read the Psalms with today's reading. Psalm 54 is from this time in David's life.

24 - 1 Samuel 24 reveals the folly of interpreting the current situation to mean it is okay to disobey God. David catches Saul in an unguarded moment and his men urge him to kill Saul, even invoking God's name to encourage David to do it (verse 4). David shows that he is not like Saul. He will not take matters into his own hands (as Saul did in chapter 13). He will wait on God and do what is right! Note again that Saul knows he is fighting against God (verses 19-20).

6 - 1 Chronicles 6 is long, but we quickly see the importance of having the priestly lineage carefully spelled out. Note the lineage of Zadok, the high priest for king David (verse 8ff). Note also that the Levites were not given land but instead were spread out throughout Israel so they could teach the Law and influence the people to live righteously (verses 54-81).

Reading 5 - 1 Sam 25; 1 Chronicles 7

25 - 1 Samuel 25 records the story of Nabal. Nabal means fool, and he certainly acts as his name suggests! Sheep shearing (verse 4) was generally a time of festivities (see Gen. 38:12) as evidenced by Nabal's later festivities and drunkenness (v. 36) so it was appropriate for David and his men to expect hospitality. David's anger flashes hot in verse 13, but David will later realize how wrong he was (note verses 26, 31). You can't kill people for being rude! David is being tempted here to act like Saul, rashly and without thought and without consulting God. Fortunately, Abigail saves David. She doesn't panic but executes a wise plan (verses 18-20). Then she delivers a brilliant speech to David helping him realize he must not take God's place (verse 26), and the Lord cares for David so why get so worked up about this minor matter (verses 28-30). The story concludes with David repenting and reining in his emotions (verse 34). Just as Abigail had said God deals with Nabal (verse 38).

1 Chronicles 7 completes the genealogy of Israel. Something new here is the addition of numbers indicating military strength of various tribes. Back to Table of Contents.

Week 19 - 1 Sam 26-31; 1 Chron 8-12

Reading 1 - 1 Sam 26-27; 1 Chron 8

26 - Chapter 26 has a deja vu feel to it, as once again Saul pursues David and once again David spares his life. Note David's strong conviction that God will take care of Saul (verse 10). He has learned from the Nabal episode! Saul's repentance seems less emotional and meaningful (verse 21) and David seems to be unwilling to believe him. Indeed, 27:4 shows that Saul continued to pursue David after this.

27 - 1 Samuel 27 finds David in desperate straits. David is at a real spiritual low here - he appears "fed up" with Saul and uncertain how much longer he can keep from getting killed. Further, he has gone to Philistia before and nearly got killed (ch. 21) so why go there again? The key in the reading is to see that David does not consult God in this, does things his own way and thus gets in all kinds of trouble. But out of this mess David does learn to seek God, and wait upon Him. Note: 28:3 marks a break in the text. The story then turns to the demise of Saul, so this material today really needs to go through 28:1-2. Initially David's scheme (and lies) seem to work perfectly, giving him the best of both worlds: the Philistines think he is raiding Israel and Israel is pleased he is raiding Philistia (verses 10-12). However, deception never works in the long run . . . .

8 - Today's reading in 1 Chronicles 8 highlights Saul's lineage.

Reading 2 - 1 Sam 28-29; 1 Chron 9

28 - 1 Samuel 28 moves the story toward a decisive climax where the threads of David's story, the Philistines and Saul will all come together. Shunem (verse 4) is in the north showing that the Philistine invasion was very serious and threatened to cut the nation of Israel in two! Saul has cut himself off from God so he now has no way to know God's will or seek God's help, but he is in real trouble (verse 6). He thus sins by consulting a medium, even invoking God's name in his sin (verse 10)! There are many questions about what exactly happened next - did Samuel really appear, or was it a trick or even a demon? Did the medium really conjure up Samuel or did God just allow Samuel to appear? The Bible gives no credence to witchcraft and her shock (verse 12) seems to say God did it not the medium, and that this was something unusual God allowed because of the crisis and Saul's hardened heart. The focus of the text is on the impending demise of Saul, not all our questions about how Samuel was "brought back" for this audience with Saul. We will have to keep our focus where the Bible's is! It is interesting to note that knowing the future often isn't the big help we think it might be (verses 18-19).

29 - Chapter 29 brings David into the story. What is he going to do in such an awkward moment? In the providence of God he is saved from having to be revealed as a liar to the Philistines or attack his own brethren in Israel!

9 - 1 Chronicles 9 offers some surprises. The genealogies are summed up (verse 1) and the entire Babylonian captivity is tidied up in one short sentence at the end of verse 1! The Levites are then discussed, in their important work in the Temple with material paralleled in Nehemiah 11 (verses 2-34). Finally Chronicles picks up the Saul story again, leading to an end of the genealogies and direct narrative beginning in chapter 10 (verses 35-44).

Reading 3 - 1 Sam 30-31; 1 Chron 10

30 - Chapter 30 says there is a cost to David's deceptions: his home has been raided while he was

away. The emphasis is on David's faith in a terrible crisis. His very life is threatened but David "strengthens himself in the Lord his God" (verse 6). He even inquires of the Lord to see if he should attempt a rescue (verse 8)! Both Saul and David find themselves "greatly distressed" but Saul goes to a medium and David goes to God! What a difference! The episode ends well, with David crediting God for it all, and being generous with what God has given him (verse 23).

31 - 1 Samuel 31 tells us what was happening in the north while David was winning a victory in the south (chapter 30). Things weren't going so well for King Saul. As Samuel foretold Saul and his forces are routed by the Philistines and he (and many others) die. The last paragraph provides a fitting end for Saul, as the men of Jabesh-Gilead rescue his body (verses 11-13). Saul's reign began with his rescue of that city and comes to its tragic close there as well.

10 - 1 Chronicles 10 echoes 1 Samuel 31, but note the verdict of God on Saul's reign and death in verses 13-14.

Reading 4 - 2 Sam 1-2; 1 Chron 11

Introduction to 2 Samuel - 2 Samuel needs little introduction. It simply continues the story 1 Samuel is telling, now stressing that it is David's destiny to be Israel's next king. While the reader is sure that this must happen the ruling house of Saul and the Philistine threat remain in the way. What will happen next? What will God do to install His choice on the throne?

1- 2 Samuel 1 begins with a phrase often used in the Old Testament to denote a major break or change in the story. "After the death of" (verses 1) signals the reader that new developments are about to take place. In verses 6-10 the Amalekite lies about his role in Saul's death, and dies for it. The chapter ends with David's lament for Saul and Jonathan (verses 17-27) showing just how genuine David's friendship and loyalty to them both really was. The book of Jashur (verse 18) is an uninspired book now lost to us. It is also mentioned in Joshua 10:13.

2 - Chapter 2 finds David king over Judah (verses 1-7) while Saul's son Ish-bosheth is made king by Abner, the commander of the army (verses 8-10). Ish-bosheth never seems like he is really in charge. Abner appears to be ruling through him. The terrible battle described in verses 12-32 appears to be an attempt to settle matters by a champions duel instead of all-out civil war, but the carnage just escalates.

11 - 1 Chronicles 11 gives us some very interesting details about David and his men. Verses 2-3 make it clear that David is God's choice to be king. Much of the rest of the chapter tells of David's mighty men and their exploits.

Reading 5 - 2 Samuel 3-5; 1 Chron 12

3 - 2 Samuel 3 shows a break in Abner and Ish-bosheth over a concubine (verses 7-8). It seems insignificant to us but whoever had ownership of the king's harem would have a strong claim to the throne (see 12:8; 16:20). Was Abner trying to make a play for the throne himself? We don't know but the relationship is ruptured and Abner begins to work for peace and to give David a unified throne (verses 9-21). Note again how often the text specifically designates David as God's choice. Unfortunately, Joab is still angry with Abner for killing his brother (2:23) and he ruthlessly murders Abner, nearly ending the quest for a united kingdom (verses 26-30). David's shows strong political savvy as he moves quickly to assure all Israel he did not order or condone this murder (verses 31-39). It is not the last time Joab will ignore David's wishes and act on his own to kill David's enemies.

4 - Chapter 4 reveals what happened with Abner dead: there is a power vacuum. Apparently two generals decide to take matters in their own hands, perhaps trying to complete an Abner-David alliance (verses 1-8). Mephibosheth's role expanded later (verse 4), but here he is referenced to show he has no chance or claim on the throne. He was five when his father died (2:11), and David ruled seven years over Judah, so he is about twelve now. That makes him too young to be a factor in the political turmoil (not to mention he is lame). David, of course, has no use for murder and lawlessness. He will wait upon God to give him the throne, and as always refuses to take it by force (verses 9-12).

5 - Chapter 5 sees David made king over all Israel. There is much emphasis here on David's humility (verses 12, 20, 25; 6:21-22). Now that the house of Saul is finally out of the way the other problem before David is the Philistines, and he promptly goes to work on them with God's help (verses 17-25).

12 - 1 Chronicles 12 gives details on the kind of army that David could now lead as Israel was unified under his command. The idols of verse 21 are burned (as we will see in 1 Chronicles 14 next week). <u>Back to Table of Contents.</u>

Week 20 - 2 Sam 6-12; 1 Chron 13-20

Reading 1 - 2 Sam 6; 1 Chron 13

6 - 2 Samuel 6 is a puzzling chapter for some, but it records a very important moment in David's rule. This point is made when we realize that 1 Chronicles 13 records the same event - God repeats what matters! The ark is transported incorrectly, in the Philistine manner and thus the ark is at risk of falling to the ground. Uzzah reaches out to do what appears to be a good thing but is struck dead (verse 7). The readings for tomorrow will show that David comes to understand what happened and why he shouldn't be angry with the Lord (verse 8). The other peculiar event here is David dancing before the ark (verses 16-23). Some have thought David danced naked as the ark was brought triumphantly into Jerusalem. This is not so. 1 Chronicles 15:27 makes it clear that David was fully clothed, wearing a robe of linen under the ephod. What David did was lay aside his royal robes to participate in the worship of God as a "common man." Michal despises him for this, even attributing evil motives to David (verse 20). David explains himself but wants nothing further to do with such a woman (verses 21-22). Thus the house of Saul will have no heir from Michal (verse 23), an important point as the story continues. A grandson of Saul and son of David could have made a strong claim to the throne. No such son will be born.

13 - 1 Chronicles 13 records the events of moving the ark and Uzzah's death.

Reading 2 - 1 Chronicles 14-16

14 - For the first time we read only in Chronicles. 1 Chronicles 14 records David's further work to establish Jerusalem as the nation's capital. Moving the ark here (2 Sam 6; 1 Chron 15) made the city the religious and political capital of the nation. The battle stories of verses 8-17 emphasize David's dependence upon God who fights for him and Israel. Saul failed to defeat the Philistines and their gods were honored (1 Chron 10:10).

Now David gains victory and destroys their false gods (verse 12). David's willingness to seek God and to obey God is the key difference.

15 - 1 Chronicles 15 tells the complete story of how the ark came to Jerusalem. Verse 13 helps us better understand what 2 Samuel 6 records. Note that David sees the Law of God as a way to "seek Him" (verse 13).

16 - 1 Chronicles 16 records David's song of praise to be used in the worship of God. It combines Psalm 96, 105 and 106. The psalm is about how and why God is to be praised, and is well worth a careful reading. The chapter ends with the curios situation of "split worship centers," with the ark in Jerusalem and the Tabernacle (rebuilt after the Philistine destruction of 1 Samuel 4?) in Gibeon (verse 39). We are not sure why David didn't consolidate all worship in Jerusalem at this time, but 2 Samuel 7 shows he fully intended to do so.

Reading 3 - 2 Sam 7-8; 1 Chron 17

7 and 17 - 2 Samuel 7 and 1 Chronicles 17 cover the same material: the Davidic promises. That makes these passages some of the most import verses in all of the Old Testament, because they shape the future of God's work with Israel. These incredible divine promises to the Davidic monarchy find their ultimate fulfillment in Jesus Christ (see Acts 2:25, 29, 34). That alone tells us they are of enormous significance. On top of all of that, this chapter is the high point of David's reign. What a place to read and study! Notice how Nathan initially "green lights" David's good intentions (verse 3). What humans think is good is often far different from what God says is

good! In verses 5-16 God then tells David that because of David's desire to build God a house, the Lord plans to build David an everlasting "house," i.e. a ruling house or dynasty (note verse 11). God's esteem for David is indicated by verse 5's use of the phrase "my servant David." That is very rare in the Old Testament. Only Moses is referred to in this way (see Joshua 1:2, 7). Not even Joshua is not called by this term. So David stands now beside even Moses! Some of these promises are to be fulfilled in David's lifetime (verses 9-11a), and some beyond his life by his son Solomon and even sons beyond that (verses 11b-16). As we continue reading in the Old Testament we will find that David's great-great grandsons were not faithful (note verse 14) but One comes who will rule from David's throne forever as the absolute fulfillment of these promises. That One is Jesus the Christ! Take a moment and browse the references in the New Testament that take great pains to connect Jesus with David and these promises: Matthew 1:1;9:27; 12:23; 21:9, 15; 22:42-45; Luke 1:32, 69; 2:4; John 7:42; Acts 2:25, 29, 34; 13:22, 34-36; Romans 1:3; 2 Timothy 2:8; Revelation 3:7; 5:5; 22:16. The chapter concludes with David's prayer of humility and thanksgiving. David's concern is for God's name (verse 26) not his own!

8 - 2 Samuel 8 serves to show the divine promises of chapter 7 (note 7:10) came to pass. God gave David rest from his enemies all around (note verses 6 and 14). We do not know why there were two priests at this time (verse 17). Possible explanations include one serving at Gibeon with the reconstructed Tabernacle, and the other serving in Jerusalem with the ark. Or it might be that one served under Saul, and Abiathar served with David during the time he was fleeing Saul, and David allowed them both to continue. Verse 18's Cherethites and Pelethites were foreign mercenaries (connected to the Philistines) who served as David's personal body guard.

Reading 4 - 2 Sam 9-10; 1 Chron 18-19

9 - 2 Samuel 9 appears to be unremarkable, until we remember that Mephibosheth could have been a rival claimant to the throne since he was Saul's grandson. Instead of exterminating the house of Saul David shows kindness to Mephibosheth, since David trusts in God's promise to establish him.

18 - 1 Chronicles 18 is part of our reading today. It deals with much of the same material we read yesterday in 2 Samuel 8. Watch for the emphasis on gold, silver and bronze that was captured. These items were saved by David for Solomon to use in the building of God's temple.

10 and 19 - Chapter 10 and 1 Chronicles 19 cover the same material: the war with Ammon. It appears to be just extending the theme of military victory begun in chapter 8, but actually sets up the events of chapter 11. Sadly an entire war gets started over a misunderstanding and bad advice (verse 3).

Reading 5 - 2 Sam 11-12; 1 Chron 20

11- 2 Samuel 11 records David's lowest moment. A key idea here is the progression of sin, as lust leads to adultery, which leads to deception and murder. Notice how the Bible makes no attempt to cover up or rationalize the sinful actions of one of its heroes. What David did is presented as the darkest possible deed, standing in stark contrast to Uriah's faithful service (verses 6-13). When Uriah won't visit his wife David decides to kill him, sending the death warrant by Uriah's own hand (verse 14). Joab improves on David's plan and Uriah dies (verse 17). David's callous disinterest in the battle report is terrible to read (verse 25). This not the David we know. Verse 26's wording is very deliberate to emphasize the sinful nature of David and Bathsheba's relationship. Read literally it says "When Uriah's wife heard that her husband

Uriah was dead, she mourned for her husband."

12 - 2 Samuel 12 picks up on the last line of chapter 11 to show God's verdict on David's adultery. Nathan handily traps David with a parable (verses 1-6) and then bores into him with God's judgment (verses 7-12).

This sin, Nathan says, comes from ingratitude and was utterly unnecessary (verses 7-8), showed that David despised God's word (verse 9), that he despised God (verse 10), and what he did caused God's enemies to blaspheme (verse 14).

20 - 1 Chronicles 20 covers very much the same material as the end of 2 Samuel 12. There is much speculation as to why Chronicles doesn't mention David's adultery. Some think that episode doesn't fit with the main theme of Chronicles, which is to emphasize the importance of worship and God's faithfulness. Others have thought it was left out because God forgave David's sin and so, from God's standpoint, the matter was "no more." Back to Table of Contents.

Week 21 - 2 Samuel 13-24; 1 Chron 21

Reading 1- 2 Sam 13-14

13 - 2 Samuel 13 begins the calamities Nathan had prophesied would strike David's house (12:10). Amnon (verse 1) is David's first born (2 Sam 3:2), and thus very important in David's house. Verse 2's last line is hard to translate, but the idea seems to be that Amnon knew marriage was impossible. Tamar gives powerful reasons for Amnon not to sin: verse 12 begins with this was "not done in Israel" (we are God's people, we have the Law, we don't act like this), then she appeals for him to be concerned for others (verse 13's "where could I take my shame?), and then ends by reminding him to be concerned for himself (verse 13's "you ... like one of the fools"). What does she mean with "the king will not withhold me from you" (verse 13b)? Since such marriages were forbidden in the law (Lev. 18:9,11; 20:17; Deut. 27:22) we can only conclude she is grasping at straws _ trying to say anything to stop this ungodly assault. Verse 21 really stands out. Of course, David can't say anything because he engaged in sexual sin as well! Verse 26 seems to show that David was suspicious of Absalom.

14 - Chapter 14 reveals Joab's scheme to get Absalom back into the king's good graces. Did Joab think Absalom would be the next king and so was siding with him? We don't know but his plan worked. The wise woman tells a sad story involving her son (verses 4-7), and gets David to agree to protect her and her son (verses 8-11). Then she skewers David by pointing out he won't afford the same kindness to Absalom (verses 12-16). Her situation involves only one family, while his involves the entire nation. She has him, but David allows Absalom to return but makes the critical mistake of really reconciling with him (verse 13). By the time two years pass Absalom's heart is hardened against his father.

Reading 2 - 2 Sam 15-17

15 - Absalom's bitterness is more than we can ever imagine. He hatches and executes a plan to take the kingdom from his father in 2 Samuel 15. Absalom begins by flattering people and complaining about the current administration (verses 1-6). Verse 11 tells that 200 men went along with Absalom innocently, but the effect will be devastating on David. He won't be able to tell who is with him and who has joined Absalom. It would appear to David that the 200 were with Absalom! David's hurried evacuation of his capital (verses 14-23) is a pathetic scene. Verse 25 stands out as a key marker of David's character. Even in a national emergency he won't resort to treating God's ark like a good luck charm (remember 1 Samuel 4?). David resigns himself to whatever God plans. Verses 31-35 treat us to a brilliant example of faith, prayer and action. David prays that God will frustrate Ahithiophel's counsel (verse 31) but then sends Hushai to be a tool in God's hands to answer that prayer (verse 34). Prayer for David was never an excuse for inaction. Success for David was never an excuse for self-glorification. He realized that God uses and blesses what we do to accomplish His ends and answer our prayers.

16 - The dramatic story continues in chapter 16. Could Mephibosheth really imagine he would receive the crown (verse 3) or is Ziba lying? We don't know. Shimei's cursing seems stupid (and could have cost him his life, verse 9) but David humbly accepts it, trusting in God again (verse 12). Ahithophel's counsel proves to be as wise as "advertised" in verse 21. If Absalom claims the royal harem he is announcing his claim to the throne and ensuring the break between him and his father is permanent. Everyone can choose up sides now without fear that David and Absalom will suddenly reconcile leaving those who joined a now existent rebellion holding the bag. The rebellion is on in earnest! Ironically the story is now back on the palace roof where all the trouble

started (verse 22).

17 - By chapter 17 we are wondering if David has a chance against Absalom's rebellion. Ahithophel's counsel is smart: David is no position to defend himself. He is on the run and without the support of the main army (verse 2). If David dies, all opposition to Absalom will collapse (verse 3). Hushai frustrates this good advice in verses 7-13. Notice the appeal to Absalom's ego in verse 11: "be gathered to you." Don't let Ahithohphel go now and get all the glory, Absalom! You lead us in battle and you will be the glorious victor! The fatal flaw in Hushai's plan is that it gave David time to organize and plan. Verse 16 may confuse the reader because we know Absalom will not pursue David at night, but Hushai obviously didn't know who's counsel would be listened to at the time he had to send the messengers to David. His only choice was to tell

David to cross the Jordan at once (verse 21). Ahithiophel clearly knows that time is on David's side and the rebellion is doomed, so he goes home and kills himself (verse 23). The next chapter will reveal that he was right.

Reading 3 - 2 Sam 18-20

18 - Today's reading ends Absalom's rebellion and its aftermath. If we were in doubt about the rebellion's outcome that ended with Hushai frustrating Ahithophel's counsel (17:14), giving David time to collect his troops, plan and resupply. 2 Samuel 18 shows David's veteran troops totally overmatch Absalom's rebels (verse 7), and many, many men die. David's concern for Absalom has been carefully spelled out (verse 5) but Joab knows how to end a rebellion: cut off the head of the monster. So he does (verse 14). Verse 18 gives one final illustration of Absalom's arrogance. His only real monument is an anonymous grave deep in the forests of Ephraim. Joab is reluctant to let just anyone carry this news (verses 19-23). Perhaps he feared for the messenger's life! David's irrational mourning (verse 33) may substantiate that such concerns were not entirely misguided. David's pain is recorded so that we will appreciate that the punishment of 12:10 was very, very real.

19 - Chapter 19 finds David mourning with misguided grief, and demoralizing his people (verses 1-4). Joab rebukes David, the only time it is recorded he ever did such (verses 5-8) but he is right. How can David grieve over the death of a rebel and not worry about his people? Even as things "get back to normal" we start seeing the markers of future trouble. Verses 9-15 find bickering between Judah and Israel, as the seeds for a split are sown that will be harvested in forty years. Why does David replace his general, Joab, with the leader of the rebel forces, Amasa (verse 13)? Verse 14 provides the answer: it was done for political reasons. We wonder if David is being generous to Shimei (verses 16-23) or is it just the one who suggested Shimei die that David didn't want to gratify. The reader will have to decide. Likewise, we don't know if Mephibosheth really did try and profit from Absalom's rebellion or whether he was slandered by Ziba (verses 24-30). David seems to want no part of such arguments. The chapter ends with a worthless man finding a reason to complain and start another rebellion (verses 40-43). The times of trouble Nathan told of have certainly come to pass!

20 - Chapter 20 shows the division that will later become permanent in the nation (verse 2). Amasa is less than a capable leader and Joab finally murders him and takes over (verses 4-12). Joab apparently dropped his sword so that Amasa felt safe (verse 8) but then produced another (perhaps it was hidden) and killed him (verse 10). To murder someone while looking them in the eye shows what a tough and cruel man Joab could be. He was, however, fiercely loyal to, and

protective of, David. Sheba's rebellion seems to have been a relatively small matter, ended with common sense on the part of a wise woman (verse 22).

Reading 4 - 2 Sam 21-23

21 - Today's reading begins the appendix of material in 2 Samuel. These chapters are not necessarily in chronological order, and they discontinue the story of stress, turmoil and warfare that 2 Samuel 12 began. 2 Samuel 21 seems to be early in David's reign, perhaps after the inquiry into Saul's house in chapter 9. The land is threatened by famine, and the explanation is that the house of Saul is under blood guilt for murdering the Gibeonites, the people who Israel covenanted with in Joshua 9. Israel should not have made a covenant with them, but they did and it must be honored. It was 400 years old and yet God expected it to be upheld! Why were the sons of Saul executed for what Saul did (verses 8-14)? They must have participated in Saul's sin and so were guilty. The law specifically forbids punishing sons for the guilt of fathers (Deut 24:16; Num 35:31). Who killed Goliath (verse 19)? The verse text says Elhanan did but we know David did. 1 Chronicles 20:5 resolves the conflict by noting that this is the brother of Goliath who was killed by Elhanan.

22 - Chapter 22 contains a psalm of praise by David that is very close to Psalm 18. Much of David's reign was a struggle. This psalm shows how he gave credit for every victory and all his success to God. The psalm has beautiful imagery of God throughout. Take special note of the connection in divine activity and human action in verses 38-41).

23 - Chapter 23 gives a fitting tribute to the men who surrounded David (note Psalm 57:14) and David's "last words." We need not take verse 1 super-literally, as if they were breathed and then he died. It is a kind of last will and testament, or last public words of David. The list of mighty men divides into three parts: the Three (verses 8-17), the Thirty (very great but not as great as the Three) in verses 18-23, and finally lesser warriors (verses 24-39). Verse 20 continues the Bible's only mention of literal snow. It is used as a figure of speech in many places but here the snow is real. Sadly we realize Uriah the Hittite, Bathsheba's husband, was one of David's trusted inner band (verse 39).

Reading 5 - 2 Sam 24; 1 Chron 21

24 and 21 - Today we complete the reading of Samuel with 2 Samuel 24. 1 Chronicles 21 is the parallel and nearly identical chapter so we will deal with them together, as both chapters are to be read today. The action here is straightforward. We are left to puzzle out, however, several questions. Why was God angry with Israel (24:1) and why was it wrong to count the people (24:3)? We do not know. Who caused David to count the people: God (2 Samuel 24:1) or Satan (2 Chronicles 21:1)? The answer is that God allowed Satan to tempt David (perhaps with pride?). The final question has to do with reconciling some of the differences in the census numbers and price paid for Arunah's (spelled Ornan in Chronicles) threshing floor. These differences may be the result of a scribal error, or it may be David paid one price for land, or even the entire Temple mount, and the other for the animals and yokes. Reconciling the census numbers is more complicated and uncertain. More important is David's determination to pay full cost for what he offered to the Lord (24:24). 2 Chronicles 22:1 tells that the threshing floor was chosen as the Temple site. Back to Table of Contents.

Week 22 - 1 Chron 22-29; 2 Chron 1; 1 Kings 1-4; Proverbs 1-2

Reading 1 - 1 Chron 22-25

22 - These readings are in Chronicles, and give us important information about David's preparations for the Temple that Samuel does not contain. 1 Chronicles 22 begins those preparations, noting that David could not build the temple due to his participation in many wars (verse 8). As David fought these wars at God's command and with God's help this may be more about the need to bring peace and safety than a mark against David's character. His place was to secure the empire, and then Solomon could build the Temple in an atmosphere of peace and safety (verse 9). The huge amount of gold and silver David stored up, from sources even outside of Israel, show how prosperous David's reign was, and how good God is at keeping His promises.

23 - Chapter 23 begins some difficult reading. These lists of names are a struggle for the modern reader but the names are important because they detail the Levites involvement and service in the Temple. Some of it is from the Chronicler's time, but it is all traced back to David. Note the change in duties with the new circumstances of being settled in the land (verses 25-26).

24 - Chapter 24 sets out the courses of the priests. By David's time there were more priests than opportunities to serve so the families were divided into 24 courses or divisions. Each course served one month out of the year, with the duties rotating among the men in their month. Verse 10 lists the eighth course, which was Zechariah's course (John the Baptist's father).

25 - Chapter 25 deals with the musicians. This is a good time to note that the instrumental music used in the Temple was ordered by God (2 Chron 29:25). Of course, attempts to appeal to the Old Testament worship system in its physical Temple to prove instrumental music should be used in New Testament worship are folly. Should we offer sacrifices and burn incense as well? We should not be embarrassed by instrumental music in the Old Testament or shy away from it. It was commanded of God and so it was used. If anything it shows that God is certainly capable of expressing a desire for that kind of music in His worship!

Reading 2 - 1 Kings 1; 1 Chron 26-28

1 - 1 Kings 1 prepares us for the end of David's reign. David is old and unable to keep warm, so a female slave is provided for this purpose (verses 1-4). What seems like a trivial note will loom large later. We then meet Adonijah, who is now the oldest of David's sons and, like David's other boys, has not been well parented (verse 6). His preparations and mannerism reminds us of Absalom. He has himself proclaimed king, and even has the backing of some high officials like Joab and Abiathar (verse 7). Joab was usually a very shrewd man but here he was badly mistaken. Adonijah will not be king and Nathan moves quickly to stop him. Note this is a very high stakes game (verse 12). Lives are at risk here, as Adonijah will eliminate all rivals to the throne as soon as he can. By verse 35 David is once again taking decisive action. Solomon is declared king, serving as a co-regent with David. But he is installed on the throne now (verse 46) so there can be no question who David chose. Verse 49 is almost funny. All those who followed Adonijah are now in rebellion to the real king! Solomon shows himself to be a gracious and generous king (verses 50-53), but we wonder what will happen when is father dies.

26 - 1 Chronicles 26 divides out gatekeepers (verses 1-19) and then concludes with other administrators (verses 20-32).

27 - Chapter 27 picks up on the secular officials ending chapter 26 and records army records. The census of verses 16-24 is a strange one. Why Gad and Asher are omitted and Aaron added is anyone's guess.

28 - Chapter 28 contains David's final public address, officially coronating Solomon (29:22ff) and explaining the foundations of his kingdom. Verses 1-9 make the Temple project priority one for Solomon. Note the conditional nature of God's promise about the dynasty of David in verse 7. David then charges Solomon to build God's house "according to the plan" God gave him (verse 19). The word for "plan" is the same word for "pattern" Moses uses of the Tabernacle in Exo 25:9, 40. So we are readied for Solomon to move to center stage and continue his father's work, even as David prepares to exit.

Reading 3 - 1 Kings 2; 1 Chron 29

2 - 1 Kings 2 begins with David's charge to Solomon (verses 1-9). The charge has two parts: spiritual matters and unfinished business. The spiritual section (verses 2-4) echoes the words of Joshua (Josh 1:6-9) and announces that the key to success is God's law. God's king must walk after God (verse 3). The rest of the chapter shows Solomon solidifying his rule. Adonijah's request for Abishag (verse 21) may seem innocent to us, but there was great political significance in possessing the women of the king's harem, as Abishag would be perceived (see 2 Sam. 3:7; 12:8; 16:21). Adonijah's request is the beginning of rebellious ideas at worst, or extremely foolish at best. Abiathar is dismissed in verse 26. We have had co-high priests up to this point, but no more. Zadok is the high priest now. We do well to remember that Abiathar was from the Ithamar clan, which is Eli's branch of the family. It was prophesied that Eli's family would be done away with and lose the priesthood and now we see that happening before our eyes. Verse 30 reveals that Joab may have been a great soldier but he didn't know the Law. Exo. 21:14 says there was to be no shelter in the Tabernacle for murderers. Shimei is put under house arrest (verses 36-37) so he cannot go to his kinsmen in Benjamin and stir up trouble. He may be one of the most foolish people in Scripture; losing his life over two runaway slaves!

29 - 1 Chronicles 29 is a great example of leadership by example. David gave freely to the Temple project and then asks others to do the same (verse 5). The response is overwhelming (verses 6-7). Notice the connection in rejoicing and giving generously for the right reasons (verse 9). Solomon is "re-coronated" in verse 22, probably a reference to a ceremony after David's death. We do not know how long David and Solomon reigned as co-regents, which explains why sometimes all the numbers (like in verse 27) don't always add up like we think we they should.

Reading 4 - 1 Kings 3; 2 Chron 1

3 - The alliance with Egypt in 1 Kings 3 is troubling. It does testify to Solomon's power, because Egyptian kings simply did not give their daughters in alliances like this. There are Babylonian records showing a rebuff of just such an offer! While it may have been flattering to receive such an offer the Law forbade marrying Canaanite women (Deut. 7:3; Exo. 34:16) and kings were not to multiply wives (Deut 17:17). If this woman was not strictly Canaanite things seem out of place here. Why enter into an alliance with Egypt? It would be better to trust in God! Verse 2 is also troubling. The "high places" were the chosen place to worship God since no central sanctuary existed at that time. More than likely they were former centers of idol worship ,and Israel was forbidden to use such places (Deut. 12:2-4, 13). Later they cause Solomon's downfall (1 Kings 11:7). The real highlight of the reading is Solomon's prayer for wisdom (verses 4-15). Solomon does well to see the people as God's people (verse 8), not his. Note God's promise in

verse 13 which the Bible will stress again and again abundantly came to pass. The episode of verses 16-28 demonstrates Solomon's great wisdom.

1 - 2 Chronicles 1 explains why Solomon went to Gibeon instead of Jerusalem to seek God (verses 3-4). Verses 14-17 testifies to Solomon's wealth but there is a note of foreboding there as the Law specifically forbade the king from acquiring many horses (Deut 17:16).

Reading 5 - 1 Kings 4; Proverbs 1-2

4 - 1 Kings 4 shows the kingdom growing and needing better organization. Saul maintained very little bureaucracy, ruling a kingdom that was a times only a loose confederacy. David had a larger court and united the country in an empire. He received tribute and had an administrative "cabinet." Solomon strengthens the kingdom even further, establishing a forced labor force, taxation system, and many officials (verses 1-19). We do well to remember Samuel's warning (1 Sam 8:11ff) about what a king would take from the people to be supported as we read these verses (verse 7). The reference to "sand" in verse 20 is the language of the Abrahamic promise. Solomon's wise leadership brings security to the country so that fortified cities are not necessary for safety (verse 25). Verse 32 tells of Solomon's literary accomplishment. While we have a number of his proverbs in the book of that name (which we begin reading today), Song of Solomon and Psalms 72 and 127 are all we have of his songs. All of this chapter emphasizes how God kept His promise to bless Solomon! However, even in the midst of such blessing there is tension. The reader notes chariots and horses again (verse 26) and one cannot but wonder if the provisions necessary to support such a large palace and court won't impose unnecessarily high taxes on the people. That very problem will come to the forefront when Solomon dies _ leading to the division of the kingdom.

Introduction to Proverbs - Since Solomon wrote so many of the Proverbs this is an ideal place for us to read them. The book of Proverbs is different from the historical material we have been reading. Its focus and concern is wisdom in a very practical way. Proverbs contains exactly what its title suggests: short, intensely practical sayings that touch on a huge variety of topics. While every culture has proverbs ("Look before you leap," for example) the Proverbs in the Bible give us God's perspective on the right and best way to live. Proverbs takes that a step further by speaking of how God actively blesses those who live wisely. Good choices make life better in the here and now is one of Proverbs' main themes. As we read Proverbs we need to keep in mind two key truths. First, proverbs, by their very nature, are general truths. They are not to be made into absolutes (note Prov 15:15; 12:21; 13:25) lest we force the Bible to contradict itself and the reality we live in. Second, just because a proverb speaks the truth that does not mean God condones what is described by that general truth. Proverbs 14:20 says that poor people have few friends while everyone likes the wealthy. That isn't as things ought to be, but Proverbs is discussing how things are. A final note: Proverbs often need little explanation. Writing notes for the reader of Proverbs can be difficult. We will focus here on the overall themes of Proverbs, and trying to work out any especially difficult sayings. At times these notes will be brief, which will allow the reader opportunity to mediate on and apply the Proverbs.

1 - Proverbs 1 contains an introduction for the entire book (verses 1-7). Note the emphasis on reverence for God being absolutely necessary to even begin this book (verse 7). The chapter's first admonition then is about evil companions (verses 8-19), a major theme in the book, and then it discusses how wisdom is available to any are willing to listen and learn (verses 20-33). The book is challenging young people (and readers today) to forsake evil companions and instead

study Proverbs to be wise!

2 - Proverbs 2 tells us that getting wisdom requires a lot of work (verses 1-4), but when you find God as the source of all wisdom (verses 5-8) you get all kinds of blessings. Note the many benefits to wisdom that are enumerated in this chapter (verses 9-22). Back to Table of Contents..

Week 23 - Proverbs 3-15

Reading 1 - Proverbs 3-5

3 - Proverbs 3 continues the emphasis on God as the source of all real wisdom (verses 1-12). Wisdom is of great value - even God uses it (verses 19-20).

4 - Proverbs 4 again implores the reader to desire wisdom. The beginning of that quest is a strong desire for insight and wisdom (verse 7).

5 - Proverbs 5 warns about sexual immorality. This is a dominant concern in Proverbs, as well it should be since Proverbs is for young people.

Reading 2 - Proverbs 6-7

6 - Proverbs 6 contains some straightforward advice about what to do when you are in trouble (verses 1-5), laziness (verses 6-11), what God hates with a special emphasis on discord (verses 12-19), and then returns again to warn about sexual immorality (verse 20-35). Verse 27 is often quoted but notice that contextually it speaks of sexual temptations.

7 - Proverbs 7 is the great chapter on adultery. In verse 14 her statement about offering sacrifices means she has leftover meat to eat. Is the young man so foolish as to really believe she sought him out (verse 15)?

Reading 3 - Proverbs 8-10

8 - Proverbs 8 personifies wisdom, calling for young people to come and listen to her. Verses 10-11 again extol the value of living wisely. Verses 22-31 speak of how even the Lord used wisdom in creation. If God acts wisely what should God's people do?

9 - Proverbs 9 concludes Proverbs' introduction and opening discussion of wisdom's value. This final chapter, almost a sermon, can be titled "The Invitations of Miss Wisdom and Miss Folly." Each way makes calls to the reader to come to her feast, but one meal is a banquet of life and the other a banquet of death. Verse 8 repeats a huge theme in Proverbs: the wise listen and get wiser, the foolish refuse wisdom and counsel. Verse 17 is famous, but what many miss is its connection to sexual immorality.

10 - Proverbs 10 begins what most people think of when they think of the book of Proverbs: simple, two line wise sayings that often feature a contrast (note the use of the term "but" repeatedly here). These proverbs form a section, beginning here and ending at 22:16. Different scholars have tried to find connecting links that tie together these proverbs, but such is very difficult to do. Although they generally make observations about life, wisdom, righteousness, or God's providence and involvement in life many proverbs cut across these lines or fall outside of any kind of classification. It seems best to just let these wise sayings stand on their own, rather than try to group them in some artificial classification. A final note that may be of more value to the reader than any "breakdown" of proverbs: break your daily reading up. Reading three or four chapters of Proverbs in a row can lead to a feeling of being overwhelmed and most of what is read being forgotten. Proverbs should be digested in bite size chunks, and is not kind to the gluttonous reader. Try reading a chapter at breakfast, another at lunch, another at supper and another at bedtime. This gives your mind more time to digest what Solomon is saying and it becomes more meaningful, memorable and more easily integrated into life. Notes on chapter 10: A major emphasis on righteousness versus wickedness begins in verse 24 and runs through 11:11. Consider underlining the words "righteous" and "wicked" or "evildoers" to make this

contrast clear.

Reading 4 - Proverbs 11-13

11 - Chapter 11 - Watch for the "caught in your own sin" theme that is sounded often in Proverbs (here in verses 5-6). Verse 14's idea is repeated in 18:1. Wisdom comes from the many, not from isolating self. Verse 22 paints a powerful word picture, doesn't it? Verse 27 asks us what we are searching for _ because we will certainly find it.

12 - Chapter 12 - Verse 2 seems to speak to our day. NASB has "a man who devises evil" while the ESV has "a man of evil devices" but either way the point is very sharp. Verse 3 furthers the thought. No one can be established in wickedness because it is an always shifting, ever changing life. Verse 9 points out the folly of pretense. Verse 11 is a needed verse in a day of Internet scams and "network marketing" schemes.

13 - Proverbs 13 works with desires, money and wisdom. Verse 7 reminds us that appearances cannot always be trusted. Verse 18's bad things happen to people who ignore instruction has been discussed in Proverbs before (see 15:32). Verse 19 mentions "evil" but it is the same term translated "harm" or "disaster" in the next two verses. The idea is to turn away from trouble. Proverbs often recommends turning away from evil and temptation (see chapter 7). The New Testament warns about evil companions (1 Cor 15:33) as does Proverbs (verse 20).

Reading 5 - Proverbs 14-15

14 - Chapter 14 has some wonderful material about the heart (note verses 10-15 especially). Verse 4 again extolls the value of work. Verse 23 warns of foolish scams and "get rich quick" schemes. Verse 34 picks up the idea of leadership, kings and rulers that seems to be developing in this chapter. We will see more on civil rulers and governmental responsibility as we journey along in Proverbs.

15 - Chapter 15 strongly emphasizes God's control of all of life (note verses 8, 9, 11, 16, and 23). There is also an emphasis on the heart (verses 7, 11, 13, 14, 15, 28, and 30). These two themes go together. People cannot see inside another person (the heart) but God can and He acts accordingly. Back to Table of Contents.

Week 24 - Proverbs 16-28

Reading 1 - Prov 16-18

16 - Proverbs 16 talks more of God in a short space than any other place in the book. God appears nine times in verses 1-11, with the king then being mentioned five times in verses 10-15. God is ordering life and the king should be an instrument of that order by reflecting and ruling as God would. Verse 30 is a summary description of the wicked man of verse 29, with his evil plans given away by his countenance. Verse 32 is a huge key to the wise life: self-control.

17-18 - Chapters 17 and 18 major in relationships and what it is to live in community with others. Many of these proverbs are (like most proverbs) crystal clear in their meaning and application. 17:19 is an exception. No one is exactly sure what "makes the door high" references. Some think of a fancy entrance that announces pride in riches, others have seen it as a metaphor for speech. 18:1 decries isolation, as read already in 11:14 and 15:22. Chapter 18 is about talk, lips, and words, ideas that are well summed up in verse 21.

Reading 2 - Prov 19-21

19 - Chapter 19 talks of poverty and wealth, being poor and being rich. Along the way we are treated to gems like verse 3 (how often have you heard someone blame God for their own foolishness?). Verse 7 breaks the pattern of two line proverbs with a three line proverb (see also verse 23). The importance of integrity is illustrated by verse 9's near repetition of verse 5. Note verse 17 - "lending to the Lord" is a powerful idea.

20 - Proverbs 20 opens with an admonition about alcohol (verse 1), an appropriate beginning as this chapter talks at length about what opposes wisdom and the best way to live (note verse 4, 10, 17, 20, 22, 23). Verse 5 is the "true friend" passage. Verse 14 is the used car buyer's verse! The wheel of verse 26 is uncertain. Some see it as a torture device but others think it is just a threshing instrument and the metaphor of separating the righteous from the wicked is being furthered. Verse 30 shows there can be great value in suffering.

21 - Chapter 21 develops thoughts on righteousness and wickedness. Verse 2 echoes 16:2, warning again of the danger of self-deception. Verse 18 is uncertain.

Reading 3 - Prov 22-23

22 - Chapter 22 has one of the most famous of all proverbs, verse 6's admonition about child-rearing. However, this verse cannot be treated as an ironclad guarantee any more than verses 8 and 9 prove that evildoers always reap calamity or that he who shares with the poor will always prosper financially. Proverbs contains general truths - we do well to keep that in focus here. Verse 16 brings an end to one collection of proverbs. Beginning in verse 17 is a new section of the book. This new section is apparent from the title, renewed calls to listen and a new style of teaching that involves couplets employing an admonition and then giving the reason for the admonition. Some have tried to find thirty sayings here that are similar to an Egyptian wisdom document with thirty sayings but such attempts fail. However, even if the writer of Proverbs did read other wisdom literature that only teaches us that God is the God of all nations and His wisdom can be seen everywhere. What is wise in Egypt would be true in Israel as well!

23 - Chapter 23 continues a mixed collection of proverbs on a wide variety of topics. Verse 17 is very powerful (note Psalm 73 in this connection). Verse 23 is a proverb that every disciple needs to memorize. The closing comments about alcohol (verses 29-35) paint a devastating picture of

alcohol's folly, and form a powerful answer to those who wish to justify it today.

Reading 4 - Prov 24-25

24 - Chapter 24 speaks more of wisdom and the right and best way to live. Verse 12 teaches us to do good when we can, and not ignore need. Verses 30-33 help us see how to become wise. One has experiences in life (verse 30), and one needs to observe what is going on around him/her (verse 31). Then one reflects on what has happened and what one saw (verse 32), leading to an understanding of the way that is wise (verse 33).

25 - Chapter 25 begins by exalting God in verse 2. God's secret are such that no one, not even a king, can find them out. Verse 16 offers wonderful wisdom in our time of excess. Verse 17 is a good example of the practical wisdom that has made Proverbs much beloved and so widely read.

Reading 5 - Prov 26-28

26 - Chapter 26 doesn't define foolishness, but it does illustrate it. Verses 4-5 are pure genius. They appear to be contradictory but instead simply teach that there is no "one size fits all" solution to life's problems. The wise person will discern what is befitting for each situation. Verses 24-26 make up a rare long proverb.

27 - Chapter 27 features some difficult proverbs. How is open rebuke better than hidden love (verse 5)? Because when one truly loves he or she won't be afraid to offer correction. Much in Proverbs has built up the need for admonition and how the wise listen to such. Being silent when someone needs reproof isn't real love. What does verse 10 speak of? The key idea here is "friend." It may mean it is better to rely on friends nearby than to go miles to get a relative's help. What does verse 13 mean? It is very similar to 20:16 and refers to teaching a fool to do better by making him suffer the consequences for his foolish action. If a man puts up his garment as collateral on a loan for a stranger, or worse for an adulteress, he is accepting a terrible risk and so you should take his garment. Only then will he learn better than to "co-sign" for such bad risks!

28 - Chapter 28 returns Proverbs to its moral footing. The last several chapters have been about day to day living and life with not much mention of God or righteousness. That changes in this chapter (note verses 2,3, 5, 8, 10, 12, 14, 18, 25). Verse 13 is one of the best proverbs in the entire book. Verse 23 is true if (as we've seen repeatedly in Proverbs) the one being rebuked is wise. Back to Table of Contents.

Week 25 - Prov 29-31; Song of Sol; 1 Kings 5; 2 Chron 2

Reading 1 - Prov 29-31

29 - Proverbs 29 closes the conventional "proverbs" part of the book. Verse 1's truth should be apparent by now. If one doesn't listen to reproof then eventually he will end up in terrible trouble. Once again we read how sin trips up the sinner (verse 6). Note the contrast in God's wisdom and man's ways in verse 11. Constantly we hear that we must let anger out or vent, etc. Proverbs says otherwise! Verse 13 varies the proverb of 22:2 a little. It is the Lord who made both the poor man and the one oppressing him, thus there is an implied threat to the oppressor. Verse 18 is often misused to back the idea that people must set lofty goals, i.e. have a "vision" for their future or perish. But the ESV makes it clear: "where there is not prophetic vision people cast off restraint." This isn't about the individual's goals and dreams but following God's word! The "curse" of verse 24 comes from Leviticus 5:1-5, which required those who knew of a crime to speak up. The proverb means the thief knows the curse but he doesn't obey the law.

30 - Chapter 30 is the first of two appendices to Proverbs. It begins with the words of Agur, someone who is unknown to us. He confesses his ignorance (verses 1-3), but we quickly realize he is not ignorant _ he is simply revealing that he trusts in God and His word not his own ideas (verses 4-6). What follows are wise sayings in longer form than most proverbs we have read. Agur likes to use a numerical form of "three, no four" to make his points.

31 - Chapter 31 is very famous. It contains the words of Lemuel. We do not know who he was either. These are the only instruction made directly to a king. The famous description of the worthy woman follows. It is an alphabetic acrostic, meaning that each verse begins with the corresponding letter of the Hebrew alphabet. Acrostics usually are written for easy memorization and/or to suggest a full exploration of the subject - from A to Z, if you will. Sadly some women have despaired as they read this amazing description, assuming they are to do all she did. Yet that fails to realize this is an idealized woman. No one person could do all she did all the time! Verse 27 is the key: she cares deeply for her household and is not lazy. The woman who pursues those goals is well on her to way becoming the woman of chapter 31.

Reading 2 - Song of Solomon 1-3

Introduction to Song of Solomon - Without doubt, there isn't anything in Scripture quite like the Song of Solomon! It is a beautiful and powerful and needed picture of the pure passions of married love. Unfortunately, understanding the Song has been hindered by false methods of interpreting it. For example, it has been used an allegory where everything stands for something else. Those who think the marriage relationship is somehow "dirty" or not to be spoken of quickly decided this was about Jesus' love for the church (and that is why we have a hymn titled "Jesus Rose of Sharon"). Yet the allegorical approach is so arbitrary and contrived, especially since no passage anywhere says Solomon is a type of Christ in any way. The first rule of Bible study is to take the Scripture at face value - why shouldn't we do that here in Song of Solomon? As long as we can accept that God made the sexual relationship to be beautiful and desirable in marriage (see Hebrews 13:4) there is no reason to try and force Song of Solomon to be anything other than what it is: a beautiful poem celebrating the joys of married love. Why should we be surprised that the God who made the sexual relationship has no problem writing of it in His Word as a great blessing? Additional notes: some see three characters in the Song - Solomon, the Shulamite girl and her "true love," a shepherd boy. A full explanation and refutation of that view is far beyond these brief notes. We will rely on the two character viewpoint as it seems more straightforward than the three character view. Changes in gender and from first person to plural speech will help us track out who is speaking in each passage.

1 - Chapter 1 - The Shulamith girl speaks to the "chorus" (perhaps her friends or other women of the court) as she discusses the wonderful character of Solomon. She desires him in a physical way (verse 2) but is drawn to his character (the "good name" of verse 3). Yet she does not feel attractive as she is a "farm girl" tanned by the sun (verses 5-6). Solomon then speaks, lavishing his praise upon her and making her feel beautiful (verses 8-10). Note verse 11's "we" designating that the chorus or friends are speaking. Solomon and the Shulamith exchange lover's talk to end the chapter (verses 12-17).

2 - Chapter 2 shows how his compliments have changed her view of herself (verse 1). She yearns for him and for physical love. Verse 3 describes kissing. Verse 4's "banner over me is love" is difficult. It may mean "he looked upon me with intent to love me." She clearly wants to be Solomon's but note verse 7. She knows there is a right time for physical love and that time is not yet! How wonderful for her to be honest with her feelings but still control herself! In verses 8-14 they talk and spend time together. They are very much in love.

3 - Chapter 3's meaning is a bit uncertain. This seems to be a dream the Shulamite girl is having - a very bad dream in which she has lost the love of her life (verses 1-5). Notice that even in her dream she desires him (verse 4) but knows that she must wait till she is married to fulfill her desire. Verses 6-11 show the wedding procession coming to the marriage ceremony. They are married and they delight in marriage (verses 11).

Reading 3 - Song of Solomon 4-6

4 - This chapter forms the heart of this great book. He is enraptured with his bride and describes her beauty in great detail. Some of these metaphors are lost on us, as today's reader is not acquainted with an agricultural society. For example, women today probably don't want their hair to be described as looking like a flock of goats (verse 1)! Yet goats descending down a mountain side would make a river of black hair that would flow and be very beautiful. In the same way, shorn sheep shine pink through their thin hair and the idea of twins clearly defines her perfect teeth, and that she has them all (verse 2). Verse 4's tower metaphor probably refers to the way she carries herself, with integrity and grace. Verse 10 offers a powerful description of the joys of wedded love. But notice she is pure (verse 12). In verse 16 she tells him she is ready for love. This verse forms the exact center of the book. In the Hebrew there are 111 lines before it (60 verses and the title) and from 5:2 to the end there are 111 more lines. The honeymoon is the highpoint in Song of Solomon! 5:1 really goes with chapter 4, as the consummation of married love is celebrated.

5 - Chapter 5 shows marriage can be grand but problems can crop up. Here she has gone to bed but is not asleep yet (verse 2). Solomon comes for her but she puts him off (verse 3). She changes her mind and decides to open the bedroom door but he is gone (verses 4-6). She has taken him for granted and now realizes her mistake. She searches intensely for him, meeting up with the friends (verse 9) to whom she describes Solomon (verses 10-16).

6 - Chapter 6 continues the "lost lover" drama as the friends ask where he has gone (verse 1). She knows - he is in the garden where they always go (verse 2). She goes there and he again praises her beauty and they make up (verses 4-13). Verses 12-13 are the most difficult in the Song. They are very hard to translate much less relate to the Song's storyline!

Reading 4 - Song of Solomon 7-8

7 - In chapter 7 Solomon again praises and describes his bride. Some have noticed this description is more vivid than the description of Chapter 4 because they are now married and can be more free with each other. We should certainly notice that while she caused a ripple in their relationship in Chapter 6 he doesn't hold it against her but is wooing her again so that their marriage can overcome problems and they can be happily together again. Some have noticed in this description and its clear exuberance for the physical side of marriage a kind of "holy lust." They share a strong desire for each other and God compliments and blesses that. We must not let our society determine our attitude toward the sexual relationship with the result that we think sex is bad or dirty or wrong. The sexual relationship is a great blessing from God when it is found in the right place: marriage! No book in the Bible may make this point clearer than the Song of Solomon!

8 - Chapter 8 ends the scene of reconciliation (verses 1-4). The book concludes with a description of true love (verses 5-7), and some beautiful advice for young people about love (verses 8-12). The last scene we see is the Shulamith and Solomon calling for one another as they did to open the book. The final invitation is an invitation to continue the joys of marriage which they share in so wondrously together!

Reading 5 - 1 Kings 5; 2 Chronicles 2

5 - After spending some time in the wisdom books of the Bible we head back to the account of the Israelites and their kings. 1 Kings 5 continues Solomon's successes. Verses 4-5 reveal why David wasn't able to do the building Solomon did: he was busy subjugating enemies. But now in the peace that followed Solomon sees real opportunity. Verse 11 finds Tyre needing food, a situation that will continue in NT times (see Acts 12:20). The laborers of verse 9 are Canaanites (compare to 9:20-21; 2 Chron. 2:17-18; 8:1-9).

2 - 2 Chronicles 2 tells of Solomon's preparations to build the Temple. Verse 6 shows good understanding that the Temple could not and would not contain God. Note that Chronicles doesn't tell of Solomon's palace building, putting the focus on the Temple. Back to Table of Contents.

Week 26 - 1 Kings 6-9; 2 Chronicles 3-8

Reading 1 - 1 Kings 6; 2 Chron 3

6 - 1 Kings 6 begin the Temple project. 1 Kings 6:1 is a tremendously helpful chronological passage. It establishes the fourth year of Solomon's reign as about 966 or 967 BC, making the Exodus about 1447 or 1446. The rest of the chapters are filled with the details of the Temple. The reader should be warned that many of these construction and architectural terms are hard to translate and sometimes the exact nature of the building is difficult to visualize. The overall message here, however, is clear: the Temple was incredibly beautiful and expensive. It was a house entirely appropriate for the one true God, the Creator and God of Israel. Verse 1's mention of the Exodus is designed to tie the Temple back to that other major event in Israel's history and say this event is just as significant. God makes very specific promises to that end in verses 11-13. Here we have a grand reference back to 2 Samuel 7:11-16, and the promises of David having a lasting dynasty. Note the conditional nature of that promise (verse 12). There is an implied warning here as well. The king and the people must not think that just because they have this house God will never leave them. (see Micah 3:11-12; Jeremiah 7:4; 26:18). Obedient hearts are more important to God than beautiful buildings!

3 - 2 Chronicles 3 adds to our understanding by noting the significance of the Temple's site (verse 1).

Reading 2 - 1 Kings 7; 2 Chron 4

7 - We read two chapters today about the Temple's construction. 1 Kings 7 deals first with Solomon's house (verses 1-12) and then turns to some final notes on the Temple (verses 13-51). Is there an implied criticism that Solomon spent almost twice as long building his palace as the Temple (verse 1)? Some of the detail in the Temple's construction is almost overwhelming but it all comes together to make the point that the Temple was simply the grandest and most extravagant building of its time. There is much speculation but little consensus about the two pillars (verses 15-22) and what their names mean. Verse 46's reference to casting the bronze in the clay tells us that a very specialized technique was used, requiring very skilled craftsman to complete.

4 - 2 Chronicles 4 contains a similar record of the amazing Temple and its furnishings. The amount of bronze and gold used for the Temple are simply staggering to contemplate (verses 18-22).

Reading 3 - 1 Kings 8

8 - 1 Kings 8 and 2 Chronicles 6 cover the same event: Solomon's wonderful dedicatory prayer of the Temple. Working the chapters in chronological order here is difficult without having huge readings on a single date. We will work with the Kings' account (today just 1 Kings 8) and add material from Chronicles as needed. Verse 2 tells us that the dedication occurred in the seventh month. Yet 1 Kings 6:38 tells us the Temple was completed in the eight month. There is debate as to what this means but it may well be that the formal dedication ceremonies were put off 11 months so as to coincide with the Feast of Tabernacles. The Feast of Tabernacles was a harvest feast, but also celebrated the end of the wilderness wanderings (Deut. 12:8-11). Solomon sees the completion of the Temple as symbolic of all of God's promises coming to pass, not only to bring them to Promised Land but to live among them (see Exodus 33:12-16 where Moses says possession of land without God would be meaningless). Verse 9 raises questions because the ark

used to have the rod of Aaron and a pot of manna in it (Hebrews 9:4). We do not know if they were removed (perhaps they were no longer needed now that they were permanently in the land?) or if they were lost during the wild days of the judges. Verses 10-11 remind us of how God came to the Tabernacle in Exodus 40:34. Solomon addresses the people in verses 12-21 with the dominant note being "praise God for keeping His promises." Solomon's prayer to God (verses 22-53) is magnificent. It asks that God would recognize the Temple as a way for sinful people to approach Him.

Reading 4 - 2 Chronicles 5-7

5 - 2 Chronicles 5 sets the stage for dedicating the Temple by bringing the ark into the house of God. The old tent of meeting is brought to Jerusalem as well (verse 5) ending the time of two places to worship. Much of verses 11-14 is not paralleled in Kings. It shows Chronicles' interest in music and musicians.

6 - 2 Chronicle 6:12-13 tells of a scaffold built above the people, and says Solomon knelt to pray. Solomon completely avoids idolatry and superstition in verse 27. Verse 29 is the core verse: please, Lord, let us keep using the Temple! Beginning in verse 30 Solomon then develops scenarios in which he hopes God will continue to be gracious, making seven requests of God. Verse 35 directly ties to the Law of Moses (see Deut 28:53). Solomon's prayer for foreigners (verse 41) is truly remarkable. Verse 56 sounds the keynote of "rest," something God had promised His people (Deut. 12:9-10). Verse 60 is one of those small verses that can slip by the reader but it tells of God's overall plans and purposes.

7 - 2 Chronicles 7 ends with the Temple dedication by telling that God sent fire from heaven (verse 1) and God's glory filled the house (verse 2). What a sight to have seen! Once again we see the joy that true worship and devotion to God can bring (verse 10). God then answers Solomon's prayer in verses 12-22, telling Solomon that faithfulness is what matters if the Temple is to be of any value. The Lord even specifically says He will cast off His people and destroy the Temple if they serve idols instead of Him (verses 19-22). Sadly that promise comes to pass, despite the warnings of prophets like Jeremiah (note his temple sermon in Jeremiah 7 that begs the people to stop thinking of the temple like a good luck charm that protects them from foreign invasion).

Reading 5 - 1 Kings 9; 2 Chronicles 8

9 - 1 Kings 9 covers much of the ground we read in 2 Chronicles 7 and 8. There is a peculiar note about Hiram not being happy with the cities given him (verses 10-13). Why is Solomon giving away cities? Is he out of tax money?

8 - 2 Chronicles 8 details many of Solomon's accomplishments. Much of what he did was very impressive but again there is a troubling note (verse 11). Back to Table of Contents.

Week 27 - 1 Kings 10-11; 2 Chronicles 9; Eccl 1-12

Reading 1 - 1 Kings 10-11; 2 Chron 9

10 - 1 Kings 10 helps us appreciate how great Solomon's kingdom really was. Sheba (verse 1) is in the south of Arabia. That means she traveled over 1500 miles to see Solomon! Some translations of verse 1 say she brought "riddles" but better is "hard questions" (ESV). Notice that all of Solomon's wealth and wisdom just bring glory to God (verse 9). As we read of Solomon's tremendous wealth (verses 14-29) we do well to remember Jesus' words in Matthew 6:29 - "Solomon in all his glory was not arrayed like one of these." Jesus uses him as the consummate example of riches! The chapter concludes, however, with a dark note (verse 26). This is a direct violation of God's law in Deuteronomy 17:16ff! What is Solomon doing?

11 - 1 Kings 11 builds off the sin at the end of chapter 10 to tell us Solomon completely lost touch with obedience and God's law. As he violated God's law regarding accumulating gold, chariots and horses so he did with multiplying wives (verses 1-3). Just as God had said in Deuteronomy 17 these women turned his heart away (verse 4). Verse 6's sad statement that Solomon did not "wholly follow the Lord" shows that while he didn't totally abandon Jehovah, he might as well have. He even built idol temples (verse 7)! Verse 9 shows us that Solomon was entirely responsible for his apostasy, especially since he had the privilege of two appearances by the Lord. God's verdict is given against Solomon (verses 11-13). There are questions about the "one tribe" of verse 13 because if ten tribes are taken two should be left. Some think this may refer to Benjamin sticking with the south, as Judah being the royal tribe would simply be assumed to be staying with the king and his family. In verse 26 we meet Jeroboam, who will be the next king. Sadly, Solomon behaves like Saul did long ago (verse 40). What will happen to this kingdom when Solomon dies?

9 - 2 Chronicles 9 contains the record of the Queen of Sheba's visit and Solomon's great wealth. Interestingly, the Chronicler does not record Solomon's downfall with foreign women. The story here closes on a high note, and then Solomon's death is recorded (verses 29-31).

Reading 2 - Ecclesiastes 1-3

Introduction to Ecclesiastes - Ecclesiastes is a marvelous, but troubling, book. It is full of statements that seem almost anti-religious, and contains a deep cynicism that makes it almost gloomy. Further, its structure is not immediately apparent so that sometimes the book doesn't really seem to "go together." The key to this unusual work is its purpose. "Vanity! Vanity! All is vanity" is the key phrase, found some 38 times. It means emptiness, futility, something transitory and unsatisfactory. That shouldn't be taken to mean life can't be good or enjoyable — only that it is a struggle to find lasting purpose. Ecclesiastes explores how to build a life that transcends the meaninglessness of this world, a life that goes beyond death. We will much here about how to live life as good as possible when it is all still vanity, still ends in death. We will also see some here about transcending death. It is fitting to read Ecclesiastes at this point in the Old Testament because many scholars believe it records Solomon's views on life as an old man. Hopefully chapter 12's good conclusion represents repentance on this wise but foolish king's part!

1 - Chapter 1 begins with a frank admission of troubles. Life doesn't change much. What has been before comes around again (verses 1-11). Solomon is determined to find meaning in this meaningless existence but it is a frustrating and difficult quest (verses 12-18).

2 - Chapter 2 tries pleasure (verses 1-11), only to discover purpose and meaning can't be found

there. There are some advantages to wisdom (verses 12-17) but all still die. Death levels the playing field. Wisdom does not transcend death. Solomon seems frustrated and uncertain where to turn next. As one writer asked "If every card we play is trumped does it matter how we play?" Thus it seems all a person can do is just enjoy the blessings of God in this life and live as best one can (verses 24-26).

3 - Chapter 3 gives God's plan for living (verses 1-8). We must take life day by day, realizing God has a time for everything to be done. Note that we need to find the right time to act, and when we do act in the right time it is beautiful (verse 11). "Beautiful" here means fitting or appropriate. From there Solomon writes about God's actions - letting man enjoy life (verses 12-13), and working everything together so that men will turn to Him, will fear Him, will trust Him and serve Him (verses 14-15). However, this beautiful and hopeful section then ends with hard facts. Often times things aren't right and often times we don't live long enough to see all things fit together properly (verses 16-22). Verse 21 has been misconstrued by some to say there is no soul, but it may just reflect Solomon's skepticism (and thus mean he is mistaken) or that from a purely human standpoint animals and people die alike, and we do not see the soul leaving the body. Alternatively, it could means there is no second chance, and no certainty about the afterlife.

Reading 3 - Eccl 4-6

4 - Chapter 4 continues the hard facts of life. The over-arching theme here is power and rulers and how people react to them. There is a return to the theme of injustice. Solomon is saying that some people in good circumstances may be able to do what he recommended in 2:24-25 but what of the oppressed? There is frustration in politics (verses 1-3), frustration with work (verses 4-6), frustration with a lack of companionship and loneliness (verses 7-12) and finally a frustration with the fickleness of people (verses 13-16).

5 - Chapter 5 contains a quiet interlude in Solomon's outcry against oppression and vanity. He reflects on God and that one ought not make demands of God but instead honor Him and accept what comes from His hand. That includes how we handle vows (verses 1-7) and not trusting in money for life's ultimate purpose (verses 8-20). Be content is a main theme here (verses 19-20).

6 - Chapter 6 is difficult. Solomon says even if you add various things to life it still won't satisfy. Add children (verse 3), or more years (verse 6), or more work (verse 7), or even wisdom (verse 8) won't fill up life and make it good. So stop dreaming for more and accept what you have (verse 9). Verses 10-12 are troubling. Solomon seems to be summarizing that to this point he has not found a greater purpose for life and so one must do as best he can and then just die. What a pessimistic note!

Reading 4 - Eccl 7-9

7 - Seven times the phrase "better than" begins the chapter. These mark a turn in the book as it turns more toward practical day-to-day wisdom. This first set of proverbs here speaks of a serious view of life, of taking life seriously and they urge us to obey God. We may not know God's entire will for our lives but we can still obey the Lord. Verses 13-14 makes clear that human wisdom cannot penetrate, change or know all of God's ways. Verses 16-17 are difficult. How can one be overly righteous? Is Solomon sanctioning some wickedness by saying "be not overly wicked?" Being over-righteous in verse 16 is an obvious allusion to a pharisaical approach. Verse 17 means capitulating and giving in to sin. Verse 21 reminds us to not take life

too seriously.

8 - Chapter 8 sounds a more upbeat note after chapter 7's very pessimistic ending. Now Solomon seems to shake off some of that depression and notes there is value to wisdom and living in a wise way. Verses 1-8 give wisdom for dealing with the king and God. In verses 9-13 Solomon again sets forth some mysteries that just can't be explained or understood, such as the mystery of unjust triumph (verses 10-13), and mystery of unfair consequences (verse 14). Once again Solomon realizes we cannot understand everything about how the world works, why God does as He does, so we must be content (verses 15-17).

9 - Chapter 9 seem to be extending the thoughts of chapter 8. Solomon has spoken of contentment, but then again he deals with some the things that make it so hard to be contented. He continues to recommend contentment (verses 7, 9) but it's a struggle when you realize you will die (verses 1-6), things don't go as we expected (verses 11-12), or when wisdom is not appreciated (verses 13-18).

Reading 5 - Eccl 10-12

10 - Chapter 10 is a collection of proverbs that don't seem to have a unifying theme to them. Contrasts seem to be at a premium here - advantages versus disadvantages or foolishness versus wisdom. Perhaps the link here is to 9:18 where Solomon extolled wisdom so now he speaks further of it. Verse 4 really challenges us but is so right. Verse 10 tells us to take time to "sharpen the saw" if we are to be effective. Verse 18 addresses slothful rulers who let things go bad and then think money is the answer to everything (verse 19). Politics hasn't changed much since Solomon's time has it?

11 - Chapter 11 has Solomon returning to the idea of how to live wisely. He has been telling us that while we cannot see all of God's plans we have to live as contentedly and wisely as possible, so here is more wisdom on how to do that. Different interpretations have been offered of verse 1. Is this the idea of charity (not seen before in Ecclesiastes) or take a risk, but don't put your eggs all in one basket? Verse 3 shows they are events beyond human understanding and control. Verse 8 again says to just be content and enjoy life as God blesses you.

12 - Chapter 12 is the climax of the book. Perhaps Solomon was old when he penned Ecclesiastes. He urges the reader to serve God ("remember" means to act decisively, 1 Sam 1:19) when young because old age is coming. Most of the metaphors for aging are easily understood here. Verse 5's "almond trees" probably references grey hair. For a moment the frustration and cynicism of Solomon pours out again (verses 7-8) but his final conclusion does find what transcends life and even death. Serve the Lord - that is what matters most and in the end, all that matters (verses 12-13). Solomon's book finishes by saying "Be happy and content _ in serving God." Back to Table of Contents.

Week 28 - 1 Kings 12-18; 2 Chron 10-16

Reading 1 - 1 Kings 12; 2 Chron 10-11

12 - 1 Kings 12 and 2 Chronicles 10 tells the sad tale of the fracture of Israel into two rival and often competing kingdoms. If we've been aware of the history of these people the division that occurs should not surprise us (see Judges 8:1ff; 12:1ff; 2 Sam 2-5; 2 Sam 19:40-43; 20:1-13 for the rift in progress). Verse 1 seems to indicate Rehoboam was reigning in Judah (see 11:43) but now proceeded north to deal with political troubles there. Sadly, while Rehoboam seeks counsel there is no discussion of prayer. Rehoboam ultimately rejects the counsel to be a "servant to the people" (verse 7), choosing instead to force the people to serve him (verses 12-15). They aren't interested in that (and the high taxes that go with it) and the kingdom divides. Verse 24 is surprising, as we don't see much spiritual sensitivity in Rehoboam. However, he was badly outnumbered he was badly outnumbered (see 2 Chron 13:3) which may have encouraged his obedience. Jeroboam's wretched sin - the introduction of idol worship in Israel - is covered in verses 25-33. It is a sin from which Israel will never recover. It is important to note from verse 28 that Israel is still worshiping Jehovah, they are only doing it through idols. Jeroboam completes the apostasy by establishing his own priesthood (verses 31-32) and setting up his own feast in the eighth month (verse 33). The northern kingdom is clearly racing away from God and is ripe for more apostasy if the current mood cannot be checked.

11 - 2 Chronicles 11 adds a key element to the story. Verses 13-17 relate that all the priests and Levites evacuated the north due to Jeroboam's outrageous sin. God's people simply cannot remain in a sinful situation and so these people must leave. However, the result is that Israel is not left without spiritual guidance or teaching.

Reading 2 - 1 Kings 13-14; 2 Chron 12

13 - 1 Kings 13 records God's effort to stop the wildfire of sin Jeroboam kindled. The young prophet calls the name of the king who will do this 300 years ahead of time (see 2 Kings 23:15-20 for fulfillment). The rest of the chapter is sad and sobering. We wonder why this older prophet (verse 11) is still in the north, and why God didn't use him to curse the altar? Beyond that we wonder why the young man is punished when the lying older prophet is not but it is not for us to judge God's ways. God used the young man as an object lesson for all to see how serious disobedience to Him really was (verse 25). Sadly Jeroboam did not listen or learn from it (verses 33-34).

14 and 12 - 1 Kings 14 and 2 Chronicles 12 are relatively straightforward here. Ahijah's message flatly rebukes Jeroboam's wife, saying of her husband that God exalted him (verses 7-8), Jeroboam failed God (verse 9), so the House of Jeroboam will be cut off (verses 10-11), the child will die (verses 12-13), and Israel will be scattered (verses 15-16). Apparently Jeroboam's wife didn't believe the prophet (verses 17). The scene then switches to the south and Rehoboam, finding him in disobedience to God as well (verses 21-31). As a result God no longer protects Jerusalem and it is sacked. The parallel account in 2 Chronicles 12:1-12 helps here. Note the failure of Rehoboam (verse 14). He didn't want to do right, and so didn't get his heart ready to seek for God.

m Reading 3 - 1 Kings 15; 2 Chron 13-14

15, 13-14 - 1 Kings 15 and 2 Chronicles 13-14 cover the same time period and kings. 1 Kings 15, however, doesn't give much space to Abijah. 2 Chronicles 13 gives us his great speech and record of his faith (verses 4-12). Don't miss it! God gave Judah the victory that day (verse 16) but alas, Abijah's righteousness would not last. He walked in the sins of his fathers (1 Kings 15:3). Fortunately, the next king was a good king, Asa. Asa bought the Syrians off so that they would attack Israel and take the pressure of his kingdom (1 Kings 15:18-20). He did not consult God in this - a disturbing note in otherwise excellent reign. There is much speculation about Asa's feet (verse 23) but no certainty what happened there. This resulted in Asa being able to build and expand the kingdom. 2 Chronicles 14 gives more detail of Asa's reign, his reforms (verses 2-4), and building programs (verses 6-7). He faced a huge Ethiopian army with faith and was given victory by God (verses 11-15).

Reading 4 - 2 Chronicles 15-16; 1 Kings 16

15 - We will begin our reading in 2 Chronicles 15 because it goes well with yesterday's reading in 1 Kings 15. 2 Chronicles 15 gives more details of Asa's reforms. Spurred by the prophet Azaraiah (about whom we nothing else) in verse 1 Asa takes on additional reforms. Verse 2 is a stellar verse that reminds us of the basic shape of being in relationship with God. How wonderful that if we seek Him He will be found! Verse 8 suggests a more extensive reformation involving the whole land. Verse 9 shows how the faithful moved in increasing numbers south so they could serve the Lord. Verse 17 is disturbing but may not be so a much a bad mark on Asa's reign, as much as it is a comment on the hard-hearted-ness of the people of the land, or may just refer to Israel because Asa had cleansed Judah (14:3).

16 - 2 Chronicles 16 largely parallels 1 Kings 15, but in verse 7 we get additional info the account in Kings does not contain! The attack from the north (verse 1) tests Asa's faith and sadly he fails. He does not seek the Lord or trust in the Lord and so is condemned (verses 7-9). His reaction to the prophet's words is terrible, as Asa appears to drift away from God (verses 10, 12).

16 - Our focus returns to Israel in the north in chapter 16. There is tremendous emphasis here on God's word coming to pass (note verses 7, 11-12, 34). Verse 7 actually condemns Baasha for destroying the house of Jeroboam even though such was God's will, apparently because Baasha did this act for his own purposes and not because he wanted to serve God. The northern kingdom is subject to all kinds of anarchy and chaos and even civil war (verse 15) as assassination follows assassination and generals replace kings. Omri (verses 21-28) finally brings some order the kingdom, permanently moving the capital to Samaria (verses 24). Yet spiritually he is no better than those before him (verse 26). His son Ahab brings Israel to a new low point (note 21:20, 25). Verses 31-32 introduce a new note in Israel's spiritual demise: a false god. Before this Israel worships Jehovah through idols (which was certainly wrong) but now they are not even worshiping Jehovah. This is wrong worship of the wrong god, Baal!

Reading 5 - 1 Kings 17-18

17 - 1 Kings 17 tells of exactly what we would expect: God acts when His people are so far from Him. Elijah suddenly appears on the scene as a mighty prophet and force for righteousness. He is not to be underestimated. He has been called the most important figure since Moses and Samuel, and he appears on the Mount of Transfiguration, appearing as the representative of prophecy. Elijah's prayer of verse 1 is nothing more than a claiming of the promises of Deuteronomy 11:16-17 and 28:23. Elijah prays that God will do what He promised He would do when His people disobeyed and God answers that prayer! As Baal was the god of rain this is a direct blow against him. Verse 9 notes that Elijah has to flee outside of Israel to find safety. Verse 16 furthers the theme of God's word coming to pass again. We do not know why Elijah stretched himself on

the boy in verse 21, but we can see that Elijah's prayer is answered. In verse 24 a Phoenician woman acknowledges God, which is ironic as a Phoenician woman (Jezebel) is now leading Israel to worship a false god, Baal! Jesus cites this story in Luke 4:24-30.

18 - 1 Kings 18 is one of the most dramatic chapters in the Bible. James 5:17 tells us that it had not rained in more than three years! Verse 21 makes clear the trouble: they are trying to worship both Baal and Yahweh (probably to secure the maximum advantages of both). Yet God has always demanded whole-hearted, undivided service. The evening sacrifice (verse 29) would be about 3 p.m. In verse 30 Elijah's quiet ways provide a stark contrast to the wild screaming of pagan practices. So Jehovah's worship and ways have always done. The twelve stones Elijah uses to build the altar (verse 31) is a clear announcement of the sin of the divided kingdom, that such a state was not God's will. The purpose of this miracle is revealed in verse 36. Notice Elijah using the covenant name of God: "God of Abraham, Isaac, and Israel" reminding Israel how God would be faithful to them, if they would be to Him. We may balk at the slaughter of the prophets in verse 40 but this is what the Law requires (Deut. 17:2-3; 13:13). The concluding word (verses 41-46) about rain contains some unusual features but the point is clear: God does what Baal cannot. Back to Table of Contents.

Week 29 - 1 Kings 19-2 Kings 6; 2 Chronicles 17-20

Reading 1 - 1 Kings 19-21; 2 Chron 17

19 - 1 Kings 19 finds Elijah the strong to now be Elijah the discouraged and weak. Verse 3 puts him far south in a time when he is needed to lead the continued resurgence of right religion in Israel. Beersheba is 100 miles south of Jezreel. Sinai is another 200 miles further south. What happened to Elijah? We do not know for certain, but James reminds us he was a man "like us" (James 5:17). People get discouraged and people can be fearful. The gentle voice of verse 12 helps Elijah to realize God doesn't always use extraordinary or dramatic means to accomplish His will. Further, Elijah's diagnosis of the situation was wrong: God can be working in ways humans don't detect. The chapter ends with a new prophet coming on the scene, Elisha (verses 19-21). But Elijah has much work to be done before the mantle passes fully to Elisha.

20 - 1 Kings 20 shows God's continued patience with Israel, as He now uses help and aid to try and woo His people back to Him. Ahab appears to be willing to be a vassal or "under-king" paying tribute but He will not submit to being ransacked (verse 9). God then rescues Israel, making absolutely certain Ahab knows He is at work (verses 13, 22, 28, 42). Ahab never acknowledges God's grace and does not follow up on the victories God gives him. Verse 36's bizarre incident shows how God's word must be obeyed, reminding us of 1 Kings 13.

21 - 1 Kings 21 is such a sad tale. Naboth is only obeying the Law in refusing to sell his land (Lev. 25:23-28; Nu. 26:7-12) and we must wonder what a king needs with another field. This is a good place to note differing views of the kingship of Israel. An Israelite king was as bound by the Law as any citizen but to Jezebel, a foreigner, she could not understand why he didn't get his own way whenever and however he wanted. Jezebel's evil plot and the ease with which she finds wicked men to help with it shows the depravity of the times. God knows what has happened and Ahab is absolutely condemned (verses 17-24). Surprisingly, Ahab repents (verse 27) but the seed of idolatry he has sown in Israel will never be rooted out.

17 - 2 Chronicles 17 provides much needed relief from all this wickedness. Jehoshaphat is the kind of king God's people need. Notice from verse 9 that teaching God's word matters!

Reading 2 - 1 Kings 22; 2 Chron 18

22 and 18 - The two kingdoms merge in the story as Ahab makes an alliance with Jehoshphat in 1 Kings 22/2 Chronicles 18. Jehoshaphat was Ahab's brother-in-law, because his son Jehoram had married Ahab's daughter, Athaliah (2 Chron. 18:1; 2 Kings 8:18) _ a marriage that becomes extremely important later. These notes follow the reading in 1 Kings 22. Jehoshaphat respects God and His word (verse 5) but he should have consulted God before pledging his support. Apparently, there is something about the prophets Ahab has assembled (verse 6) that just doesn't ring true to Jehoshaphat. Ahab, however, is not interested in hearing from a true prophet (verse 8) but Jehoshaphat insists. Micaiah the prophet speaks in this clearly biased assembly with obvious sarcasm (verse 15) but then tells what God really has to say: the campaign is doomed. Indeed, we get insight into the very throne room of God to see how the Lord is working to destroy Ahab (verses 19-23). Ahab's disguise shows he was nervous about the battle but it does not help him defeat God's intentions (verse 34) and he dies. 2 Chronicles 18:31 adds the valuable information that Jehoshaphat is only saved by the direct intervention of God. What a disaster!

Reading 3 - 2 Chronicles 19-20; 2 Kings 1

19 - 2 Chronicles 19 tells us more about Jehoshaphat. In verses 1-3 he is severely denounced for his alliance with Ahab. Having returned from the war he went back to his reform programs (verse 4). Like few other kings Jehoshaphat understood that good government begins with a commitment to the Lord (verse 6).

20 - 2 Chronicles 20 contains a story only found here, a story of great faith. Attacked by Moab and Ammon (verse 1) Jehoshaphat appeals to God (verses 6-12). In terms very reminiscent of Joshua's victory God gives Jehoshaphat the victory (verse 22). In all this joy there is an ominous note in verse 33. It seems that as long as Judah has a good king the people will follow his lead and serve the Lord. But if their ruler is an idol-worshiper they are more than ready to go along with that too. Verses 35-37 closes the reign of Jehoshaphat on a bad note, as he enters into another alliance with Israel. Remember that our reading in 1 Kings 22:49 that Jehoshaphat learned his lesson and would not sin like this again.

2 Kings 1 resumes the story of Ahab's family and the wickedness going on in the north. God is actively punishing this family, with the failure of the shipping enterprise with Jehoshaphat and now a rebellion by the Moabites (verse 1). Ahaziah then falls and is injured, tries to avoid God, but the Lord knows what he is doing (verse 6)! Ahaziah seems to have decided to kill Elijah for this word . In verses 11-14 each captain of the fifty approaches differently. The first went boldly, the second was harsh from a distance and the third was very humble. In verse 17 Ahaziah dies without a son. So his brother Jehoram became king. There is, unfortunately, also a Jehoram reigning in the south so the reader must be careful not to be confused about which Jehoram is being spoken of!

Reading 4 - 2 Kings 2-3

2 - 2 Kings 2 marks the transition to Elisha, as Elijah goes home. Elijah wants to spare Elisha the pain of seeing him leave (verse 2) but Elisha is determined to stay with him till the end. In verse 9 his request for a double portion of Elijah's spirit is understood as a desire for all of Elijah's powerful spirit, that he might be able to accomplish what Elijah did. Verse 17 may mean that some were looking upon Elisha as if he had an ulterior motive in forbidding a search, so he acquiesced. The chapter concludes with two miracles confirming Elisha's power (verses 19-25). The episode with the boys is difficult. Apparently the term "baldhead" was some sort of insult, and there may be some insult in "go up!" that would relate to Elijah's departure. Whether we understand all that is happening here or not, it is clear that God's messengers need to be treated with respect.

3 - 2 Kings 3 tells of Jehoram of the north fighting against the Moabites. In verse 2 he ends the worship of Baal but does not stop the worship of Jehovah via Jeroboam's golden calves (verse 3), so the good he did is offset by his incomplete purge of wrong religion. Interestingly, Elisha appears as a central figure in this story (verses 11-19). His word is that God will again work a miraculous deliverance for Israel. The role of music here (verse 15) is uncertain. What happened in verse 27 is also mysterious. When the Moabites saw their king sacrifice his oldest son did it renew their fury against Israel and they fought harder because their king in desperation had done such a terrible thing? Or does it mean the Israelites were overwhelmed with dread at the sight of such a spectacle that they left the battlefield? Either way, the victory over Moab was great but not as complete as it could have been.

Reading 5 - 2 Kings 4-6

4 - 2 Kings 4 contains a collection of miracles that are not dated and may not be in chronological order here. All of these miracles underline the prophet's power as God worked through him. The story of the Shunamite woman's hospitality warms the heart (verses 8-11). The story of healing her son (verses 18-37) reminds us of Elijah's raising of the widow's son in 1 Kings 17. Verse 44 concludes the chapter with the term "according to the word of the Lord." All of these signs emphasize God's power, and the certainty that what He says will come to pass.

5 - 2 Kings 5 continues the stories of the amazing works of Elisha, with the healing of Namaan. The story is a textbook example of the kind of wrong ideas that keep people from obeying God. Namaan goes to the wrong person (verses 4-5), became angry (verse 11a), had preconceived notions (verse 11b) and wanted to substitute his own ideas for God's commands (verse 12). Fortunately, a servant helped him see that God was not asking for the impossible (verse 13) and obedience followed. Verses 17-18 are difficult. Is this just a pagan man who doesn't really understand how to worship God and so brings home earth because he sees Jehovah as being the God of Israel's land, or is he beginning forgiveness when he must go through the motions of worshiping a false god? It is hard to know, but Elisha's statement "go in peace" indicates Elisha was sensitive to the difficulties a non-Israelite had in worshiping God. Gehazi's miserable greed and punishment concludes the story (verses 15-27). Elisha must not be seen as a prophet who is "in it for the money."

6 - 2 Kings 6 returns the focus to God's working in Israel. The miracle of the axe head (verses 1-7) continues the story of Elisha's great powers. It is clear that he has a relationship with God exceeding anything other prophets have. He is a "man of God" (verse 6). Next we read of God's protection of Israel (verses 8-23). Verses 16-17 are great verses on faith. How often we need to have our eyes "opened!" Verse 24 is best understood as having a period of time go by with no repentance, and so God withdraws His protective hand. The famine that results from the siege brings out the same lack of character in Ahab's son that we saw in his father (verse 31). Why do people persist in blaming God for what is their own fault? Back to Table of Contents.

Week 30 - 2 Kings 7-12; 2 Chronicles 21-24; Joel

Reading 1 - 2 Kings 7-8; 2 Chronicles 21

7 - 2 Kings 7 puts a happy end on the story of the siege we began last week, except for the man who faithlessly didn't believe the prophet (verse 2, 17-20).

8 - 2 Kings 8 caps the "tell of the great things Elisha has done" section of Kings. Once again the Shunamite woman benefits from her kindness to Elisha (verses 1-6). Of course what we notice immediately is Gehazi's presence in the story (verse 4). What is he doing here? The possibilities are that he repented and was healed, or that the story is not in chronological order. The anointing of Hazael (verses 7-15) seems to speed up the action in 2 Kings, as the tools of judgement begin to take their places. Verse 10 contains a kind of double answer. Yes, if left to normal circumstances Ben-Hadad would recover, but no, he will be assassinated and die. Elisha's deadly stare, revealing that he knew what Hazael would do, embarrasses Hazael (verse 11). The reader needs to be extra careful beginning in verse 16 because we have a Jehoram (or Joram as some translations give it) reigning in the north and a Jehoram reigning in the south too! Note God's faithfulness to His promises in verse 19. We will read more about Jehoram (verse 23) in 2 Chronicles 21. He was astonishingly wicked.

21 - 2 Chronicles 21 fills in the details of Jehoram of Judah's reign. All we need to read is verse 4 to get a grasp of how terribly evil he was. Verse 6 attributes some of the evil to the influence of his wife, reminding the reader that who we marry has a dramatic effect on our lives. The depravity of this king is seen in Elijah's letter (verse 12). The letter is very surprising as Elijah is not considered a "writing prophet" and he did not prophecy in the south. Further, it would be very near the end of his life, if not even after it. Elijah may have prepared the document to be sent later, because as God's prophet he would know the future. The fact that he writes this epistle indicates just how "northern" the southern kingdom is. Jehoram dies and no one cares, and Ahaziah takes his place (verse 20; 2 Kings 8:25).

Reading 2 - 2 Kings 9-10

9 - With 2 Kings 9 we return to what is happening in the northern kingdom, with fallout for even the southern kingdom. Elijah had been told to anoint Jehu (not the prophet of 1 Kings 16:1-7, or the son of king Jehoshaphat) but for some reason an unknown prophet is sent to do it. He is girded for action, and action is exactly what Jehu is all about. In the providence of God the kings of both the north and south end up at the same place and the same time and Jehu kills them both (verses 14-29). In verse 31 Jezebel calls him "Zimri," a name synonymous with being a traitor and assasin. In all of this Jehu is doing what God wanted him to do (although killing the king of Judah was not part of the prophecy) yet Jehu's callousness and blood-thirsty ways are very disturbing (note verse 34). Archaeological note: The Black Obelisk of Shalmanesar III, a very famous find, tells how he received tribute from Jehu. The monument mentions him by name, and pictures him. This reminds us of the rising power of Assyria, and that Jehu's kingdom was not very strong.

10 - 2 Kings 10 shows God's word coming to pass again (verses 10, 17). The dynasty of Ahab is gone, exactly as God promised. Jehu's slaughter of the priests of Baal is a stunning bit of trickery. Regrettably, although eradicating the worship of Baal was a good thing (verse 28), he doesn't go all the way back to Law and the right way to worship God. Instead the old stumbling block of worshiping God via golden calves remains in Israel (verses 29, 31).

Reading 3 - 2 Chron 22-23; 2 Kings 11

22 - 2 Chronicles 22 gives us more of the story of Ahaziah that we read in 2 Kings 8-9. Verse 7 is a key verse, showing God's work. Verse 9 is hard to translate. It seems like Ahaziah fled south from Jezreel to hide in Samaria, was brought back to meet Jehu and was fatally wounded between Jezreel and Samaria, then fled north to Megiddo where he died. He was buried in Jerusalem. The chapter then pushes the story of Judah ahead by telling of the next king in the south. Surprisingly, it's not a king at all. It is a queen and she is enormously evil (verse 10). Notice her reign is not begun or ended with the standard introductory formula we are used to. Chronicles is denying her place as a "real" ruler.

23 and 11 - 2 Chronicles 23 and 2 Kings 11 record the same story. We will follow 2 Chronicles in these notes. King Jehoshaphat's ill-advised marriage alliance has now resulted in the official paganization of Judah and an attempt to exterminate the throne of David! Verse 4's plan is for Levites who came "off duty" to stay in the Temple to make Jehoida's force as strong as possible. His planning and God's blessing bring good success. The wicked queen is executed (verses 12-15) and reforms in religion are begun (verses 16-21). Note the emphasis on the covenant with God (verse 16) so long ignored. What a good time for the people of Judah (verse 21)!

Reading 4 - 2 Chronicles 24

24 and 12 -2 Chronicles 24 and 2 Kings 12 parallel each other. 2 Chronicles 24:2 ominously ascribes much of these good times to Jehoida's influence. Some of the details of the money collection (verse 14; 2 Kings 12:13) are hard to comprehend as the translation is difficult and there is some uncertainty as to the passage's meaning. It may mean that no money was spent on vessels for the Temple until the structural repairs were made. Sadly, with Jehoida's death wickedness breaks out again, including the shocking murder of God's prophet (verse 21). Zechariah would have been like a brother to Joash! Verse 24 completes his bad reign, as the Syrians have to be bought off with the treasures of the Temple (note 2 Kings 12:18).

Reading 5 - Joel

Introduction to Joel - In today's reading we head to the Minor Prophets to read Joel. Joel does not date his message so we are not sure exactly sure where it fits in the chronology of Kings and Chronicles. However, the concern for and knowledge of Judah found here certainly suggests Joel meant his message for the southern kingdom. His theme is the Day of the Lord, a day of terrible judgment. Repentance, Joel assures, is the only possible way to get ready for this dramatic move of God. The occasion of this stark message was a devastating locust plague that did untold damage to Judah. Joel is saying "You haven't seen anything yet" - a day comes of much worse judgement. Again and again he speaks of the covenant relationship between God and His people, evident in phrases like "your God" (2:13, 26-27; 3:17), and "my people" (2:27; 3:2-3). These people were far from what God wanted them to be and so needed to learn from the locust plague and get right with God now. The wicked times of Joash certainly seem to fit this book very well.

1 - Chapter 1 details the destruction of the locusts (verses 4-5). The "nation" and powerful army (verse 6) that has come against Judah are the locusts, not a literal army. The only solution to the disaster is repentance (verse 14). For the first time we read "the day of the Lord" (verse 15). It is vitally important that the reader not associate the Second Return of Christ and Final Judgement with every appearance of this phrase. Biblically "the day of the Lord" just refers to God coming in judgment. A localized judgment on one nation can be called "the day of the Lord" (see Isaiah

13:6; Jer 46:10), and it is for that nation! Certainly there will be a final "day of the Lord" but the expression does not always mean the end of all things. Reading it as such has led to every kind of confusion and religious error. The chapter concludes with a call to pray and seek God (verses 15-20).

2 - Chapter 2 tells us more of the terrible locust plague (verses 1-11 - note the emphasis in verse 11 on the Lord's army). Verse 12 issues one of the most poignant verses on repentance in all of Scripture. Apparently there was some repentance because in verse 18 the tone shifts to blessing instead of judgment. That leads to the great Pentecost passage beginning in verse 28. Peter directly cites these verses in his sermon in Acts 2:16-21 so there is no question as to their meaning. In short, Peter says the signs you see correspond to what Joel prophesied would mark the beginning of a new age when salvation would be available to all who call on the Lord. Peter's sermon is designed to answer the questions "Who is the Lord, and how do you call on Him for salvation?" Joel 2 says there will be a day of revelation (verses 28-29), followed by a day of horrible judgement (verses 30-31). The language of these verses is nearly identical to Matthew 24:29-30 where the destruction of Jerusalem in AD 70 is described. The way out of that horrific judgment is to "call on the name of the Lord" (verse 32), which Peter tells us means to repent and be baptized, i.e. become a Christian (Acts 2:38). Indeed history records that the Christians observed the signs Jesus gave them to watch and were absent when Jerusalem was destroyed.

3 - Chapter 3 is difficult. The chapter describes a giant battle between the forces of evil and God's people in the valley of Jehoshaphat (verse 2). This does not seem to be a literal valley but may be a play off Jehoshaphat's name (literally "Jehovah judges") or a reference to his faith when outnumbered in battle (2 Chron 20). Note how Isaiah and Micah's prophecies of peace are reverse (verse 10). All the nations come up against God's people in the "valley of decision" (verse 14) but God does the deciding not men. They are all crushed and God's people vindicated. Fixing the exact meaning of these verses is difficult. From Peter's use of chapter 2 this certainly seems to pertain to the Gospel Age, and thus may reference spiritual blessings and how God protects disciples from those who stop the preaching of the Gospel. Back to Table of Contents.

Week 31 - Jonah; 2 Kings 13-14; 2 Chron 25; Amos 1-9

Reading 1 - Jonah

Introduction to Jonah - Jonah is tremendously well known but his book's spiritual value is underappreciated. He preaches during the time of Jeroboam II who we will read about in 2 Kings 14. This was a time of great prosperity in the northern kingdom, but Assyria is a mounting threat on the horizon. Jonah is sent to that empire, not the northern kingdom. The main message of Jonah is God's great concern for the entire world. Regrettably Israel did not see themselves as a light to show God's grace to all. Israel was more than happy to see the world judged, but God's attitude is very different and this book shows it.

1- Chapter 1 - Jonah is not a very admirable character, as verse 13 shows God's interest in the whole world and how Israelites are often less (spiritually) than Gentiles.

2 - Chapter 2 - This prayer is made up of pieces of Psalms, almost all of them Messianic. Note the fish obeys (verse 10) when Jonah didn't.

3 - Chapter 3 - We marvel that such a great city would repent (verse 5), but at this time Assyria was having some rough times politically that made things "ripe" for this message. The major point here is God's incredible mercy, grace and kindness (verse 10).

4 - Chapter 4 - Sadly the book doesn't end on the happy note of 3:10. Instead we are treated to Jonah's callousness and arrogance. Jonah explains his anger in verse 2 by simply admitting he didn't want God to save them! Jonah finds fault with God as He is. He doesn't do like Jonah imagined or wanted Him to do. Jonah has forgotten Israel's place as God's witnesses (see Isa. 43:1, 7-13, 20-21). But God's longsuffering mercy, that we have seen extended to Israel again and again, is truly for all.

Reading 2 - 2 Kings 13-14; 2 Chronicles 25

13 - 2 Kings 13 continues the story of bad kings for the northern kingdom. Jehoahaz does evil and the promised oppression from Syria comes (verses 2-3). Elisha had cried when he announced this, and now it happens. The change here is that Jehoahaz cries out to God (verse 4), and following the pattern from Judges the Lord sends a deliverer (verse 5). Who this deliverer is continues to be debated. Some think it is an Assyrian king, others that it is Elisha and the victory spoken of in verses 22-25, during the reign of Jehoash. If the reader does the math in verse 10 the dates will not line up correctly (as is often the case with the reigns of kings in Scripture). This is so because sons often served as co-regents with their fathers and so there is overlap in the time of their reign. Verse 14 contains Joash's poignant cry, especially meaningful since Israel's army was in shambles (verse 10). Clearly Joash cares for Elisha but he does not strike the ground with vigor and determination in verse 18, perhaps showing a lack of faith. Elisha's death and the bizarre incident of another man coming to life after touching Elisha's bones (verses 20-21) is unlike anything else in Scripture. Perhaps the story is related to show us that Elisha had made promises and those promises did not die with him. The Word of God goes on!

14 and 25 - 2 Kings 14 and 2 Chronicles 25 cover the same material. Unfortunately, Amaziah is like other kings who begin well but finish poorly. 14:7 tells of a battle with Edom. 25:5-10 gives us the details of this campaign. Amaziah hired Israelite mercenaries to help him in the battle but a prophet told him not to use them in battle. The Israelite soldiers were sent home and were angry they didn't get to participate in the spoils of battle. They raided Judean homes on their way

- which surely contributed to the friction in the two kingdoms that led to outright war (14:8-11; 25:11-28). Reading in 2 Kings alone we are stunned that Judah loses to the idolatrous kingdom of the north (14:12). But 2 Chronicles tells us Amaziah had also become idolatrous (25:14-16). He was actually worshiping the captured gods of the Edomites, an act almost incomprehensibly stupid. In the north Jehoahaz is succeeded by Jeroboam II. Jeroboam II gets very little space in Scripture (seven verses!) showing how God judges import and success. Historically, however, Jeroboam II was a very important king who expanded the kingdom to be almost what it was under David. During his reign the kingdom knew great economic prosperity but as we shall see, the people were spiritually bankrupt. Note the mention of Jonah the prophet in verse 25. This is the Jonah that was sent to Nineveh as we read earlier this week.

Reading 3 - Amos 1-3

Introduction to Amos - Amos was not a professional prophet (7:14) but a herdsman summoned by God from a small town south of Jerusalem to go north and address the northern kingdom (1:1). His message is that judgment is coming (note 2:6-8; 5:18-20). The real value of Amos is found in seeing why God is judging the northern kingdom. We might expect to read about idolatry (and certainly will) but Amos highlights social injustice as the times' chief problem (2:6-7a; 3:9-10; 4:1; 5:7, 10-12, 15, 24; 6:12; 8:5b-6).

1 - Chapter 1 would have been a great attention getter. Using the phrase "for three transgressions and for four" (meaning more than enough) Amos describes the judgment to befall all of Israel's neighbors. Make certain you note this is during Jeroboam the Second's reign (verse 1). Verse 11 recalls how the Edomites were brethren to Israel, as they are the children of Esau.

2 - Chapter 2 continues the roll call of judgment, now even including Judah (verses 4-5). One can imagine Amos' hearers loving this sermon and urging him on. But then he turns to Israel (verses 6-16) and announces their sin and the judgment to come. Note the immediate discussion of social injustice (verses 6-7). Verses 9-11 spotlight ingratitude. Verse 12 speaks of the Nazirites, those who took a vow for special service to God and who were not to touch the fruit of the vine in any form (Num 6:3-4).

3 - Chapter 3 continues Amos' withering blast. Israel expected special treatment due to their status as God's people (verse 2). But Amos asks a series of rhetorical questions about cause and effect (verses 3-7). If God is bringing forth judgement (the effect), then there is a "cause" for the Lion's roar (verse 8)! Amos says he must speak what God has told him to say, even if the message is unwelcome and unpleasant. Terrible judgment is coming (verses 13-15).

Reading 4 - Amos 4-6

4 - Amos 4 addresses the woman of the northern kingdom who lived in luxury by oppressing the poor (verses 1-3). Verses 4-5 reek with sarcasm. Notice that despite the corruption of the day worship services are still going on! God has judged the people repeatedly with many chastisements (verses 6-11) but the people are not taking note of the hand of the Lord in their midst and its meaning. Deuteronomy 28:15-68 makes specific reference to many of these judgments - if only the people had known their Bible!

5 - Amos 5 has Israel's funeral song (verses 1-3) and their only hope (verses 4-9). The references to God's creation (verses 8-9) reinforce the certainty of judgment. Who can stop the Creator of the Universe? Verse 18 announces that those who are so excited about a "day of the Lord" (like the judgments Amos announced on their neighbors at the outset of the book) need to rethink that.

The "day of the Lord" won't be good for Israel (verses 19-20). They must repent (verse 24). Verse 25 has the sense of "did you bring Me sacrifices only?" True religion is more than outward forms.

6 - Amos 6 discusses Israel's decadent and luxurious lifestyle. All will change in a terrible siege where even God's name won't be spoken because the people realize how far from Him they are (verse 10).

Reading 5 - Amos 7-9

7 - Amos 7 is a mixture of judgment and grace. Grace begins the chapter in verses 1-6 but judgment will come after the measuring line is stretched over Israel (verses 7-9). Amos is told not to prophecy any more by a false priest but he refuses to give in to those who would stop the word of the Lord (verses 10-17).

8 - Amos 8 contains visions of judgment. Verse 2's basket is "summer fruit," i.e. ripe fruit. The time for judgment is coming! The people can scarcely wait for religious feasts and the Sabbath to be over so they can go back to selling and making money (verses 5-6). Worse than any famine they would suffer in a siege will be a famine for God's word (verses 11-12). These people have no use for God's word (see 2:12; 7:10-13). Thus in desperate times they will cry for a word from the Lord and receive nothing!

9 - Amos 9 describes how God's judgment is inescapable (verses 1-6). Yet in the middle of describing the Lord's fearsome judgement there is still a note of grace (verse 8b). Judgement will have a purging effect, wiping out the wicked (verses 9-10) and sparing a remnant. What follows then is a Messianic prophecy (verses 11-15). What do these verses look forward to? We do not need to wonder. Their application is fixed in Acts 15:13-18 as James applies it to the Gospel going to the Gentiles. The language sounds like a military conquest but James says it speaks of a spiritual victory, as Gentiles come to the Lord. The blessings of verses 13-15 must be thus understood as figurative of the blessings to be found in Christ. Back to Table of Contents.

Week 32 - Hosea 1-14; 2 Chron 26-27

Reading 1 - Hosea 1-3

Introduction to Hosea - While Amos addressed the social injustices of Jeroboam II's kingdom Hosea attacked the spiritual adultery that was rampant. He did so in a most unusual style - he lived his message before the people! Hosea's book does not outline easily and doesn't always flow. It may be a collection of his sermons. In it all the love of God for His unfaithful people comes through again and again.

1 - The story is introduced in chapter 1. Hosea is to marry a woman who has turned to temple prostitution (verse 3). The first child Hosea has with Gomer seems to be his but the later children's circumstances are much more doubtful. Notice that Assyria will not triumph against Hezekiah and Judah (verse 7). Gomer's children are given devastating names: No mercy and Not my People (verses 8-9) as God renounces Israel. Hosea will return to these meaningful names in chapter 2.

2 - In Hosea 2 the sermon begins to take shape. What Hosea has done models what God is dealing with: an adulterous wife. God is doing all He can to bring His adulterous people back (verses 3-7). Sadly, Israel doesn't even realize it is God who is blessing them with the abundance they are enjoying under Jeroboam II (verse 8). Despite all her wickedness God still desires Israel and dreams of a grand day of restoration (verses 14-15). When that happens Israel will know who the real God is and stop calling Him by the wrong name (verse 16)! These people credit Baal for everything when Jehovah is the real source of every blessing. The serious judgment of God is recalled (verse 23) and reversed. These verses are used by Peter and Paul in the NT to speak of Christians (see Romans 9:25-26; 1 Peter 2:9-10).

3 - Hosea 3 describes another attempt to "rehabilitate" Gomer. Why is she called "a woman?" in verse 1? Perhaps because she has given up the right to be a wife. "Raisin cakes" were used in idolatrous worship (verse 1). She is urged to repent and put on a sort of probation (verse 3). This time of deprivation and discipline is likened to Israel's fate in days to come (verses 4). But Hosea then looks forward in verse 5 to a time when people will seek God and want to do right, serving the second David, Jesus the Christ.

Reading 2 - Hosea 4-6

4 - Hosea 4 has the language of a dispute or lawsuit. Perhaps Hosea came before the elders sitting in the city gate to hear claims and announced "God has a complaint!" The people break the Ten Commandments (verse 2) with impunity, and the priests have failed to teach who God is (verse 6). The people are so confused by idols and harlotry that they ask counsel of trees (verse 12)! Verse 13 reminds us of the immoral nature of idol worship. It was accompanied by gross perversion, temple prostitution and sexual immorality of every kind (note verse 14).

5 - Chapter 5 continues Hosea's fiery preaching against a nation given over to idolatry. Hosea still has the priests in mind, but brings in the king, rulers and even the people as the sermon continues. Verse 4 stuns us. When sin "sets in" people can't find their way back to God, can they? Verse 6 reveals that the acts of worship go on but they are vain. Verse 13 finds "band-aid" solutions instead of repentance. We will read on Friday in 2 Kings 15 of this alliance with Assyria. It will bear bitter fruit.

6 - Chapter 6 opens with what God longs to hear (verses 1-3). Unfortunately, this is fake

repentance. The reality is Israel's affection for the Lord lasts about as long as the morning dew (verses 4) that "early goes away." Thus a time of terrible judgment is coming (verses 5-11). Verse 6 makes clear God desires their hearts, not just empty worship.

Reading 3 - Hosea 7-10

7 - Hosea 7 speaks to the times Hosea lived in. After Jeroboam II died there was political turmoil and assassination after assassination (verses 4, 7). In all the troubles of the time "none call on God" (verse 7b). "Ephraim" is repeatedly used here to refer to all of the Northern Kingdom as Ephraim had become the dominant tribe. The people are like a half-baked cake - of poor quality and inconsistent (verse 8). They don't seem to understand that paying tribute to other nations to "bail them out" just makes them poorer and poorer (verse 9). Again, Hosea denounces Israel for refusing to turn to God (verse 10), and then brings that same point home again in verse 14. The people wail due to failed crops but will not turn to the Lord (verse 14)!

8 - Chapter 8 is Hosea's "whirlwind" sermon. All the idolatry and harlotry the people engaged in will be repaid. They have transgressed and acted without God (verses 1-6) and so they will reap what they have sown (verse 7). The alliances they enter into are especially repugnant to God (verses 8-10). The "return to Egypt" of verse 13 is not literal but a metaphor for the bondage the northern tribes will soon know.

9 - Chapter 9 begins a section on punishment and judgment. Hosea wants them to stop the idol festivals that they rejoice in (verse 1) because harsh and stern days are coming. Note the glory of God is withdrawing from them (verse 11). They are rejected as God's people (verse 17).

10 - This chapter focuses on the key issue of the heart (verse 2). These people's hearts were corrupt and they refused to recognize God (verse 3). They continue in idolatry (verses 5-6). Judgment for such people must come - and it will be terrible (verse 8). What God wants (verse 12) is powerfully contrasted with what Israel has done (verse 13) leading to certain destruction (verses 14-15).

Reading 4 - Hosea 11-13

11 - Chapter 11 contains one of the most moving expressions of God's love for His people in all of Scripture. When we read the Bible we always want to learn of God and these verses teach us how God feels when His people sin and determine they will not serve Him. Hosea portrays God as the hurt and disappointed father who is heartbroken by how his child acts (verses 1-4). What a view of the Lord! Even after announcing judgment (verses 5-7) God cries out in utter sorrow and dejection (verses 8-9). The Lord does not want to bring judgement on His people! What the Lord longs for is restoration which will come someday (verses 10-12:1).

12 - Chapter 12 begins with the end of Chapter 11. The chapter division here is most unfortunate. After concluding the ideas about restoration the prophet begins a long indictment against the people (verses 2-14). The prophet's sermon includes a history lesson. Jacob, their forefather, had always been a deceiver and a trickster who had a sometimes less than stellar relationship with God (verses 3-6). Ephraim is just like their forefather - tricky, deceitful and not faithful to God as they ought to be (verses 7-8)! However, while Jacob came to realize his sinful ways these people do not.

13 - Chapter 13 continues the list of Israel's sins. They have turned to idols and abominations (verses 1-3), forgetting the God who redeemed them from slavery (verses 4-5). Instead of being grateful the people have become prideful (verse 6) and so must know judgment and destruction

(verses 7-16).

Reading 5 - Hosea 14; 2 Chron 26-27

14 - Chapter 14 again gives insight into God's very heart. He shrinks from bringing judgment, pleading for Ephraim to return. Verses 2-3 contain the words God longs to hear. They need to confess that Assyria cannot save them, only God can! If they would just bring real repentance before God He would turn and bless them (verses 4-8). The book ends with a plea for wisdom. The wise man will understand that hope lies only with turning back to God!

26 - In today's reading we return to the history given to us in 2 Chronicles and 2 Kings. We are reading today in 2 Chronicles 26 and learning about a king who began well but ended poorly: Uzziah. He apparently served as co-regent with his father for a time but once he began his own reign he earnestly served the Lord. Verse 4 is tempered by the account in 2 Kings we will read tomorrow that tells of idolatry by the people (15:4). Apparently this was a time of "religious freedom" where everyone was allowed to worship as the pleased. Verse 5's Zechariah is not the writing prophet. We know nothing of this man. Uzziah expanded his kingdom and knew great prosperity, but unfortunately this led to pride (verse 16) and being stricken by God with leprosy (verse 19).

27 - 2 Chronicles 27 covers the reign of Jotham. Again we find a good king who cannot or will not demand compliance to God's law from the people (verse 2). Jotham is the first king in a long time (since Abijah, about 170 years) about whom the Chronicles have nothing bad to say. Back to Table of Contents.

Week 33 - 2 Kings 15-16; Isaiah 1-6; Micah 1-7

Reading 1 - 2 Kings 15-16

15 - 2 Kings 15 begins with King Uzziah (here given as the alternate spelling Azariah). His reign is just touched on, and then Israel's decline into anarchy and despair is recorded. Jeroboam II had a long, prosperous and stable reign (2 Kings 14:23), even if he was wicked. His successors do not enjoy that stability, as assassination follows assassination. We hardly meet a king before he is murdered. Verse 16's "would not open to him" means they didn't accept Menahem as king. His response? He destroyed their city even though they were his brethren! In verse 19 the Assyrians enter the biblical story. Menahem foolishly buys them off but inviting Assyria into the area is a terrible mistake. They will just keep inserting themselves more and more into the area, as they broaden their power base. Verse 27 begins Pekah's reign. There are some significant chronological problems with his reign if one adds up all the years. Some think he had already established a rival kingdom on the east of Jordan ("Gilead" in verse 25) and that may explain his long reign. The threat from Assyria continues to grow greater (verse 29). There are archaeological records of Assyrian actions. We may wonder why God sent Syria against Judah during a good king's reign (verse 37) but the next king explains exactly what happened (16:1, 4).

16 - Chapter 16 introduces us to one of the wickedest and weakest of all Judean kings, Ahaz (verses 1-4). He offered human sacrifices (verse 3) and not only did not take away the high places but joined in offering there (verse 4)! Ahaz shortly finds himself under attack (verses 5-6), and makes the fatal mistake of appealing to Assyria for help (verse 7). Asking Assyria to help as Ahaz did reminds us of how the Soviet Union used to "help" European countries. Those countries became puppet states for Moscow, as Judah does now for Assyria. They even send tribute to Assyria (verse 8). Isaiah 7 covers this time, with Isaiah warning Ahaz not to make an alliance with Assyria. Ahaz doesn't listen and while Assyria seems to help for the moment it is not a workable long term solution. The chapter concludes with Ahaz's foreign altar (verses 10-16), another black mark against a king that astounds us with his determination to serve any god but Jehovah.

Reading 2 - Isaiah 1-3

Introduction to Isaiah - Isaiah is considered by many to be the greatest of all the prophets. The New Testament quotes him over 400 times, showing Isaiah's huge impact, especially in Messianic prophecy. He was the dominant prophetic voice from 750-700 BC counseling kings at critical times, and preaching to a nation that needed to return to God.

1 - Isaiah 1 introduces us to this grand book. In many ways this chapter is an excellent summary of the entire book. The language reads like a lawsuit, as God puts forth His case against a sinful nation loaded with guilt (verses 2-9). The people do not know God (verse 3). Verse 7 may reference Sennacherib and his dreadful invasion. God calls for repentance (verses 10-20) showing what He desires: loyalty to the covenant and pure hearts. Vain worship is specifically attacked as useless and offensive to the Lord (verses 11-18). Notice how verses 19-20 say "eat or be eaten!" Verses 21-30 announce that a purging of these unfaithful people is imminent.

2 - Chapter 2 contains the amazing prophecy of the wonderful future for Jerusalem (verses 1-4). God will judge Judah but He is by no means through with Judah. At a Pentecost far distant God's ultimate purpose of bringing all people to Him (through the Gospel) will begin to be realized (see Acts 2). Isaiah often varies between the immediate crisis and the far future where there was hope

for great things. As fast as verses 1-5 leave us breathless with excitement Isaiah returns to the current time when judgment was coming on a people who knew not God (verses 6-22).

3 - Chapter 3 features more descriptions of the chaos and anarchy in Judah. Verses 1-15 especially single out the leadership in Judah for their failures. The situation will be so bad no one will want to be a leader (verses 6-7). Note the emphasis on oppressing the poor (verse 15). All the riches so many enjoyed would not spare them from God's judgment (verses 16-4:1).

Reading 3 - Isaiah 4-6

4 - Isaiah 4 again fills the reader with hope. God is not completely casting of Jerusalem. Great things will happen there in the future. Verse 4 makes clear that a cleansing of these people and a return to personal holiness are a huge part of God's future for Jerusalem.

5 - Chapter 5 contains the parable of the vineyard (verses 1-7). God is disappointed with the miserable, wild grapes his "vineyard" has yielded. There is no question what is meant by this story, as it is directly interpreted in verse 7. We should remember this parable when we read Jesus' many vineyard parables in the New Testament. The metaphor of "vineyard" would be easily understood by the people, but it was not a complimentary image! It spoke of God's disappointment and intent to judge His people! Verse 8 again speaks of social oppression, while verse 19 mocks the idea of God's warnings and coming. The degeneracy of these people is well spelled out in verse 20.

6 - Chapter 6 gives us a date for and an understanding of Isaiah's mission. Verse 1 would be in 740-739 BC. Notice how seeing God, even in a vision, immediately changes one's view of self (verse 5). Isaiah's eagerness to go for the Lord (verse 8) contrasts with Moses and Jeremiah's unwillingness. Verses 9-13 contain Isaiah's commission to preach and are full of very bad news: his audience will not listen to him. It is not that God doesn't want His people to listen and be saved (He certainly does) but that they refuse God's Word. Isaiah's preaching will actually confirm that Israel is so hardened in sin that all God can do is bring judgment. This text is quoted or alluded to some six times in the New Testament (for example Matt 13:14-15). It becomes the classic text to apply to people who refuse God's word. The only good news is that through judgment God is preparing a remnant who will respond to Him (verses 11-13).

Reading 4 - Micah 1-4

Introduction to Micah - Very little is known about Micah except that he was a prophet. He doesn't seem to like cities (1:5; 5:11; 6:9) and he possessed very strong convictions and courage (note 3:8). 1:1 identifies him as a contemporary of Isaiah. Usually his work is dated from 735-715 BC. Uzziah and Jotham brought a return to serving God, but Ahaz was wicked and useless. Under his reign Judah ends up as little more than a puppet state of Assyria's. We might expect Micah to attack the idolatry of the day, but he does not. Instead he discusses the hearts of the people, and how those hearts were corrupted. The heavy taxes imposed by Assyria make everyone miserable and mean the rich are oppressing the poor. This is of primary concern to Micah. His book is not easy to outline or always follow. It appears to be a collection of his sermons, so one chapter does not always flow easily into the next.

1 - Chapter 1 depicts a terrible judgment to come on Judah (verses 1-9). Verses 10-15 predicts the devastation that would fall on the towns and cities around Jerusalem by making puns on the names of these cities. For example, verses 10's "Beth Aphrah" means "House of Dust." So Micah says "House of Dust ... roll in the dust!"

2 - Chapter 2 begins with the problem of oppressing the poor (verses 1-2). Note verse 6: the people do not want to hear the truth! The false prophets tell Micah not to speak. Verse 11 describes the kind of preacher they want. Verses 12-13 speak of a remnant that will survive the judgement to come, and flourish, under the Shepherd King _ the Messiah (note 5:1-6).

3 - Chapter 3 denounces rulers and leaders of the people for their failures. What is worse than a prophet who says "peace" when God is at war with His people (verse 5)? Micah strongly contrast with the wickedness, timidity and false teaching all around him (verse 8).

4 - Chapter 4 reminds us of Isaiah 2:2-4. Micah sees past the destruction of Jerusalem to come in the near future to a day when Jerusalem is a beacon of truth to the world. This prophecy is fulfilled on the day of Pentecost when Peter preaches the first Gospel sermon (note Acts 2:17). Peace with God will result which changes man's relationship with his fellow man (verse 3). When one is right with God life is as good as it can be, and Micah employs a common figure of the good life (verse 4) to capture that idea. It won't be a kingdom of the rich and powerful but of those who have a heart for God (verses 6-8). The present problems, and judgment, are then seen to be birth pangs from which God will bring about these great things. The Jews will be taken to Babylon (verse 10) and many may not understand what God is doing (verse 12) but God is at work to exalt His (true) people once more (verse 13).

Reading 5 - Micah 5-7

5 - Chapter 5 shifts the focus from God's work through Jerusalem to God's work through the house of David. The dynasty of David didn't look like much in Micah's day. Most of the kings were wicked and they were weak kings over a tiny kingdom. A new Ruler is coming from a minor village that no one thought was important: Bethlehem (verse 2). But it was the birthplace of David and would be where the new David would be born. Matthew quotes this verse and directly applies it to Jesus (Matt 2:6). There will be a long time where it appears God has given up His people (i.e. they will be without a ruler from David's line) but God has not given up and will bring forth the Messiah at the right time (verse 3). The Messiah will stand and reign with care for the flock (in contrast to the sorry leaders of Micah's day) (verse 4). The Messiah is then pictured as defeating the people's enemies, here called Assyrians since they were the biggest threat of Micah's day (verses 5-6). The idea isn't that the Messiah literally defeats the Assyrians but that He shepherds and protects His people from all their foes. The Messiah's people, the remnant, will then be able to go forth with the Gospel (verses 7-9) conquering with God's Word. Verses 10-15 refer to God's protection of the church during this time.

6 - Chapter 6 is a covenant lawsuit. It contains God's complaint against His people for their unwillingness to serve Him. The mountains are summoned as witnesses (verse 2) just as Moses did in Deuteronomy 4:26. God has done so much (verses 3-5) but Judah will not return His love. What God desires is not more sacrificing (verses 6-7) but changed hearts (verse 8). Instead these people are wicked and cheat the poor (note verse 11). Judgement must come (verses 13-16). God actually accuses the people of the Southern Kingdom of following the sins of the notorious Omri and Ahab of the north (verse 16)!

7 - Chapter 7 contains Micah's complaint (verses 1-5). There are no leaders or good men that he can turn to for help, and none will be the friend of a godly man. So he looks to the Lord in a time of spiritual poverty (verse 7). The book ends with a song or hymn where Zion confesses sin (verses 8-10); Micah's promise is that all nations will find salvation in rebuilt Zion (11-12) with destruction and judgment for those who will not seek God (verse 13). God will shepherd His

people again (verses 14-15), leading all nations to be awed by God and what He has done through His people (verses 16-17). It is God's mercy and grace and forgiveness that will be the hallmarks of the new covenant, the fulfillment of the promises to Abraham (verses 18-20). Back to Table of Contents.

Week 34 - Isaiah 7-22

Reading 1 - Isaiah 7-10

7 - Isaiah 7 covers the material we read last week in 2 Kings 16. Here we are given the perspective of God's prophet as he tries to assist the wicked king, Ahaz, who is scared witless by the invasion of the Northern Kingdom and Syria (verses 1-2). Isaiah tells Ahaz not to panic and that God will be with him and protect him (verse 4-9). The North and Syria may have been trying to make Judah join their rebellion against Assyria, but these two smoldering torches wouldn't last (verse 4). Their plan to replace Ahaz with a king of their choosing (verse 6) would fail. Syria was crushed in 732 BC and the Northern Kingdom carried away captive in 722 BC (verses 8-9). Regrettably, as we learned in 2 Kings 16/2 Chron 28 Ahaz doesn't listen to Isaiah and makes a very ill-advised alliance with Assyria. Isaiah is then instructed to offer Ahaz any sign he would care to name (verses 10-11). Ahaz feigns sincere faith, acting as if he wouldn't dare ask for a sign (verse 12) but the prophet's response makes it clear that Ahaz doesn't really believe in the prophet at all (verse 13). The house of David will receive a sign (the "you" of verse 14 is plural): the sign of a virgin conceiving. This is specifically fulfilled in Jesus the Christ (Matt 1:22-23). How this sign was to help Ahaz is much discussed. Perhaps just the word of a coming king should have reassured Ahaz that God was protecting the house of David. The name "Immanuel" is a huge contrast to "Ichabod" (see 1 Sam 4:21) and surely should have signaled God was at work with His people! Isaiah then speaks specifically to Ahaz's day again, warning that Assyria won't be much of a friend (verse 17) and that God is sovereign over all nations, whistling for whichever world power He needs at this moment to accomplish His will (verses 18-20). The ending verses seem to depict Israel in captivity where the land grows up thick with weeds and briars because no one is there to tend it - a message about coming captivity (verses 21-25).

8 - Chapter 8 contains the longest name in the Bible (verse 1). This name is significant as Isaiah names his children with special names that fit the times. Ahaz should be reassured again, as God promises that Syria and the Northern Kingdom will not conquer him, but instead will be conquered (verse 4). The king of Assyria will come to Judah, however, and his invasion will "reach up to the neck" (verses 5-8), a reference to Sennacherib coming all the way to Jerusalem when Hezekiah was king. Isaiah calls people to reform and repent in light of God being "with us" (verses 9-10). God knows that many will oppose Isaiah and so urges him to trust in the Lord and not be bothered by people who claim he is part of a treasonous conspiracy (verses 11-15). The chapter concludes with Isaiah speaking strong words to a people who are increasingly rejecting God's law and word, and thus setting themselves up for nothing but darkness and silence from the Lord (verses 16-22).

9 - Chapter 9 opens with good news for the lands of Zebulon and Naphtali (verse 1). They were the first invaded by Assyria but Matthew 4:15-16 fixes the understanding of these verses as being Messianic, and that these lands would be the first to see the Messiah. Sadly, verse 2 tells us the prophecy was not understood (see John 1:46; 7:52). These verses speak of war implements being put aside and even destroyed (verses 3-5) as a Deliverer is coming. But it is not a great warrior that comes but a Child (verses 6-7). This is the child Immanuel (7:14). This is Jesus the Christ. The titles applied here leave no doubt that the Messiah is deity. The chapter concludes with a sharp turn toward bad news, with four stanzas of judgment (verses 8-21). This material is primarily directed toward the north (note verses 9, 21). Note the repetitive phrase "anger not turned away... His hand is stretched out still" in verses 12, 17, 21.

10 - Chapter 10 continues the note of judgment from chapter 9 (note the "anger... hand" phrase again in verse 4). Verses 1-4 may well apply to Judah. Verses 5-19 announce that Assyria is simply a tool in God's hands to do His bidding. Assyria certainly doesn't understand that (verse 7) but it is so. Assyria actually blasphemes Jehovah, saying they will do to God what they did to other (false) gods (verse 11). So when God is done with Assyria He will punish them (verse 12). Note Assyrian arrogance (verses 13-14) in all they claim they have done. The ax in God's hand shouldn't boast (verse 15)! In all that God is doing once again we hear there will be a remnant of God's people spared (verses 20-34). Note the reference to Gideon's victory (verse 26). Isaiah calls for the people who will be attacked by Assyria (verse 24), who's towns and cities will be overrun by the Assyrian invasion (listed in verses 28-32) to trust in God and His deliverance (verses 33-34).

Reading 2 - Isaiah 11-13

11 - Isaiah 11 is one of the most powerful Messianic prophecies in all Scripture. From the fallen tree of the house of David (think especially of the time when there would be no king at all over Judah after the destruction of Jerusalem in 586 BC) there will come a unique and special Ruler of Rulers. It is just the right lineage that makes Him King (verse 1) but the Spirit of the Lord (verse 2), giving Him every endowment to be the ideal King. He will not judge by appearance (verse 3) but with righteousness, helping the oppressed (verse 4). His kingdom will be marked by peace and security for all (verses 6-9). These verses are often misused to refer to some literal paradise on earth . But why should they be any more literal than verse 4? Who makes "a rod of His mouth" literal? Paul identifies the fulfillment of these verses in Romans 15:12 as occurring in his day as the Gospel brought all men to the Lord and provides them with spiritual security. The Gospel calls all who will (and not all will, note verses 14-15) to come to the Lord (verses 11-16).

12 - Chapter 12 contains imagery from the Song of the Red Sea (Exodus 15) as it celebrates the great trust and faith that marks the new relationship with God chapter 11 opens up. God is very much the center of this song.

13 - Chapter 13 begins a series of words to foreign nations (chapters 13-23). The careful reader will draw two main lessons from these chapters, even as he/she battles some of the obscurity and difficulty of various verses. First, these chapters announce God's sovereignty over all nations and all peoples. Second, these chapters give the reader a "vocabulary lesson" in prophetic speech. We will note several "stock images" that Isaiah uses that are used throughout Scripture, and that when we are familiar with them make understanding prophetic material throughout the Bible much easier. Verses 2-3 announce that God is summoning an army. Note verses 6 and 9 carefully. The expression "day of the Lord" often means only one thing to people: the end of all time brought on by Jesus' return, ushering end Judgment Day. Isaiah clearly doesn't mean that here as this oracle is directed to Babylon (note verse 19). The "day of the Lord" is a day of judgment but sometimes, as here, it is a local judgment on one nation and not the whole world. Readers who substitute "The Second Coming" everywhere they see "Day of the Lord" will make a mess of things quickly. Verse 10 uses standard prophetic language for governing authorities and rulers (stars) to be shaken out of their places as Babylon and its government falls. Alternatively this may simply indicate that the nation will be plunged into darkness - unable to know which way to go with no guides to help them. Verse 11 steps beyond just Babylon to announce judgment for all the world that does as Babylon has done. It is the "end of the world" for Babylon for certain (verses 17-19).

Reading 3 - Isaiah 14-16

14 - Chapter 14 is the song of victory over Babylon. There is a great contrast to the fortunes of Jacob (Israel) in verses 1-2 when compared to Babylon's fate. God has much still for Israel but Babylon will be completely wiped out (verses 3-23). Much controversy has surrounded verses 12-15 as some have speculated these passages describe the origins of Satan. These verses, in context, speak to a "man" (verse 16) and obviously speaking to the proud and arrogant kings of Babylon. If there is a secondary application here to Satan the rest of Scripture does not mention it or make use of it. The chapter closes with a word of judgment about Assyria (verses 24-27) and Philistia (verses 28-32). The prophet's point is that if God can break these powers He can break any power, including Babylon (note verse 27). Verse 28's time frame would be 715 BC.

15 and 16 - Chapters 15-16 are a word of judgment against the Moabites. This prophecy shows detailed knowledge of the Moabites. Parts of it are used by Jeremiah in Jeremiah 48. Note the emphasis on Moab's pride in 16:6.

Reading 4 - Isaiah 17-19

17 - Chapter 17 deals with Damascus, the capital of Syria. Isaiah announces that it will cease to be a city of importance (verse 1). The occasion of judgment on Syria will also be an opportunity to bring judgement on the Northern tribes ("Jacob," verse 4) but Israel will have a remnant left (verse 6) something promised to Syria. Judgement is discussed again (verses 7-11), and Assyria enters the picture once more (verse 12) even as once again Isaiah reveals that God will judge the Assyrians too (verse 13). Verse 14 may be speaking of Sennacherib's men who were such a terror to Jerusalem in the evening but in the morning were dead men (2 Kings 19:32-37).

18 - Chapter 18 has a word for Cush or Ethiopia. There is some question who the messengers are in verse 2 and where exactly they are sent. However, the emphasis in this message is that God is in control (verses 4-6) of all, even a powerful and exotic nation like Ethiopia. A day will come when even Ethiopia is impressed with God's power (verse 7)!

19 - Chapter 19 introduces us to more of the "prophetic vocabulary." Verse 1's "riding on a swift cloud" shows that the Lord can "come" in judgment, and that not every judgment is The Second Coming and End of All. This chapter brings judgment to Egypt. God is coming in judgment on Egypt, not the whole world. What do we make of the verses at the end of the chapter that speak of Egypt and Assyria being blessed (verses 16-25)? It seems best to see these as a "spiritual capture" of a pagan people by the Gospel. A literal altar (verse 19) is not possible as this would violate the Law (Lev 17:8-11). Verses 21-23 use the language we have seen about nations "knowing the Lord" in places like Isaiah 2, helping settle our understanding here to be the blessing of the Gospel calling all people to the Lord. Israel's place in this is to share, not be the preeminent nation, as all people serve the Lord (verses 24-25). That is truly remarkable!

Reading 5 - Isaiah 20-22

20 - Chapter 20 describes a strange sign that Isaiah actually became or did to represent Assyrian domination of Ashdod. There is some question as to when exactly to date this invasion (verse 1). Sargon ruled from 722-705. "Naked" in verse 2 doesn't necessarily mean absolutely without clothes, but probably indicates Isaiah went about in a loincloth or slave garb to show that Egypt and Cush, like Ashdod, would be enslaved (verse 3). Whatever he did was designed to attract attention to his message. Verse 4 describes the short tunic that captives wore in shame that is depicted on ancient monuments. The point of Isaiah's dramatic prophecy was not to trust in

Egypt to save from Assyria, and that God was the one in control and so they ought to look to Him not foreign alliances for security!

21 - Chapter 21's first ten verses describe the judgment to come on Babylon. "Oil the shield" in verse 5 refers to making ready for battle, as the leather shields of the day needing to be supple. Babylon isn't making those preparations, but instead will be caught feasting and partying. Verse 9 is used symbolically in Revelation 18:2. Once again we see the value of developing a "prophetic vocabulary" as we read in Isaiah. Edom is addressed in verses 11-12 . The names of the places here are in Edom, but the term "Dumah" means silence and may be chosen for its ominous overtones. The sad question is "How long till morning?" implying a time of darkness and suffering. The bedouin tribes of Arabia are addressed in verses 13-17 with the same message of impending judgment. It is recorded that Sargon (king of Assyria) did attack Kedar in 715 BC.

22 - Chapter 22 makes a sharp point: since Judah acts like the pagan nations around her she will be condemned and know doom just as they do! There is laughter and excitement (verse 2) perhaps after Sennacherib's defeat but Isaiah looks further into the future and sees the destruction of 586 (verses 5-8). This chapter well describes the hearts of the people from the time of Hezekiah all the way to 586. There was a willful ignorance of God (verses 12-14) and an absolute refusal to repent. Shebna, a high official who appears again with Eliakim (verse 20), in 36:3; 37:2, is specifically rebuked for arrogance (verses 15-19). In the place of this bad man who plans without being mindful of God will be Eliakim, who will do right (verses 20-25). The verses sound messianic in places but seem to have real fulfillment in Eliakim, even though Jesus uses the language of verse 22. Is the key there literal? Probably not, but represents being entrusted with authority. Yet in the day of judgment the government system (the peg of verse 25) will collapse. Back to Table of Contents.

Week 35 - Isaiah 23-35; 2 Chron 28; 2 Kings 17

Reading 1 - Isaiah 23-25

23 - Isaiah 23 gives a word of judgment to the commercial trading powers of the day, Tyre and Sidon. The news of Tyre's fall reaches their trading fleet in a far off port (verse 1), leaving them homeless. Notice that pride is specifically singled out as the reason for their fall (verse 9). Verses 15-17 tell that Tyre will return after seventy years and start up commerce and trade once more. Verse 18 is very difficult since there is no evidence that Tyre ever used her vast wealth to help God's people. Perhaps it just means that God uses commerce for the good of all mankind and help His purposes.

24 - Chapter 24 depicts a massive judgment on the entire earth (verse 3). This is the first chapter in a series of messages that are a distinct unit (chs 24-27) and must be held together, for Isaiah says that out of the judgment on the world will come salvation. The material in this chapter isn't that difficult to understand. What is up for much discussion is the "when" of "Isaiah's apocalypse." We may not be able to give a definitive answer (yet!) to that question, but can surely benefit from seeing God in action, and understanding His control of the entire world. One of the key ideas in Isaiah is that God is fully in control and moving everything toward His intended outcome. Verses 14-16 present an interesting break from the destruction as God is praised, but then we are right back into doom and destruction (verses 17-23). Note again the "prophetic vocabulary" of passages like verse 19 and 23. Verse 20 references the metaphor of being drunk on the wine of God's wrath, an image that is repeated throughout the Bible and best explained in Jeremiah 25:15-17.

25 - Chapter 25 praises God for complete victory. Verse 8 is used in Revelation 7:17 - more of the "prophetic vocabulary" we are building as we read in Isaiah.

Reading 2 - Isaiah 26-29

26 - Isaiah 26 continues the imagery of judgment, now contrasting all that happens to the wicked with the safety and security to be found in the city of God. The wicked just don't get it (verses 9-11) but God's people certainly do. Verse 19 is one of the clearest statements of resurrection in the O.T. (see Daniel 12:2 for the other passage that speaks of resurrection in the O.T.). Verse 21 connects this chapter back to the material in chapters 24-25.

27 - Chapter 27 introduces us to Leviathan (verse 1), a mythical sea-monster that pagans believed in. "Wake up, pagans!" Isaiah shouts. "God is stronger than your fake gods!" The Lord has established His vineyard (verse 1), probably a reference to His people (remember the vineyard parable in chapter 5). Verses 4-5 are difficult, but may mean that God's anger against His people has been expended and so He is no longer judging His people but now set against their enemies - but even then He wishes even the enemies could be restored. All of God's action leads to the time when there will be the perfect harvest of all who want to serve Jehovah (verses 12-13). Regardless of race or heritage they will be welcome to the "mountain at Jerusalem" - surely a reference to the Gospel call that begins in Acts 2 in Jerusalem.

28 - Chapter 28 begins a series of judgment messages (chs 28-35) that are full of woes. Verses 1-4 describe Israel before its fall at the hands of the Assyrians in 722. They are proud, arrogant and drunk. Verses 7-13 employ the image of being drunk on God's wrath (see Jer 25:15-17). It is as if the prophet says "You want to drink? Then drink this!" Verse 10 asks if they are children that need to be explained that God's law is the law? Then a foreign nation (Assyria and captivity) will

have to teach you (verse 11), for God's Law is the Law (verse 13). Isaiah then turns his attention to the kingdom of Judah. Those in Jerusalem (verse 14) need to learn from watching their neighbors to the north. They need to trust in God (verse 16) and not themselves, for their own plans will be annulled (verses 18-22). The chapter concludes with a parable from agriculture (verses 23-29). As the farmer does exactly what is needed at the right time so is the action of the Lord for His people.

29 - Chapter 29 is about Jerusalem here given the name "Ariel" which may mean "hearth of the Lord." Verse 8 explains that this is directed to Mount Zion. The people of Jerusalem should expect much tribulation (verses 1-4), perhaps during the siege of Sennacherib, but should also expect deliverance (verses 5-8). Yet these people are a people who must drink the wine of God's wrath eventually (verse 9) because they refuse to see God's message (verse 10) or truly worship and serve Him (verse 13). They sit in judgment of God (verse 16). Criticizing God is foolish for in a little while He will reverse everything so that Lebanon (famous for its forests) will be the place of farming, the field shall become a forest, and even more the deaf shall hear, the blind shall see, and people will be joyful in the Lord (verses 17-19), while the scoffers will be destroyed (verses 20-21). In short, if you doubt God just wait _ He can do far beyond anything we might imagine and is always doing exactly what we didn't think possible! The amazing work of God is designed to bring God's people back to Him (verses 22-24).

Reading 3 - Isaiah 30-32

30 - In Isaiah 30 we again find people ignoring God's word. Isaiah had warned that seeking Egypt's help against Assyria was folly (see chs. 18-20). Yet some are certain Egypt can save them from disaster, but are only bringing disaster upon everyone with their stubborn disobedience (verses 12-14). The key verse here is verse 15. It's not foreign alliances that will help but trust in God! Verse 18 looks beyond the current times of despair and sin to see a time in the future where God will, by His grace, bless richly. Through all the adversity God will purify Himself a people (verse 20). Who is the Teacher of verse 20? Some translate it as a plural and take it to be the prophets and priests who taught the Law and who hid themselves during the times of idolatry. Others translate it singularly and think it speaks of the Lord. Verse 33 announces a "Topheth" or "burning place" (ESV) has been prepared for the enemies of God's people. In other words, God has a place where He will judge and punish those who defied Him. Here this may even be a reference to eternal hellfire.

31 - Chapter 31 continues the theme on trusting in God, not in Egypt or warhorses (verse 1). God is in control and can handle the troubles of the moment (verse 4), and will protect His city (verse 5). Note the strong prophecy of what was to befall Assyria (verse 8)! A sword would deliver Judah, but not the sword of men. An angel's sword will be the deciding factor (as we will see in Isaiah 37).

32 - Chapter 32 features reversals (verses 1-8). This text is very Messianic, looking forward to a day when a true King will rule in righteousness (verse 1). What is right and what is wrong will be abundantly clear, along with who is doing what is right versus what is wrong (verses 3-8). Isaiah then returns again to the present day to address women living in luxury without thought of God (verse 9). Trouble was coming, and coming soon (verse 10)! This may be a reference to the invasion of Sennacherib in 701 BC that terrified Judah. Things will change for the better when the Spirit comes (verse 15), perhaps a reference to the people getting a "new heart and new spirit (as in Ezek 11:19) from the fright of the Assyrian invasion and even more seeing the deliverance

of God. Others see this as a prophecy of the outpouring of the Spirit in Acts 2 as foretold in Joel 2. Both views have their merits and warrant study. The basic message remains: God is the One who can bless with peace and security.

Reading 4 - Isaiah 33-35

33 - Isaiah 33 addresses the Assyrian threat again, but this time from a basis of hope. Assyria will be destroyed (verse 1). Those who trust in God (verses 5-6) lean upon the Lord and know salvation from their enemies as He arises to judge and save (verse 10). The invasion of Assyria certainly terrified Judah (verses 14-15) but God will save (verses 22). Even though the city is like a ship with rigging that cannot hold its mast in place or set sail (verse 23) there will be plenty of spoil. Perhaps this speaks of the Assyrians leaving so much on the battlefield after being smote by the Angel of the Lord. The last verse is difficult but may look forward to a time of ultimate safety when sin is forgiven in the time of the Messiah (verse 24).

34 and 35 - Chapters 34 and 35 are a unit. Chapter 34 contains the bad news of judgment and destruction on the enemies of God while chapter 35 carries the good news of the redemption and glory of God's people. Neither chapter seems to speak to a particular period of history but summarize what Isaiah has been saying about the need to trust in God and stand with Him. Edom seems to stand for all the ungodly here (verse 5). 35:1 marks a strong contrast with chapter 34. Isaiah likes to use contrasts to make his point, and here he speaks of a wonderful land instead of the stark useless lands of the previous chapter (34:9-13). Jesus uses the good news proclaimed in verses 5-6 as His answer to John the Baptist in Matthew 11:2-6. That settles that Isaiah is looking ahead to Messianic times. It will be a grand time when the way to God will be clear and people will come to the Lord joyfully (verses 8-10).

Reading 5 - 2 Chronicles 28 and 2 Kings 17

28 - Today's reading takes us back to the historical books, as we catch up on what the kings were doing during Isaiah's time. 2 Chronicles 28 goes with 2 Kings 16 that we read two weeks ago (week 33). It gives us more details about Ahaz's wicked reign. Despite all of God's attempts through both chastisement (verses 5-15) and the prophet of Isaiah's encouragement (especially in Isaiah 7-8) he persisted in evil. Assyria becomes a player in the situation at his (ill-advised) invitation (verse 16). He stubbornly refused to turn to God (verses 23-25). At his death we can only hope for something better in his son, the next king, Hezekiah.

17 - 2 Kings 17 tells of the end of the Northern Kingdom. The chaos and assassinations and Assyrian intrusion into Israel's situation finally culminated in a vassal king, a term that means Hoshea recognized Assyrian authority and that he was little more than a governor of a province in the Assyrian empire (verse 3). He tried to go behind Assyria's back and hire Egypt to help free him from Assyria (verse 4). It didn't work. Assyria punished Israel by besieging and destroying its capital (verses 5-6) and deporting her people to far off lands. The Northern Kingdom is no more. The time is 722 BC. The Bible then goes to great lengths to make certain the reader understands exactly why this horrific fate happened to what had been God's people (verses 7-23). Note the emphasis on how Israel acted like the Canaanite peoples who had lived there before them (verses 8, 11, 15). If such crimes resulted in the Canaanites being removed from the land could it be any different for God's people? The chapter ends with a discussion of the mixed up situation of the people the Assyrians brought to live in the land the Northern Kingdom previously occupied. Religious practices got no better (verses 29-32), with a sad synthesis of idolatry and the worship of Jehovah springing up. God tried to work with these peoples (verses

35-39) but they would not listen (verse 40). They become the forefathers of the mixed race people the Jews despise in New Testament times, the Samaritans. Back to Table of Contents.

Reading 1 - 2 Chron 29-31

29 - Today's reading takes us back to 2 Chronicles, where we read of Hezekiah's marvelous reign beginning in chapter 29. Hezekiah is given special status in verse 2, where he is directly linked to King David. Notice that he got started on doing what God wanted right away (verse 3). The rest of the chapter is dedicated to his efforts to restore the worship of God. He set out on a four stage restoration process: re-consecrating the Levitical personnel, (verses 4-14), directing them to purify the Temple, (verses 15-19), rededicating the sanctuary and altar, (verses 20-30), and then finally encouraging the populace to renew their presentation of sacrifice, (verses 31-36). The fact that it took eight days to "take out the trash" of the temple (verse 17) shows just how wicked Ahaz had been. It is notable that the credit for this restoration is given to God (verse 36).

30 - Chapter 30 tells of the first feast to be celebrated in the newly cleaned up Temple: the Passover. Hezekiah tries to bring all who know God to Jerusalem for this special celebration (verse 1). The Law made provision for those who were unfit at the time of the Passover to wait till the second month to observe it (Num 9:9-11). Fittingly Numbers 9 speaks of those who miss the Passover because they were far from home on a journey - a fitting description of the nation who had gone so far from the Lord! Regrettably many in northern Israel still don't get it and will not worship God (verse 10), although some do avail themselves of this great invitation (verse 11). Verse 20's "healed" may be taken in the sense of pardon since some of this observance was not exactly as the Law specified. It is folly for people to try to use Hezekiah's Passover as a model for doing worship today any way they wish, since what was done here wasn't exactly as prescribed in the Law. Note that Hezekiah prayed for forgiveness (verse 17), which the Lord graciously granted. Who would want to begin worship today saying "Lord, we are doing this wrong, so please pardon us?" This is clearly an extraordinary occurrence when people far from the Lord were doing the best they could to get going in the right direction again and again, God was very gracious to them. It is hardly a model for people today who know what God desires in worship but want to do as they please anyway! That is far from the spirit that Hezekiah was restoring in this chapter.

31 - Chapter 31 documents the good giving the people were involved in again. This was necessary to keep right worship operating. Hezekiah doesn't want what just happened to be a momentary or one-time thing. So he sets the example of giving personally (verse 3) and everyone followed his lead (verses 5-7). Verses 16's "three" probably should be "thirty" (see 1 Chron 23:3).

Reading 2 - 2 Kings 18-19; 2 Chron 32

18 - This reading gives us more on the life of Hezekiah, as we read today in 2 Kings 18. Kings summarizes his religious reforms (verses 1-12 - note especially verse 6), giving more space to the terrible invasion of Sennacherib (verses 13-37). Hezekiah quickly realizes his mistake in rebelling against Assyria (verse 14), and in a surprisingly desperate act strips the gold off the Temple to buy Assyria off (verse 16). It doesn't work and Assyrian continues its invasion. Apparently the Assyrians have gotten wind of Hezekiah's religious reforms and believe that he has offended the gods by removing the multiple altars in Jerusalem (verse 22). They even try to act as if God has sent them (verse 25)! Verse 27 is not a pretty verse, but it certainly makes the horrors of siege warfare vivid and real. The Assyrians then make the crucial mistake of insulting God (verses 33-35).

19 - Chapter 19 details the arrogance and blasphemy of the Assyrians crashing down upon them. They have insulted the one true God (verse 7), and God moves to action. First, the Assyrians hear of an Ethiopian army advancing on them (verses 7, 9), but they do not all withdraw to deal with this threat (verses 10-13). Hezekiah then brings Sennacherib's blasphemous letter before the Lord, noting that He is "God of all the kingdoms of the earth" (verse 15). God then takes more drastic actions to protect Hezekiah and Jerusalem. In one night an angel destroys the Assyrian army (verse 35). Sennacherib does go home (verses 36-37), where he is assassinated in 681 BC as Isaiah prophesied in verse 7.

32 - 2 Chronicles 32 parallels much of the material in Kings. It does, however, link the destruction of the Assyrian invasion force more closely with Hezekiah's reforms and faith in God (note verses 1, 8). Hezekiah's end is not as good as we would hope (verses 25-31). Verse 30's tunnel connecting the spring of Gihon to the pool of Siloam inside the city walls involved a tunnel of over 1700' through solid rock. Under threat of the Assyrian invasion it was dug by teams working on both ends at the same time — and they met exactly in the middle. It is still considered to be an amazing engineering feat and is visited by tourists in Jerusalem today who can still see the inscription to Hezekiah inside it. Chronicles finishes with Hezekiah's reign and life and all its ups and downs by giving him a favorable summary (verse 32). We, however, aren't done with Hezekiah. Next week we will read more of Hezekiah in Isaiah.

Reading 3 - Isaiah 36-37

36-37 - Isaiah 36-37 gives us Isaiah's perspective on Sennacherib's invasion (that we read about in 2 Chronicles 32 and 2 Kings 18-19). This material is almost word for word the same as the account in Kings. The fact that God saw fit to record this material three times (Kings, Chronicles and now here) does stress its importance to the reader. Note again the blasphemy of God (36:7, 15, 18-20), which virtually guarantees God will intervene (37:16, 23-29).

Reading 4 - 2 Kings 20, Isaiah 38-40

20 - 2 Kings 20 tells us Hezekiah's near-death experience. Verse 1's "in those days" is indefinite. However, comparison with 18:2 would make Hezekiah only 39. The news of his imminent death must have been a tremendous shock. Verse 6 seems to indicate this material is chronologically out of order and occurred shortly before the Assyrian invasion we just read about (note as well Isaiah 38:6). Perhaps Kings places this material here because this event and the one to follow don't show Hezekiah in a very good light, bridging the way to Mannaseh, the next king. Hezekiah's request for a sign (verse 8) seems to betray a lack of faith. If God says you will be healed you will be! Verse 9's "sundial" is better translated steps. It seems a stairway had been constructed from which one could tell time. The chapter then finishes with the miserable telling of Hezekiah's pride (verse 13), leading Hezekiah to do foolish things (verse 13 - showing a rising power all your wealth just tempts them to come and get it!), and then being indifferent to God's rebuke (verse 19).

38 - Isaiah 38 gives us Hezekiah's psalm (not recorded in Kings or Chronicles) upon being delivered from the death sentence of sickness (verses 9-20). Hezekiah lays bare his emotions and thoughts upon realizing he would die (verses 10-14), and then changes to giving God thanksgiving for deliverance (verses 15-20). Verses 15-16 are very difficult and uncertain. Verse 17's concern about the forgiveness of sins is remarkable. Verse 18 reflects the uncertainty and lack of knowledge about the state of the dead found often in the Old Testament. It is the New Testament where we learn fully about life after death.

39 - Isaiah 39 tells the story of Hezekiah's pride and folly as recorded at the end of 2 Kings 20.

40 - Isaiah 40 launches the second half of the book. While chapters 1-35 spoke of judgment and destruction due to wickedness and sin, the books now prophetically looks past those dark days to a time of comfort and God healing and blessing His people again. The opening words of verse 1 set the tone for the rest of the book: comfort. God is doing something great and new (verses 3-5), verses that John the Baptist fulfills. Don't marvel at such a word because God's word does endure and come to pass (verses 6-8), for God is such a great and powerful God (verses 9-31). Verses 18 and 25 sound for the first time what becomes a dominant note for the next 12 chapters: God is alone, absolutely unique and unlike anything or anyone. If the reader will underline in the verses that make this declaration in a distinctive color the main theme of Isaiah's message here will become obvious. Verse 27 notes that the wrong way to go with all this understanding of God's greatness and transcendence is to say "He is too great to see or care about us." Wrong! He renews and strengthens the weak (verses 29-31). Put your hope in this God and He will be there for you!

Reading 5 - Isaiah 41-44

41 - Isaiah 41 continues the words of comfort as God speaks to the nations (verse 1). He is bringing an invader to Babylon, Cyrus (verses 2-7), that His people in Babylonian captivity should not fear (verses 8-10). God's people will be redeemed and exalted once more (verses 11-20). This amazing restoration will cause all to know that Israel's Lord is God indeed (verse 20). Nothing the nations do, and especially not their gods, can stop what God will do (verses 21-29). They are powerless before Him!

42 - Isaiah 42 begins the Servant Songs. At first we might be uncertain who the Servant is (verse 1) but having the Spirit, helping the weak and bringing justice (verses 1-4) mark Him as the Davidic king of 11:1-5. This is Jesus the Christ. The Lord is doing something great and incredible, something that is awesome and takes incredible power and strength (verses 10-17). Unfortunately, God's people don't get it and don't seem to want to get it (verses 18-25). We will see Isaiah alternate between descriptions of God's great actions and activity intersperses with a rebuke of idolatry and an unwillingness to see and realize who God is on the part His people. These verses say that Israel has failed to be what God wanted, and thus they had to be chastised (verses 24-25).

43 - Isaiah 43 moves back to comfort by saying that even though Israel was faithless God is still faithful, and He will redeem Israel once more (verses 1-7). This speaks of the restoration of Judah after the Babylonian captivity. God affirms His uniqueness again (verses 10-11). Verse 14 fixes this prophecy to the return from Babylonian captivity and uses imagery from the first Exodus to describe it (verses 16-21), despite Judah's persistent refusal to honor Him (verses 22-28).

44 - Isaiah 44 again moves to consolation and comfort. Jacob has been faithless but God still want to honor and use His people (verse 1). "Jeshuran" appears to be a term of endearment meaning "upright." Verses 3-5 speak of the new covenant (note the emphasis on the Spirit being outpoured in verse 3, as in Joel 2). Verse 5 speaks of Gentile conversions, again showing God's desire for all to come to Him. Verses 6-8 affirm God's uniqueness, sounding the main message of these chapters again, while verses 9-20 deliver a withering (and funny) blast against idolatry. In contrast to dead and powerless gods the real God will deliver Israel (verses 21-28). For the first time the instrument of deliverance is named: Cyrus, the king of the Persians (verse 28). When

Isaiah spoke this word the Persians weren't even an empire. God demonstrates His incredible power by naming a king hundreds of years before he is even born! Back to Table of Contents.

Week 37 - Isaiah 45-63

Reading 1 - Isaiah 45-48

45 - Isaiah 45 sets Cyrus before the reader as God's instrument (verse 1), called by name (verse 4), all of which strongly emphasizes God's sovereignty in all that happens (verse 7). Some are confused by verse 7's statement about creating "calamity." God is not the author of evil or wickedness (James 1:13) but He can and does bring disaster upon those who defy Him. Verse 13 speaks of Cyrus again, looking forward to the return of the exiles recorded in Ezra. Verse 15 says God "hides Himself" referring to God as invisible or more probably that His ways are past finding out. Note again the main theme of God's uniqueness and singular position as the only God in verses 5, 6, 18, 21, and 22.

46 - Chapter 46 begins with the announcement that Babylon's gods will be thrown down (verse 1). Bel was the chief god of Babylon. Nebo was his son. Again there is sharp satire on idolatry (verses 6-7). God's unique position is highlighted in verses 5 and 9, while God's specific power to prophecy and accomplish His purposes is singled out in verses 10 and 11.

47 - Chapter 47 speaks of the humiliation of the city that worshiped these false gods, Babylon. Note their claim to deity in verses 8 and 10 ("I am, and there is no one besides me") contrasted with God's claims. False religion and arrogance won't stop the real God (verse 11)! Astrologers and astrology are condemned in verses 12-15. Such only lead people away from God, ending in judgment and destruction.

48 - Chapter 48 returns to speak of Judah, but it does not paint a very flattering portrait. Judah is faking interest in God (verse 1b), and they are obstinate (verse 4). All that has been said blasting idols has to be said to the people of God too (verses 5-8). Yet still the Lord loves Judah (verses 12-16). Verse 19 contains the key phrase "offspring like sand" that evokes the promises to Abraham from Genesis 12. Verse 20 announces liberty from Babylonian captivity. Yet verse 22 injects a sad note of reality into the prophecy's fond desire for a people who would truly love God.

Reading 2 - Isaiah 49-52

49 - Isaiah 49 gives us the second of the Servant Songs (verses 1-12). In chapter 42 the Servant sounds like it might be Israel, but here it is plain that Israel cannot be God's servant. Israel has failed and must be called back to God (verse 5). Beyond even that important task (stated again in verse 6a), the Servant will work to bring to salvation to all men (verse 6b, note also verse 12 and 22). This is the True Servant, the Messiah, who will begin His mission first with the Jews and then expand it to all men. Verses 14-23 comfort Jerusalem. Great things are ahead of her, for God has not forgotten her (verses 15-16). These verses seem to speak beyond just Jerusalem's rebuilding under Ezra and Nehemiah but to the spiritual blessings that flow from her beginning in Acts 2. Verse 24-26 offer hope for the captives who will return. Is there implicit in verse 24 the accusation that God couldn't bless and care for the captives as they return? Isaiah answers such wrong thinking forcefully! It is their sin that has caused the problem, not a "power shortage on God's part" (50:1-2)!

50 - Isaiah 50 contains the third Servant Song (verses 4-9). All of this will not be explained until chapter 53 but already we see suffering for others when the Servant is righteous (verses 5-6) and a determination to trust in God in the midst of adversity (verses 7-9). Who will be like the Servant and also trust and obey God (verses 10-11)? Verse 11 condemns the self-sufficient who imagines that he is in light (in contrast to verse 10's darkness). Such a "self-made" walk leads only to disaster.

51 - Isaiah 51 calls to the righteous of 50:10, urging them to listen (verse 1), look (verse 2), give attention to God's law (verse 4), and so trust in God (verse 7). The emphasis here is to trust in God and what He can do. Beginning in verse 9 there is an increasingly urgent call to trust in God, rouse up, and depart from Babylon (52:11). "Rahab" in verse 9 may be Egypt (see 30:7) or may be the name of a mythical monster (see Psalm 89:10). Either way the point is God's power to subdue their enemies. Verse 10 is full of Exodus imagery. The "ransomed" will return ... from captivity (verse 11). Jerusalem has drunk of the wine of God's wrath (verse 17) a metaphor best explained in Jer 25:16-17 (see also verses 21-22). But a day of reversal has come. God is not punishing Judah any longer, but now is will help her return from captivity (verses 21-22).

52 - Isaiah 52 sets up the "why" of the captives return. They have been oppressed and sold into bondage, but such caused God's name to be despised (verse 5). Foreign nations spoke disparagingly of Jehovah. Since His people were "down" it was assumed He was not very powerful. Nothing could be further from the truth! God has great strength and power to restore (verses 6-12). This is very good news, the kind of news that makes the messenger beautiful (verse 7). Then Isaiah turns his attention to the One who buys ultimate redemption, who makes freedom from sin possible: the Suffering Servant (verses 13-15). Many are familiar with Isaiah 53 but do not realize the description of the Messiah there begins in chapter 52. The poem is perfectly symmetrical, with five stanzas of three verses each, beginning and ending by exalting the Servant. Verse 15's "sprinkle" certainly evokes the idea of atoning sacrifice. Many will be stunned by who He is and what He does, and many will not understand His amazing work.

Reading 3 - Isaiah 53-55

53 - Today we continue the majestic Suffering Servant song that began in 52:13. Chapter 53 contains the four stanzas that complete the song. Remember, this text is explicitly applied to Jesus so there is no question as to who the Servant is (see Matt 8:17; John 12:37-41; 1 Peter 2:23-24). Note the parallelism, as the "arm of the Lord" (verse 1) means the strength of the Lord. By message (word) and power God has revealed Himself in and through the Messiah! But the Messiah is not what people expect. He grows up out of "dry ground" (verse 2), a reference to the House of David in utter disrepair. Notice the Messiah is not handsome or popular (verses 2-3) but instead is believed to be "getting what He deserves" from God (verse 4). Verses 4-6 are the center stanza and represent the center of the Messiah' work: He bears the punishment for our sins. Calvary is described in three short verses, and yet there may be no better description of what happened there. He is the voluntary sacrifice for our sins, a willing victim (verses 7-9). Most of the people of "his generation" didn't care what happened to Him, nor understand it (verse 8). Matthew 27:57ff fulfills verse 9 exactly, the kind of stunning prophecy that only comes from God. Verses 10-12 end as the Song began: shouting for joy and exalting the Servant. What happened to Jesus is the work, ultimately, of God (verse 10). "His soul" here is an expression meaning "Him," or referring to His life. Verse 10 goes on to list three results coming from His sacrifice: He will see His offspring (spiritual posterity, the new Israel), His days are prolonged (a reference to His resurrection), and He accomplishes God's purposes. Jesus is our substitute, the one-time sacrifice making atonement for all (verse 11), the source of our righteousness because we can only be right when we are forgiven. Without the Cross that couldn't happen, and so the Servant is glorified for His saving work (verse 12). Words fail this writer in the presence of this incredible chapter. This one paragraph seems so miserably

insufficient. The salvation of all mankind depended upon Jesus living Isaiah 53. Praise God that He did!

54 - Chapter 54 shifts gears to consider the future of Israel. Some want to apply this to the restoration of the Jews from Babylon but that seems weak. It is better to see this as the result of Servant's work. The cross leads to the church! Paul cites verse 1 in Gal 4:27 and applies this to the church, fixing our understanding. The worldwide expansion of the church (verse 3) happens before our eyes in Acts. God's love for His people are powerfully portrayed in verses 6-8. Note the import of the "eternal covenant" (verse 8b). That idea flows through the rest of the chapter, as God promises security and safety for His people (verses 9-17). The glowing city of verse 12 will be found again in Revelation 21:10-27.

55 - Chapter 55 contains such an incredible plea from the Lord, unmatched for warmth and concern. Note the emphasis on stopping foolish false religion that is worthless (verse 2). Come and share in the covenant of the Messiah that was made to David (verse 3)! Come to the Lord (verses 6-7). The words of verses 8-11 do more than look back on the plea to return, showing that God forgives and offers grace as no man would ("my ways are not your ways") but look forward to His plan to restore and save, a plan that He will execute and certainly cause to happen. God's ways are greater and more powerful than anything we could imagine _ and God brings those grand plans to pass!

Reading 4 - Isaiah 56-59

56 - Chapter 56 offers a stark contrast to what was before. God is calling, but His people are far from what they ought to be. Salvation is truly for all nations (verses 3-8), an emphasis the Jews of Jesus' day seemed to have completely missed. Jesus cites verse 7 when He cleanses the Temple, a particularly pointed moment since the area of the Temple that had been turned into a bazaar was the only place where Gentiles could worship (see Mark 11:17). John 10:16 reveals that Jesus knew Isaiah very well (verse 8). The chapter concludes with a sharp denunciation of the leaders of God's people and how they have failed (verses 9-12).

57 - Chapter 57 goes exactly where we knew it would when we saw the failure of the religious leaders in chapter 56. This is a vivid description of wholesale apostasy, perhaps matching the time of Manasseh. Manasseh persecuted the wicked (verse 1, see 2 Kings 21:16) and revived Molech worship, offering even his own sons to this false god (verse 5b, see 2 Kings 21:6). Verse 2 speaks of the righteous being dead, killed for their faith. The apostate mock the faithful (verse 3) and descend into every kind of perversion and evil (verses 4-13). Terms like "bed" and "nakedness" and the imagery of prostitution fit perfectly the spiritual adultery of those times. For the unrepentant there is no hope (verses 20-21) but again, incredibly, God offers grace to those who would come to Him (verses 14-21). Note especially the beautiful and tender terms of verse 15.

58 - Chapter 58 discusses fasting. The people were involved in a fast to call upon the Lord and know His ways (verse 2). However, it wasn't "working" (verse 3). Isaiah explains why: the people were not doing what was right, they were not obedient to God (verses 4-6). Fasting should glorify God and lead to obedience (verses 6-14). God hadn't ordered fasting. He wanted His people to turn their attention to do what He had commanded instead of crying out to Him when they were in trouble. They needed to live obediently and stop using God as an "insurance" policy.

59 - Chapter 59 continues with the problem of unanswered prayer from chapter 58, now explaining in very clear terms the problem: sin, not a lack of power on God's part (verses 1-2). That sin is then clearly spelled out (verses 2-8). In verse 9 the consequences of sin are listed. Verse 10 speaks of groping in broad daylight (note John 12:35-40). The innocent man is victimized in a world like this (verse 15). So God arises and puts on His armor to bring judgment and retribution (verses 16-20). The new covenant is clearly seen in verse 21.

Reading 5 - Isaiah 60-63

60 - Today we will read great notes of restoration that outstrip a return from captivity and rebuilding literal Jerusalem. Much of this seems to speak beyond that physical city to the church itself (note Gal 4:26). Further, Revelation 21 draws on Isaiah 60 to speak of heaven itself, the place where the church will rest for all eternity. The return to physical Jerusalem is here being used as a model of a much grander work of God to be accomplished beginning in Jerusalem in the future. There is a heavy emphasis on all nations coming to Jerusalem for salvation (verses 3-14). In verses 15-22 God guarantees the conquest of His kingdom and the exaltation of her people. Verses 19-20 are the ultimate word for the people of God: He will dwell with them and they will be in His presence. Revelation 21:23 and 22:5 place this great promise in Heaven, something those in the Kingdom now can look forward to someday.

61 - Chapter 61 is the song of the Anointed Servant. Jesus uses this when He preaches in the synagogue in Luke 4:17-21 and to answer John the Baptist's question in Luke 7:22. Jesus' use of this defines Him as Spirit anointed, and on the mission God sent Him to accomplish. To Isaiah's hearers it would sound like something about returning from captivity, but only Jesus can really "fill up" these verses. Note verse 6 and its promise of a new priesthood. The citizens of this grand new kingdom sing out in praise (verses 10-11).

62 - Chapter 62 continues the idea of restoration. Zion is here seen as a woman yearning for her husband, with the emphasis on God's action to find and restore her (verses 3-4). Some translations have "Hephizbah" in verse 4 where the ESV renders it "My Delight Is in Her" and "Beaulah" is given as "Married." These are terms that speak to close relationship with the Lord. This chapter is about more than a physical city that needed rebuilding! Notice again how God desires all to be saved (verse 11). The church is given four marvelous names in verse 12.

63 - Chapter 63 is full of dark notes of judgment and vengeance (verses 1-6). Edom was the long standing enemy of Israel, going back to the very womb (Genesis25:23ff). Edom seems to be used here symbolically of all those who would attack the people of God. The Lord will deal fully and finally with these enemies in His time. Isaiah remembers God's past actions and grace to His people (verses 7-14), leading Him to ask for mercy (verses 15-19) for a people who don't deserve it. The people of God are pitiful here - they feel as if Abraham and Jacob won't claim them as relatives (verse 16) and as if God has forsaken them (verse 17). Some of this sounds almost irreverent but we remember that Isaiah was called to bring people back to God. If they would not return then they would be hardened _ and that is what we see here. Verses 18-19 are very difficult and fraught with translation issues. This may look forward to the Babylonians treading down the temple. Back to Table of Contents.

Week 38 - Isaiah 64-66; 2 Kings 21-23; 2 Chronicles 33-35; Nahum

Reading 1 - Isaiah 64-66

64 - Isaiah 64 is a prayer to the Father for mercy on His people and action on their behalf. Humility and confession characterize this prayer (verses 5, 8), a welcome contrast to the hard heartedness we have seen before. Some have used verse 11 to say this is not from Isaiah's pen, but the Bible can speak of events long before they occur (note Lev 26:31 and Isaiah 39:6).

65 - As Isaiah draws to a close it doesn't end with "and they lived happily ever after. Instead chapter 65 rebukes idolatry and explains why God has not acted to save and deliver (verses 1-7). But even in this action a remnant shall be saved (verse 9). The Valley of Achor was where Aachan caused Israel so much trouble (Joshua 7:26). There will be a refining process, as judgment separates out the true servants from the false (verses 13-16). God is doing something new, so dramatically new and different that it is termed a whole new world (verse 17). All that was before - the special physical nation, its temple, rites and sacrifices - will all be abolished. Verse 20 is notoriously difficult but may mean that time has no meaning in this new work of God, something certainly true in heaven. All will be safe and secure in this new Kingdom (verses 21-25). Verse 25 confirms that this is looking to the time of the Messiah, as Isaiah repeats what we read in 11:6-9 here.

66 - Chapter 66 finishes this grand book of prophecy. There are differing views of the time frame of this prophecy. Some term it reproach of those who think they can capture God in a box, perhaps by rebuilding His temple. Others see this related to the time of the Messiah, a view that seems to be almost necessary and certain as the chapter progresses. Several truths are, however, clear. God loves the humble heart (verse 2), and will judge those who engage in wickedness, acting decisively (verses 4-6). Again the idea of a new work, something God is doing that is very dramatic and incredible, is presented (verses 7-8), a work that God will not abandon but will cause to happen (verse 9). This surely seems to speak to the Messiah and Gospel age. Jerusalem will then know peace (verses 10-14), at a time when the Lord will bring judgment on her enemies (verses 15-17). Verse 17 singles out apostates. This intervention or move of God causes a great gathering of those who want to serve the Lord (verses 18-23). The desire of God is found in verse 18, with the sign of verse 19 could be the cross or even Jesus' resurrection - the means to accomplish God's wish. The nations listed here come from the furthest points on the compass, reinforcing the idea of all nations coming to worship. Notice the incredible promise to make priests and Levites out of Gentiles who come to serve the Lord (verse 22), echoed in the promise that all shall be able to worship (verse 23). This cannot be anything in the literal Temple for such would be a violation of Moses' Law. It must instead look forward to the time when the Gospel calls all people to come to the Lord. Thus "new moon" and "Sabbath" are not literal either but simply poetic images of worship. The last word in Isaiah, fittingly, is once again a strong word of judgment on the enemies of God. He will accomplish His plans - and those who try to stand against Him will be utterly vanquished (verse 24). There is no peace for the wicked (48:22; 57:20)!

Reading 2 - 2 Kings 21; 2 Chron 33

21 - We turn back to the records of Judah's kings as we read in 2 Kings 21 today. The pictures of disaster and judgment so vividly drawn by Isaiah are now given substance, as we learn why God cast His people off. Manasseh begins reigning in approximately 698 BC. His reign is arguably the worst of any Judean king. He leads Judah to do all that the Canaanite nations did that God destroyed (verses 2, 9), guaranteeing a similar end for Judah. Verse 3 connects him directly to Ahab - how awful! The prophets of verse 10 are not known to us but their words will surely come to pass. Verse 16's "innocent blood" may well be those prophets. His son Amon then comes to the throne (verse 19) and unfortunately is a "chip off the old block." He leads Judah deeper into sin and idolatry. Verse 22 heartbreakingly says "he abandoned the Lord." How sad!

33 - 2 Chronicles 33 also covers Manasseh and Amon's reign. Note how verse 3 makes specific mention of Hezekiah's reforms, making it clear Manasseh undid all of Hezekiah's reforms. The surprise comes in verse 12: Manasseh repented! This information is only in Chronicles and provides a good end to a bad man's life. His prayer (verse 19) is not included. The Prayer of Manasseh, in the books of the Apocrypha, was written much later and is not authentic. Sadly Manasseh's repentance did not affect his people (verse 17) or his son (verse 22).

Reading 3 - Nahum

Introduction to Nahum - The target of the prophecy is Judah's longtime nemesis, Assyria and their capital city, Nineveh. We saw God's mercy directed there 100 years earlier in Jonah. Now we find people who have "repented of their repentance" and so God closes the story. Nineveh was a huge city, with 8 miles of wall that averaged 50 feet in breadth. The great palace of Sennacherib, with its 71 rooms and 27 gateways with winged bulls has been uncovered by archaeologists. Interestingly, as Nahum mentions in 2:6, a flood played a vital role in the destruction of Nineveh, as flood waters tore down her walls. We are not sure if Nahum spoke during Mannaseh, Amon, or Josiah's time but his message fits somewhere in this time.

1 - Chapter 1 begins by referencing both Jonah's work (beginning of verse 3) and Nahum's message (end of verse 3). Verse 11 probably references Sennacherib. In verses 12-13 we get total reversal. Assyria's power is shattered, Judah's is established. Note that in verse 12 God's justice and judgement are said to apply Judah too. Verse 15 is a transition verse, moving into the description of Nineveh's fall, and saying as Assyria's false religion is destroyed, so true religion is established.

2 - Chapter 2 uses common images for destruction of attack, failures of defenses and a verdict of judgement to describe what will happen. These themes will be repeated in chapter 3. Verse 2 shows how after the fall of Israel the prophets reclaimed the name "Israel" and applied it to Judah. Verse 6's talk of a flood accords with what history tells us of Nineveh's fall. Verses 11-13 use lion imagery. Nineveh was the lion's den, and Assyria was the lion but God is against her (verse 13) and so she will be destroyed.

3 - Chapter 3 rings with battle imagery in verses 2-3. The reader can practically hear the battle! Thebes was famous for being on the Nile and using water to beautify and protect her (verse 8) as Nineveh did. She and her allies (verse 9) were crushed (verse 10). "Drunk" is Jeremiah's favorite judgment metaphor, meaning "drunk on the wine of God's wrath" (Jer 25:15-17). Assyria was notorious for unspeakable atrocities and violence visited upon those it conquered. All would delight in her end and the end of her evil (verse 19).

Reading 4 - 2 Kings 22-23

22 - We return back to the story of Judah's kings in today's reading. 2 Kings 22 tells of good king Josiah. Verse 1 sets the date as 641 BC. Verse 13 shows that when someone has the right heart and is trying to do right receiving more information about what God desires results in more obedience, not arguing and complaining that the current situation must be "good enough." Since

Zephaniah and Jeremiah both prophesied during Josiah's time it is interesting to find the king consulting a woman, Huldah (verse 14). God's graciousness toward Josiah is recorded in verses 15-20.

23 - 2 Kings 23 records more of Josiah's massive reforms. Verse 9 is obscure but seems to mean that these priests didn't officiate at the Temple, but they did eat with the other priests. Verses 16-20 record the fulfillment of the prophecy of 1 Kings 13. That was 300 years before, but God's word came to pass just as the prophet predicted! Verse 22 doesn't mean other Passovers hadn't been celebrated but that this one was unique _ perhaps because it had been so long since this was done the people really put their hearts in it. Verses 26-27 may seem harsh to the reader. After all, the people have repented and are serving the Lord. Why must disaster still come? The account in Chronicles will help us better understand what was going on in Josiah's day and why God's judgment was not averted. Verse 29 records Josiah's death in 609 BC. Shallum replaces Josiah (verse 30). He is also known as Jehoahaz (see Jer 22:10). Egypt promptly replaces him with a new king, who will be their vassal, Jehoiakim (verse 34). This is the evil man who burned the scroll of God's word in Jeremiah 36.

Reading 5 - 2 Chron 34-35

34 - 2 Chronicles 34 is a good place for us to develop a time line of Josiah's life. He was 8 years old when he began to reign (verse 1), 16 years old when he began seek God (verse 3), 20 years old when he began purging idols (verse 3b). When Josiah was 25 Jeremiah was called (Jer 1:2), and when he was 26 he started the Temple repairs (verse 8). Note how Chronicles makes clear that Josiah forced people to worship only God by destroying every idol (verses 6-7). That point is emphasized in verses 32 and 33. Josiah's reforms, it turns out, were only very superficial. He served the Lord with a whole heart but many of the people only went along because he made them. This figures large in Jeremiah's people, because God was not fooled by people "going through the motions" who didn't really want to serve Him.

35 - 2 Chronicles 35 recounts Josiah's Passover and death. Was God really with Pharaoh Neco (verse 21)? It certainly appears so (verse 22) and leaving us to wonder why a good king disobeyed this word. Back to Table of Contents.

Week 39 - Habakkuk; Zephaniah; Jeremiah 1-10

Reading 1 - Habakkuk

Introduction to Habakkuk. This amazing book deals with a problem every believer in God has: why is there evil in this world? When will God stop it? Habakkuk's book is not specifically dated but the invasion of the Babylonians (1:6) gives us some reference. He appears to be speaking toward the end of Josiah's reign or during the chaotic years of wickedness after it. We know nothing of the prophet but as we read his book we can all understand his dilemma and learn from how he resolved it.

1 - Chapter 1 introduces the prophet's problem (verses 1-4). Everywhere he looks he sees violence and sin. How long will God put up with this? God's answer comes quickly (verse 5): not long! God is raising up the Chaldeans (another name for the Babylonians) to bring His judgment upon the Jews. They will make siege mounds (verse 10) and take every city. That seems to answer Habakkuk's complaint, but he then has a second problem (verses 12-2:1). How can God use people even more wicked than the Jews, the Babylonians, to punish the Jews (verse 13)? The Babylonians were an idolatrous and wicked nation that used hooks to drag off their captives, and then sacrificed to their implements of warfare! Shouldn't they be the ones being punished, not doing the punishing?

2 - Chapter 2 gives God's great response to Habakkuk's troubles. Notice how God will entertain honest, reverent questions! The Lord's answer is that He will, in His time (note verse 3) deal with Babylon too, and the righteous must trust in God to do what is right (verse 4). God says "Don't worry Habakkuk. Evil will not last, only righteousness. The future belongs to the righteous because the prideful will be destroyed. Do you trust Me to do this?" The chapter then pronounces woe upon woe (verses 6, 9, 12, 15, 19) upon Babylon. God will deal fully with this wicked nation! In stark contrast to the silent idol (verse 19) is the silent worshiper who in deep reverence bows before God, recognizing His sovereignty and righteousness.

3 - Chapter 3 finds Habakkuk being that worshiper. He constructs here a psalm that is very much like Psalm 77 and 18, psalms that also depend heavily on the language of the Red Sea deliverance. In verse 11 the sun and moon are symbols of God's created order and permanence. Their interruption shows God's power over all things. Verse 16 is key. Habakkuk says he will quietly wait for the judgment of God and for God's actions. When that invasion comes (verse 17) Habakkuk will still trust in God (verse 18) to do right and save His people. God's justice may not be immediately apparent to us, and it may not be immediately administered, but we must learn as Habakkuk did that God does judge rightly and so must we "live by faith" in God

Reading 2 - Zephaniah

Introduction to Zephaniah - The man who may have fed Josiah's hunger for God and zealous reforms may have been Zephaniah. Prophesying during Josiah's time (1:1) Zephaniah uses the term "day of the Lord" more than any other prophet. A day of terrible judgment was coming if God's people didn't change _ and soon. Some think Zephaniah may have prophesied late in Josiah's reign instead of early, which would then mean his message lays bare the pretend repentance of the people as their king made them serve only Jehovah.

1 - Chapter 1 begins with a bang. God is bringing massive destruction (verses 2-3) on His people and the city of Jerusalem (verse 4) because of their persistent wickedness (verses 4b-6). Zephaniah's favorite expression "day of the Lord" appears for the first time in verse 7 where

Judah is the sacrifice God is preparing. Note in verse 8 that the king (Josiah) is not to be punished but his sons, just as Huldah prophesied in 2 Kings 22. Complacency and indifference to God and His judgment are singled out in verse 12. Verses 14-18 give us a great definition of what the "day of the Lord" is. It is a time of catastrophe, destruction as the judgment of God is visited upon a people. Note especially that "day of the Lord" does not mean the Second Coming of Christ. That is the ultimate and final day of the Lord but the prophets use the term often to refer to a localized judgment of God, as here in Zephaniah.

2 - Chapter 2 tells Judah what they ought to do: repent! Verse 1 pictures a gathering together to repent. Verse 3 urges repentance to be seen in works: seeking God and doing His commands. Only the humble are admonished because nothing can be done with the rest. The good news is that while other nations are completely judged (verses 8-9), God will spare a remnant of His people (verse 9). Note the word to Nineveh (verses 13-14), echoing what we read in Nahum.

3 - Chapter 3 begins with a focus on Jerusalem (verses 1-8). The charges of verse 2 are fearful: (1) she obeys no one, (2) she did not trust God, (3) she did not draw near to God. Bad leaders are a further problem (verses 3-5). The chapter closes with a hopeful note of restoration (verses 9-20). Lips made vile by serving idols would be purified to worship God (verse 9). The Messianic era is described as a time of great joy (verses 14-20). While they couldn't celebrate the feasts in a foreign land, God will bring them back (verse 18). The day of the Lord is a terrible judgment but ultimately it purges the people of God as He restores and blesses them again (verse 20).

Reading 3 - Jeremiah 1-4

Introduction to Jeremiah - This book is one of the most emotional and intense in all of the Old Testament. It contains the collected sermons of Jeremiah that he preached over a 40 year period, from the time of King Josiah to after the destruction of Jerusalem in 586 BC. This book records Jeremiah's stern and fiery preaching, as well as his own struggles of faith and the persecution he endured. The most problematic part of reading Jeremiah is that it is not in chronological order. The wise reader will watch carefully to see exactly when each message was delivered.

1 - Chapter 1 introduces us to Jeremiah, and dates his book as beginning in 627 BC (verse 2). Verse 5 makes abortion wrong, period. Note there are more negatives in Jeremiah's charge than positives (verse 10), something unfortunately dictated by the times he lived in. Verses 11-12 contains a pun in the Hebrew. The word for "almond branch" (verse 11) sounds very similar to the word for "watching" (verse 12). Nearly all of Jeremiah's preaching would be dominated by the threat of Babylonian invasion, the boiling pot from the north (verses 13-15). Jeremiah's major theme is that the Jews have forsaken God and even worse, gone off to serve idols (verse 16).

2 - Chapter 2 contains word picture after word picture, something Jeremiah does so well. That begins with the picture of an unfaithful wife (verses 1-8). Note the powerful indictment of verse 13 that sounds the theme of 1:16. In verse 25b the people announce they are so steeped in sin they can't stop!

3 - Chapter 3 continues the sermon of chapter 2 in verses 1-5. The idea here is that contrary to how people act when a spouse is unfaithful, God will take them back if they will just turn to Him! Verse 6 identifies these messages as set in Josiah's time. We read of idolatry with some surprise due to Josiah's vigorous reforms but verse 10 explains so much. The people were faking their return to God! It was not done with a whole heart. Remember 2 Chronicles 34:32-33? Verse 16 seems to say the ark of God was missing from the people, perhaps taken by one of the many

Egyptian raids on Jerusalem. Verses 17-18 give us a glimpse of Messianic times. Verses 21-25 paint the picture of what repentance would look like.

4 - Chapter 4 makes it clear the people were pretending in their service to God. They say the right things, even using God's name (verse 2) but they have not removed their idols (verse 1). Verse 2 ends with a clear allusion to the promises of Abraham. These people need to break up their hard hearts (verse 3). Jeremiah injects a personal note in verse 10, because he feels God has let His people be deceived by allowing false prophets to lie to the people. Jeremiah laments the fate of Judah in verses 19-26. This is a powerful lesson to those who preach today. We may deliver a sober message of God's judgment but we should never rejoice that people are away from God and will be lost. Jeremiah hurt for his people! Verse 22 is astounding. Verses 23-26 present Genesis' creation language, but show it being reversed out as God brings judgment.

Reading 4 - Jeremiah 5-7

5 - Jeremiah is a book full of action and chapter 5 begins an "acted out sermon." Jeremiah will go looking for a righteous man (verse 1). Unfortunately, none can be found. People talk religion but won't live it (verses 2-3). Jeremiah wonders if maybe this problem is only found in the poor (verse 4) but fares no better with the "movers and shakers" in society (verse 5). Verses 8-9 remind us that idolatry in Bible times involved sexual perversion of every sort. Verses 10-19 detail that judgment is coming, but note verse 18: it won't be a full end because of God's purposes! Verses 21-31 enumerate that appalling judgment must come (note verse 23) particularly because of a lack of a social justice and concern for the weak (verses 25-28). Verse 31 reveals again that Josiah's reforms did not take hold in the people's hearts.

6 - Chapter 6 gives a picture of an invasion, but verse 8 shows it is only a picture of things to come if there is not repentance. Jeremiah complains he has no one to tell this dark news to (verse 10) but God wants everyone told (verses 11-15), whether they listen or not. Verse 20 shows the temple is still in operation. Why then is God bringing judgment? Verse 19 shows that their worship was nullified by their disobedience! Note the invader from the north (Babylon) in verse 22. So it will constantly be in Jeremiah. The chapter ends with God making Jeremiah His assayer of metals (verses 27-30), and Jeremiah's assay report reading "worthless metal."

7 - Chapter 7 is one of Jeremiah's most important sermons. He stands in the Temple and warns of misguided trust in the Temple building. The emphasis upon externals instead of the heart was absolutely destructive to these people who thought judgment could not come upon them as long as the Temple stood in their midst (verse 4). The people must stop oppressing the poor, stop violence and stop idolatry (verse 6) if they want to be God's people and enjoy His blessing! Verse 11 was used by Jesus in Matthew 21:13, as He cleansed the Temple. His audience would be quite familiar with the context of the quotation and how Jesus was comparing them to the wicked people of Jeremiah's time! Verse 12 references Shiloh where the Tabernacle was when it was over-run by the Philistines and the ark was captured in Eli's time (1 Sam 4:10ff). So don't think having a building to worship God in guarantees His protection! The people have become so enmeshed in pagan practices Jeremiah's prayers cannot help (verse 16). Verses 22-25 serve as a sad summary of Israel's history. Verse 29 speaks of the custom of cutting hair as a sign of mourning. It was time to mourn! The supreme abomination, idols in the temple itself, was actually happening (verse 30). Verse 33 directly quotes Deut 28:26, where Moses had warned this would happen if they disobeyed God.

Reading 5 - Jeremiah 8-10

8 - Chapter 8 answers the question "Why won't the people repent and return?" The answer, in part, is false prophets who deceived the people. The people won't return (verses 4-7) because they have false prophets lying to them (verses 8-12). Instead of repenting the people trusted in their walled cities (verse 14). Again, we see reliance on "we live in the city of God, Zion" in verse 19. The time to repent had past (verse 20).

9 - Chapter 9 can be difficult because it can be hard to know if God or Jeremiah is speaking. Either way the material deals with a people who are trusting in being God's covenant people. The chapter opens with much about deceit - the very opposite of what God is (verses 1-6), and how they refuse to know God (mentioned twice, verses 3 and 6). God spells out the trouble in verse 13. Verses 23-24 are crucially important. What they were so proud of didn't matter at all, while they were lacking in knowing the Lord. Notice they are called to not just know about God but to know Him - His character and who He is.

10 - Chapter 10 presents some translation difficulties, but its point is clear: God is greater than lifeless idols. Verse 11 actually appears in Aramaic in the middle of a chapter of Hebrew. Some think it may start the rest of a chapter as an answer to Babylonian captors who were trying to urge the Jews to serve false gods. Watch how Jeremiah takes on the pain of his people (verses 19-25). There is no self-righteous snobbery in Jeremiah, delighting to "tell people off." He hurts for his people who are dooming themselves to captivity. His prayer for humility (verses 23-24) is amazing and should be copied today. Back to Table of Contents.

Week 40 - Jeremiah 11-20; chapters in chronological order

Reading 1 - Jeremiah 11-13

11 - Chapter 11 highlights the word "covenant." The term appears repeatedly and much of this chapter sounds like Deuteronomy, the book of the covenant. Verses 9-10's conspiracy is the attempt to make alliances with foreign powers rather than trusting in God. The chapter ends dismally: a threat is made on Jeremiah's life (verses 18-23).

12 - Chapter 12 connects to chapter 11, as it contains Jeremiah's lament or complaint about his miserable state. Verse 2 makes this sound like it was Josiah's time but we are not sure. God's answer (verses 5-13) is that it will get harder for Jeremiah (verses 5-7), and the real sufferer was God Himself who has been abandoned by His people (verses 8-13). Unexpectedly, the chapter ends with a note of grace and restoration (verses 14-17). God's mercy for His people is amazing!

13 - Chapter 13 is the Parable of the Dirty Underwear (verses 1-11). Some have argued that Jeremiah did not make two trips to the Euphrates River (a journey of 800 miles) but to a nearby town whose name sounded like Euphrates. The reader will have to make us his/her mind on this. The point of the parable is clear: Israel was as close to God as a persons' undergarments are to him (verse 11), yet as no one wants to wear dirty, ruined undergarments so God is casting Judah away from Him. Verses 12-14 seem to employ a common saying "Wine in every jar" or "wine for all!." Jeremiah says there will be wine for all, but it will be the wine of God's wrath (see Jer 25:15-17)! Verse 21 is very difficult but seems to say the nations they seek as allies for help will then rule over them. All of this is coming upon them because of their sin. The people seem incapable of repentance (verse 23), and so must be judged.

Reading 2 - Jeremiah 14-16

14 - In chapter 14 God is using drought to try and get His people's attention. Verse 7 sounds good but it is the fake repentance of 7:9-10. God has been reduced to a visitor, who will not stay in this wicked land (verse 8). Again Jeremiah is told not to pray for these people for nothing can avert judgment now (verses 11-12). Once again we see the role false prophets are playing in keeping the people in sin (verses 13-18). The chapter closes with Jeremiah praying for God to act for His name's sake, not for these wicked people (verses 19-22).

15 - Chapter 15 is God's response to that prayer: He will not relent. Even if Moses and Samuel prayed for Judah (verse 1) the wound Mannaseh made is fatal (verse 4). Jeremiah responds in complaint (verses 10-18). He hates his role of being a troublemaker (as people view him) and believes he is a righteous man who is suffering more and more. God tells Jeremiah he needs to repent of such accusations, speak the truth and refuse to conform to the people (verse 19). If He will do so God will deliver and save him (verses 20-21). Jeremiah's struggles with his difficult message, persecution and the tough times he lived in ought to encourage all of us today!

16 - Chapter 16 again has Jeremiah living his message. He is not to marry or attend funerals because a time will come when there will be too many dead for funerals (verses 6-7) and it is not the time to feast and be merry (verse 8). Verses 11-12 hold the key to the chapter. When people asked Jeremiah about his peculiar lifestyle (being unmarried would be odd) he was to have a ready answer. The chapter then ends with a note of grace and restoration (verses 14-21).

Reading 3 - Jeremiah 17-20

17 - Chapter 17 tells us how serious the problem is: sin is engraved in the people's hearts (verse

1). Jeremiah sets the "two ways" before them, calling them to trust God (verses 5-8). Yet their hearts are corrupt (verses 9-10). For the fourth time we hear Jeremiah pour out his heart (verses 14-18), this time with an emphasis on being protected from his enemies. The Chapter closes with a stirring sermon on not profaning the Sabbath (verses 19-27).

18 - Chapter 18 invites us to go on a "field trip" with Jeremiah to the potter (verses 1-11). The word "potter" is closely related to the terms used of Jehovah's work, especially in creation. The imagery of God as a potter would be a well-known figure for Jeremiah to use. Perhaps the biggest key here is to see that God's plans are not completely fixed yet. There is time to repent, but the bitter reply of the people (verses 11-12) leaves little doubt what must happen. Instead of appreciating and responding to Jeremiah's stirring preaching (and visual aids) the people just make threats against his life (verse 18), and once again Jeremiah prays for God's protection (verses 19-23). Verse 23 sounds so harsh to our ears, but is only Jeremiah agreeing with God and praying that the Lord will do as He has said, for there is no other choice.

19 - Chapter 19 uses pottery again, but this time the pot is completed and dried. This must indicate a different time in Jeremiah's preaching, when the time and opportunity for repentance are now gone. Verse 4 speaks of the blood of innocents, reminding us of 2 Kings 21:16 where Mannaseh sacrificed children. Nothing can be done with such a bad "pot" except to break it (verse 10). Jeremiah then announces judgement (verses 11-15). This sermon will not be well received.

20 - Chapter 20 tells us of Pashhur beating Jeremiah and locking him up (verses 1-2). Jeremiah never backs down, giving Pashhur a new name and saying he is responsible for the judgment to come because his lies reassure people who ought to be repenting (verses 3-6). Jeremiah then complains bitterly to God (verses 7-18). He argues that the Lord "persuaded" him (verse 7) to do this job (better than "deceived" since God never promised visible results). However, Jeremiah admits he cannot keep his message to himself (verse 9), the sure mark of a true and faithful messenger for God. Yet Jeremiah's faith doesn't keep him from understanding reality and dealing with its troubles (verse 10). Jeremiah seems to arrive at a place of faith (verse 12), only to plunge back into despair (verses 14-18). The gritty realism of this book is one reason it is so valuable to us today. We can expect discouragement when we bring God's message to unhearing peoples as well _ and we must learn to persevere on as Jeremiah did!

Reading 4 - Jeremiah 22, 23, 26

Special note: Jeremiah is not arranged in chronological order so reading it straight through becomes complicated and sometimes confusing. We will read it in chronological order, reading all of the chapters that go with each king's reign. This arrangement accounts for the "skipping around" we will do in our reading.

23 - After Josiah died in battle, he was replaced very briefly with his son Jehoahaz (2 Kings 23:30). But as Pharaoh returned home from the battle he passed through Judea, claimed it as his own vassal state and put the king of his choosing on the throne, Jehoakiam (2 Kings 23:31-34). Jehoahaz ruled only ninety days. His brief rule is covered in Jeremiah 22, along with other kings. Verses 1-10 call for righteousness and faithfulness to God, much as Jeremiah had preached during Josiah's reign. Josiah is the dead king of verse 10. Shallum in verse 11 is another name for Jehoahaz. He "went away" to Egypt and died in chains there (verse 12). Evidently, even though his three month reign was short, it was long enough for him to plan big palaces (verses 13-14) and do wickedly (verses 16-17). Why wasn't he more like his father, a true king (verses 15-16)?

Verses 18-23 deal with Jehoiakim, he reigned from 609-597. As we will see as we read further in Jeremiah he was enormously evil. Verses 24-30 give us a brief word about the king after Jehoiakim. Coniah or Jehoaiachin also rules only three months (2 Kings 24:8). Note the denunciation of the promise to David from 2 Samuel 7. God's people are so far from Him that God is taking radical steps - even leaving David's throne empty for a time. Jeremiah will watch these developments carefully.

23 - Chapter 23 is not dated but it's time fits Jehoahaz and Jehoiakim well. Verses 1-8 rebuke the leaders of the people as bad shepherds. However, in the midst of this dark sermon Jeremiah speaks a word of grace (verses 5-8). "Righteous Branch" is a Messianic title from Isaiah 11:1. These verses seem to have in view the church as a grand re-gathering of the people who care for God. This "second exodus" will be foreshadowed by the return of Judah from Babylonian captivity (verses 7-8). Verses 9-40 single out false prophets as particularly guilty of leading God's people astray (verse 13). Verse 17 may be false prophets telling people that all is well, that Egypt will protect them from Babylon. They don't rebuke sin and idolatry but speak from their "own heart" to preach a message people wanted to hear. Verse 28 contains a proverb meaning "what value has straw compared to wheat?" Jeremiah was apparently taunted with the phrase "what is the burden of the Lord" according to verse 33.

26 - Chapter 26 is the first chapter specifically dated to Jehoiakim's evil reign. Verse 1 dates the material at 609 BC. The sermon commanded in verse 2 may well be the sermon in chapter 7, or one very much like it. Verse 4 defines really listening to God as "walking in My law." Shiloh is mentioned in verse 6 because it is where the Tabernacle was, but was apparently overrun by the Philistines (1 Sam 4-5; see also Ps 78:59-60). God is warning His people not to assume that because they have His worship center God will protect them. While some argue for Jeremiah and repentance (verses 17-19), others oppose him and cite the example of Uriah the prophet (verse 20). We do not know anything about him, but he gave his life for speaking the word faithfully. As we read this dismal story it is clear that this book is not just about the prophet Jeremiah, but is illustrating the wrong kind of response to God's Word.

Reading 5 - Jer 25, 35-36, 45

25 - Chapter 25 is set in Jehoiakim's fourth year, 605 BC (verse 1). This year marked a change in governing affairs in Judea, as Babylon defeated Egypt and took Judea from Egyptian control. Daniel 1:1 tells us this was the year Babylon took the first captives, including Daniel, Shadrach, Meshach and Abednego. Remarkably, Jehoiakim kept his throne. He was now a Babylonian vassal but he was still ruling. Verses 5-6 give an excellent summary of Jeremiah's preaching. Nebuchadnezzar is termed God's servant in verse 9, keying off the prophets being called God's servants in verse 4. Since Judea would not listen to those servants God was bringing a servant they would be forced to listen to! Verse 11 starts the 70-years of captivity "clock" at 605 BC. Verses 15-17 are so important to our prophetic "vocabulary." Here the metaphor of the "wine of God's wrath" is introduced. We will read much of nations being "drunk" or "staggering" or "God's cup" _ terminology that builds off these verses. Verse 26 contains a coded reference to Babylon. We are not sure why Jeremiah encoded it, but the message is clear: even Babylon will answer to God.

35 - Chapter 35 introduces us to the Rechabites. This nomadic tribe lived in tents and refused wine (verses 6-7). Because of the invasion of Babylon (in 605) they had left their farms (verse 11). This chapter is designed to show that while this clan obeyed their father (verse 10), the Jews

had not obeyed or listened to their Father (verse 15).

36 - Chapter 36 is stunning in its wickedness. These events seem to have taken place late in Jehoiakim's first year as king (verses 1, 9). Jeremiah's preaching becomes the center of attention (verses 11-16), showing that some still have good hearts but even then it is clear that some are afraid for Jeremiah and Baruch's safety (verse 19). Verse 22 says this happened in December. Verse 24 is the key to the story and Jehoiakim's era. God's patience and grace are as amazingly wonderful in verse 28 as Jehoiakim is wicked. How could anyone burn a message from God? How could God care so much He wrote the message again?

45 - Chapter 45 reveals that Baruch wasn't happy with his assignment (verse 3). Verse 4 echoes the call of Jeremiah from 1:10, but there building and planting are mentioned. Here nothing so positive is referenced. God does assure Baruch that his life will be spared (verse 5). Jeremiah is a book that tells the honest reactions of people to God and His Word, even when that reaction is from God's servants and is "I am weary!" Back to Table of Contents.

Week 41 - Chapters in Jeremiah in Chronological Order

Reading 1 - Jeremiah 27, 28, 29, 24

27 - In 597 BC Jehoiakim rebelled against Babylon (2 Kings 24:1) but died before Nebuchadnezzar's troops arrived to quell the rebellion. His son Jehoaiachin had only been reigning 90 days when Babylon arrived, pulled him off the throne and took him in chains to Babylon along with ten thousand other captives (2 Kings 24:8-17). We read of Jehoaiachin in Jeremiah 22:24ff where he is called Coniah. Zedekiah was made king in his place. He would reign for 11 years. Chapter 27 begins Zedekiah's rule in 597 BC (verse 1). A summit was occurring in Jerusalem where various minor powers were debating whether to submit to Babylon or try and rebel. Jeremiah assured them all that God was using Nebuchadnezzar as His instrument and they must submit (verses 4-11). Zedekiah receives the same message (verses 12-15), as do the priests and people (verses 16-22). The chapter ends with a note of hope (verse 22).

28 - Chapter 28 tells the story of a false prophet, Hananiah who doesn't like Jeremiah's sermon on submitting to Nebuchadnezzar. He claims there will be no seventy year captivity, but that within two years the captives will return (verse 3). Jeremiah says he wishes it were so (verse 6 - perhaps tinged with sarcasm), but that it will not happen. Hananiah will pay with his life for his lies and two months later he is dead (verse 17), a powerful sign to all the people that Jeremiah was a true prophet and his words should have been heeded.

29 - Chapter 29 is a letter Jeremiah wrote to the captives in Babylon urging them to be good citizens and to settle in for a long stay (verses 5-10). It would be discouraging to hear of seventy years of captivity because that means most of the captives won't live to return home but God offers a good word (verse 11) of future hope to the captives. "Seeking with a whole heart" will be the key for those who return (verse 13). We know nothing Shemaiah (verse 24) but he is very unhappy that Zephaniah has not stopped Jeremiah from preaching and letter writing!

24 - Chapter 24 completes our reading about the exiles in Babylon. Jeremiah has a vision of two baskets of figs, one good and one bad (verses 1-3). The Lord then explains that contrary to what people might think the captives just taken to Babylon were not the bad people experiencing God's judgment. They are the good figs (verse 5) who will someday be restored to Judah. Verse 7 speaks of having a heart to know the Lord. This doesn't mean they couldn't know the Lord before or that God somehow over-rode their free will. It simply means their situation would cause them to have a new perspective on serving God. The people still in Jerusalem must have been congratulating themselves as being the "really" righteous but God disabuses them of that notion (verses 8-10).

Reading 2 - Jeremiah 37, 21, 34

37 - Chapter 37 moves the time forward to around 588 BC. Around this time Zedekiah foolishly (and in violation of Jeremiah's word) rebelled against Nebuchadnezzar (2 Chron. 36:13). Verse 2 sums up Zedekiah's reign. Verse 4 is ominous. Verse 5 is what the people were always hoping for: rescue from Egypt. Jeremiah tells them it won't last (verses 9-10). Jeremiah's unpopular preaching results in him being misunderstood and falsely imprisoned. Notice that Zedekiah is such a weak king he sends to Jeremiah secretly (verse 17). These are terrible and difficult times as Babylon begins to descend upon Judah for a final time.

21 - Chapter 21 is dated shortly before the siege of Jerusalem begins (verse 2). Note the heavy emphasis on God fighting against Judah (verses 4-7). Verses 11-14 give what God wants from

kings of the House of David: justice and help for the oppressed. Kings like Zedekiah had miserably failed to do this _ and punishment was coming.

34 - Chapter 34 begins with a tough word for Zedekiah (verses 1-5). An honorable death is good news but not death in Babylon! The rest of the chapter (verses 6-22) discusses how the people freed their Hebrew slaves (a good thing) but then reneged on their repentance (verse 16). Reading this with 37:11 gives us the full story. The people freed their wrongfully held slaves, but when the Babylonian army departed to deal with Egypt the people then took the slaves back. Babylon had gone for now, but the Lord says they will return (verse 22). He is bringing them back!

Reading 3 - Jeremiah 30-33

30 - Today we read four of the most important chapters in the Old Testament. In the midst of a terrible siege Jeremiah breaks from his "doom and gloom" preaching to speak a word of consolation and comfort. The main question Jeremiah answers is "Is God done with Judah?" Such would certainly look to be so to besieged Jerusalem. Babylon is about to wipe them off the map. Yet in chapter 30 Jeremiah, at precisely that time, says good things are coming (verse 3) and that God is not done with Judah (verse 11). Their need is for grace because they cannot heal themselves (verses 12, 15). God will give that grace (verse 17), and a day will come when one of their own (not a foreigner) will again occupy the throne (verse 21). Their relationship with God is not terminated (verse 22), even as the wrath of God punishes their sin (verses 23-24).

31 - Chapter 31 speaks of a time of joy to come when the people return from Babylon (verses 4-5). This return is seen as a model of God's greater work, bringing all people to Him (verse 1, cited by Paul in Rom 9:25-26 and Peter in 1 Pet 2:9-10 and applied to Gentiles). The people will return in repentance (verse 9), as God does this great work (verses 10-14). Verse 15 reminds us how Rachel died on the way to the Promised Land (Gen 35:19). But God comforts Rachel (verse 16), bringing her children back from captivity. Again, the key question is "Is God done with the Jews" and verse 17 answers it again decisively. The slapped thigh of verse 19 is a figure of sorrow. God still cares for His people after all their sin (verse 20). Verse 27 then stretches the horizon beyond just the return from Babylon to talk of even greater things in the future. God will use the Jewish people to do something really marvelous: bring the Messiah who will inaugurate a new and better covenant (verses 31-34). These verses are laced with relationship language ("be their God") and speak of people who choose to know God based on being taught of Him, instead of just being born racially into the nation of God's people (verse 34). This covenant will be written on the heart. This is not a slap at the Law of Moses but again refers to people wanting to serve God, instead of being made to do so. Forgiveness of sin _ real forgiveness of sin, not just the foreshadowing of it by animal sacrifice _ will be the hallmark of this new covenant (verse 34). Space fails to discuss all these verses mean, but it is the only place in the O.T. where the term "new covenant" is used. It is the basis of Jesus' proclamation of the Lord's Supper (Luke 22:20) and is quoted twice in Hebrews (chs. 8 and 10) and alluded to in many other places in the NT.

32 - Chapter 32 has Jeremiah live the message he preaches. In the middle of the siege he buys a field from a relative to keep it in the family as the Law prescribed (verses 8-12). Who would buy land an invading army was camped on? Jeremiah then reverently prays to God, bringing His uncertainty and puzzled questions before the Lord (verses 16-25). God answers His questions by saying (1) nothing is too hard for God (verse 27), (2) the city will be destroyed, but (3) the

people will be restored to the land again (verses 36-44).

33 - Chapter 33 completes the book of consolation. This was a terrible time where desperate measures were called for (verse 4). Verse 8 tells us exactly what the captivity was: a purging of God's people. The chapter ends with a wonderful restating of the Davidic promises. We do well to remember the promise of verse 17 was qualified in 1 Kings 2:4. Jesus does become the ultimate fulfillment of these promises. Some wonder about the priests mentioned here (verses 18, 21) but Isaiah 66:21 talks of the day Gentiles will be priests. This is a reference to Christians, a "royal priesthood" (1 Peter 2:5) serving the Lord.

Reading 4 - Jeremiah 38, 39, 52

38 - Jeremiah 38 must be late in the siege. The number of fighting men appears to be reduced (verse 4), famine has set in (verse 9), and many have deserted (verse 19). Things aren't going well. The spinelessness of the king is sad to see (verse 5). The constants are Jeremiah's continued preaching of judgment and Zedekiah's continued refusal to act. He will listen to Jeremiah and seems to believe he is a prophet of God, but he stubbornly refuses to do what Jeremiah tells him to do (verses 14-23). Since Babylon will surely punish a rebellious vassal king just what does he hope Jeremiah will say? He must be hoping Jeremiah will promise divine deliverance, something Jeremiah has steadfastly guaranteed will not happen. Note his self-interest and concern for self - being put ahead of what would spare the city being burned (verse 19)! Jeremiah does not lie in verse 26. He is just not obligated to tell them everything that happened.

39 - Chapter 39 records the fall of Jerusalem. The siege lasted some two-and-a-half years. Zedekiah's plight is pathetic (verses 6-7) and is not helped when we remember it was his own fault. This is what happens to those who do not listen to God! In contrast, God cares for Jeremiah through the Babylonians just as He promised (verses 11-14). Verse 13 lists titles of various officers, not names. The material about Ebed-Melech reinforces how God keeps His promises to the faithful (verses 16-18).

52 - Chapter 52 provides a sad summary to Jeremiah. Verse 6 reminds us of the horrors of siege warfare. Cannibalism was common as the besieging army starved out the city inhabitants. Some speculate that Zedekiah and his men breached the wall (verse 7) in a cowardly attempt to escape under cover of darkness. Note the burning of the Temple and demolition of the city occurred a month after the city fell, directed by Nebuzaradan (his name means "Butcher") who apparently came to Jerusalem to direct its destruction (verse 12). What happened to civic officials in a rebellious Babylonian province? They were put to death (verses 24-27). This chapter is sad but its ending is encouraging. A king of David's line is in prison. Jeconiah (or Jehoiachin, see Mat 1:11) is freed, and given a place at the king's table (verses 31-34). God's promises live!

Reading 5 - 2 Kings 24-25; 2 Chron 36

24 - Today we return to Kings and Chronicles to read the history that Jeremiah lived in. 2 Kings 24 highlights that sins of Mannaseh demanded punishment (verses 3-4). Verse 8 occurred in 597 BC. Jehoiachin is on the throne when the Babylonians arrive to punish the Jews for the rebellion Jehoiakim began. Thousands are taken captive, including Ezekiel (verse 14). Note the use of the phrase "cast them from His presence" (verse 20). Such wicked people could not live on God's land (see Jer 7:15)!

25 - 2 Kings 25 reads very closely to Jeremiah 52. It goes on beyond the destruction of Jerusalem in 586 to tell of Gedaliah who governed the people who remained in the land (verses 22-26). We

will read Jeremiah's more detailed account of Gedaliah's governorship next week.

36 - 2 Chronicles 36 also tells of Judah's decline and destruction. The fact that Jerusalem's fall is recorded in three different books should signal the reader how important this city and this story really is. Don't let the repetition become boring, but rather let it make the point God wants emphasized! Verses 14-16 make that point loud and clear! Note how the seventy years of captivity are not an arbitrary number but are linked to the Sabbath (verse 21). Chronicles ends on a high note too. After 70 years of captivity there was a change in Babylon and the new Medo-Persian king Cyrus proclaims that peoples can return to their homelands. Ezra is the story of that return. After reading more in Jeremiah, and reading about life in Babylon we will read Ezra. <u>Back to Table of Contents.</u>

Week 42 - Lamentations; Obadiah; Jeremiah 40-51

Reading 1 - Lamentations

Introduction to Lamentations - We begin reading Lamentations today. This sad book is anonymous, but probably was written by Jeremiah. Its date is obviously after the 586 BC destruction of Jerusalem and the Temple. The lamentation of this dreadful event centers on God's role. It was essential that people understood that God had destroyed the city, or they would not learn the much needed lesson that should come from such devastation. The book is also arranged as an acrostic (except chapter 5), with each verse beginning with the corresponding verse from the Hebrew alphabet. Thus it gives the "A-Z" of suffering, doom, and sorrow over Jerusalem.

1 - Chapter 1 begins by identifying Judah's allies that she hoped would defend her from the Babylonians as "lovers" who have now deserted her (verse 2). Verse 5 sounds the main theme: what has happened to Jerusalem is God's doing. Verse 8 graphically depicts spiritual adultery. The temple itself has been desecrated (verse 10). What could be worse? Confession like what is found in verse 18 is the only answer. The chapter ends with a prayer that Babylon will be judged too (verses 21-22).

2 - Chapter 2 drives home a single idea: God is the one who brought about this suffering because His wrath against sin has severe consequences. Notice verse 9's famine of God's word. Instead of listening to Jeremiah the people listened to false prophets (verse 14), bringing upon themselves utter destruction. We will see in Obadiah how people laughed and delighted in Judah's fall (verses 15-17). The horror of siege warfare is pictured in verses 19-22.

3 - Chapter 3 introduces a tiny note of hope in the midst of such despair. Yes, God has chastised His people (verses 1-18), but God will show mercy again (verses 19-39). Verse 22 is key. "Steadfast love" or "faithfulness" is God's covenant love. It is God's love for His people that is faithful because it is based on God's promises, not the faithfulness of God's people. Hope is found in this great God (verse 24), and so Jeremiah says we just need to do right, wait on God and keep waiting on Him (verses 25-26). God didn't want to afflict His people (verse 33), so the Jews need to repent and turn back to God (verses 40-42). Look at the strong and beautiful language of verse 44. Sin has a high price! Jeremiah's thoughts turn to his own suffering and he again hopes in God (verses 52-57) who saved him.

4 - Chapter 4 portrays the distress of the siege. The situation is so awful that Jeremiah says the lucky ones are the dead (verse 9)! The root of their troubles goes to bad leadership (verse 13). Instead of depending on God Judah always looked to foreign alliances to save her (verse 17), but such hopes were vain. Chapter 5 is not an acrostic. It is a prayer for mercy, appealing to God's heart in tender terms. The first part is a description of the affliction of God's people (verses 1-18) followed then by praise for God's abiding power (verses 19-22). Note verse 7. It is true that their parents had been idol worshipers but they had joined in and served idols too! Jeremiah knows only God can restore the devastated city and her people. Lamentations fittingly ends with his heartfelt prayer for God to do just that. Before we see how God answered that prayer we will turn to two other prophetic books.

Reading 2 - Obadiah; Jeremiah 40-42

Introduction to Obadiah - This little book discusses the impending destruction of Edom. In 586 the Edomites assisted the Babylonians, turning against their brethren (the nation of Edom comes from Esau, Jacob's brother, see Gen 25:21-26). So Obadiah prophesies that Edom will know

God's wrath for mistreating His people. Edom was located in the south, down by the Dead Sea and just knew that in the cliffs and caves, with their fortresses carved out of the rock, they were invincible. They were dead wrong.

1 - Chapter 1 is short and direct: Edom will be judged. Verse 3 reminds us of Jeremiah 49:16, and the condemnation of pride found there. Remember that Esau is the father of the Edomite nation (verse 6). Verse 11 speaks of the 586 destruction of Jerusalem. Verses 13-14 indicate that Edom helped the Babylonians, even turning over escaping Jews to the invaders. Verse 15 is the theme verse for the book. Verses 19-21 say Judah is to return from captivity, but Edom does not. They are doomed and the nation will be no more.

40 - Jeremiah 40 begins the story of what happened in the aftermath of Babylon's devastation of Jerusalem. The captain of the guard is preaching Jeremiah's sermon (verses 2-3). How ironic! Gedaliah is the son of a good man, Ahikam (verse 6). Ahikam saved Jeremiah's life in 26:24. Why did Jeremiah elect to stay with these ungodly "bad figs" (ch. 24)? He seems convinced it is his task to keep bringing God's word to these people. What a faithful prophet. Note the people are "gathering" (verse 12) because there has been no planting and farming for more than two years. They have to get what they can from what is growing wild. Verses 13-14 are ominous. Even worse there is no effort made to consult the Lord or see what He would have Gedaliah do. Gedaliah seems naive and worse, doesn't pray or ask Jeremiah for help.

41 - Chapter 41 shows how real the threat from Ishmael was (verse 2). Why he assassinated Gedaliah we don't know but it seems to be related to the Ammonites trying to continue the instability of the region (40:14). Ishmael was a descendant of David through Elishama (41:1; 2 Sam. 5:16) and so may have desired the office for himself. Verse 8 may reference stores of hidden food that were put away during the war. Verse 17 is terrible. Once again the people make up their mind without consulting God. They are terrified of Babylonian reprisal, as once again the Judean province causes problems (think of the dead Babylonian garrison, verse 3), but they should do What God says if they want true safety!

42 - Chapter 42 plays the last verse of the "We won't listen to God" song that has been sung throughout Jeremiah. The people come with big promises to listen to Jeremiah (verses 1-6) but we read in 41:17 makes it sound very much like these people have their minds made up. Which is worse - people who defy God's word like Jehoiakim did or people who feign interest and promise to obey with no intent of doing so? Notice the word of God doesn't always come immediately even to a prophet like Jeremiah (verse 7). Jeremiah responds with a promise if they will heed God's word (verses 9-12), a warning of what will happen if they don't listen (verses 13-18), and then finishes by exposing their hearts (verses 19-22). He knew all along they had no intention of staying in Judea!

Reading 3 - Jer 43, 44, 46

43 - Chapter 43 records the wretched response to Jeremiah's words. The people deny he is a prophet of God (what happened to What they said in 42:2-3?), refuse his message and even ascribe bad motives to him (verses 2-3). Off to Egypt they went, taking Jeremiah with them (verses 5-6). Jeremiah then places some stones in some mortar (verse 9) that one day Nebuchadnezzar will place his throne on. The very king these refugees sought to escape would come to Egypt, and when they saw the stones and Nebuchadnezzar they would be reminded of Jeremiah's words and know the prophet was right. Babylon did invade Egypt in 568-567 BC.

44 - Chapter 44 completes their story, showing how evil they were. One of the main functions of this material may be to turn all hope to Babylon. After reading of these ungodly people it is clear that they will not obey God and cannot be the remnant God will work with to continue His promises. These people had seen and heard so much (verses 2-6) but learned nothing from it (verse 7). In verses 15-19 the people are extremely defiant, announcing that all the bad things that came upon them came when they stopped worshiping idols, not because of it! There is a heavy emphasis on women being involved in idolatry and even leading their husbands into wrong doing that is very troubling here (verses 15, 19). Verses 24-25 are very dark words of judgment: "you just do that! If that is what you think will save you, then go ahead!" But it will not save them (verses 26-30).

46 - Chapter 46 begins our final section in Jeremiah: the word to foreign nations (chs. 46-51). The key theme in all of these chapters is God's sovereignty over all peoples, not just the Jews. Also heavily emphasized is the sinfulness of pride. Nearly every nation is condemned for arrogance (46:8; 48:14, 28, 42; 49:4, 16; 50:31-32). The historical setting of this chapter's message to Egypt is the historic battle of Carchemish in 605 BC where Babylon defeated Egypt assuring that Babylon would be the new world power, not Egypt (verse 2). Note the use of "day of the Lord" in verse 10 to mean judgement on a nation, and not the end of the world. Verse 13 mentions an invasion of Egypt by Babylon. Four dates are viewed as possibilities for that invasion (604, 601, 588, and 568) but scholars are divided which occurrence this references. Verse 25 frames the defeat of Egypt as a defeat of her (false) gods.

Reading 4 - Jeremiah 47-49

47 - Chapter 47 contains a word of judgment on the Philistines. The date of this attack by Egypt (verse 1) is unknown. It would be a terrible judgement, so bad that parents would leave their children behind (verse 3). Verse 5 speaks of "gashing yourselves," which may be mourning behavior or might be an attempt to get the attention of idol gods.

48 - Chapter 48 condemns the Moabites. They were destroyed by Babylon in 582. This chapter condemns Moab for her pride (verses 7, 29-30). The image in verses 11-13 adds to that, as the metaphor employed speaks of wine aging peacefully in the cask. Moab felt very self-satisfied and secure, but had ignored God. Verse 40 speaks of Nebuchadnezzar. The chapter ends very appropriately, adapting Numbers 21:28-29. The reference there is to a campaign by the Amorites against Moab in which Moab was defeated and a victory song was composed. Once again, Jeremiah warns, Moab will know the pain of defeat, and need to rebuild Heshbon (verses 45-47).

49 - Chapter 49 condemns Ammon (verses 1-6), Edom (verses 7-22), Damascus (verses 23-27), and Kedar and Hazor (verses 28-33) and Elam (verses 34-39). Ammon had unfairly taken land not their own (verse 1) and was guilty of pride (verse 4). Interestingly, the word to Ammon ends with a note of grace (verse 6). Edom lived down in the cliffs and caves south and east of the Dead Sea, but her fortresses should not have made them feel secure against God's wrath (verse 16). The word to Damascus (verses 23-27) is a word to Syria, because Damascus was its capital. Verse 25 may be the city residents speaking. Kedar and Hazor (verses 28-33) were desert people. The Babylonian attack (verse 30) is recorded on The Babylonian Chronicle. God is concerned even about people living far off in the desert that few other nations notice! Elam (verses 34-39) was a close neighbor of Babylon's. From beginning to end of this prophecy God is the actor, the One doing everything.

Reading 5 - Jeremiah 50-51

50 and 51 - Today we finish Jeremiah by reading chapters 50 and 51. These are huge chapters (almost equaling all the material to the other nations combined) with a single focus: Babylon. These chapters are important because they balance Jeremiah's preaching of "submission to Babylon." If people wondered about submitting to an evil nation these chapters now assure them that God knows what Babylon is about and will, in His time, judge them as well. These messages were delivered in 594 BC (see 51:59). Some of the highlights of these chapters are 50:5, where God's people see the work of God and it causes a return to the Lord. 50:15, 28 announces vengeance for God's temple as a reason for judgment. 50:18 shows that we can learn what God will do by what He has done. Assyria brought judgment but was then judged. So it will be again. 50:31-32 follow that up by renouncing Babylonian pride. Verse 34 uses the term "Redeemer" that is also used in Ruth. It references a strong family bond. God still cares for His people! Verses 41-43 are taken from 6:22-24 with one change: now Babylon hears a noise in the north instead of Israel! 51:1 uses an atbash cipher ("Leb-kamai" for Chaldea), as in 25:26. Why Jeremiah encoded this word is unknown. 51:14 begins a section where Jeremiah says God has the power to do anything (and thus can destroy Babylon), and idol worship is foolish and of no help whatsoever. The rest of the chapter pictures Babylon in its death throes - confused, exhausted, demoralized and finally destroyed. God's people need to get out of the city (51:45), for Babylon will fall for all her evil deeds (51:49). Why is this valuable word from God to be cast into the Euphrates (51:63)? It then models what will happen to Babylon itself: it will sink into disaster (51:64). Back to Table of Contents.

Week 43 - Ezekiel 1-15

Reading 1 - Ezekiel 1-3

Introduction to Ezekiel - This prophetic book tells us of God's word to the captives in Babylon. Ezekiel was taken there in 597 BC and tirelessly urged repentance so that the lesson of the captivity would not be wasted. Unfortunately, often the people did not want to hear his message. So, while Daniel was in the court of Babylon, and Jeremiah was at home in a land full of wicked people soon to be judged in 586, Ezekiel was with the people in captivity. His work helps us understand them and their God. His book divides very neatly based on that 586 destruction: chapters 1-24 tell how Jerusalem must fall, chapters 25-32 say foreign nations must fall, and then chapters 33-48 provide comfort for the Jews.

1 - Chapter 1 gives us the setting for Ezekiel and opens with an amazing vision. Verse 1 seems to mean Ezekiel's thirtieth year, making him thirty. That is the year one entered into service as a priest (Num 4:3) so would be significant to him since he was a priest (verse 3). Verse 2 marks the time as 593-592. The rest of the chapter contains an astonishing vision of God (verses 4-28). God is seen in His chariot, a battle wagon, carried by cherubim. It is a vision of holiness, standing in stark contrast to Jerusalem's sins. Verse 5 tells us of the cherubim, the bearer of God's throne or chariot. There are other references to cherubim in Scripture (1 Chron. 28:18; Psalm 18:10; Gen 3:24; Exod 37:6; Rev 4:6). Apparently, the cherubim group together to look like a chariot, each have four wings, and wheels beneath them. They do the bidding of God and go wherever He directs. It is very important that we not be consumed by the details, trying to decide what everything "stands for," but instead concentrate on the big picture: God's awesome holiness and power. Notice that God is separate from even the cherubim (verse 22) because He is God and supreme in holiness.

2 - Chapter 2 describes Ezekiel's call and commission. "Son of Man" (verse 1) becomes the normal title for Ezekiel. It is used over 90 times to refer to him, and is used to mean Ezekiel is a frail and weak man. Verse 3 speaks of "rebellion," a term used many times in this book to describe a people who have not just "missed the mark" though they were trying to do right. These people rejected God for idols! The commission given to Ezekiel is very tough (verse 5) and puts no premium on visible results but instead faithfulness from the messenger.

3 - Chapter 3 finds Ezekiel eating the message of God (verses 1-3). Eating the scroll signifies how the prophet would totally absorb God's message - it would go all through him. Unfortunately, what was sweet to him would be rejected by the captives (verses 4-11). Ezekiel is then transported by God to his audience (verses 13-15) and told he has the responsibilities a watchman has (verses 16-27). Ezekiel's role was to warn Israel of the coming threat: judgment of God (note verse 18). What do we make of Ezekiel's muteness in verse 26? It may not mean total speechlessness, but that Ezekiel would speak only the message of God. It could mean Ezekiel, for a time, was mute except for preaching the specific message of chapter 4.

Reading 2 - Ezekiel 4-6

4 - Chapter 4 needs to be understood against the backdrop of what we read in Jeremiah. False prophets were telling the people there (and in Babylon) that the 597 captivity would be short-lived and the captives would come home soon (see Jer 28:3). The city would not be attacked or besieged. Ezekiel acts out a very different message (verses 1-8) with a very different meaning (verse 13). The "griddle" of verse 3 is difficult. It may have been an iron pan that was used as a

siege wall, or protection for the "attackers" of Ezekiel's little city. Verse 4 says Ezekiel will lie on his side as part of the sermon, but it does not mean he laid there 24 hours a day. The number 390 in verse 5 remains unexplained, despite many attempts to add, subtract or divide it into something meaningful. Somehow it represents the punishment given to the ten Northern Tribes. Then, in verse 6, Ezekiel faces south, representing Judah for 40 days. Again what the number of days represents is uncertain. The bread of verse 9 is made of many ingredients, implying there isn't enough of any one ingredient to make a loaf. The rations of verses 10-11 are sparse, amounting to about a half a pound of bread and one pint of water. God graciously allows a priest another way of preparing his meal (verse 15) as verse 12's requirements were so repulsive to Ezekiel.

5 - Chapter 5 continues Ezekiel's "visual aid" preaching. Ezekiel shaves his head, a sign of mourning (verse 1) and then destroys the hair. This signifies that one-third will die inside the city, one-third will die by the sword, and even the last third will lose part of its people (note verse 12). This terrible judgment would be so awful that it would serve as a warning to other nations (verse 15).

6 - Chapter 6 attacks the mountains, the place of the idol worship known as the "high places." The refrain of verse 7 is repeated four times (verses 7, 10, 13, 14). That this would be said so often points out that they do not know the Lord. Remember, "know" speaks of relationship with God, not just understanding the facts about Him.

Reading 3 - Ezekiel 7-9

7 - Chapter 7 begins four speeches that emphasize that judgement was coming and was coming soon. Note from verse 2 that the end spoken of here is not the end of the world and second coming of Jesus, but it would be the first time the Israelites had no place to worship God. Verse 10's rod is Nebuchadnezzar, and its "blossoming" says the time has come. Verses 12-13 describe judgment coming so quickly that business deals end up being meaningless. This may refer to the Sabbatical Year when all land reverted back to original owners. No one would gain from such a transaction because in just a few years no one will be in the land! The response to this threat in Judea is weak and lame (verses 14-27). They cannot get an army together (verse 14)! While they obsessed about wealth it could not save them and there was nothing to buy (verse 19). Verses 20-22 speak of the Temple. So the Judeans will be chained together and taken to Babylon (verse 23).

8 - Chapter 8 begins in the early fall of 592 or 591 (verse 1). Ezekiel is taken in a vision to Jerusalem so that he can see the incredible moral depravity and wickedness of the leaders of his nation. The idol of verse 5 is called an "image of jealousy" because God is a jealous God (Exodus 20:1-3). We do well to be reminded that the jealousy of God is not a fickle emotion but the righteous response to something or someone who has usurped His place. Incredibly, Ezekiel then sees the elders secretly worshiping idols (verses 7-12). They are rationalizing this wickedness by saying God has forsaken them (verse 12). This is key for Ezekiel, because it shows that the captivities of 605 and 597 were not seen as punishments to the people but failures by God! Tammuz, the god of fertility who "died" in the fall was revived in the spring by crying, is being worshiped in the temple (verses 13-14)! The sun is being worshiped as well (verses 15-18). The twenty-five men in verse 16 could be one man from each division of the priests and the high priest. What "branch to the nose" means (verse 17) is uncertain.

9 - Chapter 9 shows the glory of God leaving the Temple. God's house has become polluted with

idolatry and wickedness so the Lord decides to move out! An angel comes and marks the righteous who mourn the idolatry of the times (verse 4). Some wonder what good it did to be marked since righteous people did die in the siege and slaughter (see Ezek 21:3-4). But not all suffering is punishment. The mark simply means God knows who is His _ that alone would be tremendous comfort. Verse 10 speaks of justice and "reaping what was sown." This is always God's way!

Reading 4 - Ezekiel 10-12

10 - Ezekiel 10 continues the action of chapter 9. The key action here is verse 4. Ezekiel sees the glory of God that infused the temple, and indicated God dwelling there, leaving. It is a stunning development. From the Holy of Holies the glory of God goes to the temple's doors. God's house has become polluted and defiled and so God is moving! We do not and will not understand all the details of the cherubim here (as we did not in chapter 1) and some verses are very hard to picture (like verses 9-14). The point here is clear, whether we can puzzle out all the details. Verse 18 tracks God's glory out of the Temple and verse 19 finds it now at the east gate. God is leaving His house! Deuteronomy 31:17 promised this would happen. God abandons His Temple!

11 - Chapter 11 continues the story. Key to understanding the chapter is to realize there are two groups of Jews, one in captivity and the other in Jerusalem. This chapter shows that the future of the people lies with the captives, not those back home. The men of verse 1 are evidently prominent and well known men. Verse 3 shows the work of the false prophets. Jeremiah consistently taught that the people must submit to Babylon or be destroyed (see Jer 29:4-5). These false prophets tell the people to fortify and make ready for war, instead of building houses and living the quiet lives of good citizens. God expresses the verdict using their terminology (verse 7). These wicked leaders will not die in the city. They will not get to be even (partly) correct, able to say "We died in the city." Zedekiah and his prices were caught trying to escape and were judged at Riblah (2 Kings 25:1-7), down at the border as verse 11 predicts. Ezekiel's concern for his people is seen again in verse 13. God answers the prophet's question by saying that the people in Jerusalem are hopeless. They think they are the remnant, but they are not (verse 15). God is using the captivity to purge His people (verse 16). These people needed a new heart (verse 19) and God was working to give them just that. But as for the people in Jerusalem _ there was no hope for them (verse 21). The climax of the chapter is verses 22-23. God's glory leaves the Temple and Jerusalem and is gone. Jerusalem is on its own now. What will protect them from Babylon?

12 - Chapter 12 contains another visual aid sermon (verse 3). While God has given up on the people in Jerusalem God is still teaching and trying with the remnant in exile. Verse 10's prince is Zedekiah. The talk of "covering his face" is ironic since Zedekiah is blinded before bringing brought in chains to Babylon (Jer 52:11). Verse 22 refutes a common idea (from the false prophets) that nothing ever comes of these doom and gloom messages, or at least nothing will come of them for a very long time. Verse 23 says clearly the time of Jerusalem's end was very near.

Reading 5 - Ezekiel 13-15

13 - Chapter 13 condemns the false prophets who contributed so much to Judah's problems. They whitewash or plaster over the rebellious schemes of the leaders by applying God's seal of approval to them (verse 10).

When the storm comes the people will see that the plaster didn't do the job they were told it would do (verse 12). Verses 18-19 expose divination and sacrificial rituals used as part of the false prophet's lies. True prophets were put to death during this time (remember Uriah was killed, Jer. 26:20ff).

14 - Chapter 14 returns to the remnant in Babylon. These are the people God wants to work with but verse 3 tells us these people would worship idols if they just could! Ezekiel tells these men with divided hearts that they must repent or be punished. Verse 9 doesn't mean God deceives people, but it does mean that if a person does not desire the truth God will allow him to believe a lie and be deceived (see 2 Thess 2:10-12). The chapter closes with a stirring message that Jerusalem will be destroyed and the presence of a few righteous people will not stop that destruction.

15 - Chapter 15 is the parable of the useless vine. The people of Judah might question whether God would really destroy His chosen people. Ezekiel's answer is that what makes a vine valuable is that it bears fruit (verse 1). A vine is good for nothing else. The wood from a vine is too soft and crooked and weak to be used for any kind of building. The vine is a common symbol for Israel (see Gen 49:22; Psalm 80; Isaiah 5:1-7). The parable is then applied to Judah and Jerusalem (verses 6-8). Verse 7 speaks of the Babylonian invasions in 605 and 597. Judah survived those but fire was waiting for them again. Back to Table of Contents.

Week 44 - Ezekiel 16-30

Reading 1 - Ezekiel 16-18

16 - Chapter 16 speaks to people who were not convinced they were a worthless vine. A discussion of Israel's history was in order to correct arrogance and pride. The chapter contains very stark language, but it is appropriate in light of the sexual immorality that surrounded idolatrous practices in the Old Testament. Verse 2 introduces the chapter's key. The history lesson beings in verse 3. Jerusalem was begun, as a city, by the Hittites and the Amorites. No one thought the city important at first (verses 4-5). "Rubbed with salt" was part of the way a new baby was cared for (verse 4). Then God made His name dwell there (verses 6-14). The "spreading of a garment" over her is the symbol of marriage (Ruth 3:9). Yet despite all the blessings of God Jerusalem simply used those blessings for evil (verses 15-21). She did not remember her humble beginnings or God's blessings (verse 22). She is worse than a prostitute because a prostitute gets paid for her "services," while Judah offered herself to the idols of the surrounding nations for free (verses 30-34). Again the remember theme is noted (verse 43). She is like her Hittite and Amorite "parents" (verses 44-45). These people are so wicked God promises that when Sodom is restored they will be restored as well (verse 53). Verse 60 echoes the idea of remembering once more, but now it is God who remembers and who, amazingly, offers grace to a wicked people.

17 - Chapter 17 uses a parable of two eagles to help the people understand the sin of making foreign alliances. The parables (verses 1-10) tells of Babylon (verse 3) planting or making Zedekiah king (verse 5). He was not a great king but a low vine with very limited powers (verse 6). He sought to rebel against Babylon with the help of Egypt, the second eagle of verse 7. The interpretation (verses 11-24) announces that Judah is not to rebel or count on Egypt (as they did - see 2 Chron 36:13). Again a message of Ezekiel's concludes with God's grace as He replants the tender twig (the house of David), making reference to the Messiah and His kingdom (verses 22-24).

18 - Chapter 18 is the great chapter on personal responsibility. The people in captivity were complaining bitterly that their parents were the reason they were in Babylon (verse 2). It is important to realize Ezekiel is not teaching righteous children never suffer for their parents' wrongdoing. For example, the children of alcoholics do suffer though innocent. What Ezekiel contests is that God punishes the innocent for the sins of others. That doesn't happen! Ezekiel tells the story of three generations of men, one righteous, one wicked and finally one righteous. These illustrations may be rooted in the lives of Hezekiah, wicked Manasseh and righteous great-grandson Josiah. The chapter's point is summarized in verse 20. God does not want any to die (verse 23) and so allows people to repent and change. When they do God changes His verdict on their lives. These people needed to stop blaming others and start repenting! Verse 31 shows that getting a new heart is not something requiring a miraculous direct operation of God but something the sinner can do when he changes his ways, exactly what Ezekiel hoped the people would do.

Reading 2 - Ezekiel 19-21

19 - Chapter 19 may carry on the conversation of chapter 18. Ezekiel may be dealing with the question "Should we trust our leaders back home?" His answer is sharp and clear: no! They are like the wicked man of 18. Verse 2 starts the metaphor of Judah as lions, as lions are a common figure for the Davidic dynasty (Gen. 49:9; 1 Kings 10:19-20). The first cub is Jehoahaz (verses

3-4), the son of Josiah. He only reigned three months, was taken to Egypt and died there (2 Kings 23:31). The second cub (verses 5-9) is Jehoiakim's son, Jehoaichin. He was no better than the others. The chapter concludes by developing the metaphor of Judah as a vineyard again. Note the vine destroys itself (verse 14), which is exactly what Zedekiah did.

20 - Chapter 20 gives a history lesson. Verse 1 is set in July/August of 591 or 590 BC, putting it very close to Jerusalem's destruction. Watch the emphasis on God acting for His name, His reputation (verses 9, 14, 22). The message is straightforward, detailing Israel's history of apostasy and God's longsuffering grace and mercy. Verse 37 uses a figure of speech drawn from shepherding. The shepherd counts his sheep as they pass under the rod for inspection, counting, etc. The idea here is of ownership. Verse 39 is dark and sarcastic: just go do evil since that is what you want so much! The material beginning in verse 45 goes with chapter 21. It is a word of judgment to the south (the Negeb). The people claim they cannot understand Ezekiel's message but how could they miss it? The south is Judah!

21 - Chapter 21 continues the word of judgment from the end of chapter 20. Now we see why the people "couldn't" understand Ezekiel's words (20:45). They don't want to hear this bad news (verse 7). Verse 10 is difficult but the "wood" is the rulers who have been called "branches" earlier (19:11). Babylon will stand at the crossroads, its king trying to decide which way to go and what country to destroy (verses 20-21). The false prophets in Jerusalem will tell the people Babylon will not come (verse 23) but they will! Verse 26 says destruction is coming for the priest ("turban") and king ("crown"). Even the Ammonites will be destroyed by Babylon (verses 28-32).

Reading 3 - Ezekiel 22-24

22 - Ezekiel 22 contains three messages. First, Jerusalem is corrupt (verses 1-16), secondly, the people are impure (verses 17-22) and third, all of society has failed (verses 23-31). Highlights here include the idea that the captivity was a purging (verse 15), and that leadership had utterly failed the people (verses 25-27). "Dross" in verse 18 is the base metals that refining removes so as to have pure silver or gold.

23 - Chapter 23 uses some very stark language about spiritual adultery. We may be made uncomfortable with these descriptions but we do well to remember they simply mark out the depth of relationship God had with His people, and how they were in spiritual adultery. This chapter is like chapter 16, but here the emphasis is on alliances not idolatry. Chapter 16 stresses the beginnings of Israel's history while this material looks at the recent past. Jerusalem should have learned from her sister's example but she did not (verse 11). Removing ears and nose is a figure for deportation (verse 25). The real trouble is that she forgot God (verse 35). Verses 36-49 summarizes much of chapters 20-23. God's people had done wrong for so long they were worn out with adultery (verse 43) and so only judgment could stop their sin, teach them, exact vengeance and show who the Lord is (verses 48-49).

24 - For so long Ezekiel has been preaching that judgment is coming. In chapter 24 that terrible day arrives. The date in verse 1 would be January 588. The siege lasts approximately 18 months (see Jer. 39:1-2). Ezekiel tells the parable of the cooking pot (verses 3-5), saying that Babylon will kill and murder without rhyme or reason. The contents of the city will be deported and then the pot (the city) will be burned (verse 11). Then we read of an incredibly difficult burden for Ezekiel. God takes his wife from him (verses 16-18) and Ezekiel was not to mourn her loss in any way. This naturally causes people to wonder what Ezekiel is doing, acting so callously

(verse 19). Ezekiel tells them God will destroy the Temple and they should accept God's will and agree with Him in this horrible judgment (verse 22). Verses 25-27 may not mean Ezekiel was entirely mute but that when the news of what God had done in Jerusalem reached Babylon people would finally realize Ezekiel was right all along and listen to him.

Reading 4 - Ezekiel 25-27

25 - Ezekiel 25 begins a series of messages to Israel's neighbors. Some of these nations delighted in the downfall of Judah (Ammon and Moab) while others had even helped the invaders (Edom and Philistia). Ezekiel warns that God knows what each nation has done and is sovereign over all people, not just the Jews. The messages begin to the east of Judah with Ammon and then move clockwise to Moab, Edom and Philistia. The wise reader will watch to see what God charged each nation with so that we can profit from these gloomy words even today.

26 - Chapter 26 begins a three chapter section dealing with Tyre. To the modern reader Tyre is nothing more than a dot representing a single city on the map of ancient Canaan. Why does God concern Himself with this one city? The answer is that in ancient times Tyre was an economic power that flexed her might throughout the Mediterranean. It was a seaport and center for trade. Her wealth made a significant player in Mideast politics. One of the main themes in the messages against Tyre is the condemnation of pride. Verse 1 dates the message in 586 BC. Tyre thought Jerusalem's ruin guaranteed her own prosperity (verse 2) but such was not to be (verse 3). The words of judgment ring out, shocking with their prophecy of total destruction (note verse 4 and 14). What would we think of a prophet today announcing New York or London would become a bare patch fit for nothing but drying fishing nets?

27 - Chapter 27 sees Ezekiel composing a lament for Tyre (verses 3-9) in which is discussed as if she were a beautiful ship. Note her pride at the end of verse 3. Her trading partners are listed from far and near (verses 10-25) showing her worldwide economic powers.

Reading 5 - Ezekiel 28-30

28 - Ezekiel 28 contains a final word against Tyre. Her king is the fountain of the people's pride, since he thinks of himself as a god (verse 2). But he was merely mortal (verses 8-10) and would die like any other man when God brought foreign opponents against Tyre. The chapter concludes with a lament song for the king (verses 11-19) and a warning for Tyre's neighbor Sidon (verses 20-26). The material for the king of Tyre reminds the reader of the Garden of Eden, but the Bible makes no application of this to the devil or his origins. Thus we must not draw conclusions about Satan from material specifically directed to the king of Tyre (verse 12). Verses 14-16 simply say that Tyre enjoyed a blessed and elevated position, i.e. God allowed them to prosper. Sidon is also warned of coming judgment (verses 20-26). Note the emphasis on "then they will know that I am the Lord," a phrase that repeatedly occurs in Ezekiel. There is a marvelous note of grace and restoration for Israel at the end of the chapter (verses 25-26).

29 - Chapter 29 addresses Egypt. Ezekiel contains seven messages to Egypt, more than any other book. Ezekiel contains so much about Egypt because it was still a superpower in Mideast politics in Ezekiel's day, although they were on the decline. Beaten by Babylon in 605 at Carchemesh she was still scheming to get back the land taken by Babylon then (which included Judah). This worked out perfectly for Judah, as they were anxious for an ally to help in their rebellion against Babylon. In fact, in 588 the Egyptians advanced against Babylonian forces invading Judah, providing temporary relief to Jerusalem. They were defeated and Babylon returned to finish off

Jerusalem. Verse 1 dates chapter 29 from January 587, right when all this maneuvering was happening. So we see that Ezekiel is warning the exiles not to be deceived into thinking Egypt would "save" Judah. Her glorious history, large army and big plans to replace Babylon as the dominant superpower would not change anything: she would be defeated because God was against her. Again we see pride and arrogance as part of God's main case against a country (verse 3). Verse 6 says leaning on Egypt is like using a water reed (a hollow plant like a cattail) for a walking staff - it would immediately break! Judah's dependence on Egypt ultimately let them down. Verses 11-13 speak of "forty years," probably meaning a generation of Egyptians would know a time of desolation and unimportance as a world power, thanks to Babylon's devastation. Verse 17 dates this second message in 571 BC, making it one of the last messages to Egypt. Nebuchadnezzar's soldiers wore themselves out against Tyre, with their armor chafing and rubbing them bald in a difficult campaign (verse 18) but would be "compensated" with Egypt.

30 - Chapter 30 continues the dark words of doom for Egypt. Its message for the captives in Babylon was plain: Egypt would not defeat Babylon and would not rescue Judah or them. Verse 20 dates another message to Babylon in 587, after Egypt's failed attempt to stop the Babylonian invasion of Judah (see Jeremiah 37:5ff). Egypt's arm was broken when it failed (verse 21), and now they would be punished further (verse 22-26). The scattering here is a reference to Egypt's army, not the people of Egypt. Egypt was attacked and further defeated by Babylon in 568-567 (see Jeremiah 43:10-14). Back to Table of Contents.

Week 45 - Ezekiel 31 - 45

Reading 1 - Ezekiel 31-33

31- Chapter 31 now tells the story of Egypt's condemnation using the parable of a tree (verses 1-9). Verse 3 might should read "a cypress" instead of Assyria, focusing the message on Egypt not Assyria. The tree is great and grand (verses 4-9) but it is cut down and her allies abandon it (verses 10-15) and those who relied on it suffer as well (verse 17).

32 - Chapter 32 continues God's strong words of judgment for Egypt. Verse 1 gives the date as 586/585. The lamentation for the Pharaoh (verses 2-16) says that Egypt is a like a great sea beast, caught and left on the beach to rot and be food for scavengers. Verse 17 is also dated in 586/585. This final word to Egypt announces that she will take her place in the Graveyard of Nations - great powers God humbled and overthrew. Just as Assyria (verse 22) and so many others were destroyed by God so shall God do to Egypt. Today's reader may be tempted to be bored by these repetitive messages to Egypt. Instead, we should see God's power and sovereignty over all nations. These chapters reinforce our need to trust God rather than in men. He alone holds power—all power —in our world.

33 - Chapter 33 is the famed "Watchman" chapter. This sounds very much like 3:16-21 where Ezekiel is commissioned, and chapter 18 where individual responsibility is emphasized. This re-commissioning may be because new responsibilities are coming his way as his message is seen (finally) to be true. It is a time of hope. Ezekiel no doubt endured very rough treatment, as Jeremiah did. But verse 10 shows his preaching was paying off, as the people finally began to get it. Even so, there is a still a note of whining and complaint in their "confession," yet God does no one wrong (verse 20)! Verse 21, dated in 587/586, brings Ezekiel complete vindication. 24:27 contains Ezekiel's prophecy of this very event, and now his mouth is opened (verse 22). The exiles would have many questions now. Are they the remnant or is God planning to use the feeble group left over there under Gedaliah (see Jer 40-41). Verse 24 indicates the people in Judah were still trying to claim remnant status and saying they could claim Abraham's promise. God says they aren't the remnant and won't last (verses 25-28). The exiles had listened to Ezekiel to be entertained (verse 31), but now they were really listening (verse 33).

Reading 2 - Ezekiel 34-36

34 - The tone of Ezekiel changes dramatically beginning in chapter 34. Before Ezekiel has spoken repeatedly of judgment and condemnation for Judah's sin. Now he looks forward to a time of restoration, and beyond even that, to the time of the Messiah. As the exiles receive the devastating news that Jerusalem and the Temple have been demolished Ezekiel brings a word of comfort: God is not done with the Jews, and a bright future exists for God's people! Some of these messages will be hard for us to completely understand but if we are careful not to contradict the rest of Scripture and we keep things in context we can gain much from Ezekiel's preaching. Verses 1-10 blast the leadership of the people for their utter failure. Note the repeated emphasis on "My sheep." The leaders were God's stewards, thus they had failed God. In even better news the True Shepherd was coming (verses 11-24), One in the spirit of David who would truly care for His people as a shepherd should. Verses 23-24 picture Jesus the Good Shepherd (Jno 10:11), ruling and reigning. Verses 25-31 return to language that would bring a smile to any exiles' face - they would return to dwell securely in their land again. This does not have to be literal (any more than the reference to David in verses 23-24 is literal) but may picture the return from captivity while envisioning even something greater in the future: God's people prospering

spiritually under the Messiah's rule.

35 - Chapter 35 answers the question many exiles would ask: how can we go home when there are enemies like Edom there? God's answer is that Edom will be judged and destroyed. "Mount Seir" (verses 2-3) describes the area of Edom (see Gen 36:8, 9). Edom thought they could grab the land that had been Israel and Judah's (verse 10) but this land grab would not work (verse 11). Note Edom's pride in verse 13.

36 - Chapter 36 addresses the land itself, assuring it that its people are coming home. The long series of "therefores" show the basis for judgments to come (verses 1-7). Verses 13-15 speak of a land that had a reputation for being "jinxed." Yet the house of Israel would return to their land (verses 16-38). The nations around them mocked God because His people were carried away captive (verse 20), but because of God's concern for His name (verses 22-23) He would return them to the land (note verse 36). The people who return will be different (verse 25), they will care about their relationship with God (verse 26). They will have a new heart and a new spirit! The key to all these good blessings is the people's repentance (verse 31).

Reading 3 - Ezekiel 37-39

37 - Chapter 37 contains two visions, the Valley of Dry Bones (verses 1-14) and the Two Sticks (verses 15-28). Neither is hard to understand. The dry bones represent Israel, a nation that is dead in captivity with no hope whatsoever. God revives them, doing something only God could do. The two sticks are specifically interpreted (verse 19). Mormonism tries to say this is a vision of the Bible and the Book of Mormon. This does not and cannot work. God says this is about nations, not books! The vision looks forward to when all of God's people are united under one king, David (verse 24). Since David was dead when the prophecy was given we are forced to look for a figurative meaning. The vision looks forward to the Gospel's call, assembling all who have a heart for God ("walk in my rules and be careful to obey my statues"), to be God's people (verses 27) and follow Christ (the David of verses 24-25, remember 33:23-24). This vision looks forward to the church and its blessed relationship with God.

38 and 39 - Chapters 38-39 are not difficult chapters to understand, but their specific application is very difficult. Their main point is that God will protect His people when they return to their land. A horrible and terrible enemy will invade but God will utterly destroy them, leading to peace and safety in the land. The defeat of this apparently invincible army by the Lord would convince the people of God they are safe and they will serve the Lord again. Beyond these general ideas, certainty is very difficult. We do not know of any historical ruler known as Gog, nor are we completely certain where Magog, Meshech and Tubal are. Some try to make this into a future battle scene, but 38:11 hardly looks like modern day Israel (with all its armies and defenses), and the weapons of 39:9-11 are not anything any modern army would use. The reader must not try to force these chapters into some system of end-time speculation or contrive to fit these happenings into the evening news. The chapters speak of God fighting for His people (38:18-23), granting an enormous victory of unparalleled dimensions (39:1-16), the enemies' bodies being food for scavengers (39:14-21). All this will reassure Israel (39:22), and the nations around them (39:23). 39:25 summarizes the chapters: God will restore these people He had to punish. We must be content with what the text says and not speculate beyond it.

Reading 4 - Ezekiel 40-42

Today we begin the final section of Ezekiel, his amazing vision of a new and stunning Temple.

Some have tried to make this into a prophecy of a literal temple that will be built someday in Jerusalem during the supposed thousand-year reign of Christ (the premillenial view). Yet in this temple we see the Levitical priesthood (43:19; 44:15), sacrifices for sin being made (43:19-22, 25-26; 44:27) and even circumcision (44:9) _ all done away by Christ and the new covenant! Some have tried to see the church in this vision, but even that seems problematic. When this vision was given the people of God were in disarray. Their capital and the temple had been in ruins for many years. They had no king of David's line and apparently little hope of being constituted as a country ever again. Thus it is probably best to see this as just a wonderful vision of rebuilding the temple and the nation to serve God. It is a message to give hope to people who desperately needed it. God has vowed to protect the nation (chs 37-38) but where will they worship? Much of this language reminds us of the Tabernacle instructions in Exodus, meaning these chapters seem to point toward a "second Exodus," and a homecoming to serve God.

Chapters 40-42 - The visions begin in 573 (40:1). A divine messenger appears carrying measuring instruments (40:3). He then measures and marks out the new temple (40:5 through chapter 42). The cubit here is probably 18" (40:5). Some of the terms used for the building are uncertain and vary from translation to translation. Beginning in 42:15 the area of the temple is measured. The NKJV and NASB give the measurement in "rods," which would make it huge _ almost a square mile in size. The ESV and NIV render the measurement in cubits, which makes it more in keeping with the sizes given for the rest of the structure.

Reading 5 - Ezekiel 43-45

43 - Ezekiel 43 contains the most important aspect of the vision: God's glory returns to the new temple (verses 1-12). The emphasis is that God's return makes them His people again - just like when the Tabernacle was indwelt. It is all that any Jew in exile could ever hope for.

44 - Chapter 44 discusses the priests that will serve in the Temple. Interestingly, once God uses the east gate to come in it is permanently closed because God came through it (verse 2). The prince of verse 3 is probably the people's leader. Verses 5-9 forbids the use of foreigners in the temple service. Verses 10-16 allow only the family of Zadok to serve in the Temple. Zadok was David's high priest and was faithful to Solomon when Adonijah tried to usurp the throne (1 Kings 1:32, 38). The chapter concludes with details of the appearance and behavior of the priests (verses 17-37). Some of this sounds strange to us but emphasizes how they are set apart to God's work.

45 - Chapter 45 again reminds of the Law prior to Israel taking Canaan, as the land was divided out. The priests are given a share (verses 1-7), and the leaders are urged to deal rightly with the people and use a just balance (verses 8-12) and offer the correct sacrifices (verses 13-20). Back to Table of Contents.

Reading 1 - Ezekiel 46-48

46 - Ezekiel 46 continues discussion of the "prince" and the various feasts that will again be observed before the Lord when the people return from exile (verses 1-18). The places for offerings and kitchens are also laid out (verses 19-24).

47 - Chapter 47 depicts a mighty river that flows from the Temple, getting ever deeper as it goes. It is so powerful it makes the Dead Sea fresh again (verse 8). Everywhere the river flows plants sprout and bloom and fish thrive. Is this just a picture of the blessedness the people who return can expect from the Lord? Verses 13-23 describe the dividing of the land, just as in Numbers 34.

48 - Chapter 48 continues the tribal allotments. The Levites are given allotments and the city will have twelve gates, three on each side. The last verse of the book is significant: the city will be named "The Lord is there" showing that God will again dwell with His people. While there is much here we may not be certain about it is clear Ezekiel provided the hope and comfort the people in exile needed to sustain faith until the seventy years of captivity would end. But what did faithful people do who lived during this time of captivity? Could one be faithful in exile? Tomorrow we begin answering that question by reading Daniel.

Reading 2 - Daniel 1-3

Introduction to Daniel - This book is exciting, interesting, and very important. It teaches us how to stand up for righteousness, do right and live right in very difficult times and circumstances. Its visions bridge the gap from Malachi to Matthew by telling us significant events that will occur during the intertestamental times. More than anything else, it sets forth the sovereignty of God. His people may be in captivity (due to their sin) but that did not mean God was weak or powerless. It is also important to note the New Testament usage of Daniel. Jesus' favorite self-title, "Son of Man," comes from Daniel 7:13, while His Olivet Discourse (Matt. 24; Mark 13; Luke 21) is full of imagery from Daniel, particularly the "abomination of desolation." Other apocalyptic sections of the NT (2 Thess 2; Revelation) draw heavily on Daniel's imagery.

1 - Chapter 1 begins with the date, 605 BC (verse 1). Babylon came to Judah three times (605, 597 and 586), with each "visit" progressively more violent and destructive. In 605 Nebuchadnezzar was content to take young men back to Babylon to train for civil service. God's sovereignty (a major theme in Daniel) jumps to the fore right away (verse 2). God is the main actor in Daniel! Note this further emphasis in verse 9 ("God gave") and verse 17 ("God gave them"). Daniel's career would span from 605 to 538-535, making his whole term of service approximately 65 years (verse 21).

2 - Chapter 2 contains Nebuchadnezzar's dream of future kingdoms. Note Daniel's humility and determination to give God the credit (verses 20-23, 28, 30). Daniel says the statute represents four empires (verses 31-43): Babylonia (gold, 605-539 BC), Persia (silver, 539-331 BC), Greece (bronze, 531-146) and Rome (iron, 146 BC-AD 300). Verses 44-45 focus our attention on God's everlasting kingdom to be established in the days of the Roman empire (see Luke 3:1ff; Luke 20:17-18; Mark 15:43).

3 - Daniel 3 brings Shadrach, Meshach and Abednego back into the picture. Where Daniel is during this troubling event is unknown and not discussed in Scripture. The entire chapter gives us a look at a showdown between God and Nebuchadnezzar. Notice the emphasis on what

Nebuchadnezzar did and the repetitive refrain "he had set up" the image. This is Nebuchadnezzar challenging God (note verse 15b)! Fortunately, Shadrach, Meshach and Abednego refuse to knuckle under (verse 12), and refuse to reason from consequences (verses 17-18), choosing instead to die for what is right than compromise. What courage! The identity of the fourth person in the furnace (verse 25) is unknown - perhaps an angel or even Jesus. The chapter that began with a decree to worship an idol then ends with a decree honoring the one true God (verse 29)!

Reading 3 - Daniel 4-6

4 - Daniel 4 might be titled "Temporary Insanity," as God teaches Nebuchadnezzar a needed lesson in humility. Verse 17 is the main point of this chapter: the Most High rules, not men! Verse 13's term "watcher" is a very unusual term for an angel used only in this chapter. Daniel shows great courage in giving the true interpretation of the vision, as it was certainly not something that would make Nebuchadnezzar happy to hear (verses 19-27). Verses 34-37 close the chapter by reconnecting to verses 1-3. The message that God is in control was needed not only for foreign rulers like Nebuchadnezzar but exiled Jews who wondered if they would ever get back to their homeland.

5 - Daniel 5 is the story of Belshazzar, a bad king who deliberately defied God (verse 2). Verses 30-31 record the end of the Babylonian empire as the Medes and Persians take Babylon. There is much discussion of verse 31's Darius, perhaps the royal name for Cyrus, the first Persian king.

6 - Daniel 6 presents the familiar story of Daniel and the Lion's Den. It is not surprising Daniel would be installed in the new government (verse 2), as his fame as a wise man would be widespread. Daniel's prayers (verse 10) are courageous because he could have prayed secretly. Verse 24 is a powerful warning against jealousy. As Nebuchadnezzar had done before, so now Darius praises the One true God (verse 25).

Reading 4 - Daniel 7-9

7 - Chapter 7 begins the vision section of Daniel. These chapters are fascinating, exciting and famously difficult. Verse 1 dates this vision in 556. Verse 4 has wings being plucked, clearly referencing a reduction of pride and power. Probably corresponds to Nebuchadnezzar's insanity. Verse 5's bear appears to be the Medo-Persian empire, though "raised up" is difficult. There are many different ideas about the three ribs in his mouth. Verse 6's leopard is Alexander and his swiftly won empire. The four heads signify the division of the empire among his four generals, Antipater, Lysimachus, Seleucus and Ptolemy, when he died. Much is made of the symbolism of the ten horns in verse 7 but the Bible does not invest the number "ten" with any specific meaning. The scene then cuts away world powers to a throne scene in heaven (verses 9-14). The throne here reminds us of Ezekiel 1 and Revelation 4. God is seen as "the Ancient of Days" because in Daniel's world old age was respected and venerated. God exercises complete sovereignty over the terrible beast and kills it (verse 11). The phrase "Son of Man" is Jesus' favorite term for Himself, used heavily throughout the Gospels (note also Acts 7:56). Thus, even though the figure is not called Messiah here, Jesus uses Daniel's language to speak of Himself cinching its meaning. Jesus is the One who receives an everlasting Kingdom in the days of the last empire (as in Daniel 2's vision). The interpretation of this is very straightforward (verses 16-18), at least until we come to the identity of the fourth beast. Some think he must be Rome due to parallels in Revelation but it is crucial with apocalyptic visions that they be allowed to stand on their own. John may use Daniel's images but he can, and does, put his own meaning on them. It seems better to see the fourth beast as the evil Antiochus Ephiphanes. Note he is destroyed

before the Son of Man receives the kingdom (verses 11, 26), while Rome continued during the time of the kingdom. Verse 24's ten kings maybe the Seleucid line being put down. Verse 25's time reference is difficult. As seven is viewed as a perfect number this may be saying evil will last only half as long as God's work. The time of temple desecration under Antiochus was about 3.5 years, so that may fit, or it may just be a figure for a remarkable, sudden judgment. Don't lose sight of the main meaning of this vision, even as we puzzle over the details. The emphasis and import of all this is verse 27. God reigns and rules and His people will know victory and triumph!

8 - Chapter 8 again looks to the time between Malachi and Matthew with very specific prophecies of what will happen then. Daniel's message would encourage God's people when persecuted to persevere and not give up because God will triumph over every enemy! Verse 1 gives the time as 553-552 BC. Daniel sees the Medo-Persian empire overrunning the entire earth (verses 3-4, 20), and then being defeated by a goat (verse 5) that symbolizes Greece and Alexander the Great (verse 21). When Alexander died his empire was divided among his top four generals (verse 8, 22). Out of those kings would come one king who would persecute the Jews and try to usurp the place of God (verses 10-14). This is Antiochus Ephiphanes, the Syrian king of the Seleucid line, who tried to stamp out Judaism, erecting an idol to Zeus in the temple and defiling the altar by offering swine on it in 168 BC. He threw down various leaders ("host of heaven" verse 10, see also verse 24) and stopped the temple's offerings (verse 11). The time of verse 14 is difficult but may be the 1150 or so days until the Maccabees took Jerusalem and cleansed the temple. Why is this vision said to refer to the "time of the end" (verse 17)? Many suggestions have been made but best may be the idea that this would be the end of God's wrath on Israel. Daniel knows this isn't The End, as he speaks of the restoration of the Temple. God finally struck Antiochus dead (verse 25b). It is comforting that not even Daniel understood everything about this vision (verse 27) just as we surely don't today!

9 - Chapter 9 contains Daniel's great prayer for his people to be allowed to return home from exile. The material in Daniel's prayer is not difficult (verses 1-19). Daniel has been reading Jeremiah 25 (verse 2) and realizes it is time for the people to return from Babylon. He pleads with God to do as He has promised! The emphasis on God's name and righteousness in this prayer is notable. The divine answer (verses 20-23) is very difficult. Prolonged discussion of all these passages is beyond the scope of these brief pages. Some think it points to Jesus and His work (and Jesus does reference Daniel in Matt 24:15-16) but this solution is not without difficulties. Usually if the reader believes the times to be literal the outcome is to take this as a reference to Jesus. If the times are viewed more figuratively and indefinite then the end of that perspective is to see this as dealing with Antiochus Ephiphanes. This author is impressed that much of what is said in verse 24 seems to apply to Jesus and only to Jesus. The reader will have to study and make his or her own decision. Note that verse 25's "Messiah" (NKJV) should be translated "anointed one" (meaning it could be Cyrus, Isaiah 45:1 or some other person). Who the "he" is of verse 27 is also difficult. Certainty in all the details eludes us but we can keep our focus on the certainty that God is active and will keep His promises (the context is God's promise of seventy years of captivity). In this, even in a difficult text, we find and hope and encouragement.

Reading 5 - Daniel 10-12

10 - Daniel 10 provides a brief respite from the complexities of the visions in chapter 9 and 11. The chapter stresses that events on earth can only be understood from a heavenly perspective, as

we see that God is working out His purposes here. Verse 13 demonstrates this, as heavenly warfare is detailed. The "prince of Persia" wants to stop the messenger from delivering the message so that it cannot be implemented. "Latter days" in verse 14 may be the events toward the end of the Jewish dispensation. What a scene all of this makes, and how it fuels our anticipation of the final dramatic vision of Daniel!

11 - Chapter 11 shows us the Persian empire (Xerxes is the fourth king of verse 2), Alexander and the Greeks (verse 3), and the division of Alexander's kingdom upon his death (verse 4). Two of the four generals who received his empire were Ptolemy (Egypt) and Seleucus (Syria). Verses 5-45 detail, with amazing accuracy, the battles between these two families to control Palestine. There was an attempt to make an alliance by marriage (verse 6) but the peace was only temporary, as Ptolemy III invaded Palestine pushing back the Seleucids (verses 7-10). Wars and counter-attacks followed down through the years (verses 11-16). Once again a marriage alliance was planned (verse 17) but it failed. By verse 18 the Seleucid ruler is Antiochus III. When he tries to conquer Greece the Romans defeat him. He dies two years later (verse 19). His brother Antiochus IV (Ephiphanes) succeeds him in 175 through deceit and intrigue (verses 21-23). Antiochus attacked Egypt, now ruled by Ptolemy VI, but the invasion didn't fully succeed (verse 27), so he attempted it again in 168 BC (verse 29). This time Rome issued an ultimatum to leave (verse 30), utterly humiliating Antiochus. On the way home he vented his spleen on the Jews and Jerusalem (verses 30-31). Antiochus set up an idol in the Temple and thoroughly desecrated the Temple. Incredibly, some Jews went along with him in his attempt to install Greek culture in Judea and stamp out the old ways, but war broke out. Led by Judas Maccabee and his brothers the Jews fought to stop Antiochus (verse 32). Some joined the Maccabeean cause insincerely (verse 34) but the fight was on. Up to this point the vision matches history so well its interpretation is not difficult. Verses 36-45 are notoriously difficult. This writer knows no solution that solves every problem. The temptation is to keep reading this as applying to Antiochus, but some of what occurs here does not seem to fit him. Others see this as skipping ahead to the end of the world, but such seems dubious. What is clear is that we have a king who exalts himself above God (verses 36-39). Verse 37's reference to "beloved of women" is very difficult and uncertain. Verses 40-45 then portray a giant battle against this wicked king in which he attacks Israel (the "glorious land," verse 40) and is defeated. The purpose of the chapter is to say that wherever righteousness is, evil will try to destroy it _ and that God will ultimately deal with evil. So be faithful!

12 - Chapter 12 finishes the vision with a "time of trouble" (verse 1). God protects His people through all of this, and there will even be a resurrection of the dead (verse 2). This resurrection has prompted much speculation. Is it a symbol for national revival after Antiochus' persecution? Note that it is a resurrection of the evil and the good. Is this once again pressing the message of faithfulness, now urging people to think about the eternal reward for serving the Lord (verse 3)? That would surely be a message of comfort and hope that would strengthen the Jews. The message is sealed (verse 4) until the right time. The final reference in the book then is to 1290 days (verse 11) and 1335 days (verse 12). The 1290 days may relate to the three years the Temple was profaned under Antiochus' control. The meaning of the additional 45 days of verse 12 is entirely unknown. Notice that the book urges faithfulness and perseverance in the face of suffering and trials even at its end. We may never solve the mystery of all the details and numbers here but we can learn and profit from Daniel's overall theme: be faithful unto death!

Back to Table of Contents.

Week 47 - Ezra 1-4; Haggai; Zechariah 1-8

Reading 1 - Ezra 1-2

Introduction to Ezra - What happened to the small remnant of Jews who returned to their shattered homeland and destroyed capital after the Babylonian captivity? Ezra and then Nehemiah recount their story. Ezra's book divides into two parts, both of which precede Nehemiah. Chapter 1-6 give the history before Ezra, while chapters 7-10 tell what happened once he arrived in Jerusalem. It is important the reader realize the book opens in 539 BC but Ezra doesn't arrive till 458 BC. Nehemiah arrives 13 years later in 445.

1 - Chapter 1 records Cyrus' decree to return the Jews to their homeland. Remember, this was prophesied in Isaiah 44:28-45:1, hundreds of years before Cyrus lived. The Sheshbazzar of verse 11 is mysterious. He is not Zerubbabel and is only mentioned a few times. He may have been a Persian official responsible to the government.

2 - Chapter 2 lists the names of the families returning. This list shows who is a true Israelite in contrast to the Samaritans in the north who give the Jews so much trouble. Note that priests of uncertain lineage could not serve until God could be consulted with Urim and Thummim (verse 62). We do not know exactly how Urim and Thummim were used but it is of value to see that God's people didn't act without being certain of His approval.

Reading 2 - Ezra 3-4

3 - Ezra 3 begins in September-October (verse 1), about three months after the exiles had arrived home. The priest takes over, leading religious revival (verses 2-7). In the spring of 536 (verse 8) construction on the Temple began.

4 - Chapter 4 summarizes all the different attempts to stop the efforts of the Jews. Chapter 3 tells of the start of the work. Chapter 5 records that the work on the Temple took twenty years to finish. Chapter 4 explains why it took so long. In consecutive order Ezra details the attacks of those who made the reconstruction of Jerusalem so difficult. Verses 1-5 are set in Cyrus' time (539-530), verse 6 in Xerxes' day (485-465), while verses 7-23 take place during Artaxerxes' reign (464-424). Notice both temple building and wall building are discussed here (verses 2-3, 12). Verse 24 then resumes the story of the temple's reconstruction during the time of Darius I (522-486). Make certain that you read 5:1-2 to set the stage for our reading in Haggai and Zechariah. What did these men say that restarted the work? We will see tomorrow!

Reading 3 - Haggai; Zechariah 1

Introduction to Haggai - Haggai is one of the few successful prophets in the Bible. Indeed, very few prophets ever saw their audience accept and act on their preaching, but Haggai and Zechariah did. The entire focus of Haggai's preaching was "Get back to building the Temple." For eighteen years the work had been left unfinished. Haggai's emphasis is "Thus says the Lord" (some form of phrase "the Lord says" occurs 19 times in 38 verses!) and happily people responded with repentance to his authoritative preaching.

1 - Chapter 1 dates this as August or September of 520 BC (verse 1). The people had rebuilt their homes (verse 4) but God's house was still in ruins (verse 4b). The result was that the promised prosperity (remember Ezekiel's prophecies?) did not come to pass (verses 6, 9). The repentance of the people (verse 12) brings on a great word of encouragement and comfort (verses 12-13). It only took 24 days for Haggai's message to bring about change (verse 15)!

2 - Chapter 2 begins one month after chapter one (verse 1). The questions being answered in verse 3 expose what people were thinking: the new Temple was small and plain. How could these poor returning exiles possibly build anything to match what Solomon and his unlimited budget and numerous craftsman constructed? The people were thinking of giving up because their efforts appeared so feeble and lame. But God makes great promises to them (verse 5) and is ready to honor their work if they will just keep at it! Verse 7 is difficult. Some apply this to the Messiah, others the church and its global mission for all (see Eph 2:21-22; 1 Pet 2:4-9). Jesus' presence would give that temple greater glory (verse 9). The reader should note that Zechariah gives his first message between Haggai 2:9 and 2:10. The question of verses 11-14 has to do with "contagious holiness" and "contagious sin." Haggai asks "If you touch something that is holy does that cleanse you and make you holy?" The answer is "No" (verse 12). However, if you touch something unclean you do become unclean. Disobedience is "contagious." Bad attitudes effect everyone. That is what happened to these people, and it rendered everything they did unacceptable to God (verses 13-14). Attitude matters to the Lord! If they will keep on working God will bless them (verse 19). Haggai's final message deals with "shaking the nations" (verse 21), God's total overthrow of pagan powers (verse 22). Zerubbabel is not the Messiah (verse 23) but he does stand in Christ's lineage. In these bad times God is saying "I have not forgotten my promise to David (2 Samuel 7)." God is still working in and through these people. But for God to use them they had to be obedient and rebuild the Temple!

Introduction to Zechariah - Zechariah is often called the prophet of hope. His book shows an interest far beyond just rebuilding the Temple. Zechariah wanted to renew the people's spirituality. So his book is full of apocalyptic visions to help the people grasp key spiritual truths that would encourage them to keep trusting in God even as they faced hostile enemies around them. Some have thought that Haggai worked with those who were dedicated to the Lord, while Zechariah may have tried to rally those who were weak and uncommited. There is tremendous emphasis in Zechariah on the promised Messiah _ something of special note to Christians today.

1 - The message of chapter 1 fits between Haggai 2:9-10, a time when the people were discouraged (verse 1). Verse 6 is key. God's word did overtake these people's wicked forefathers! The answer to Zechariah's question was "Yes!" Thus the people are admonished to fully return to God and remain faithful to Him! Everything depends on this. Verse 7 begins a series of eight night visions that Zechariah saw in February of 519 BC. The first is of horsemen, one of whom is riding on a "sorrel" or dappled horse (verse 8). These horsemen are God's night patrol. Were the Jews asking when God would "shake" things up (as Haggai promised, 2:20), and is God still angry with us even though the time of punishment is over (verses 11-12)? Verses 16-17 contains the comfort and assurance the people needed. The next vision (verses 18-21) depicts the nations that have scattered God's people. Perhaps this is Assyria, Egypt, Babylon and the Persians or, alternatively, "four" may just suggest completeness (like the expression "the four winds"). The message is God would raise up powers to destroy these nations (verse 21). Haggai's shaking is coming so be patient!

Reading 4 - Zech 2-5

2 - Zechariah 2 continues the visions. The measuring line vision (verses 1-13) is a challenge. It is hard to keep up with the angels here and to know if this is spiritual or physical Jerusalem. The vision's message is that God protects His people (verse 8). Note that Jews were living in Babylon and becoming like her (verse 6). They needed to come home. The vision does seem to look beyond just physical Jerusalem to a time when all people can be in covenant relationship

with Him (verse 11).

3 - Chapter 3 brings Joshua the high priest to the fore. He stands before the Lord in filthy rags (verse 3), probably a symbol of his and the nation's sins. The high priest represented all the people (Exo 19:6). Satan accuses Joshua (verse 1), meaning Satan points out the people's sins before God. How can God have fellowship with such people? But what Satan has failed to account for is God's grace in forgiving His people (verse 4). Speaking of forgiveness naturally leads to discussion of the coming Messiah, the Branch. "The Branch" is a very Messianic title (see Isaiah 4:2; 11:1; Jer 23:5; 33:15; Zech 6:12). The stone of verse 9 is uncertain but clearly represents God's favor and blessing and forgiveness for His people.

4 - Chapter 4 continues the visions with a vision of a lampstand and two olive trees. The lampstand vision isn't explained until verses 10b-14. First Zechariah receives a word about Zerubbabel (verses 6-10). Here God encourages Zerubbabel to persevere. From a human standpoint the people didn't have the might or strength to do the job ("flatten the mountain") but God would help them. Zerubbabel will complete the Temple (verses 7b-10). The bad attitudes of Verse 10 will be replaced with rejoicing. The lampstand, according to verse 10b, appears to symbolize God's ability to see everywhere (cast light into the darkest corners of the world). The two olive trees perpetually feed it with the oil it needs (verse 12). But who are the anointed that the trees stand for? It is natural to see them as Zerubbabel and Joshua, the governor and high priest of Zechariah's time. Perhaps it looks forward to Jesus, who is both king and priest.

5 - Chapter 5 has two visions, a huge flying scroll (verses 1-4) and a woman in a basket (verses 5-11). These visions push Zechariah's theme of spiritual renewal. The first vision deals with what seems to have been prevalent sins of that time, stealing and lying. The second vision represents the cleansing of all sin from the land.

Reading 5 - Zechariah 6-8

6 - Zechariah 6's vision of four chariots (verses 1-8) obviously corresponds to the first vision. The Bible does not tell us what the colors here represent (verse 2) so we must not speculate. These chariots go forth to watch and execute the will of God throughout the earth (verses 6-8). Verse 8's precise meaning is uncertain. It may be that God rests now that His cause is vindicated. The vision of crowing the high priest (verses 9-15) contains some strange features, such as the names from verse 10 being changed in verse 14. Again we read of the Branch (verse 12) the Messianic title. Joshua the high priest is crowned priest and king but he cannot really fulfill this prophecy. Instead it points to Jesus, the Branch, the Messiah, who would build the temple of God, the church, for all to come into.

7 - Chapter 7 is two years after the night visions (verse 1), making this 518 BC. It answers a question about fasting (verse 3). God's answer is simple: all this fasting is something the people came up with (verses 5-6), not Me! What God desires is people to live for Him and do right (verses 9-10) not come up with all kinds of extra religious rituals!

8 - Chapter 8 continues the idea of needing to obey God. Note the heavy emphasis on "thus says the Lord." This is God's word and it begins with a wonderful message of comfort and reassurance (verses 1-8). God goes on to speak of grace for His people (verses 11-15), but then strongly reminds them to do what their fathers failed to do: be obedient (verses 16-17). The direct answer to their question about fasting is then given (verses 19-23). The fasts will become feasts as God continues to work with His people to bring about salvation to "men from the

nations of every tongue" (verses 23). This looks forward to the day when the word of the Lord will go forth from Jerusalem (verse 22) as seen in Acts 2. Back to Table of Contents.

Week 48 - Zechariah 9-14; Ezra 5-6; Esther 1-6

Reading 1 - Zechariah 9-11

9 - This chapter begins one of the toughest sections of Scripture. The visions in chapters 9-14 are very difficult but stress judgment on heathen nations and the coming King (chs. 9-11), and the rejection of the shepherd and the final victory of God's kingdom (chs. 12-14). Chapter 9 opens with judgment upon Syria (verse 1) and surrounding nations (verses 2-8). Is this Alexander the Great conquering the world? But a greater King is coming (verses 9-10) who will be a King of peace. This is directly applied by Jesus to Himself in Matt 21:4-5, as Jesus makes His triumphal entry. The chapter then closes by talking of God fighting for His people and the great victories the people will be granted (verses 11-17). Some see the Maccabean Wars (and their unexpected triumph) here (note verse 13).

10 - Chapter 10 features an unexpected and difficult transition from battles to asking for rain (verse 1). The connections to what went before is uncertain. What is clear is that God is fed up with people seeking idols (verse 2) and bad leaders (verse 3). Despite all of this God will graciously bring His people home again and make them strong (verses 6-12), perhaps a reference to the call of the Gospel and its marvelous provisions. As Ephraim (verse 7) did not exist in Zechariah's time that seems to force this to be not literal.

11 - Chapter 11 begins with doom and destruction. The building of verse 1 may be the temple (note Jer 22:23). It is bad leadership that has caused this fall (verses 4-6). Zechariah fires the bad shepherds (verse 8). There are numerous explanation for who the "three shepherds" are, but we just don't know. We do know the staff called Favor is the covenant the people broke with God (verse 10). Sadly, God's shepherd and work is not valued - instead he is paid wages so poor they are an insult (verses 12-13), verses later to be applied to the money Judas received for betraying Jesus. The other staff stands for Union (verse 13), which is now taken away, either standing for the unity between Judah and Israel that should have been in place or internal unity among the Jews. God then uses bad shepherds to punish the people (verses 15-17).

Reading 2 - Zechariah 12-14

12 - Zechariah 12 starts the second prophetic word. The term "on that day" appears sixteen times. Jerusalem will be attacked (verses 2-3) but God will defend it, with Judah being given strength from God to destroy all nations around them (verses 5-9). The action is not hard to understand, what is difficult is the application. Is this a real battle, or does this speak of the Gospel's victories? The reader will have to make his/her own decisions here. Things get a little easier in verse 10. There is movement away from images of physical deliverance to spiritual deliverance. By looking upon the Messiah people will be moved to repentance. This is directly quoted and applied to Jesus in John 19:37. Verse 11 references the mourning for Josiah when he was killed at Megiddo (2 Chron 35:20). Verse 12 uses language from the Day of Atonement to talk of mourning for sin.

13 - Chapter 13 continues from chapter 12 by using new covenant language (see Jer 31:31-33) to speak of forgiven sin. Idolatry will be cut off from this new repentant people the Messiah rules (verses 2-3) and there will be no more false prophecy (verses 4-6). There is a sharp turn in verses 7-9 as the Shepherd is smitten at God's command. Jesus applies this to Himself in Matt 26:31-32, fixing the interpretation. When the Shepherd is struck His people are scattered and refined down to a small remnant (verses 8-9).

14 - Chapter 14 pictures God's sovereignty as King of Kings. First Jerusalem is attacked but God routs her enemies without there ever being a battle (verses 1-9). The result is God being established as the King over all the earth. Again, the facts are fairly clear but the application is uncertain. Some think this may be speaking of the AD 70 destruction of Jerusalem and God's preservation of Christians. Others argue that this is spiritual Jerusalem (Heb. 12:22; Gal. 4:26) which is attacked by the world. Verses 12-15 announce a plague on those who attack Jerusalem, resulting in all of God's enemies going down in defeat (verse 15). The remnants then turn to the Lord (verses 16-19), something that surely sounds like converted Gentiles in the church age. A holy kingdom in installed (verse 20) where everything is clean and nothing unclean is allowed in (verses 21-22). Many of these blessings seem best to apply to the church: a redeemed, cleansed people.

Reading 3 - Ezra 5-6

Ezra 5-6 - Now we return to Ezra to see the results of Haggai and Zechariah's preaching. It is clear Ezra wants us to focus on the providence of God (note 5:1-2 and 6:14). No time is spent discussing the actual building but instead another episode of attack and slander is reported (5:6-17), which God will defeat. The letter from Tattenai makes clear the Jews were using the authority of Cyrus, some twenty years earlier (5:13) as their authority. Note the confession in what they say about their history (5:12). The Babylonian captivity has had a good effect. Darius searches in the archives (6:1) and the relevant records are found in Ectbana, a strong testament to their authenticity (6:2). Darius authenticates the decree and adds his own provisions to what is done in Jerusalem (6:3-12). Similar records of Persian support for local cults has been found by archaeologists. The chapter concludes with rejoicing at the completion (finally) of God's temple (6:13-22). Darius may be designated the "king of Assyria" (verse 22) to symbolize oppressing powers. It is not inaccurate - Persia did rule the lands of Assyria.

Reading 4 - Esther 1-3

Introduction to Esther - The book of Esther occurs between Ezra 6 and 7, so we read it now in its chronologically correct place. Having journeyed back to Jerusalem with Zerubbabel to see the plight of the returning captives Esther takes us back to palaces, kings and intrigues (as in Daniel). Esther takes place in the capital of the Persian empire during the reign of Xerxes (486-465 BC). Interestingly, there is no explicit or specific mention of God in this book. However, God's sovereignty and providence are found on every page.

1 - Chapter 1 begins with the greatness of the Persian empire. Ahasuerus (his Persian name in Hebrew) is the king more widely known by the Greek version of his name, Xerxes (verse 1). The "third year of his reign" would be 483 BC (verse 3). Esther is filled with authentic details of Persian life, including mentioning the royal colors, purple and white, of Persia in verse 6. The riches of Xerxes are put on display in an incredible banquet, where each man could drink as he pleased (verse 8). There has been much speculation why Vashti would not appear for her husband (verse 12) but no one knows for certain. What is certain is that Xerxes thought this could result in widespread domestic problems and so took decisive action (verses 16-22).

2 - Chapter 2 advances Esther's story by telling how she came to be in the palace. There is an ominous foreshadowing in verse 10. The Jews had learned already to protect their identity. Sometimes people do not understand the particulars of how Xerxes selected his new wife but verses 12-14 make clear it was not a beauty pageant. Esther should not be blamed _ she is a helpless victim of the king's whims. The break from Esther's story to tell of Mordecai's

faithfulness to the king (verses 19-23) seems odd but will be very important later. Xerxes was murdered in his bedroom in 465 BC. Such plots were a part of the life of any king.

3 - Chapter 3 adds the villain to Esther's story: Haman. Why doesn't Mordecai bow down to Haman? Jews can bow down to a man (see 1 Sam 24:8; 2 Sam 14:4; Gen 23:7). Perhaps Mordecai saw it as idolatry. Or maybe Mordecai just did not approve of Haman but this independent judgment will cause problems. The casting of lot to determine "fate" was a huge part of Old Testament life and culture (verse 7). Esther points people to Who really controls life and it is not a mindless set of dice.

Reading 5 - Esther 4-6

4 - Chapter 4 heightens the drama. Will Esther go see the king? No one just wanders by and chats with the king (verse 11). Look at Mordecai's faith in verse 14. He is sure deliverance will arise, and believes God may have brought Esther to the kingdom for "such a time as this."

5 - Chapter 5 tells us Esther will not be executed for approaching the king (verse 2). Her plan is masterful and wise, and shows careful planning. Haman, in contrast, is seen as a foolish loser who cannot enjoy all he has because of one person who won't do to suit him (verse 13)!

6 - Chapter 6 heightens the tension. We are ready to see how and when Esther will reveal the plot against her people to the king but instead we are taken to the palace's sleeping quarters to see a king who cannot sleep (verse 1). Now the prior reporting of the assassination attempt against Xerxes makes sense (verse 2). Haman's pride is on full display (verse 6) but he is humbled (verses 10-11). What has happened only foreshadows the greater disaster about to befall this wicked man. All of this, of course, is God working seemingly random events together to do His will. Back to Table of Contents.

Week 49 - Esther 7-10; Ezra 7-10; Nehemiah 1-9

Reading 1 - Esther 7-10

7 - Esther 7 completes Haman's downfall. Verse 4's ending is very obscure and uncertain. His moment of glory turns into disaster and he can't even beg for mercy without getting in more trouble (verse 8).

8 - Chapter 8 settles what the Jews can do about Haman's day of destruction. The law cannot be changed but they will be allowed to defend themselves (verse 11). This would be more than enough to convince most people not to mess with the Jews.

9 - Chapter 9 tells us what happened on the day massacre was planned. Instead of destruction the Jews rout their enemies. Verse 26 gives the origin of the Feast of Purim. The name comes from the Persian word for "lot." Haman cast lots for them, but God overruled his decision!

10 - Chapter 10 completes the story. Esther begins by telling of the greatness of Xerxes and ends with the greatness of Mordecai!

Reading 2 - Ezra 7-10

7 - Ezra 7 takes us back to Jerusalem and the people who returned from Babylonian captivity. Since the last king we read about was Darius (6:12) approximately 57 years have passed. One of the key ideas here is God's providence, "the hand of the Lord" (verse 6). Ezra comes to Jerusalem in 458 BC (verse 7). It is very troubling to read that some in Judea do not know the Law (verse 25). Ezra has his work cut out for him.

5 - In chapter 5 external problems and pressures give way to internal troubles. Nehemiah deals with a lack of food, people being forced to mortgage their property, oppressive taxation forcing people to borrow money, and some even having to sell children into slavery (verses 2-5). Note Nehemiah's emphasis on doing what is right at once (verse 11). Verse 14 dates Nehemiah's time in office from 445-432 BC. At a time when people were impoverished he refused to tax the people more to pay for all the entertaining a governor must do (verses 15-19). Nehemiah modeled for the people what he expected of them!

6 - Chapter 6 ratchets up the tension with a plot to assassinate Nehemiah (verses 1-9), and an obscure scheme involving the Temple (verses 10-14). Shemaiah is a false prophet and seems to be trying to entice Nehemiah to go into the Temple, which he could not do since he was not a priest (verse 11). Verse 15 notes that the work was not stopped and gives all the credit to God (verse 16). Nehemiah's leadership skills are amazing.

Reading 5 - Nehemiah 7-9

7 - Chapter 7 tells of an empty city that now needed to be populated. Verse 3 reports some defensive measures Nehemiah took. Opening the gates later in the morning would avoid surprise attacks at dawn. The rest of the chapter contains a genealogy (verses 6-73), largely similar to Ezra 2. This genealogy connects the inhabitants of Jerusalem to the people who returned home from captivity. God is working to rebuild and now refill the city.

8 - Chapter 8 begins the great Watergate Revival. This interrupts the story of repopulating Jerusalem, resumed in chapter 11. Ezra's sudden reappearance (verse 1) has prompted all kinds of speculation and discussion about how this material fits with Ezra's work in Ezra 7-10. It does seem fitting here that the wall is rebuilt and now the people can serve the Lord and Ezra leads

them to do so. The people's desire for the Law (verse 3) and reverence for it (verses 5-6) are a delight to see. Note the emphasis on understanding God's word so it could be obeyed (verses 8-12). In an additional Bible study group (verse 13) Ezra leads the leaders to reinstate the Feast of Tabernacles (verses 14-18).

9 - Chapter 9 sees the people repenting and turning to God with renewed zeal (verses 1-3). This sets the stage for recommitting to God's law and God's covenant in chapter 10. The prayer of confession (verses 6-38) is a wonder. It recounts the history of Israel, noting again and again how often God's people had failed and how gracious God had always been. Back to Table of Contents..

Week 50 - Nehemiah 10-13; Malachi; Job 1-11

Reading 1 - Nehemiah 10-13

10 - Nehemiah 10 lists those who "re-covenanted" with God (9:38). Why Ezra's name does not appear here is unknown. The specifics of this new effort to serve God faithfully are then carefully spelled out (verses 29-39). The reader should note the absence of idolatry here. The Babylonian Captivity finally was sufficient to purge this recurrent evil from God's people. It will not trouble them again.

11 - 12 - Chapters 11-12 resumes the story of chapter 7, as new people move into the city (verses 1-24). Those who were willing to move in to the city are given special recognition (verse 2). Nehemiah then gives some additional lists, noting settlements outside of Jerusalem (verses 25-36) and a list of priests (12:1-26). The wall is rededicated with great rejoicing (12:27-43). Verse 43 sounds a note of joy unlike almost anything else in the Old Testament. The Temple's services provided for as they should be (12:44-47). The picture here is of Nehemiah's good work bringing out the intended results of Jerusalem's safety, security and restored interest in obeying God's law.

13 - Chapter 13 concludes Nehemiah in a most unlikely way: many of the old problems Nehemiah and Ezra worked to eradicate rear their ugly head again. Only in verse 6 do we learn that Nehemiah has been away - perhaps for more than ten years. What we just read about being fixed and rededicated (12:44-13:3) seems to have been compromised, as the Temple is now home to Tobiah (verses 4-5), a problem Nehemiah fixes forcibly (verses 7-8), and then re-cleanses the Temple (verse 9). The portion the Levites were to receive had to be restored (verses 10-13), and the Sabbath was not being observed (verses 15-22). Finally the problem of mixed marriages is again addressed (verses 23-28). Interestingly, when Ezra hears of mixed marriages he pulls out his own hair (Ezra 9:3), but Nehemiah responds by pulling out the offender's hair (verse 25)!

Reading 2 - Malachi 1-4

Introduction to Malachi - Malachi is the last word of God to the Jews for 400 years. It is a unique and different book, because the people of God are in a unique and different place in their development and history. For so long we have read prophets that railed against idolatry or promised captivity but there is none of that here. The people have returned from captivity and are not idol worshipers. But God's people are not faring well spiritually, and Malachi comes to point to some crucial areas of life that where repentance is needed. Malachi's work challenges us in a time of spiritual apathy and disinterest in God's law. There are no datable events in Malachi but it may fit during the time Nehemiah was away or during his second term as governor.

1 - Chapter 1 begins the book in its unusual dialogue style. Malachi speaks for God and for the people in a question and answer format. The expression "Yet you say" occurs eight times (1:2,6,7; 2:14,17; 3:7,8,13). The people are challenging that God even loves them (verse 2) but their place back in Judea while Edom (the children of Esau) lay destroyed was proof positive of God's love (verses 3-5). God then has a question for the people: where is the honor due Me as a Great King (verse 6)? The people don't seem to think they have dishonored God (verse 6b-7) but by offering sick and diseased animals they are despising God (verses 8-9). Such offerings are an insult (verse 12-14). Note the people's general attitude toward worship is "How dull and boring it is!" (Verse 13). Again, such only insults God.

2 - Chapter 2 begins with a rebuke of the priests (verses 1-9). They are despising God with these

sorry sacrifices and so God will despise them. Verse 3 is strong language but just speaks how the punishment fits the crime. They treat God with contempt, so He will treat them with contempt. The priests are also charged with failing to instruct and teach the people in what is right (verse 7). In verse 10 the rebuke turns to all the people, not just the priests. Once again we confront the evil of intermarriage with foreigners (verse 11) and now a second evil is spelled out: divorce (verses 12-16). Apparently Jewish men were divorcing their Jewish wives to chase after foreign women! The tears of these put-away wives are pictured as putting out the fire of the altar and thus keeping God from accepting their worship (verse 13). The Hebrew in verse 15 is notoriously difficult. The reader should consult different translations to try and get a sense of the meaning here. God's verdict on divorce is clear (verse 16). The chapter concludes (in a fine example of poor chapter divisions) with the people's complaint that the promised prosperity had not materialized (verse 17). The prophet will deal with this complaint in chapter 3.

3 - Chapter 3 answers the question of 2:17: "Where is the God of justice?" Malachi's answer is He is on the way, and this isn't such wonderful news for these who have treated the Lord with such contempt (verses 1-5)! The "messenger" of verse 1 is identified in the New Testament as John the Baptist (Mt 11:10-14; Luke 7:27). John will prepare the people for a coming of the Lord that will bring judgment on sinners (verses 2-3). God's nature doesn't change (verse 6) and so those who have failed to reverence God must be punished (verse 7). The reader can almost hear the people in verse 7 saying "Return? Why we never left!" but their failure to tithe is just one more example of their contempt for God (verse 8-10). The people complain that the promised prosperity hasn't materialized and that they are too poor to tithe. Malachi says their lack of prosperity is because they don't tithe, and is not an excuse for it. More blasphemous and false charges against God are rebuked in verses 14-15. Fortunately some still love the Lord and turn to Him (verses 16-18) but the Lord knows those that don't love Him (verse 18).

4 - Malachi 4 concludes the Old Testament with a strong warning of judgment in verse 1. This verse may reference the destruction of Jerusalem in AD 70. The book ends with two admonitions: remember the Law of God (verse 4), and watch for a prophet like Elijah who will come to prepare the way for the Messiah (verses 5-6). That prophet is John the Baptist (Mark 9:11-13; Luke 1:17) who preached and even acted much like Elijah did. This would be the last word from God for more than four hundred years, but it told God's people exactly what to do while they waited: obey the Law of Moses and watch for the prophet who would point to the Messiah.

Reading 3 - Job 1-3

Introduction to Job - The list of what we don't know about Job far exceeds any list that could be put together of established facts. For example, we don't know when it was written, or even who wrote it. There is debate about its theme. Many use this book as the classic reference on human suffering, and the age-old question "Why do the good suffer?" However, this writer does not believe that is the key to Job, noting that Job is never given an answer to that question. Instead the book pivots on the idea of 1:9: does Job serve God simply because it pays to do so? Job believes he serves God because God is God and thus worthy of His adoration and worship. But will Job abandon this when life becomes cruel and hard? At its most fundamental level the book then is about holding on to one's integrity and faith. Integrity is living life in accord with what you believe is right. Job believes God is good and kind and that he has done nothing to deserve the terrible suffering that comes his way. So when life doesn't make sense and is assaulting him at every level will he continue to serve God or will he give up his faith?

1 - Chapter 1 begins by setting before us a man who is as righteous and morally upright as possible (verse 1). Job is the man who is living according to the precepts and principles of Psalms and Proverbs (think Psalms 1). Thus we expect him to be blessed by God, and he is (verses 2-5). Satan then enters the picture (verse 6). There is much we might want to know about the scene here that the author of Job does not tell us. His concern is that we see that Satan is not a legitimate son of God and that he is not equal to God, but far less in power than the Lord (verse 12). Note the concern about "cursing God" (verse 11). That crystallizes what this struggle between God and Satan is about. Verses 21-22 make it clear that Satan has lost round one. Job blesses God instead of cursing!

2 - Chapter 2 continues the emphasis on "integrity" (verses 3 and 9). Job is absolutely blameless but continues to do what he believes to be right even when he doesn't understand what is happening to him. His wife urges him to commit suicide (blaspheme God so as to cause God to strike him dead) in verse 9 but Job refuses. He refers to her as a "foolish woman" (verse 10) which doesn't mean she is dull or stupid, but a fool as it is used in Proverbs and Psalms: one who mocks and scoffs at God (see Psalm 14:1).

3 - Chapter 3 begins the book's main section where Job's friends make long speeches that he responds to with equally long speeches. Unfortunately, this is where many readers decide to skip to the end to see how it all turns out. That is a terrible mistake that we want to avoid. By understanding what Job and his friends are talking about we can watch the plot of this amazing book unfold. In this chapter Job makes clear his desire to die. Instead of celebrating his birthday (as everyone does) he curses the day of his birth (verses 1-10). He wishes he had been still born (verses 11-12), and even now longs for premature death (verses 20-23).

Reading 4 - Job 4-7

4 - Chapter 4 is the first of the friends' speeches. All of these speeches press the same point: the wicked are punished and the righteous are blessed here on this earth. They articulate the point of view found in general terms in Psalms and Proverbs (note Psalm 1; Proverbs 10:27-29; 12:21, 28; 19:23). Each friend opens with a different tact, with Eliphaz beginning more carefully, the friend concerned that Job's faith not slip away. Bildad is harsher and Zophar is the harshest of all. The speeches will get progressively more bitter and insults fly (note 11:12; 12:2; 15:2; 16:3; 26:2-4). The difficulty is that Job doesn't disagree with the friends. He agrees that you reap what you so (see Job 9:2) but knows he is not wicked. So why is he suffering so? Eliphaz says it is because Job has sinned (verses 7-8) but as readers we know this is wrong. He recounts a vision he had (verses 12-16) that leads him to the (obvious) conclusion that men are sinners before God (verse 17).

5 - Chapter 5 contains more of Eliphaz's certainty that Job is a sinner. Note verses 2-4, cruelly blaming Job for his children's death. He argues that trouble doesn't grow on its own, someone plants it (verses 6-7). God is at work in this world to make sure the wicked get what they deserve and the righteous are blessed (verses 12-16). Eliphaz concludes by saying "If you will just turn back to God, Job, then He will surely bless you again" (verses 17-27).

6 - Chapter 6 features Job's first replies to the argumentation of his friends. He says that in such affliction a person can say things they don't really mean (verse 3). He renews his wish to die (verses 8-10) as life for him is completely empty. He dares the friends to point out his sin (verses 24-27).

7 - Chapter 7 continues Job's lament. He is afflicted with boils (verse 5) and completely miserable. Job wishes God would let him alone but instead feels as if God is treating him like the sea monsters in the deep that have to be carefully guarded because they are a threat to humanity (verses 11-12). Such seems ludicrous to Job; he is no threat to anyone and only wishes to die (verse 16). Even if Job has sinned he wonders why such can't be pardoned for soon Job will be dead and not matter to anybody (verses 20-21). Why is Job getting such "special attention" from God?

Reading 5 - Job 8-11

8 - Chapter 8 is the first of Bildad's speeches. He bluntly attacks Job with little concern for his feelings. He announcers that sinners get what they deserve, even implying Job's children were sinners (verse 4), while urging Job to repent and return to God. The way he has always been taught is what he believes and wants Job to believe too (verses 8-10). Tradition and long standing wisdom are Bildad's guide. Just come back to God and all will be well, Job (verses 20-22)!

9 - Job answers Bildad in chapter 9. God has all power - no one can rebuke, reprove or stand before such a God (verses 1-12). But if God is so powerful why doesn't He help Job? Job does begin to blame God for his troubles (verse 22 and 24). Even if Job puts on a happy face (verse 27) he still will be condemned (verse 29). Job longs for a referee or arbiter to stand between him and God so that Job can speak freely and prosecute his case that God isn't running the universe properly (verses 32-35).

10 - Chapter 10 continues Job's pleas, now more and more directed toward God. Job wants to make his case to God (verses 1-2), and to ask and question God about how He has treated Job (verses 3-7). God made Job (verses 8-17), in which Job speaks wonderfully of God's creative power. Once again Job ends then by longing for God to let him be (verses 18-22).

11 - Chapter 11 introduces us to Zophar. He offers a stiff rebuke, saying that God has actually overlooked some of Job's sin and that Job is getting less than he deserves (verses 1-6)! What Job needs is to be humbled so that he will repent (verses 13-20). Back to Table of Contents.

Week 51 - Job 12-27

Reading 1 - Chapters 12-14

12 - Chapters 12-14 are Job's response to Zophar. In chapter 12 Job laments his situation (verse 4) and dares to say that his friends are wrong: the wicked actually prosper on this earth (verse 6). God has all power, as nature shows (verses 7-12), and God can do as He pleases (verses 13-25). But for Job this means God is responsible for what has happened to him, a point he takes up further in chapter 13.

13 - In Chapter 13 Job says his friends are just trying to defend God (verses 4-8), but he wants to speak with the Almighty (verse 15). The fact that he dares to speak as he does argues for his innocence because he is taking his life in his own hands by asserting his integrity and righteousness (verse 14). Job is certain that if he could simply take his case to God he would prevail (verses 16-27). Beginning in verse 28 and continuing through chapter 14 Job then laments again his miserable situation.

14 - Chapter 14 is a sad and dark chapter. However, in verse 14 Job may be asserting some kind of faith in the resurrection and afterlife, though in an Old Testament setting Job does not understand everything about this. Yet Job ends this speech totally despondent and in complete despair. He seems to be without hope.

Reading 2 - Job 15-17

15 - In chapter 15 Eliphaz vents his anger on Job. He insults Job for being arrogant (verse 7), and asks if Job thinks he is so much smarter than everyone else (verse 7-13)? All men sin before God (verses 14-16) so Job should stop denying the obvious: what is happening to him has happened because he is a bad man. The wicked cannot stand (verses 20-21) and know pain and suffering for their deeds at once (verses 29, 32). Eliphaz carefully includes all that Job has known: fire (verses 30, 34), attack (verse 21), lost possessions (verse 29) and a ruined house (verse 28).

16 - Job's response in chapter 16 shows just how miserable Job is. His friends aren't helping him (verse 2). Job feels that while he has not attacked God, he is being attacked by God (verses 6-14)! Job calls for all to remember the terrible injustice done to him (verses 18-22). Note his continual emphasis on his innocence (verse 17) and his desire to meet with God (verse 21).

17 - Chapter 17 has Job's continued plea for justice, but he speaks candidly of death because he does not believe he will live long enough to be vindicated. Mixed in with these sad notes are plain criticisms of his friends and their thinking (verse 2). The point of view of the friends is given in verses 8-10; they are upright men shocked to see Job in such a state. They seem glad to denounce Job. Verses 11-16 reveal Job on the edge of despair. He has no hope except to die and what kind of hope is that (note verse 15)?

Reading 3 - Job 18-20

18 - In chapter 18 we get another dose of the same reasoning the friends have pounded Job with since the beginning: God blesses the righteous and punishes the wicked. Bad things have happened to you, Job, so that must mean you are wicked. "Stop insulting us!" (verse 3) and "Realize that you must be very evil to receive such punishment" (verses 5-21) announces Bildad. The words about a wicked man's sons dying must have been particularly hard for Job to bear (verse 19).

19 - As another round of debate kicks off in chapter 19 Job ratchets up the increasingly

infriendly dialogue by announcing his irritation with his friends (verses 1-5). In verses 6-21 Job then turns his attention to complaining about God, and charging God with abandoning him and causing him every kind of trouble. What could be worse in a patriarchal society than children mocking you (verse 18)? Incredibly all of this bitterness ends with a statement of trust (verses 23-29). Job expects in some way to finally see God (verse 26b). We will see that more and more Job fixes on an audience with God.

20 - In chapter 20 Zophar answers. It is beautiful poetry with much parallelism. Unfortunately, it is also more of the same line that evildoers are punished immediately by God (note verse 5). Evildoers suffer in the here and now (verses 15, 18) because they are wicked (verse 19) and so God punishes them in this life (verses 23, 27-28).

Reading 4 - Job 21-23

21 - Now it is Job's turn as in chapter 21 he blunts the friends line of reasoning with a direct assertion that the wicked do indeed prosper (verses 7-16). Much of what he says here echoes what the friends have been saying (21:7 relates to 20:11 for example) showing that Job is hearing what they say - he just doesn't agree with it. Even when the wicked directly refuse God (verses 14-15) they are not punished. The wicked are not struck by God (verse 17) and if one says their children will suffer for what they did (verse 19, answering Zophar's suggestion in 20:5) Job says the wicked person ought to pay for his own sins (verse 20). Indeed, Job says, it doesn't seem like it makes any difference whether you are good or bad (verses 22-26). All die alike. Job concludes by saying "I know what you are thinking - I am wicked. But ask any traveler and he will tell you the wicked do well in this world" (verses 27-34).

22 - Chapter 22 has Eliphaz' response. Again we see the tension rising noticeably as Eliphaz continues the accusation that Job is wicked (verses 5, 7, 9). In verse 17 he quotes Job from 21:14. He finishes by urging Job to repent so that all will be well (verses 21-30).

23 - Chapter 23 is short, giving Job's opening salvo in response to Eliphaz. Job doesn't know everything about what is happening to him or why but he is absolutely certain he is not a sinner and so he refuses to repent (verses 1-7). To do so would be to compromise his integrity, all that he has left. Note again Job's desire to talk directly to the Lord (verse 3). He is not a sinner (verses 11-12). Job then begins to talk of how God, in some ways, is above our rules and so cannot be engaged in conventional debate (verse 13-17) though Job longs to make his case to God.

Reading 5 - Job 24-27

24 - Chapter 24 continues this line of thought. Why doesn't God just crush the wicked (verse 1)? Job wants to see God's justice demonstrated by knocking down the evil. The wicked do evil (verses 1-4) while the poor's plight is so pitiful (verses 5-12). Verses 18-25 sound so uncharacteristic of Job's argumentation that some translations have "You say" at the beginning of verse 18 so this is the argument of the friends. In verses 22-25 he again challenges their thinking that God is on the side of the righteous by saying God helps the wicked! In verse 25 Job throws down the gauntlet: show me I am wrong!

25 - Bildad takes up the challenge in chapter 25. God is all-powerful (verses 1-2) and God sees all so no man can possibly be considered righteous before Him (verse 4).

26 - Chapter 26 begins a long section of Job's speeches that are essential in the book. Job says he understands and agrees with the amazing power of God (verses 1-14). God does have all power and might. Although unspoken in this chapter Job's point hangs in the air: why doesn't God use

His power to exalt the righteous and put down evil?

27 - In chapter 27 Job again announces he is innocent and he will not repent (verses 1-6). Integrity is more valuable to Job than his life (verse 5). If you attack Job and his integrity then he hopes you will be cursed (verses 7-12). Job reflects on the fate of the wicked (verses 13-23), verses that are difficult to find in Job's mouth. Some think this is a speech of Zophar's because it reflects the conventional thinking that the wicked are struck down in the here and now. But Job may simply be summarizing their arguments for pushing forward to his masterpiece on wisdom in chapter 28. Back to Table of Contents.

Reading 1 - Job 28-30

28 - Chapter 28 is one of the most important chapters in the book. It signals a change in Job and a determination to seek God in faith. Job says that man can mine the earth to find its riches (verses 1-11) and that wisdom has greater worth and is more scarce than such treasures (verses 12-19). But where can wisdom be found (verse 20)? Wisdom comes only from God (verses 21-28)! Verse 28 is extremely important. Wisdom is found in fearing the Lord. This statement is found at the beginning of Proverbs (1:7) and at the end of Ecclesiastes (12:13) but is right in the middle of Job! The way to wisdom is through submission to God. Job is realizing that he cannot get help from any human. He must run to God, not away from Him. Job has hit bottom but now begins a steady ascent upward that will prepare him for the face-to-face encounter with God he so desires.

29 - Chapters 29-31 contain Job's last speeches. In chapter 29 he reminisces about how happy he used to be before he was struck down. Job goes out of his way to remember his own good deeds (verses 12-17), a clear answer to the many charges that he hasn't care for the poor (see 22:16). It is of import that when Job recounts righteousness he doesn't do so in terms of worship or sacrifices offered but instead in terms of helping others.

30 - Chapter 30 contrasts strongly with the previous chapter's warm tone. It's theme is "How miserable I am now!" Note the use of "but now" in verses 1, 9, 16. Job says he has no honor from men (verses 1-15), no blessing from God but instead pain and suffering from God (verses 16-23), and no one extends benevolence to him (verses 24-31). There is an emphasis here on how all his relationships - both with his fellow man and with God - are messed up. Job's lament over his lost honor and his lost relationship with God says much about him.

Reading 2 - Job 31-33

31 - Chapter 31 contains Job's oath of innocence. This takes the form of "If I have done _____ then let me be cursed." The only way one would dare to say such is if he was truly innocent. Job says he is innocent of sexual sin (verses 1-4), lying (verses 5-8), adultery (verses 9-12), has given his slaves equal rights (verses 13-15), and shown care and compassion for the needy (verses 16-23). Job then turns to secret sins, like coveting (verses 24-25), secret idol worship (verses 26-28), and rejoicing at his enemies' demise (verses 29-30). He polishes it off by saying he has practiced hospitality (verses 31-32) and is not a hypocrite (verses 33-34). Job then wishes he could "sign" his statement of innocence (verses 35-40) and "go to court" against God to hear the charges God would make and answer them. Job is sure he could answer every charge and would wear his innocence like a crown (verse 36). The reader should note this chapter makes an excellent counterpart to Proverbs 31's worthy woman. Job is the worthy man!

32 - In chapter 32 something unexpected occurs: a new character speaks. Elihu is a bit of a puzzle. Apparently he has been here for some time, listening and sitting quietly as he waits for the older men to speak wisdom (verse 6). In some ways he echoes what the friends have already said (34:7 see Eliphaz at 15:16; 34:8 see Eliphaz at 22:15; 34:11 and Bildad at 8:4; 35:5-8 and Zophar at 11:7-9 and Eliphaz at 22:2-3, 12). But more than that his speech prepares us for God's final and climatic speeches. He doesn't provide the final answer but he points to it, saying much that anticipates God's final answer. He emphasizes God's transcendence, that God always does right and there are very real limits to human understanding. These are key themes in God's final

speech. The friends have said that God is just and so Job must be wicked. Job says he is not wicked so God must be unjust. Elihu says there may be more here than that - and that God may have other purposes for suffering than just punishing the wicked. Suffering might be a warning to keep one from sinning, for example (33:16-28; 36:8-11, 15). In short, Elihu moves Job closer to God. That may be the only thing short about Elihu _ he is quite wordy. It takes him 24 verses to say "I'm about to speak!" His concern is about God's reputation and especially Job's charge that God is in the wrong (verse 3). He respects age and has waited because he is young (verses 6-9) but now he feels he must speak (verse 10, 17-20). While the friends are giving up, thinking only God can answer Job (verse 13) Elihu has much to say. He promises no special treatment for anybody (verse 21) so get ready for some straight talk!

33 - Chapter 33 contains Elihu's opening salvo, a speech on introducing the idea that suffering can be God's way of delivering us from sin and keeping us from sinning. The reader should note this is an important part of the why-do-the-righteous suffer question. Suffering may give us strength of character, preparing us to deal with sins ahead of us. Elihu continues his wordy introduction in verses 1-7, saying Job can easily refute him because he is just a man (verses 6-7). He then quotes and summarizes Job's position: that God has done Job wrong, afflicting an innocent man as if he were God's enemy (verses 8-11). But Elihu notes that Job is wrong (verse 12) because God is transcendent and greater than any man (verses 12b-13), that God gives man revelation to save him (verses 14-17), and most of all that suffering has other purposes, notably to warn people away from sin (verses 19-33). Nightmares can be an illustration of this: God warning someone (verses 15-18) and the terror of the nightmare changes how a man lives. Physical suffering can do the same (verses 19-22). The sufferer need only a word from an intercessory angel and he is healed and so thankful that he didn't continue in sin (verses 23-28). God wants man to be saved and does not delight in hurting man (verses 28-29). Elihu is making the case for God's justice and Job's righteousness, something the friends did not do.

Reading 3 - Job 34-36

34 - In chapter 34 Elihu continues his rebuke of Job, even accusing Job of pride and sin (verses 7-9). He counters Job's complaint that God treats the righteous and wicked alike (see 9:22; 10:3; 21:7-8; 24:1-12), and strongly defends God (verses 10-30). Note particularly verses 10-12 where Elihu says God does not do wrong _ ever. Job may not understand what God is doing but God is not doing wickedness (verse 17). Elihu particularly emphasizes the power of God - showing no partiality (verse 20), seeing all that men do (verse 21-22), pulling down the mighty (verse 24), and striking down wrongdoers (verses 25-28). This is God's consistent pattern of work, so even if God is silent, not offering any reason for His actions (verse 29), who can charge God with doing wrong? Elihu ends with an another attack on Job (verses 31-37). These verses are hard to translate and seem to shame Job for his lack of humility. Elihu wonders if a man is punished for his sin and repents (verses 31-32) would Job accept such or would he charge God with being unfair? What Job says about God numbers him with the wicked (verses 35-37).

35 - Chapter 35 reproves prideful thinking. Elihu says "Do we really imagine that we are so important to God that He must answer us?" Note the theme of verse 3 (found also in 34:9) of "will man serve God if it profits him nothing?" This directly connects to the book's main question, found in 1:9. Elihu's answer is that man doesn't add to or take away from God (verses 5-8). Job needs to stop imagining that he is so important that God must respond to him and explain His actions! Further, Elihu notes that people call out to God when in trouble (verse 9) but they forget God when things go well (verses 10-11). Elihu argues that because of pride and

ngratitude God does not answer people (verse 12). Is he taking a thinly veiled shot at Job by saying this? Elihu finishes by saying Job is taking advantage of God's silence and mercy (verse 15) to charge God with doing wrong.

36 - Elihu keeps this train of thought on into chapter 36, as more and more he highlights God's power. Elihu has much to say about God's might (verses 5-12), an idea that prepares the way for much of what God says. He mentions that God works through various situations and circumstances to teach us (verses 8, 10, 15). Again Elihu is working the idea that suffering can be instructive. He cautions Job not to let the terrible circumstances he is in cause him to sin (verses 17-21), and reminds Job of God's great power and transcendence (verses 22-23). For Elihu God's power means He has the right to be the Ruler of the universe and all that is in it - and is above question. As an illustration of the power of God Elihu discusses meteorology, even showing a remarkable understanding of the rain cycle (verses 24-33).

Reading 4 - Job 37-39

37 - Chapter 37 continues Elihu's speech, amplifying and discussing the power of God as observed in nature. Verses 1-5 discuss thunder, verses 6-13 discuss winter. Verse 13 says we don't always understand why God does as He does. Verse 14 is Elihu's central thesis: think about what God can do, Job! God is the Creator (verses 15-20). God is the Almighty who does right and is worthy of our reverence (verse 23). Note that Elihu's speech is not said specifically to end. In some ways, God picks up and continues Elihu's speech.

38 - As if appearing on cue God arrives as Elihu speaks of His power and justice. For so long Job has been crying out for God to appear and now Job will get the opportunity to present his case. The reader should realize that God does not simply attempt to shut Job up by overwhelming him. Instead God carefully shows Job how little of God's way he really knows and understands. God is controlling chaos and evil - even if Job doesn't recognize it. Job has never doubted the power of God but he needs to see that just as God works in nature so God works with humans and the moral order of the universe to accomplish His will. Just as humans don't understand all that God does in nature (and some of that seems awful, wondrous and even silly) so we will not understand all that God does with people but God is at work and God is accomplishing His purposes. Take note that God says nothing about Job's suffering - a fatal blow to those who wish to construct this book into "the" answer to the question of why good people suffer. God speaks first about His wisdom and power in nature (chapters 38-39) and then on how He is sovereign over evil (chapters 40-41). Chapter 38 begins with heavy irony. Job has said he wants to ask God some questions, but the Lord says "I will go first - I want to ask you some questions" (verses 1-3). What follows then is a giant discussion of all kinds of creation (verses 4-21), and weather phenomena (verses 21-41). In some ways God is saying "Do you think you could do a better job of running the universe?" Watch how verse 22 reminds Job that not only is he ignorant of much of how G:od does, the world isn't Job's but God's! Further, everything God does isn't just for people, but sometimes for the land or animals (verse 26). Can any question make plainer how powerless men are than God asking "Can you kept the constellations bound together?" (verses 31-32). Verse 39 introduces the idea of God's work with animals, the major idea of the next chapter.

39 - In chapter 39 God asks Job "What do you know of the animal kingdom?" The animals that are chosen are not necessarily animals that we might have chosen. God chooses to exhibit His ways an interesting collection of very different creatures, like the wild donkey (verses 5-8), the

wild ox (verses 9-12), or even the ostrich (verses 13-18). The lesson here is that God makes creatures that appear odd and crazy to us if that pleases Him. A bird that doesn't fly and can outrun a horse - how weird is that?

Reading 5 - Job 40-42

40 - Job's repentance starts the chapter (verses 1-5). He has lost his desire to be vindicated. However, God is not done. Having shown that there is more to God's work in the world than Job realized God now turns to discuss evil and chaos. Verses 6-14 should not be read as God browbeating Job, especially since Job always agrees that God is great in power and might. Instead God is challenging Job to consider if He has the "arm" (verse 9), or strength and power, to keep evil in check. The illustrations that God uses of this are the Behemoth (verses 15-24) and the Leviathan (chapter 41). Much has been done to try and identify which animal fits the characteristics and descriptions given here, without success. Behemoth looks some like a hippo, and Leviathan resembles a crocodile but at key places the similarity breaks down (verses 17-18; 41:18-21, note especially 41:33). Further talk of the created animal kingdom seems out of place anyway, since God has already spoken of animals in chapter 39. God is now talking about justice and doing right - and it is to these two mysterious creatures that God appeals. An investigation of other places in the Bible that use Behemoth and Leviathan reveals that they are used frequently in the myths of the time and even in Scripture to represent evil and disorder (see Isa. 27:1 (perhaps evil powers at the end time); Psalm 74:14ff (Egypt); Psalm 104:26 (the great unknown terrors of the deep)). Here in Job God uses these two beasts to represent evil and chaos which God keeps in check by His power. The message is clear: God keeps the world, even evil, under control. He isn't asleep or absent. He is sovereign in His power to keep evil from overrunning everything. Job has charged God with letting evil run amok, and not running the universe as Job would like it (9:21-24; 24:1-12). God powerfully points out here that Job cannot contain evil (verse 14). Only God can do that — and He does! The first speeches make the point that God is Creator, now God wants Job to see He is Savior as well. Thus, God is saying that He is not Job's enemy but His friend. This doesn't answer every question about evil in this world but is certainly a comfort. God is in control of Behemoth and Leviathan. God is in control of evil!

41 - In chapter 41 we meet the Leviathan. Anything that Job does to attempt to control evil, as personified by the terrible monster Leviathan, will fail (verses 1-8). Yet God easily tames the awful beast (verses 9-11).

42 - Chapter 42 brings this great book to a close. Job speaks with repentance and contrition in verses 1-6. Job realizes that it is the purposes of God that matter, and that God has the power to bring His purposes to pass (verses 2). The term "repent" in verse 6 can be comforted, and so Job may be saying he is comforted by seeing God's control of creation and evil. It is clear Job has learned much about himself and God. While never claiming to know everything, he repeatedly misunderstood God's actions while demanding a fair trial. Now he understands how little he knows, and that he lacks the basis necessary to call God into court. The Lord has clearly shown Job the limitations of his experiences, both with creation and with moral forces. God is seen now as one who balances and directs the powers and needs of all creatures, letting each creature live out its freedom. Creation is not a puppet with God's hand shoved up its back. Creation is truly free _ and that includes (whether we understand it or not) the freedom to rebel against God and make evil choices. God does what we cannot: keep all of this under control and balanced. Job's friends are rebuked (verses 7-9) because they misrepresented God to Job. Job was right when he said he was innocent and he was right in not giving up his integrity to satisfy their view of the

world. In the end this means God is vindicated. Job does not just serve God because he is blessed. He does not understand, or even agree with, everything God is doing. Note that God does not tell Job about the conversation of chapters 1-2 with the devil. But Job never doubts he must serve God. So, Satan is the loser. Job serves God because God is God, and worthy to be served. The book ends with Job blessed again, with special emphasis on his daughters (verses 10-17). Job closes our reading of the Old Testament for the year. Congratulations on reading so much of God's precious Word!

Back to Table of Contents.

The Reader's Companion for the New Testament

INTRODUCTION TO MARK - This is an easy Gospel to read. There is little background information given or needed. Mark just begins with the main actors and action of his story. He tightly focuses on Jesus, telling us how Jesus feels and what Jesus does. "Immediately" is one of Mark's favorite words. The book was probably written for a Roman audience that would appreciate and understand power and a Man of decisive action.

1 - John the Baptist seems to have intentionally chosen by his lifestyle and clothing to identify himself with the Old Testament prophets, rather than trying to be part of the "religious establishment" (verse 6). Jesus then bursts on the scene, changing men's lives (verses 17-27), and teaching without any mention of rabbinical traditions or precedents but with His own authority (verse 22). He quieted demons (verse 25, 34) because such could only give Him an undesirable recommendation. No one wants to be commended by a demon! Some puzzle why Jesus asked people not to tell about His great work (verses 44-45) but when this leper violated Jesus' request the Lord could hardly move around and Jesus' wisdom is vindicated.

2-3 - These chapters introduce the two controversies that dogged Jesus throughout His ministry: separation with sinners (2:17) and the Sabbath (2:23ff, 3:1-6). The key to the controversy in 2:24ff is to remember that Jesus and His apostles were not violating Moses' Law but rabbinical traditions about what could and could not be done on the Sabbath. Jesus points out the hypocrisy of the Pharisees by asking why they don't condemn David, who really did break God's law (verse 26), and why with their traditions they destroy the Sabbath's real intent (verse 27)? Chapter three continues these controversies, and we meet the Herodians (verse 6). This was a political party dedicated to keeping the Herodian family in power. Strange bedfellows for the straight-laced Pharisees indeed! Don't get lost in Jesus' discussion of an unforgivable sin (verse 29). This is simply the sin of the hard heart that refuses all evidence, and will not repent. A heartfelt concern about having committed this sin would of itself show that one has not done so!

4 - Verse 2 introduces Jesus' favorite teaching method: parables. Jesus told parables to gain and hold people's interest, as well as to sift the casual hearer from those truly interested in His message (note verses 12 and 25). So Jesus urges His listeners to use their ears to really hear, to really listen (verse 9). Mark concludes the powerful message of Jesus with a powerful miracle (verse 39), leaving us, the readers, asking "Who can this be?"

5 - This chapter introduces three hard cases which would impress Mark's audience with Jesus' jaw-dropping power. The demon-possessed man always brings out questions about Jesus sending demons into the pigs (verse 12), why He would do that and why they wanted to go there. The truth is we don't know, and aren't told because it is not important to the purpose of the story. We need to get our eyes off the pigs and look at the man who was healed. We also need to note that if you ask Jesus to leave (verses 17-18) He will! In verse 19 we get a change of strategy, as Jesus usually forbids this (see 1:44). But this area was heavily Gentile, which may account for Jesus allowing this man to become His messenger. Verse 41 contains Aramaic, the common language of the common man in Palestine. Mark translates it for his readers, showing us that his intended audience was not Jews in Palestine.

Applications from This Week's Readings

Jesus had no interest whatsoever in placating the religious establishment or perpetrating their stifling man-made traditions that they bound as if they were from God. Examine yourself and your own ideas about how to worship and live as a Christian. Ask yourself "Do I bind what God has not? Am I stifling God's ways with my self-made traditions?" Back to Table of Contents.

Week 2 - Mark 6-10

6 - Some are confused by verse 5's lack of miracles, but it is not Jesus suffering a "power outage," but a lack of faith in the crowd (note verses 3 and 6). Their faithlessness limited Jesus' work because they didn't bring more to Him to be healed! The sad story of John the Baptist is inserted now by Mark. Verse 17's Philip is not the Philip of Luke 3:1 but another relative named Philip. Herod Antipas was visiting him in Rome, met Herodias and talked into her running away with him. John the Baptist reproved them for living in adultery (verse 18), and it cost him dearly. The chapter concludes with two more illustrations of Jesus' power. Verse 37 speaks of denarii. It was a day's wage, meaning that this is eight to ten months of pay! Verse 48 says it was between 3:00 and 6:00 a.m.

7 - Again Jesus and the Pharisees tangle. Jesus sternly rebukes all their human traditions, derived from long debates by various rabbis, which end up neatly nullifying God's law. Verse 11 tells how they got around caring for parents by simply saying "I've dedicated those funds to God's work." It appears that one didn't even have to give those monies to the Temple then, but could just say "they are dedicated to God," freeing him to change his mind later (after his parents were gone). What sophistry! We are not used to a Jesus who appears unwilling to help (verse 27) but we cannot hear His tone of voice or see the twinkle in His eyes. Is He testing this woman's resolve and faith? In verse 33 Jesus takes special care to let this deaf-mute man know what He is doing.

8 - We have had 5000 fed, but the disciples don't fully understand Jesus' power so Mark gives us all another illustration by telling of the feeding of the 4000. For those seeking more signs can help, but for those with closed hearts no sign will be given (verse 12). Why Jesus heals the man of verse 22 in stages is unknown to us. It is clear that Jesus does not want His disciples telling the world He is the Messiah (verse 30) until they understand what being the Messiah means: He will be killed and rise again (verse 31).

9 - The chapter begins with the key promise of verse 1. It doesn't matter how folks want to define the "kingdom" it is clear Jesus thought it would come shortly. Any teaching that has the kingdom to be something yet future is therefore obviously flawed. Verse 7 makes the point of the Transfiguration: Jesus is of primary importance. We may not ever grasp all that happened there but we can get that. Moses and Elijah probably represent the Old Testament (the Lawgiver and the Great Prophet) but Jesus is the One who matters now. That is why John the Baptist came as His forerunner (verse 13). We may wonder why the disciples could not handle the demon possessed boy of verses 17-25 but Jesus tells us: they were intimidated and lost their faith. What was needed was prayer that restores faith and power (verse 29). So much is made of the unknown man in verse 38, particularly if one tries to rebuke false teaching. Yet this man is not a false teacher for Jesus approved him! If Jesus rebukes false teaching, wrong religion and hypocrisy (and He does!) then His disciples can and must follow His example. Verse 50b probably references purity.

10 - The teaching on divorce and remarriage is remarkably clear (verses 1-12). While much has been made about exceptions the tenor of Jesus' teaching is simple: if you are married, stay married! The rich man of verses 17-22 ought to surprise us. In Jesus' day the belief was that the rich must be very righteous for they had been so blessed. Jesus shows how such blessings can get in the way of really serving God - a warning we do well to consider carefully. Verse 37 shows a very carnal view of the kingdom. This was a consistent problem with Jesus' audiences. Verse 38

uses "baptism" to speak of an immersion, but not in water, but in suffering. Jesus tries to counter their mistaken view of the Kingdom with the "serve first" teaching of verses 42-45.

Applications from This Week's Readings

An emphasis in these chapters is Jesus doing the most incredible and amazing things. Meditate on the power of Christ. How can you have more faith in Him? How does seeing His great power help you feel more safe and secure knowing He will help you and answer your prayers? Back to Table of Contents.

Week 3 - Mark 11-15

11 - Mark now begins the last week of Jesus' life. On Sunday Jesus enters Jerusalem in triumph, hailed as the Messiah (verses 9-10). On Monday He curses a fig tree that promised fruit but did not deliver (like the Jewish nation), and then stops the use of the temple as a marketplace (verses 12-17). We need to be careful with verse 23's statement about faith. First, the apostles indeed had done much that seemed impossible, like walk on water and cast out demons. Second, other passages inform us about prayer and what we should ask for, and that needs to be factored in to all we believe about prayer.

12 - This is one of Jesus' sharpest and clearest parables. Israel was often compared to a vineyard (see Isaiah 5:1ff), so the meaning here is easy to grasp (verse 12). Jesus deals with their "impossible" questions easily (verses 13-27), but they cannot handle His (verse 35)! Jesus quotes Psalm 110 where God says to David's master (or Lord) "Sit at the place of prominence." But how could that be? David was the greatest king. The Messiah would be his son. How could the son be greater than the father, especially when that father was David? Jesus is pushing them to recognize that David's son would be Divine and so be a greater king than even David. However, they don't see it. Do we?

13 - This chapter is the subject of so much speculation and controversy. Yet if we simply look at the questions the disciples asked (when will the Temple be destroyed, verses 1-4), and remember that they didn't understand that Jesus would leave so had no basis to be asking about a Second Coming, we will come out just fine. Watch how the chapter repeatedly addresses Jesus' listeners. Whatever this is about they would see it, it would happen in their lifetimes, they needed to be warned, and they needed to be ready (note verse 30). Verse 14 uses the term "abomination of desolation" but Luke has "armies" letting us know exactly what this is about: the destruction of Jerusalem by Rome in AD 70. Some get lost in the language of verses 24-27 but it simply judgment language from the Old Testament prophets (see Isaiah 13:10-13; 19:1ff).

14 - Mark shows Jesus in control of everything, including the timing of His death, despite what the chief priests wanted (verses 1-2). Verses 8-9's praise should give every disciple determination to imitate this example and to do whatever we can, no matter how small it may seem. Why the secrecy in planning the Passover (verse 12)? It would provide an ideal setting for an arrest — out of the way and private. But Jesus is determined this Last Supper will not be interrupted. The hymn of verse 26 is probably Psalm 118. Don't miss the end of verse 31. Peter's denials are famous but all the apostles pledged themselves to Jesus. Could verse

51 be talking about Mark? Verse 62 is an emphatic claim to be the Messiah, combining Psalm 110 and Daniel 7:13-14.

15 - Going to see Pilate was necessary because the Jews could not enact capital punishment (verse 1). The effect as Mark walks us through Jesus' sham trial with Pilate is for us to see Jesus' absolute innocence, the lust for blood on the part of the crowd, and Pilate's sad and cowardly weakness. Verse 23 tells us Jesus refused the common painkiller offered to the condemned. Jesus' crucifixion takes place around 9:00 A.M. (verse 25). The land would be dark from noon till three o'clock (verse 33). It is easy to miss what Jesus' death means but verse 38 makes sure we don't: Jesus opens the way up to God.

Applications from This Week's Readings

These chapters show how what people wanted Jesus to do and what they wanted His kingdom to

be were far from reality. How do we try to remold the Kingdom to fit our own grand designs and delusions today? Will we listen to Jesus and let Him be the King He is? Back to Table of Contents.

Week 4 - Mark 16; Galatians 1-4

16 - Make certain you note how no one has any expectation of a resurrection (verse 3). This is powerful evidence for those who want to argue an apostolic conspiracy stole Jesus' body. Verse 9 introduces a serious textual question: are these verses authentic? Various translations footnote or italicize these verses, giving them an air of uncertainty. However, the verses actually teach nothing new or different. The only question is did Mark write them? Further, while acknowledging some important manuscripts do not contain them, there is excellent evidence based on very old documents that they are authentic and should be treated as such. Verse 17 may cause some to wonder why we don't have these signs today. Granted, if this were the only verse about signs we might conclude we should have them, but verse 20 tells us they did have the signs, while other texts tell us more about signs and how long they would last. In effect we do have the signs as we read about them in our Bibles!

Introduction to Galatians - This is one of the first epistles written (perhaps in the early AD 50's). It brings the Jerusalem Conference's results (Acts 15) to the churches in the province of Galatia that Paul and Barnabas established in Acts 13-14. A new teaching had taken root there, the result of "Judaizers" who taught that a Gentile must become a Jew before he can become a Christian. What will Paul say about this new hybrid Gospel?

1 - Galatians begins abruptly. Usually Paul has some words of praise for his readers but here there are none. Paul repeatedly develops his apostolic authority and authenticity (verse 1). Verses 8-9 leave no doubt where Paul stands on adding to the Gospel, do they? Paul then retells his conversion and its aftermath to assure his readers that he didn't borrow his teaching from men (verses 11-23).

2 - Trying to mesh the visits to Jerusalem mentioned here with the record in Acts quickly becomes very involved and complex. More than likely, verse 1 references the Jerusalem Conference. Paul subtly (and not so subtly) keeps introducing his main ideas, as in verse 5. Lest anyone think Paul is subservient to Peter we are told of Peter's hypocrisy (verses 11-14). Paul then emphatically states his main point: no one can be made right with God by their own deeds (verses 16-21). While Jews knew about sacrifices for sin and the Day of Atonement they were sure that God's person, a person in the covenant, would be marked by keeping the Old Law. Thus, Gentiles had to keep the Law if they were going to be "in." Paul says law keeping isn't the way "in," faith is! He will also go on to say it has always been that way (3:6). Of course, Jews would not like that at all. We are being treated like every other sinner, they would protest (verse 17)! But a life-giving relationship with God comes through faith in Christ (verse 20).

3 - Verse 1's strong tone shows us how concerned Paul is about his brethren in Galatia. He appeals to the spiritual gifts they see in their midst (verse 5) as proof positive that what he preached was the true Gospel from God. Further, Abraham was "in" with God prior to Moses' Law because he was a person of faith (verse 6). Because of his faith God made promises to Abraham, promises that included blessing all nations (verse 8, 14). This promise, that was made hundreds of years before the Law of Moses, finds its fulfillment in Christ (verses 16-17), not in Jewish pride. Paul knows Jews will ask "Why then did God give the Law?" His answer is that the Law restrained sin (verse 19) and led us to Christ (verse 24). Notice that verse 26 shifts from "we" and "us" to "you," being inclusive of all of Paul's readers. The blessings promised to Abraham that come through Christ are available to all who will put on Christ (verse 27). All can be "heirs!" (verse 29).

4 - Christ has come to make us heirs, so don't go back to the way of slavery! Be an heir, be a child (verse 5) who can call God "Father" (Abba is an Aramaic word for father). We can do that when we receive the testimony of the Spirit, now contained in the New Testament (verse 6). Verse 10 probably speaks of the Jewish holy calendar and its many feast days and Sabbaths. After being so stern with the Galatians Paul is tender in verses 13-15, remembering how he was sick among them. Did that illness affect his vision (verse 15)? Paul makes one more appeal for them to remain free from those who would bind the Law upon them by presenting an allegory (verses 21-31). This is a surprising allegory, because we expect Judaism to be linked to Sara, Abraham's real wife. Instead Judaism is tied to Hagar, the slave woman who bore Ishmael. Christians are the real children of Isaac, the real children of promise, Paul says (verse 28). Ishmael persecuted Isaac (see Genesis 16:15; 21:9-10) just as the Gentile Christians were being persecuted then.

Applications from This Week's Readings

Our readings this week and last week work together to show us Peter failing twice. Why did Jesus select a man like Peter, given some of his problems? What does this say about God's willingness to work with less than perfect people? Think also about Peter and quitting. Did Peter give up? Will you quit if and when you fail Jesus spectacularly? Back to Table of Contents.

Week 5 - Galatians 5-6; Ephesians 1-3

5 - Verse 6b contains a beautiful statement of how faith and works must go together. Paul knows these brethren well but does not seem to know the troublemaker(s) by name (verse 10). By verse 15 Paul is transitioning from the doctrinal portion of the letter refuting the Judaizers to say, in a practical way, the church must get along. The NIV has "sinful nature" instead of "flesh" in verse 16, a translation that leads to misconceptions of every kind. "Walk in the Spirit" just means to walk according to God's will, or to walk with God, or be led by God. The teaching of the Spirit, contained in the Bible, controls how we live (see verse 25).

6 - Again Paul urges building strong relationships among brethren (verses 1-2). Verse 11 may again refer to an eye illness, but it also serves to authenticate the letter. Paul apparently took the pen and added these last notes personally so the Galatians would know it was from Paul. While has the pen Paul revisits his main theme once more: don't let anyone add Judaism to the Gospel (verses 12-16).

Introduction to Ephesians - Ephesus was an important port city in the New Testament world. At the end of the 2nd missionary journey Paul established the church (Acts 18:19-28), returning on the 3rd journey and staying approximately two years (Acts 19:8-10). This epistle is one of the prison epistles (Ephesians, Philippians, Colossians and Philemon) that Paul wrote during Roman imprisonment (AD 60-62). Paul writes to help with issues of unity, using the terms "in Christ" about thirty times, more than any other book in the NT. Understanding who we are "in Christ" (chs. 1-3) helps us "walk worthily" (chs. 4-6).

1 - verse 5 mentions "predestination" as does verse 11. We must realize the Bible teaches predestination! What it does not teach is Calvinism's idea that individuals are individually chosen by God, regardless of their actions, to be saved or lost. God has decided, chosen, or destined, the group of people who serve Him to be saved. We decide if we want to be in that group. Verse 9 speaks of the "mystery," which we will read more about in 3:3. A "mystery" is something we cannot know without God revealing it. Verse 13's seal is difficult. An official wax seal on a document indicated it was genuine. The Holy Spirit has worked to certify their Christianity is genuine. Note that a seal is very public and can be seen by all so this cannot refer to some mystical work in a person's heart. Perhaps this references the gift of miracles, a very public demonstration of the transformation of Christianity peculiar to NT times.

2 - Verse 3's "by nature" means "by habit." Unfortunately we have had to fight against so much misuse of verses 8-9 that we may miss their point. We are saved by grace and should be so thankful for it! Verse 11 makes plain that Gentiles particularly should be thankful for God's grace. By grace the Law of Moses ("the middle wall," verse 14) between Jews and Gentiles was broken down. Paul may have in mind the hostility between the two groups as well, so that peace should reign among disciples (verses 15-16).

3 - Verses 3-4 make it plain we can understand the Bible. Paul had a revelation (the mystery of how Gentiles were to be included in the Kingdom, verse 6), and when we read what Paul wrote we can understand it too. Gentiles being "in" was certainly not understood before (verses 8-9), but is known now, Paul announces. Such grace given to all is a cause for praising God (verses 14-22). God is amazing!

Applications from This Week's Readings

Reading Ephesians makes us more mindful of God's grace and our responsibilities to "walk worthily" as a result. Focus your attention in chapters 4-5. Can you identify some specific areas of your life that need to be improved in light of the admonitions here? Back to Table of Contents.

Week 6 - Ephesians 4-6; Philippians 1-2

4 - There is a heavy emphasis on unity in this chapter as Paul brings his teaching about all being saved by God's amazing grace to its point: walk worthy (verse 1). Paul speaks of gifts that benefit our unity and work together (verse 7), but someone might ask "How can Jesus give gifts?" He ascended on high (verse 8), defeating every enemy to do so. Parenthetically Paul speaks of that ascension in verses 9-10, but then returns to the theme of gifts in verse 11. You may want to write in the word "gifts" beside verse 11 to help you see the flow of thought: "And He Himself gave gifts to be ..." In verse 17 Paul turns his attention from how brethren treat each other to how Christians act in the world.

5 - Verses 1-5 continue chapter 4's "how to walk outside" theme, emphasizing purity. Judgment is used as a motivator for correct conduct in verses 13-14. Verse 21 opens up the idea of submission. Paul then details the various roles we find ourselves in and how we function in them. "Submit" means to yield to another. It does not mean one is inferior. Chauvinism finds no refuge in these beautiful verses that describe how a wife willingly follows her husband's leadership because he sacrificially loves her as Christ loves the church (verses 22-33). Christ doesn't mistreat His church or act as a tyrant or dictator over us. How then could anyone find such an idea for the Christian home here?

6 - Verses 1-4 contain famous admonitions about children. These simply continue Paul's discussion of roles in life begun in 5:21. The Lord is powerful and mighty (verse 10) but this does not negate our part in fighting against and defeating Satan and his helpers (verses 11-12). Spiritual warfare is real. Paul does not say such is a figment of our imagination or that the devil is a myth. He sees Christians locked in a struggle with a crafty and truly evil opponent. The armor of God and prayer equips one in this battle. "Praying in the Spirit" (verse 18) refers to praying with the Spirit's help or in harmony with His revealed will.

Introductions to Philippians - The good church at Philippi began beside a river and was helped by an earthquake (Acts 16:12-40). Paul loved these brethren dearly. He took the occasion of writing a "thank you" note for their support to urge them be unified and have real joy. There is little rebuke in the epistle, outside of a few words about grumbling and quarreling (see 2:2-3, 14-15; 4:1). Instead Paul uses his own example of how he is coping with his circumstances (he is in prison, 1:13) and to urge them to imitate Jesus.

1 - In NT times it was common to begin a letter with the sender's name (instead of putting it at the end as we do) and then to follow that salutation with a word of prayer (verses 3-11). Notice how love and thinking are beautifully combined by Paul in verse 9. What a different idea about persecution and suffering is found in verse 29. Do we feel privileged to be able to suffer for Christ as Paul says the Philippians were?

2 - Some of the most awesome words ever written are found in verses 5-11. Paul is able to succinctly summarize Jesus' incarnation and death as a means to motivate the Philippians to be unified and care for each other. If Jesus humbled Himself how can Christians ever be arrogant and prideful? Paul wants the Philippians to "work out their own salvation" (verse 12), meaning they are to take an active role in their growth and strengthening as disciples. When we do that we are connected to God who is working in us (verse 13). These two verses are a powerful illustration of both human effort and God's grace being brought together. Verse 25 mentions Epaphroditus. We know little about him, except he was an important disciple in the church at Philippi, had brought funds to Paul (4:18) and then became very ill (verses 26-30).

Applications from This Week's Readings

Consider memorizing Paul's grand statements about Christ humbling Himself in Philippians 2:5-11. Even if you don't commit it to memory read it over several times. Then think about where you can give yourself up to serve others. Live out Phil 2:5-11 today! Back to Table of Contents.

Week 7 - Philippians 3-4; Hebrews 1-3

3 - Verse 2's "dogs" is a reference to the Jewish teachers who wanted to circumcise Gentile Christians. We may wonder how Paul managed to overcome his past as a persecutor to be such a force for Jesus, but verses 12-14 tells us how he did it. We can learn much from his example. Notice how apostolic example is crucial for Christians (verses 15-17; also 4:9).

4 - "Gentleness" or "reasonableness" in verse 5 references a spirit of kindness that is necessary because the Lord's coming is close (verse 5b). What does Paul mean by this? Either he wants to remind the Philippians that the return of Christ could happen at any time, or that by our dying (a possibility at any time) we go to see the Lord. Perhaps Paul means all of these ideas to some extent. Christians must live like Jesus could come at any time because He could. Verses 15-16 provide good information about how churches need to send directly to preachers in the field, instead of forming a missionary society or bureaucracy of networked churches under one large church.

Introduction to Hebrews - The book of Hebrews has an unjustly deserved reputation for being hard to understand. So, many avoid it and thus miss out on a book designed to help Christians in times of trial. It is true we don't know the author's name (perhaps Barnabas?) but his identity is not the key to Hebrews. The key to understanding Hebrews is to remember it is a "word of exhortation" (13:22). The book was written to exhort and encourage discouraged Christians to persevere in the faith. Hebrews encourages us by showing us the greatness of our High Priest, reminding us not to harden our hearts like those who displeased God, to see that God is fulfilling the great promises to Abraham in Jesus (and we are the recipient of those blessings), and even presents great examples of men and women who refused to give up and "by faith" served the Lord. This book will be wonderfully encouraging to us if we will just let it!

1 - Verses 3-13 end all discussion about Christ's deity and equality with the Father. Angels are important, powerful and even helpful to us (verse 14) but they have never been addressed or treated like Jesus Christ has been. He is divine!

2 - Verses 1-4 form a parenthesis, keying off of 1:14's "angels." The "word" (verse 2) is Moses' Law. Note the purpose of miracles in verses 3-4: confirm the message of God. Verse 5 rejoins the thought of Christ's preeminence begun in chapter 1. But how can Christ be so great if He was human? The answer is Jesus was "made a little lower than angels" (verse 9) for the purpose of salvation. How is Jesus "made perfect" (verse 10)? This is priestly language, used in other places to refer to the installation of the high priest. The Hebrew writer is arguing that Jesus is set aside for His work as Savior, He is installed in the office of Messiah, by His suffering. That suffering also equips Him to help us, His brethren (verses 14-18).

3 - Verse 1 is the only place Jesus is called an apostle. The designation fits well, however, because apostle means "one sent on a mission with the authority to carry it out." The Hebrew writer then contrasts Jesus and Moses (verses 2-6), using the metaphor of house building. Each built a house (a people or family) but Jesus' house is greater. As Moses' people were on a journey to the Promised Land so are Christ's. However, some didn't reach the physical Promised Land due to an "evil unbelieving heart" (verses 7-19). What a warning for the people following Jesus to the real and eternal Promised Land!

Applications from This Week's Readings

Hebrews urges us to see Christ more clearly that we might be encouraged to persevere and continue serving Him. How does the material in Hebrews 1-3 help you better appreciate Jesus?

Back to Table of Contents..

Week 8 - Hebrews 4-8

4 - The comparison between Israel of old and Christians today from chapter 3 continues in verses 1-13. The key term is "rest," used here of the Promised Land and heaven. Those without faith cannot enter into God's rest (3:19; 4:2). The rest has been ready since creation (verse 3), some must enter into it, and the since the Israelites did not enter into it (verse 6), the rest remains (verse 9). Will we be the people of faith who enter into heaven by faith and trust in Jesus Christ? Verse 14 picks up the idea of "high priest" begun back in 3:1. Look how practical and encouraging verses 14-16 are!

5 - The Hebrew writer now gets to his point about Jesus as high priest. High priests are appointed (verse 1), gentle (verse 2), and called (verse 3). So it is with Jesus (verses 5-7). The point is strengthened by showing Jesus praying in the Garden in agony (verses 7-8). In this "school of suffering" Jesus "learned" or experienced trials fully as a man, as we do. He is therefore fully qualified to be our high priest, a subject the author would like to say more about but cannot because of spiritual immaturity (verses 11-14).

6 - This chapter continues the rebuke of 5:11-14, speaking of a lack of spiritual maturity. Verse 4 should not be taken as proving there is an unforgivable sin, but instead speaks of a mindset that will not repent and so cannot be forgiven. The readers need to get busy diligently applying themselves so as to grow in the faith (verse 12) so they will be able to endure (verse 15). God won't fail us or lie to us (verses 17-18), we have Jesus the High Priest and the certainty of our hope as an anchor (verses 19-20). Therefore, we must not forsake the Lord or His way!

7 - One of the keys to perseverance in Christ is seeing and appreciating His role as our High Priest. It is to this key point that Hebrews now returns, linking up with 5:10 (note also 2:17; 3:1; 4:14) after a small detour on maturity (5:11-6:20). The chapter plays off Abraham's meeting of Melchizedek in Genesis 14 and the prophecy of Psalm 110:4. Verse 3 doesn't mean Melchizedek was an angel or had no parents. It just means he is not a priest according to genealogy. His parents are unknown, not non-existent (note verse 6). The argument is made in verse 7: if Abraham paid tithes to Melchizedek then Melchizedek is greater than Abraham. That means since Jesus is a priest from Melchizedek's line, not Abraham's, He is greater than Abraham too. But for Jesus to be a priest there must be a change in the Law, for Jesus could not serve as a Aaronic priest (verses 12-14). The Law of Moses was weak (verses 18-19) so a change should be welcomed as it betters our situation (verses 22-28).

8 - Jesus is not only a better High Priest than the Law of Moses could have ever had, He is serving in the perfect, heavenly Tabernacle (verses 1-6). This is the real Tabernacle. The one Moses constructed was only a shadow or model of the heavenly reality (verse 5). Jesus also serves under the new covenant prophesied by Jeremiah long ago (verses 7-13). Note Jeremiah's emphasis on knowing God (verses 10-11). In the New Covenant knowing God (equated with having God's law in mind and heart) will be essential to being accepted by God. This covenant also provides direct and real forgiveness of sin (verse 12).

Applications from This Week's Readings

Hebrews has much to say about the human part of Jesus, the suffering Son. What Jesus did for us was very hard for Him. Do we understand that, or just assume His earthly ministry and death were easy because, after all, He was the Messiah? Give some more thought to the difficulty of leaving heaven, of the suffering in Gethsemane, of the embarrassment of being executed before your mother and friends as a criminal. Then give thanks to our High Priest that He was so willing to come that we might have a High Priest who can sympathize with our weaknesses and temptations! Back to Table of Contents.

Week 9 - Hebrews 9-13

9 - Verse 5 ends with "cannot now speak in detail," simply meaning that time does not permit a fuller conversation about the earthly Tabernacle. Instead, the author presses forward with the idea of covenant ratification in blood. Verse 8 is speaking of heaven, and makes clear that Moses' Tabernacle was not sufficient (verses 9-10). Christ enters the better Tabernacle, heaven (verse 11), and makes atonement with His own blood (verses 12-14). Covenants, or "testaments" (verse 15) must be ratified with blood. Moses' covenant was so ratified (verses 18-22), and so Jesus' is as well (verses 24-28).

10 - Verses 1-4 make plain that sin was not dealt with fully and finally under the terms of the Mosaical covenant. While animal sacrifices provided forgiveness (see Lev 4:20, 26, 31, 35) it was only forgiveness in view of Jesus' work to come on the cross. Animal blood alone cannot atone for sin ever. Those very sacrifices should have reminded the worshipers of their own sinfulness and that a better sacrifice was needed (verses 3-4). Jesus is that great once-for-all sacrifice (verses 11-14). The massive development of Jesus as High Priest of a better covenant with a better sacrifice is brought to a head with verse 19's "therefore." With Jesus we have confidence we could never have under Moses' Law and so must not vacillate but be strong, helping and encouraging other disciples (verses 22-25). "The day" (verse 25b) is judgement day. We see it approaching by faith. Picking up the theme of judgement day the Hebrew writer describes the awfulness of turning away from the only sacrifice for sin (verses 26-31). The chapter concludes with a plea not to give up Christianity and lose the reward of heaven (verses 32-35).

11 - This chapter is not hard to read. The key is to see that it connects to 10:32-35 and the theme of endurance. It is terribly unfortunate that chapter 11 has become known as the Hall of Fame of Faith because that destroys the very point the author wants to make. These aren't super-Christians who are superior to everyone. These are set before us as examples of ordinary men and women who persevered due to their faith despite every difficulty. The point is they did it and you can too! The Hebrew writer is imploring his readers to do as others already have: live by faith and not give up!

12 - From start to finish Hebrews is about encouragement to persevere and now the author uses even the example of Jesus to do that (verses 1-4). The "chastening of the Lord" (verses 5-11) is hard for us. We don't always understand why hardship comes into our lives. Neither did the recipients of Hebrews. But the author wants them to think of it as a proof that they are God's children rather than somehow showing that God has forgotten them (verses 8-9). Hard times can have a positive effect on our character if we will let it (verse 11). The Hebrew writer reminds them of Esau's failure (verses 16-17). It is not that Esau couldn't repent but that once he started his life in one direction he couldn't find a place to make a u-turn. This is a sober warning about apostasy! Verses 18-24 use the imagery of mountains to again make the point that perseverance matters. If Mount Sinai and the Law of Moses (verse 18) was important, how much more is the new covenant, symbolized by Mount Zion (verse 22)? We must not "refuse Him who speaks" (verse 25). Judaism will be shaken (verse 27), perhaps a reference to Jerusalem's destruction in AD 70, but Christianity will never be removed. We must be true to it (verse 28).

13 - This chapter concludes Hebrews with some fairly straightforward, direct admonitions. Verse 9 informs us that some were being troubled with rules and regulations about food, but foods don't build up spirituality. That leads to the writer using food and eating sacrifices to make a point

about Jesus, the Christian's sacrifice. Verse 13 sounds the familiar note of being ready to suffer and to persevere in Christ. It may seem strange that such a long book is described as "few words" (verse 22) but given the vastness of the topic Hebrews isn't as long as it could be. Timothy is mentioned in verse 23. This may be the Timothy that traveled with Paul, but we have no way of being sure.

Applications from This Week's Readings

The best application of these chapters is to look at chapter 11's pattern "by faith he/she did _____ " and then decide what you are doing by faith. How are you persevering as a disciple of Christ "by faith?" What visual evidence is there of your walk with Christ and faith in Him? Are you pressing forward or turning back? Back to Table of Contents.

Week 10 - Colossians 1-4; Luke 1

Introduction to Colossians - This is another prison epistle of Paul's (see 4:3, 10), written shortly after Ephesians. There is no doubt that it was written to combat false doctrine that was spreading in Colossae, though all the dimensions of the troubles are not known. Paul is concerned about true knowledge (see 1:9), and that false religious practices like asceticism and the worship of angels cease at once (see 2:8, 16, 18, 21-23). A major feature of this heresy seems to have been that God is far off and inaccessible. The result is a warm epistle that helps us focus on Christ Jesus as the center of all we are, and to realize that He has come here for us and to save us. What reassuring truths!

1 - Verse 3 begins an introductory prayer, just like Ephesians. Verse 6 reminds us of the rapid spread of Christianity throughout the Roman Empire. Ephaphras (verse 7) will be mentioned again in 4:12. Verse 13 should lay to rest all question about the Kingdom's present existence. If we are not in it now we are still in domain of darkness. We need not look forward to some earthly kingdom and a thousand year reign. Christ is king over His kingdom (the church) even now! Some have misunderstood verse 15's "firstborn" as making Christ a created being. Such cannot be, according to the very next verse which sets Christ above all creation (verse 16). "Firstborn" can mean the first one born, but it can also mean "position of preeminence" and be conferred upon one (see Psalm 89:27; Jer 31:9; Exo 4:22). No one can give birth order, but one can be treated with the status accorded to a first born. That is its meaning here. If there is any doubt about Jesus' divinity and deity just read verse 19. All that makes God deity rests in Jesus Christ (note 2:9 as well). Note how Paul rejoices in suffering (verse 24) as his example strengthens the Colossians and only verifies his apostleship.

2 - Laodicea (verse 1) is about 11 miles from Colossae. Verse 2 makes plain how important growing up and maturing really is. This is essential if we are to avoid being tricked by false doctrine (verse 8). Verses 11-12 are powerful verses to use in the case for baptism. If someone says "baptism is a work" read these verses to show that such is right: baptism is a work of God! Verse 13 introduces the Gentiles, and as Paul develops this thought it seems some of the trouble may have been some form or offshoot of Judaism. Paul demands the Colossians separate themselves from this carnal religion and its false taboos (verses 20-23).

3 - The Gospel is for all, even barbaric tribes like the Scythians (verse 11). All that we do must be done "in Christ's name" or by His authority (verse 17). Paul's emphasis on how we must work hard because we work for the Lord is well needed today (verses 23-24).

4 - Paul mentions Tychius (verse 7). He was a highly trusted traveling companion of Paul's, who carried this letter, the letter to Philemon and probably the Ephesian letter too (see Acts 20:4; Eph. 6:21; Col. 4:7; 2 Tim. 4:12; Tit. 3:12). Mark's mention in verse 10 puts a happier face on his failure in Acts 13:13 (cf. Acts 15:37; 2 Tim 4:11). The mention of men like Aristarchus, Luke and Demas helps us see how many co-workers Paul relied on in his work. Verse 16 mentions a letter to Laodicea, which some now assume is a lost epistle (as if God would allow inspired letters to be lost!). This letter is probably the epistle to the Ephesians which was meant to benefit all the churches in that area, and shows every characteristic of being a "cyclical" letter.

Introduction to Luke - this Gospel is a magnificent and powerful portrait of Jesus. Written in the mid 60's to a government official (1:3) it stresses several key themes. These include the verifiable evidence that Jesus was real and that Christianity is not a fairy tale, the troubles money cause a disciple, the work of the Holy Spirit, how the Gospel is for all (even Gentiles), and what discipleship is about. Caution: the chapters are long so the daily readings might take longer than usual.

1 - Verse 3 names Theophilus as the recipient, in all probability a real person. Luke has a concern in both of his books for showing how the Gospel is accepted by the powerful and intelligent. Verse 9 - there were too many priests so lots were used to determine duties. This was an important job and one would only get to do it once in a lifetime. Verse 27 - Luke ties Jesus to the promises of David regularly (see 33, 69). Verse 67 - the Holy Spirit is a continual theme in Luke-Acts.

Applications from This Week's Readings

Re-read Colossians 4:5-6. Paul wants the Colossians (and us) to take our influence very seriously. Others are watching us and listening to us, and they make judgement about the Kingdom and Jesus from what we do. Pray about this and be especially aware of your influence this week. Back to Table of Contents.

Week 11 - Luke 2-6

2 - Verse 7 shows not a cute and cuddly scene (as portrayed today) but one of appalling poverty, dirt and humiliation. Jesus was born into just about the worst set of circumstances we can imagine. Verse 10 - catch "all people" - the Gospel is for Gentiles too! Verse 25-26-27 - the Spirit is emphasized again. Verse 44 - we wonder how they lost Jesus but Mary and Joseph probably expected he was in a big crowd of family and so assumed they would see him at the end of the day when the group stopped for the night.

3 - Verse 16 - the Holy Spirit's baptism here is something that promises power, but "fire" speaks of judgment (see the next verse). The big question in chapter 3 is the genealogy of verse 23. Why is it here? Why isn't it exactly the same as Matthew's? The answer to the first question is because it shows Jesus' connection to all men, going back to Adam not just Abraham. It also makes the point that Jesus was a real man, something easy to forget. The differences in the genealogies of Matthew and Luke have many possible explanations. Some think this is Mary's lineage via Levirate marriage or adoption.

4 - Verses 1-13 - watch how Jesus defeats temptation by using the Scriptures. Verse 1 emphasizes the Spirit's work, but the practical outgrowth of being led by the Spirit is knowing your Bible so you can use it to overcome the devil! Verses 14-30 show Jesus being rejected at Nazareth, His hometown. They cannot get over knowing about His humble origins. Jesus stings them by talking of Gentiles that God worked with instead of Israelites in verses 26-27.

5 - Verses 1-11 show the kind of obedience Jesus is looking for: immediate, and without question. Verses 33-39 are often misunderstood. Jesus speaks here of what is inappropriate, and even foolish to do. It is just the wrong time to fast, He says. That will come later, but now is the time to pay attention to Me.

6 - Does Jesus break Moses' Law and endorse situation ethics in verses 1-5? No. What the disciples did was a violation of rabbinical traditions, not God's Law. Jesus cites what David did not to endorse law breaking (He even says David did what was "unlawful," v. 4) but to point out that the Pharisees were guilty of selective prosecution. They wouldn't attack David for what was wrong but they did attack Him for what was not! Verses 24-26 contain "woes" that are not in Matthew's Sermon on the Mount. This has been called the Sermon on the Plain and probably contains the common message of the Kingdom Jesus preached everywhere. Verse 40 is a key verse on discipleship.

Applications from This Week's Readings

Think about what you have seen of Jesus. Would you have followed Him if He called you (5:10)? He is! Are you pursuing Jesus Christ? The easy answer is "Of course." But how are you pursuing Jesus? What kind of following are you doing? Back to Table of Contents.

Week 12 - Luke 7 - 11

7 - Once again we find a Gentile accent in Luke (see verse 9). Many have wondered if John the Baptist had real doubts in verse 20 or if he was only making an opportunity for two disciples to meet Jesus. Yet there seems to be little reason to doubt that John was doubting! Jesus was not doing what many thought the Messiah would do. In Jesus' answer He reminds John of what Isaiah prophesied the Messiah would be about (see verses 22-23). Jesus didn't do just any miracles but the prophesied works of the Messiah. The scene of verse 36 is a little bizarre for us but customs in that day had everyone reclining at table. Further, it was not uncommon for people to come and go when a famous person was being entertained for a meal. The guests ate but it was perfectly acceptable to come and sit along the wall, watch and listen to the dinner conversation.

8 - Verse 21 tells us more about discipleship: it involves doing. We need to ask ourselves "What am I doing in Jesus' name?" The story of the demoniac man and the pigs in verses 26-40 always leaves us scratching our heads a little about the demons' request to attack the nearby swine. The text doesn't tell us why they asked for this, or why Jesus allowed it. There is just much we don't know about the demoniac world. Luke wants us to look at the healed man (verse 35), not the pigs!

9 - In many ways Luke's Gospel answers the question of verse 9. Don't miss the great discipleship sayings of verses 23-26. "Taking up the cross" does not refer to the sufferings of life, having ornery in-laws or a sick child. Worldly people have all of this too! The cross here is the peculiar responsibilities of discipleship, especially those that lead to a death of self. Verse 40 makes us ask why the disciples couldn't cast out the demon but Jesus tells us in verse 41. They lacked faith, apparently being intimidated by the demon. The final discipleship sayings of the chapter emphasize that we don't follow Jesus to get riches or a grand home (verse 59), that important family matters like funerals are not more important than the Kingdom (verse 60), and that Jesus is requiring single minded devotion to Him that does not look back in regret (verse 62).

10 - Jesus commissions the Seventy to go out and preach. The result is the rolling back of Satan's dominion (verse 18). We then get two stories about what it is to be a disciple. Unfortunately, often times the story of the Good Samaritan (verse 29ff) gets bogged down in discussion of whether it means I must stop to help change a stranger's flat tire. Please remember the story is not about a man who is inconvenienced because his donkey threw a shoe. The man is bleeding to death! This story involves doing for others and the next story speaks of listening to Jesus (Mary in verse 41). Discipleship consists of both action and thought. We hear Jesus and we do Jesus' bidding, particularly for others.

11 - Note the emphasis on persistence in prayer (verses 5-13). In our instant society this is much overlooked. Verse 30 includes Gentiles again, this time the Ninevites.

Applications from This Week's Readings

There is much in these chapters that challenges a lame and weak version of discipleship that says "I go to church three times a week so God must really be impressed with me." Am I becoming like Jesus? Am I bearing my cross daily? Am I denying self? Do I serve others or just self? Back to Table of Contents..

Week 13 - Luke 12-16

12 - Verse 10 catches our eye, for a sin that will never be forgiven is unimaginably horrible. Many wonder "Have I done this and so am irrevocably lost?" In the context Jesus is speaking of those who reject Him despite all His works done by the power of the Spirit. They even attribute that power to the devil (11:15). Such a hard heart will never ask for forgiveness and so will not be forgiven. It is not that God won't forgive, it is that these will not humble themselves and ask. By being concerned about having committed this sin one reveals that he or she is exactly the kind of person Jesus is not talking about here! Remember, God will forgive any sin that we will repent and ask Him to forgive (1 John 1:9). Chapter 11 goes on with parables about a rich fool and servants who are and who are not ready for their Master's return. There is an urgency to the Gospel's demands (verses 49-59) that many miss, especially if they have many possessions.

13 - The idea of repentance percolates to the front in verses 1-9. Some ask why the Pharisees warned Jesus in verse 31? They may have been lying or, they may have been sincerely trying to help. Not all Pharisees were bad.

14 - Jesus tells stories at the dinner table that illustrate key aspects of discipleship. Luke again sounds the theme of the "outsiders" (Gentiles) coming in while Jews will not (verse 23). Some of Jesus' most powerful sayings on discipleship end the chapter. The Lord does not mean "hate" as we use the term (verse 26) but "love less." By comparison to our devotion to Jesus our ties to family are as nothing. Don't take this lightly, Jesus says. Count the cost of following Me first (Verses 28-35)!

15 - The three Lost and Found parables are among Jesus' most famous. However, the key to them all is probably verse 2 and the concluding story of the Elder Brother (verses 25-32). God's grace and forgiveness are freely given out to those who are most undeserving. Will we rejoice at this or piously pout?

16 - The parable of the unjust steward (verses 1-13) certainly surprises us. Did Jesus commend a thief? Yes and no. Jesus commends him taking action to secure his future, not his stealing. The parable urges disciples to be as diligent securing their future (verse 9). Note the emphasis on money again in Luke. Verse 16 is also difficult. Some see the idea of great effort, of taking vigorous action to get into the Kingdom. While many lessons can be learned from the story of the Rich Man and Lazarus (verses 19-31) we do well to focus on its main points: what we do here affects our eternal destiny, and once there our destiny cannot be changed. In verse 29 we read of "Moses and the Prophets," a Jewish expression for the Old Testament, i.e., the Bible.

Applications from This Week's Readings

What rich material for us to pray about as we contemplate our discipleship! Repeatedly we have seen the contrast between the self-righteous and self-satisfied and Jesus' demands for something more. Where am I in these chapters? Am I a Pharisee or a disciple of the Christ? Back to Table of Contents.

Week 14 - Luke 17-21

17 - Verse 4 puts repentance before us again. Don't make more of verse 6 than Luke wants. Other passages teach us more about praying in God's will. Jesus is just emphasizing the power of faith, not that we should be transplanting bushes. Verse 16 shows us another Gentile does the right thing. A key statement about the kingdom is found in Verse 21. The kingdom is about God's rule and reign in our hearts, and should not become some institution. It is "within us." The section beginning verses 22 is difficult. It may be about Christ's second coming, or it may speak of Jesus' judgment on Jerusalem. Either way the focus on preparedness is clear. The wording about "two ... and one being taken" means some will be ready and others won't.

18 - Don't make the mistake of deciding God is a crabby judge from the parable in verses 1-5. Jesus' point is that if a mean judge will help someone in need how much more will our great God? Luke's money theme re-enters with the Rich Young Ruler (verses 18-27). Notice that not everyone is commanded to sell everything - just this man. Why? Because that is what he needed to follow Jesus. We all are called to give up whatever is in the way of serving Christ first. Notice how the blind man can see that Jesus is the Messiah promised to David (verse 39). Jesus' signs confirmed to those who would see that He was the Christ.

19 - Zacchaeus forms a huge contrast to the Rich Young Ruler of chapter 18 who would not give up his money to be right with God. Jesus concludes that story with the shocking saying that a Gentile can become a "child of Abraham" (verse 9). Gentiles can be in too! Amazing! Notice the wrong thinking about the kingdom that permeated the people (verse 11b). This is why Jesus was often reluctant to reveal Himself as the Messiah or make plain statement that He was (and is) the King of Kings. The people of His day did not understand the kind of kingdom He had come to establish. The parable of the money (verse12-27) may seem harsh but verse 26 is the key: you are responsible to do with what you have.

20 - In verse 17 Jesus quotes from Psalm 118:22, a psalm about a king being threatened with danger and delivered. We meet the Sadducees in verse 27. Jesus destroys their contention that there is no life after death in verse 37. God would say He was the God of Abraham, Isaac and Jacob if they were dead. Since He says He is their God then they must be alive. The use of Psalm 110 in verse 42 is familiar but sometimes misunderstood. The first line could be translated "God said to the King." The Jews understood this to be the Messiah, a son of David. But how could David speak of a descendant as his king? How could a descendant be greater than the forefather, especially when the forefather is David? The Jews didn't know but we do: the descendant of David who is greater than even David is the divine Jesus Christ!

21 - This chapter is considered to be one of the most difficult in the Gospels, but it doesn't have to be. A couple of clues in the text help tremendously. First, notice the question of verse 6. Many want this to be an End of the World/Second Coming passage but that isn't the disciples question. Second, get the time frame of verse 32. Whatever all of this means it happened in the first century. I believe the chapter speaks to the judgment on Jerusalem brought about by Roman armies in AD 70 (see verses 20-21, 24). This best fits the warnings and context of this chapter. The difficult language of verses 25-28 simply echoes the language of the Old Testament prophets when they warned of impending doom and judgment (see Isaiah 19:1).

Applications from This Week's Readings

Did you notice in this week's reading how meeting Jesus forces people to decide what they will do with Him? Jesus pushes people to repent when He is with them. Some resist. Some repent. You are meeting Jesus now by reading about Him. What will come about in your life from this meeting? Back to Table of Contents..

Week 15 - Luke 22 - Acts 2

22 - Verse 15 highlights how important the Last Supper was to Jesus. He took great pains to make certain He was not arrested prior to this Passover because what He instituted here was and is so vital. The Passover feast featured several cups of wine (verse 17), but the order of the Supper is to be bread, then cup (verses 19-20). Verse 36 warns the disciples to prepare for opposition instead of widespread acceptance as before. Want to defeat temptation? Verse 40 shows prayer to be a powerful tool in the war against darkness (verse 53). We may wonder how Jesus saw Peter as he spoke (verse 61) but as Jesus was shuttled from fake trial to fake trial He could easily have been going right through the courtyard at the crucial moment.

23 - The charge against Jesus changes here (verse 2) because a Roman court won't care about Jesus' crimes against Jewish tradition and law. Verse 4 is the first of many statements of Jesus' innocence. In verse 8 the Lord meets John the Baptist's murderer, Herod Antipas, and refuses to answer him. Why would Jesus waste words on Herod Antipas, who only wants to see a dog-and-pony show? The criminal (an insurrectionist, not a thief) of verse 42 has caused much anguish because he is saved without baptism. But Jesus can save who He wishes as He wishes. Further, baptism is part of the Gospel age, which had not yet begun.

24 - Watch carefully and see if you can find anyone who believed Jesus would rise from the dead. That ends the foolish speculation that a disciple stole His body. None of the disciples expected a resurrection so why would they stage one? The Old Testament really is all about Jesus (verse 27), and the Gospel really is about repentance and forgiveness of sin (verse 47). Verse 49 references the promise of the Holy Spirit, who will be a major actor in Acts.

Introduction to Acts - Acts is the sequel to Luke. Its main purpose is to show that the work of God begun in Jesus is continued in Jesus' followers, the New Testament church. It lets us watch disciples and discipleship in action.

1 - Luke enjoys showing bad questions, as we see in verse 6. The disciples were still stuck thinking about a physical kingdom! On the Sabbath you could walk a little more than a half mile on the Sabbath without violating rabbinical tradition. This is the "Sabbath's day journey" of verse 12.

2 - This is one of the most important chapters in the Bible. Note the key role the Holy Spirit and the Scriptures play in "birthing" the church. People get confused in verse 1 and fail to realize that "they" refers to the apostles (1:26). The apostles are the only ones who receive this special baptism, not the entire 120 assembled. Confusion reigns again in verse 4, where some try to make this ecstatic utterances. It is clearly foreign languages, as the people assembled can understand what is said (verse 11). Peter begins his sermon at nine o'clock in the morning (verse 15) and it is full of Scriptural references. Verse 34 again brings Psalm 110 to the fore to point out Jesus' superiority to David. Jesus is King and Messiah (verse 36b).

Applications from This Week's Readings

We have witnessed, via Luke's inspired pen, the most important events in human history: Jesus' death on the cross and resurrection three days later. The first question is "Do you believe what Luke wrote here?" It is credible and authentic history. So, the second question is even more important: "Will you follow Jesus?" Back to Table of Contents.

Week 16 - Acts 3-7

3 - This wonderful story is very straightforward. The man is healed and Peter preaches the sermon of Acts 2 again. Verse 19's expression "times of refreshing" is difficult. It may simply be the refreshing blessings of being in Jesus Christ, or it may refer to the restoration of all things (verse 21), speaking of the New World established by the Messiah. Verse 25 connects Peter's sermon (and Jesus) to the grand promises made to Abraham in Genesis 12. The Bible's theme of redemption echoes from cover to cover!

4 - Luke wants us to see Peter's courage (verse 8). What has happened to the man so timid he would not stand up to a servant girl the night Jesus was betrayed? He is now "filled with the Spirit!" Notice how authentic and beyond question New Testament miracles are (verse 14). The benevolent spirit of verse 32 would be important as so many Jews, now Christians, were remaining in Jerusalem. Luke loves to introduce us to major characters with a quick preview before they come fully on stage. So we meet Barnabas in verse 36.

5 - The church has been attacked in chapters three and four by outside enemies, but now finds itself with internal problems. What if Christians fail to manifest basic integrity? God makes an example of Ananias and Sapphira. Evidently they acted as if they gave all the purchase price of the land when they actually kept some back (verse 2). Verse 12 shows how Jewish the early church was. They are still meeting in the Temple. At first verse 13 appears to contradict verse 14, but verse 13 probably means few would just stand and listen unless they were willing to join, or it may mean no one would meddle with the church. Gamaliel sums Acts for us in verse 39. God is at work here!

6 - Racism and mistrust of foreigners is not a new problem. There were many out of town Jews among the first church, and they weren't being treated right (verse 1). The apostles are concerned about missing prayer time first, then teaching time (verse 4). We could learn much from this. Again, we see Luke's emphasis on the Holy Spirit in verse 5. We aren't certain what Stephen was preaching but we can deduce from verse 11 that he may have been among the first to see that Christianity was completely separate from Judaism. Did Stephen's face really glow (verse 15)? Perhaps, or it could be an expression for inner confidence that gave a gleam to his eyes.

7 - Stephen's sermon stresses two themes: the Jews have been continuously blessed and they have continuously rejected God. He develops this by tracing out Jewish history, something his audience would have loved to hear, but it is a history full of warts and blemishes. Verse 9 begins the theme of rejection. It is furthered in verses 25, 35, 39, and brought to a head in verses 51-52. For Stephen it is not ignorance (as Peter said in 3:17) but willful rebellion that is at work here. Stephen is often portrayed as seeing Jesus as he died but verse 56 is prior to being stoned, and the vision may not have continued during the stoning. This is the equivalent to a lynching, as the Sanhedrin did not have the power of capital punishment.

Applications from This Week's Readings

Did you notice how much praying was going on in these chapters? How is the praying here different from your praying? Reread the prayer of 4:24-30. Can you adapt that prayer to be yours, so that you will be asking God for more courage to speak of Him and His way? Back to Table of Contents.

Week 17 - Acts 8-12

8 - Luke characteristically gives us a brief introduction to a major character in verse 1. Stephen's death is something Paul never forgot. Verse 5 has the church starting to branch out in a natural direction: Samaria. Samaritans were looked down on by Jews but knew something of God and His law. Some of the most important information about the miraculous gifts of the Spirit is recorded in verses 14-19. Note that at baptism one did not receive a miraculous gift. This eliminates Acts 2:38's "gift of the Spirit" from being miracles. Further, we learn here that only apostles could give the power of miracles to Christians. This safeguarded the gifts from the very kind of profiteering Simon envisions, but it also means that since there are no apostles today there can be no miraculous gifts given. Verse 23 is difficult in the NASB, having "gall of bitterness." This simply means "full of bitterness. We wonder if God miraculously grabbed Phillip in verse 39 or if that just means Phillip left. It could be either.

9 - Don't miss the significance of this story to Luke. He tells it three times in this book (chs. 9, 22, and 26). It is a powerful record of how one truly seeking God can make a dramatic change when he realizes he is wrong. Verse 13 finds Ananias (obviously not the Ananias struck dead in ch. 5) arguing with God! God's patience is amazing. Galatians 1:15-24 tells us that there is a three year time period in between verses 25 and 26. The ability of the church to make a mistake with brethren is also well illustrated in verses 26. Once again Barnabas appears, encouraging and helping (verse 27).

10 - Cornelius is a "God-fearer" (verse 2). These were Gentiles who were attached to the synagogue and believed in the one true God but were not circumcised. Sometimes people think if God would just show them a vision they would understand all they were to do but Peter's vision still requires him to think about it and it takes some time for him to "get it" (verse 17). For the rest of Acts verse 35 serves as a kind of summary statement: the Gospel is for all and now it will go to all. The baptism of the Holy Spirit in verses 44-47 is just the kind of remarkable sign necessary to get Peter's attention and assure him that Gentiles can be admitted to the kingdom of God. There are only two cases of Holy Spirit baptism in Acts (here and Acts 2) showing us that it was not common, nor should we expect it today.

11 - Luke is determined that Christianity will not be just another party in Judaism like the Pharisees or Sadducees. Peter's defense of what he has done is crucial to establishing that Christianity is for all. Notice that the charge against Peter is not baptizing Gentiles but eating with them (verse 3)! Verse 19 connects Luke's story back to 8:4. What happened because of the persecution? The Gospel went north to Samaria (chapter 8), then there are three incredible conversion stories (the Ethiopian, Saul, and Cornelius). Now Luke picks up the story of the Gospel's spread by showing its arrival in Antioch. Verse 20 is very important. Cornelius' conversion paves the way for all Greeks to come to Jesus. The famine of verse 28 occurred in AD 45-47, meaning the church is now more than twelve years old.

12 - The events of this chapter can be reliably dated to AD 44. This is Herod Agrippa I, the brother of Herodias (see Mark 6:22). Verse 5 shows how the church's answer to troubles was prayer. Verse 15 keeps us from thinking the early Christians were always perfect paragons of faith. They were praying but did not have much faith God would act on their prayer! Don't miss the contrast in verses 23-24. Evil men who try to stop God's work are removed (even Josephus records Herod's death) and the Word of God goes on.

Applications from This Week's Readings

In these chapters we see God using so many people: Stephen, Ananias, Barnabas, Dorcas, Peter and Paul. Most are just common people who gave themselves over to God's work. What if Ananias never goes and sees Saul? What if Barnabas doesn't introduce him to the brethren in Jerusalem? Think carefully: are you making yourself available to God's work, big or small? Pray about God using you just like He used His people in Acts. Then look for any place to be used and get to it! Back to Table of Contents.

13 - Mark the action of the Spirit again (verse 2), a constant theme in Acts. Paul sharpens this theme by identifying the real struggle: the devil versus the Spirit (verses 9-10). The sermon that begins in verse 16 is not well known but uses Scripture powerfully to make the case for Jesus as Messiah to a Jewish audience. Verse 48 may seem to speak of sort of predestination but don't be confused. God has predestined all who will obey His word to be saved. How do you get into that group? You do as these did: you believe and obey God's word.

14 - Miraculous signs are so badly misunderstood today. Verse 3 reveals their purpose: confirm the message and messenger. Paul and Barnabas preach again, a short sermon, beginning in verse 15. Watch how it does not appeal to Jewish Scripture but instead to nature and its proofs of God. They adapted their approach to their audience. Once again Luke leaves us uncertain if we are seeing a natural event or a miracle (verse 20). The text just doesn't say if Paul was dead or only appeared dead. Of more importance is Paul's great courage. He goes right back into the city! Verse 27 closes the first missionary journey on a very triumphal note. I wonder if we would have felt as good about it given all the persecution. Instead of complaining, Paul and Barnabas are happy to accent God's work through them.

15 - The Jerusalem Conference is a crucial event in the early church's history. For some twenty years Christianity has been viewed by some as simply a party or sect of Judaism. The increasing acceptance of Gentiles has made this more and more complicated to pull off. Christianity appears to some to be a breakaway movement of its own that needs to be reined in (verse 5). Peter, Paul, and Barnabas all cite examples to prove God doesn't require Gentiles to become Jews first before becoming Christians (verses 7-12). James cinches it by citing Scripture, showing that God always desired all people to come to Him (verse 17). What of the regulations bound on Gentiles (see especially verses 20 and 29)? These are probably best understood as the means to make social interaction between Jewish Christians and Gentile Christians possible. Gentiles need not become Jews but they could not act like full-fledged pagans either.

16 - Take a moment and check the map in the back of your Bible to see where these missionary tours occur. Lystra and Derbe are in present day Turkey. Verse 11 details a key moment in world history: the gospel goes to Europe. After Acts 16 the emphasis of Scripture is toward the west and Europe, as Asia largely turns away from the Gospel. Where the Gospel went education and progress followed. Much of our current world situation is explained by Acts 16:11, isn't it? Verse 13 helps us see that there could not have been many Jews in Philippi, because if there had been as many as ten they would have had a synagogue and not been down by the river. The end of verse 14 is just a wonderful way of crediting God for Lydia's conversion so that no one will think it was a result of Paul's oratorical skills. God opened her heart through the preaching of the Word, not through some "better felt than told" experience that some get and others are denied. We may chuckle a little in verse 37 as Paul asserts his rights as a Roman. These magistrates could be in real trouble if Paul decides to report them. Being a Roman citizen had privileges!

17 - Luke continues several key themes here. One of those is that preaching should be based in Scripture when possible (verse 3). The other is that the Jews rejected the Gospel, and so are responsible for the persecution Christians were receiving (verse 5). Verse 11 is often used to plea for verifying all that is done from the Bible. The verse does teach that but it really stresses character. Many of the Athenians lack that kind of heart (verse 32), and the chapter closes with a low moment for Paul. The Gospel doesn't gain much of a foothold in Athens, but watch Paul. He

never quits.

Applications from This Week's Readings

These chapters highlight the inevitable advance of Christianity because some very brave people were willing to take great risks to preach Jesus. They risked ostracism, misunderstanding and persecution. What are you risking to speak of Jesus and advance the Kingdom? Back to Table of Contents.

8 - The decree of verse 2 was made in 49 AD. Notice that both Jews and Christians alike are victed from Rome. The government does not, at this time, see a difference in the groups. That vill change. The Jews continue to be the Gospel's greatest obstacle (see verses 6 and 12). Paul is nvolved with vows twice in our readings this week. The vow of verse 18 may be the Nazirite ow of special dedication and thanksgiving to God. One took a vow, then after completing it pecial offerings were made and the hair was cut (see Numbers 6). The Second Missionary ourney ends in verse 22 and the Third Journey follows immediately (verse 23), as Paul heads ack to territory he believes will be fruitful.

9 - These two episodes about John's baptism (Apollos in 18:24ff and this one) go together. In he New Testament world there was confusion about Jesus and John and some didn't have the vhole story. It is of interest that a lack of knowledge about the Holy Spirit in verse 2 cues Paul to he reality that their entire Christianity is suspect. We get some honesty about what drives idol eligion (money, verse 25) followed by another look at Paul's courage (verse 30).

?0 - Verse 4 lists these men's names because they were delegates from the various congregations vho were sending money to Jewish Christian's relief (see 1 Corinthians 16:1-4). Worshiping vith brethren, particularly observing the Lord's Supper, was very important for Paul. He waited o he could be with the brethren at Troas (verse 7). What a contrast to too many who make little ffort to worship when "on the road" or even at home! As Paul gathers the elders from Ephesus te stresses how he has faithfully proclaimed all of God's word (verse 27). Verse 35's saying of esus is famous, but what many don't realize is that it is not in any Gospel. It must have come rom Paul's own conversations with Jesus or from other who knew Jesus and told of what He aid and did (see 21:16).

?1 - This text is fairly straightforward. Paul is going to Jerusalem with money to relieve Jewish Christians in need and show how Gentile Christians cared about their brethren (see Acts 24:17; Romans 15:25-28. This concern drives him to Jerusalem, even as he is warned of impending langer (verses 4 and 11). What catches our attention is this business with Paul and the four men vith a vow (verses 20-26). What is Paul doing getting involved in the old Jewish religion, we vonder? Remember that Judaism was more than just a religion, it was also a way of life. It was a :ulture, a lifestyle. Paul never told people to give up that lifestyle, or to deliberately do things to ffend Jewish sensibilities. He circumcised Timothy to avoid offense (see 16:3-4), and the Ierusalem Conference's decision encouraged Gentiles not to offend Jews (see 15:23ff). What Paul does here is affirm that he isn't trying to force Jews to become Gentiles. Keeping old :ustoms, like eating only kosher foods, was fine. However, if you asked Paul if they could be saved by those things he would have said "Certainly not!" (see Galatians 2:16) and he had no tolerance for the false gospel that Gentiles had to be circumcised (i.e., become a Jew) first before they could become Christians (see Gal. 1:8-9; 5:4-6). There was a difference in Jewish culture and Jewish religion. Paul was a part of that culture _ it was how he grew up and who he was _ but long ago he gave up trying to be justified by Jewish law to find grace in Jesus Christ (see Romans 7).

?2 - As you read this chapter watch how Paul stresses his continuity with Judaism and that rather being a Law-destroying rebel he is actually the best kind of Jew. He even argues with God to get the right to teach Jews (verse 19)! Some have tried to find a contradiction in verse 9 and the account in Acts 9:7, but together the accounts tell us they heard something but didn't understand what they heard. Verse 17 has Paul "cutting to the chase," as he doesn't mention his preaching in Damascus or time in Arabia (see Acts 9:20ff; Gal. 1:17). Verse 22 shows that Paul's real problem wasn't that he had committed crimes or was evil. The trouble was Jewish exclusivism and unwillingness to admit Gentiles could be accepted by God just as Jews were.

Applications from This Week's Readings

Our readings show how Paul kept butting heads with the Jews, and after giving them a fair chance he would move on to better prospects. Do you ever get weighed down having the same religious arguments with the same people again and again? Be like Paul and move on to someone who will really listen instead of argue and cause trouble! Back to Table of Contents.

Week 20 - Acts 23-27

23 - Much has been made of verses 4-5, and the apparent disrespect Paul shows the High Priest. Many explanations are possible. Perhaps Paul's poor eyesight kept him from seeing who was speaking (especially plausible if the High Priest were not in his priestly garments). Maybe it is sarcasm and irony, as Paul is saying "No real High Priest would act like you are acting." Maybe Paul lost his temper and just said something he shouldn't. In such a place as this Paul seems to sense that he cannot receive a fair trial so he disrupts the proceedings with a careful statement (verse 9). Verse 12 makes us chuckle as we think of hungry would-be assassins but it ought to show us how serious these threats were, and how quickly they expected to act. Lysias took the threats seriously, as his immediate action and large accompanying force shows (verses 23-24). Felix (verse 26) was appointed by Claudius in AD 52.

24 - This chapter is fairly straightforward. Listen to Paul as he connects himself deeply to Judaism and God's Law. Christianity is not some outlandish new idea, Paul says, but exactly what God planned all along (see verse 14). Verse 17 references the collection for the brethren Paul brought (see Romans 15:25ff).

25 - As politicians come and go Paul can't seem to make any headway toward freedom, so in frustration he claims the right of a Roman citizen to go to Caesar (verse 11). In verse 13 we meet Agrippa II, the son of the Herod Agrippa who was struck by God in Acts 12. Agrippa II, Bernice and Drusilla (Acts 24:24) were brother and sisters. Verse 27 makes clear the issue Luke is pushing: Paul's innocence. . In some ways Paul seems almost to have become a sideshow or novelty being used by high officials for entertainment

26 - Paul uses his position, even if it is as a novelty, to preach one of the most stirring sermons ever. The theme again is Paul the Good an d Obedient Jew (note verse 6). Verse 18 gives us an excellent summary of the Gospel message. Is Agrippa mocking Paul or genuine in his statement of verse 28? We cannot hear his tone of voice so we do not know. The chapter ends with Paul being vindicated by the Roman government again (verse 32). Luke is letting everyone know that Paul (and Christianity in general) have not broken Roman law.

27 - Make certain you are consulting a map as you read Luke's travelogue in these last two chapters. Most Bibles have a map of Paul's journeys. The main point of these two chapters concern the difficulties of sea travel, Paul's courage and his innocence. Repeatedly Luke mentions little touches like Paul's liberty in verse 3 to show his audience that Paul certainly is not a bad man. Verse 9 dates the voyage, telling us of "the Fast" or Day of Atonement, which would be in October. Some translations have "Euroquilo" or "Euroclydon" in verse 14. It is simply a north-eastern or terrible storm. Verse 17 tells how desperate the situation was. They try to bind the ship up, and they are afraid of the sand bars off North Africa's coast. If they go aground there the ship will be battered into splinters and they will all die. Verse 28 mentions fathoms, a nautical measure equal to about six feet. Verse 34 shows how Paul combined faith with practical reality. God would do His part. They must be ready to do theirs.

Applications from This Week's Readings

We have now read Paul's conversion story three times. Why is it presented so many times? What proof does it offer for the power of the Gospel to change a person? Paul was very ready to explain his own conversion, from what led up to it to how Jesus changed him. Are you as ready to tell your own story? We do not encounter the Lord in blinding light like Paul did but we had to have some encounter with Him through the Word. Why did you obey the Gospel? How are you different now for having done so? What is your conversion story? Back to Table of Contents.

28 - Again, we are impressed with Paul's practicality as even a great apostle can gather wood (verse 3), and his courage and faith show when bitten by a snake (verses 3-4). Verse 11 has the sound of an eyewitness, doesn't it? It must have been exciting (and occasionally terrifying!) to travel with Paul. If our admiration of Paul knows no bounds it is tempered by the realism of verse 15. Even Paul could use encouragement and enjoy being with brethren! The preaching Paul offers (verse 23) is again scriptural, and again it fulfills the pattern of all Acts: some believe and some don't (verse 24). When verse 31 closes Acts we may wish we knew more of Paul's final situation but the book isn't about Paul. It is about the work of God which goes on and prospers even to this day.

Introduction to Romans - Romans is unlike any book in the New Testament. It is the only epistle Paul wrote to a church he had never visited. It is common to view Romans as Paul's great summary of his teachings on salvation. However, Paul never wrote long theological treatises. He wrote to churches in trouble to help them do right. The church in Rome had unity problems between Jews and Gentiles as revealed in chapter 14. Therefore, much of what Paul writes in this letter highlights the term "all" and "everyone" so that he can appeal for unity. Watch in the opening chapters how Paul will say that all of them, Jew and Gentile, are sinners, are saved the same way, and are servants of the Lord.

1 - Verses 8-15 reveal Paul's desire to come see them. Note the three times Paul says "God gave them up" in verses 24, 26, 28. Although chapter 1 is usually applied to Gentiles only many of these sins can be found in Old Testament Israel (note verse 32 - an appeal to people who know something of God's law).

2 - Paul knows some of his readers will excuse themselves from the indictment of chapter 1. "I haven't done all of those things, I'm not like that!" they will protest. Paul replies that saying "I am not as bad as others so I must be alright" won't work. All are sinners (verses 1-10). Verse 12 doesn't mean Gentiles had no law whatsoever, but not the written codified law like the Jew had. Verse 14's idea is that Gentiles didn't know enough to write a Bible but they knew enough to keep from doing evil. Everyone knows something of right and wrong (verse 15). In verse 17 Paul begins an attack on the Jews. They are not as perfect as they claim. In the judgment God won't ask "Did you have the law?" but "Did you do it?" The advantage of circumcision was that it put one in the middle of the law and the people who had the law. But if you don't honor the law and obey it then the advantage is lost (verse 25).

3 - Verses 1-2 are surprising. We expect Paul to say "None" but there were advantages to being Jewish. Unfortunately many Jews did not take advantage of those advantages and so were condemned (verses 3-4)! Would someone then argue that if God condemning sin shows Him to be just we ought to sin more so God will be seen as more just (verses 5-7)? Such is outrageous and cannot be so (verse 8). Paul will deal with such wrong thinking further in 6:1. Our understanding of verse 12b may be helped by adding "habitual" here. No one does good constantly, consistently, and continually. Verse 23 has Paul's major point for this section. That bad news is followed by good news (verse 24). Verse 25 speaks of "propitiation," meaning to remove God's wrath through an offering. Look at the emphasis on unity and oneness again (verse 30).

4 - Once again, Paul shows his understanding of his audience. Some will object to what he is teaching by pointing to Abraham. Now there was a fine fellow! Surely God accepted him based

on all the good things he did! No, says Paul, that's not the case. Abraham was "justified" or "counted righteous by faith." Here Paul sets forth an entirely different kind of righteousness not based on never sinning, but obtained through faith as a gift of God. It is based on forgiveness not perfection. Verses 6-7 beautifully illustrate what "counted righteous" and "reckon" or "impute righteousness" means. Those terms just means "forgiven." The man counted righteous by God is the man forgiven by God. Verse 9 sounds out the unity theme again A Jewish Christian might say "Oh, yes, justified by faith, but not just any believer can be justified, but the circumcised believer only." No, Paul says, Abraham was right with God prior to circumcision (verses 10-12). Thus Abraham can be the father of all who believe, not just the Jews or circumcised. Anyone with faith can be a child of Abraham! Paul even argues that if the promise of blessing depends on law keeping then it will never be fulfilled because no one keeps the law perfectly (verse 14). The chapter ends by showing that Abraham's faith is a model for us today (verse 22). Be like Abraham and trust in God!

Applications from This Week's Readings

A right relationship with God can be obtained because (1) we are right (we have never sinned) or by (2) faith in God. Since none of us are sinless the way of faith becomes critically important. Read 4:20 again. Is your faith strong like Abraham? Do you trust in God to forgive your sins and count your righteous? Pray about your faith this week and consider reading Abraham's story (beginning Genesis 12) to build up your faith. Back to Table of Contents.

5 - Faith changes everything, even how we suffer (verses 1-3). How does the Spirit pour out God's love in our hearts (verse 5)? By telling us of the cross (verses 6-8). Verse 12 begins a difficult section. Paul wants to illustrate how one person's actions have affected all humanity. Who can Paul use to illustrate this? Adam and Jesus are the only possible choices. So Paul says that just as it was in Adam's case where one man's sin had such terrible effects even so now the act of the one man Jesus Christ has brought about a universal effect. Notice Paul doesn't write here of conditions. There is no talk of how we are condemned or saved. Thus, if we try to read more into chapter 5 we will end up in trouble. Let's be content with Paul's simple idea: just as one man's sin had terribly destructive results so one Man's righteous act has incredibly constructive results. Note verse 19 as it troubles some. Paul may mean here that all men are treated as sinners (i.e. all die physically).

6 - Verses 1-5 set forth how all in Christ now via baptism. Note that if baptism is not necessary to salvation then Paul's argument fails. In verse 6 some are charging Paul with loose theology that results in sin. Is the net result of being saved an indifference to sin? Absolutely not, Paul says! Instead we need to see ourselves as slaves of righteousness, not sin (verses 15-23).

7 - Paul is still answering the question of 6:15. He has spoken of a new relationship in Christ (6:18ff) and now speaks to the legitimacy of that relationship for Jews. They can "marry again" (be in Christ) because they died to the Law (think of baptism, 6:1ff). Notice that we can't blame law for our sins, it is our passions at work (verse 5). So verse 6 concludes: we cannot continue in sin, we now live in the Spirit. Verse 7 then begins a new question: since we had to be delivered from the Law is it evil? Paul says "Of course not!," but the material it works with (the human heart) is rebellious and thus the Law is doomed to fail. Verse 11 reminds us of the Garden of Eden. Satan based his entire attack on the law of God. He used it to deceive Eve and kill her (spiritually). Paul concludes by talking about the "wretched man" who tries to do right, knows the Law is right, but still fails (verses 14-25). Such a person can never be right with God for he sins despite his efforts not to do so. There has to be a better way....

8 - The better way is found in Jesus (verse 1). A liberation has taken place because Jesus is greater than the sin power personified in the last chapter (verses 2-3). In verses 5-11 Paul talks of how these freed people live: they follow God's will instead of selfish desires. Paul then goes on to talk about the relationship we have with God when we are "in" the Spirit (verses 12-17). This language throws some but Paul isn't speaking of something mystical or based in feelings. The Bible speaks freely of knowing God and being in God or Christ (note John 15:1-7; 1 John 2:24). This just means to be in relationship with God, to submit to Him and be controlled by Him. So it is here. We are controlled by the Spirit (who uses the Word to teach us what we need to do so we can do right, verse 16). This will lead to a glory that all Creation is waiting for (verses 18-24). As we wait the Spirit helps us, even with our prayers (verses 24-25). These verses have been subject to much debate as to "how" the Spirit does this, but we don't know. Let us just rejoice that He does! Verse 28 does not say everything is good but that God can work good through anything, even tragedy. Verse 29's reference to predestination does not mean individuals are predestined, but that those who will choose God will be chosen by Him. All of this works together to assure the person who follows the way of faith, who is Spirit-led and controlled, will have victory (verses 31-39) for God is working for him!

9 - But what of those who are still trying the Law way to be justified, Paul? Chapters 9-11 deal

with this question, particularly since it appears Gentiles were disdaining Christian Jews as somehow inferior since they were a minority in the church. Remember, Romans is about unity. The key verse is verse 6. A true Jew is one who receives God's word (see 2:28-29). Indeed, there were physical descendants of Abraham, like Esau (verses 11-14) that God did not use. God works as He will (verses 19-24). The rejection of the Jews was even prophesied (verses 25-31), so don't criticize God and how His Gospel works!

Applications from This Week's Readings

These are difficult chapters. Much remains here that we may not fully understand in one reading. However, several truths are clear. We cannot be right with God by our own righteousness or efforts (ch. 7). We need Jesus and we need to be controlled by the Spirit (ch. 8). If we will follow Jesus God will do more than we can imagine to see to it we are saved. If we won't follow Jesus we may well end up like obstinate and stubborn Jews who missed the Kingdom due to their self-righteousness (chs. 9-11). So we need to ask: am I truly seeking Jesus? Am I Spirit-led, i.e. do I let Scripture command my life? Am I trusting Jesus or my own righteousness? Focus then on the end of chapter 8 and thank God for His mercy, care and decisive actions that will bring us home to Him. Back to Table of Contents.

10 - The reason so many Jews reject Christ is because they want to do it themselves (verse 3). There are only two ways to be saved: obey perfectly (verse 5), or travel the road of faith (verses 5-17). Regrettably, many of the Jews have rejected the way of the faith as prophesied (verses 18-21). It isn't that they haven't heard (verse 18), or they are offended at Gentiles being "in" (verse 19), or that it is too hard to figure out (verse 20). They are disobedient and stubborn (verse 21)!

11 - So what is the final word on Jews? Is God done with them? Paul says "Certainly not!" (verse 1). There will always be a remnant who is faithful (verse 5), even if many do reject Jesus. In fact, Paul wonders if the flood of Gentiles into God's kingdom might ultimately provoke Jews to jealousy and cause them to come too (verses 11-15). In poignant verses reminding Gentiles not to get too full of themselves Paul portrays the people of God as an olive tree (verses 17-24). That tree was full of Jewish "branches" to start with. Yes, some of those branches were cut off due to disobedience and wild branches (Gentiles) were then grafted in (verses 17-19). But being grafted in is not a cause for boasting or carelessness (verses 20-23). Perhaps those broken off branches (unbelieving Jews) will come to faith and be put back in (verse 24). Indeed, all true Israelites (real followers of God) will be saved (verse 26).

12 - As Paul often does, he moves from doctrine to admonition. The key teaching of this chapter is at its beginning: take your body and use it for God's service in every way possible. Notice how all of life here is depicted as "worship" or "service" (verse 1b). To do this requires a radical change in thinking (verse 2). Since every member of the Body of Christ does not have the same abilities and talents we need to think correctly of self (verse 3) and then use what we have to serve others (verses 4-8). Mark carefully the many different "jobs" or abilities people can have in serving the Lord and other Christians.

13 - Some might wonder if a lack of revenge and retribution will result in lawlessness. No, because government is appointed to take care of these problems. Scripture uniformly urges obedience to civil authority (see 1 Tim 2:1-2; Titus 3:1; 1 Pet 2:13-17) because, as Paul teaches here, civil government provides services to its citizens and is a God-ordained means of maintaining order. Thus we should submit to it. Naturally Paul does not mean we should disobey Christ to obey civil government, nor does Paul mean every government pleases God (note verse 3b). Verse 8 should not be seen as a prohibition against all borrowing (note Matt 5:42; Luke 6:35) but merely commands that we pay what we owe, and particularly in this context that we pay the taxes owed government (see verse 7). What does Paul mean in verse 11 about salvation being near? It is a difficult verse. Paul may just be referring to the reality that in God's scheme of things there is only one major event left, final judgement. Every day draws us closer to it.

14 - This chapter has been the subject of misuse and much debate. If we are good students, however, we can see from the outset some principles that rule out many problems. For example, Paul is content to leave both weak and strong in their respective states. That means Paul cannot be discussing matters of right and wrong for if someone is in sin Paul wouldn't let them stay in such a state, would he? Instead Paul says God accepts both weak and strong as they currently are (verse 3). Paul's tone is also notably milder than when he deals with false teaching and sin (compare this to Galatians). So, what is Paul concerned about? The eating of certain kinds of foods and the celebrating of certain days. Probably these are foods sacrificed to idols or foods that were not kosher according to Jewish dietary law, and the days mentioned are probably Jewish feast days. We have seen much in this epistle about unity and here Paul gets down to the

troubles at hand. Jews wanted Gentiles to eat as they did, and abstain from what they abstained from. Gentiles were appalled at Jews who continued to participate in Jewish feast days, and who refused to eat meat sacrificed to idols (see verses 10, 20-23 - Paul will not tolerate forcing one view on others). Both sides were judging the other side as inferior. Paul says these particular matters are of no concern to God, and thus all judging must stop (verse 13). Don't lead or push others into sin who do differently than you (verses 14-21). Don't violate your own conscience and don't look down on others who do different than you in these matters of judgment (verses 22-23)! A modern day example might be of converting a Jew, who is uncomfortable working on Saturday even though he is now a Christian. Should we (the strong) make him work on Saturdays? No! Can he, however, force everyone else to stop working on Saturday due to his scruples? No, Paul says.

Applications from This Week's Readings

The Roman church was urged to get along, to help each other, to be understanding on non-important differences so they could be united. Ask yourself, "Am I helping the unity of the local church where I am a member?" Back to Table of Contents.

Week 24 - Romans 15-16; 1 Thess 1-3

15 - The first thirteen verses finish the thoughts of chapter 14. Paul is urging the brethren to serve one another so Jesus has already done. That is the remedy to the disunity and troubles in Rome: humble attitudes that see how we are all alike, all need Christ, and all need to do what Christ has done. Verse 14 to the chapter's end fill us in on Paul's travel plans. Note verse 16 and the contribution. This money is much more than just a cash contribution. For Paul it symbolizes Jew-Gentile relations and the full entrance of Gentiles into God's scheme (see also verses 26-27).

16- This material gets overlooked as just a bunch of names. It's much more than that! We get a good look into a NT church, what it was like, and who made it up. For example, from these names we note several things; that women can and should serve in important ways in the church (Priscilla (verses 3-4), Mary (verse 6), Junia (verse 7), Tryphena, Tryphosa and Persis (verse 12) are all female names). Further, we see that the church is made up of a diverse group of people. Nereus, Hermes, Persis, Herodion, Tryphosa, Tryphena, Amplias are all slave names. So at Rome the church would be made of slaves, former slaves, and freemen. What a collection! Verse 17 gives rise to people "marking' troublemakers. However, the idea isn't putting a mark on people but rather "watch" or "keep your eye on him."

Introduction to 1 Thessalonians: This congregation was founded in Acts 17:1-9 by Paul. Jewish persecution drove Paul away and so he wrote back to Thessalonica, a populous and important city, to try and help the brethren he had to leave too quickly. He wanted to encourage them, deal with some false charges and answer some of their questions. The date of this epistle's writing is fairly well fixed as AD 51 or 52, making it early in the NT canon. One of the keys to watch for is the expression "as you know." Paul appeals to their personal experience with him throughout the epistle.

1 - Verse 1 mentions Silvanus, another name for Paul's companion, Silas. In verse 5 we can hear the echoes of charges against Paul. The church is commended for its evangelistic interest in verse 8. Note how repentance has worked major changes in the Thessalonians in verses 9-10.

2 - Paul sets forth his philosophy of preaching in verses 3-6. He will not trick, fool, or flatter to gain converts. Instead he shows the gentle and careful concern a parent exhibits (verses 7 and 11). Verse 9 probably references Paul making tents to support himself. Jewish persecution is singled out in verses 14-18 as the work of Satan. Note how Satan does have an affect on God's workers and what they can do. Satan can hinder us!

3 - Verse 1 speaks of Paul in Athens in Acts 17, anxious about how the new church in Thessalonica is fairing. Timothy's report was thrilling to Paul (verses 6-10). Verse 10 has a very strong term for praying. It is a word translated elsewhere as "begging" (see 2 Corinthians 8:4).

Applications from This Week's Readings

Thessalonians brings much of the truth of the Gospel to bear in our lives in a very practical way. The Thessalonian brethren were changed by the Gospel. Focus on 1:8-10. Am I changed by the resurrection of Jesus the Christ? Am I evangelistic? Have I truly repented? Am I eagerly waiting for the Lord's coming? Back to Table of Contents.

Week 25 - 1 Thess 4-5; 2 Thess 1-3

1 Thess 4 - Thessalonica was a pagan city with pagan morals, particularly regarding sexual activity. Paul urges purity and self-control (verses 3-7). Verse 4's vessel can refer to one's own body or one's spouse, but either way it means to be chaste and pure. Verse 6 reminds us that sexual sins (like adultery) take something from another we have no right to possess. The chapter concludes with great comfort for the Thessalonians who were sure that brethren who had already died ("fallen asleep," verse 13) had missed everything. No, Paul, says. Jesus will bring those brethren with Him when He returns again.

5 - Paul builds off the end of chapter 4 to talk more of Jesus' Second Coming. Yes, it will catch many unaware and so be terribly unpleasant (verses 1-3) but it will also bring vindication and salvation for Christians (verses 9-11). Some quick admonitions close the epistle, including a word about quenching the Spirit in verse 19 that may puzzle some. It simply means to suppress the influence of the Spirit as He was directing that church through spiritual gifts like prophecy. Verse 22 is not well translated in the old King James, resulting in much misunderstanding and misapplication.

Introduction to 2 Thessalonians - Paul's interest in the Thessalonians doesn't end with sending a single letter. While still at Corinth (Acts 18) he receives further word about the Thessalonian church. So he wrote again to set matters straight as persecution was leaving the church at the point of despair, and to repair damage done by a counterfeit Pauline letter. He also wanted to encourage the brethren not to forsake their normal duties in life simply because Jesus could return at any time.

1 - Verses 6-10 ring with a vengeance and victory, sounding like the book of Revelation. Judgement brings terror to evil doers and vindication to the righteous. That day will come, Paul says, so don't quit!

2 - This chapter is one of the most difficult in the New Testament. There are numerous translation difficulties (sometimes "he" can be "it" or vice versa), and we don't know what Paul had already taught them that he is relying on to guide them (verse 5). Their main concern was they had missed the Second Coming (verse 2). Paul says that can't happen because first there must be an apostasy (verse 3), which we cannot identify with certainty, and then the "man of sin" has to be revealed (verse 3b). There are many opinions about the "man of sin's" identity. Some see the pope here, others a certain Roman emperor demanding worship, others see the Roman Empire in general. Perhaps Paul is saying that Roman persecution will get worse, but Jesus will deal with Rome so don't lose your faith in the meantime. Whatever we make of the difficulties in verses 3-9 the point of verse 15 is clear: stand fast. Loving the truth is the key to standing fast (note verse 10).

3 - The epistle ends with a note about church discipline directed toward those who don't receive apostolic instruction (verse 6). It seems some were quitting their jobs because Jesus might return any day. Paul understood the possibility of Christ's return but that doesn't mean we can sit down and do nothing until He does come (see verse 12).

Applications from This Week's Readings

Persecution and patience are main themes in Thessalonians. Have you ever been persecuted? Is it harder to endure overt threats, like the seizure of property and jail, than the more subtle persecutions of our day? What are you doing to "stand fast" against the work of Satan? Back to

Table of Contents.

Week 26 - 1 Timothy 1-5

Introduction to 1 Timothy - The epistles of 1 and 2 Timothy and Titus are unique because they are not written to churches, but to young preachers to strengthen and encourage them. Timothy was Paul's beloved "son in the faith" (see Acts 16:1; 1 Tim 1:2), who seems to have been a little doubtful about himself and his abilities. 1 Timothy was probably written from the imprisonment reported at the end of Acts in the mid-sixties.

1 - Verses 3-7 makes it plain Paul has reports of problems and wants very specific issues dealt with by Timothy. Verse 18 tells us that God had called or spoken of Timothy's work in high terms, though we do not have those prophecies recorded. As Paul always looked back on the Damascus Road call so Timothy is reminded of the charge God gave him. Verse 20's "handed over" refers to church discipline (see 1 Cor 5:5).

2 - In the first four verses Paul reveals his "filter" for observing all of life: how can this help the Gospel's cause? Even his prayer for politicians (verse 1) is for them to create the climate in which the Gospel will flourish (verse 2). Paul wants what God wants (verse 4). Verse 6 ends by saying it is now the right time, the appropriate time, to tell of the great truths about Jesus. "Lifting holy hands" (verse 8) must not throw us. Many prayers in Scripture are accompanied by a lifting of the hands to beseech heaven's help (see 1 Kings 8:22; Neh 8:6; Psalm 63:4; 134:2). Unfortunately, this practice is now identified with Pentecostalism, but Paul certainly wasn't thinking of today's charismatic groups when he wrote 1 Timothy! Verse 9 contains important admonitions about modesty, but we should note that Paul here is concerned with over-dressing. These verses are probably in the context of the worship assembly and so warn about coming to church to show off one's fine clothes. However, since immodesty is dressing to draw the wrong kind of attention to one's body the application to under-dressing fits just as well. Verse 15 is difficult. Notice that Paul goes from "she" to "they" in the same sentence! "She" may reference Eve (verse 14) but clearly is representatively used here speak to all women. This is probably best understood to mean that women who remain in their role as a woman (instead of trying to usurp a man's place, verses 11-12) can be saved. Is Paul thinking about the woman's nature and that Eve was deceived and so saying women can be saved as they are, i.e. as women? So, instead of trying to depart from their role and be what they are not (men) they should cherish and be happy to do what God made women to do. What a timely teaching for today!

3 - Elder and deacon qualifications are fairly straightforward. Their application to every circumstance and situation is where we run into trouble sometimes, but a full discussion of that is simply not possible in this limited format. Mostly they are not that difficult to understand. Verse 8 certainly is not giving license for today's social drinking. We need to remember the vast differences in biblical wines and wine now. Further, one can say "stop lying constantly" without okaying some lying. Verse 16 uses the term "mystery" because without God's revelation we would never know these great truths (see Eph 3:3-5).

4 - This chapter straightforwardly tells us apostasy is coming. We always need to be careful of those who offer some "higher" spirituality by abstaining from what God has made and declared good (verses 3-4). Verse 8 offers a needed admonition to our society that adores perfect physical bodies but has no place for character.

5 - Verse 9 is talking about widows who are cared for from the church's treasury. Verse 12 says younger women may cast off their first "faith" or "pledge." That may mean their pledge not to marry a non-Christian, or that they marry a pagan and lose their faith. The crucial distinction that

the church cannot do everything individuals can do is firmly established in verse 16. Note that verse 18 teaches that the church can financially support its elders for their work. Verse 23 has wine as a medicine, not as a beverage.

Applications from This Week's Readings

While chapter 4 is discouraging in its direct prophecy of troubled days ahead much in 1 Timothy prepares him (and us) for times of apostasy and false teaching. What in 1 Timothy have you read that prepares you to be more effective for Christ in the religiously-tough times we live in? Back to Table of Contents.

Week 27 - 1 Timothy 6; 2 Timothy 1-4

6 - Verses 1-2 help us see that slavery was tolerated in New Testament times because it was a fixture in that world. The church's purpose wasn't to remodel society. Paul returns again to the theme of boldness, reminding Timothy that Jesus didn't shirk from telling the truth before Pilate (verse 13). The "deposit" of verse 20 is the teaching Paul committed to him (see 2 Tim 2:2).

Introduction to 2 Timothy - This is the last epistle Paul wrote. Imprisoned in Rome (see 2 Tim. 1:8, 16; 4:6-13) in approximately 67 AD he knew that his execution wasn't far off. This epistle picks up the theme of boldness and confidence that 1 Timothy touched on and furthers it substantially. Timothy seems discouraged and Paul wants to remedy that in this letter.

1 - We know little of Timothy's family (mentioned in Acts 16:1) but it is clear that Eunice and Lois had a huge impact on Timothy's life (verse 5). But Timothy seems to have lost his courage (verse 7). Paul strongly urges him to press the cause of Christ fearlessly (note 2:3-5; 4:5). What is "what I have committed to Him" (verse 12)? Some translations have "what I have been entrusted with" which makes it even more difficult. This may be Paul's own salvation (in keeping with his idea of death being a victory, an encouraging idea for Timothy) or it may be the Gospel message Christ gave Paul to preach. That is how Paul uses the idea two verses later in reference to Timothy (see also 1 Tim 6:20). Verse 15 singles out of Phygelus and Hermogenes, which may mean they were leaders.

2 - Verses 11-13 contain Paul's beautiful "trustworthy sayings." Verse 13's last line should not be taken to mean God saves the unfaithful anyway. It just means that God will always be faithful to His promises and Word, even if we are not. Timothy must watch carefully not to be contaminated (verses 20-21) with bad attitudes and actions (verses 22-26) if he wants to be useful to God.

3 - The "last days" mentioned in verse 1 are the time of the Christian era (Acts 2:17). Paul believes he and Timothy were living in them at that time, and that this last era would be a difficult time for God's people. Jannes and Jambres (verse 8) are not mentioned anywhere in Scripture but in New Testament times were believed to be magicians in Pharaoh's court. Verse 11 cites the troubles of the first missionary tour (Acts 13-14). The value of Scripture and its origin is cemented forever in two of the most famous verses in the Bible (verses 16-17). In context they are attached to verse 15, a reminder to Timothy to keep reading his Bible. What a needed admonition!

4 - After the disappointment of Demas (verse 10) we read an encouraging note about Mark (verse 11). He had left Paul on the first missionary tour but with Barnabas' help (Acts 15:37-38) is now serving God effectively. Note that Paul bears no hard feelings toward him. In verse 19 we meet Priscilla and Aquila again. They were faithful co-workers with Paul (Acts 18:2; Rom 16:3; 1 Cor 16:19).

Applications from This Week's Readings

Re-read Paul's final statements in 2 Timothy 4:6-8. Picture yourself at the end of your life. You know the end is coming and coming soon. Could you say what Paul says here? If not, why not? Pray about staying the course, or making the changes needed to be able to live like Paul and have his confidence. Back to Table of Contents.

Week 28 - Titus 1-3; Philemon; Jude

Introduction to Titus - This letter is like 1 and 2 Timothy because it addresses a young preacher. However, it lacks any admonition about courage or zeal. We know little of Titus (he is only mentioned 12 times in the NT) but he seems to have been a remarkably effective preacher, even when working in difficult places and with difficult brethren. This epistle gives Titus some advice and encourages him to persevere (see 3:8).

1 - Much discussion has been raised over elder qualifications (verses 5-9). Again, extensive discussion of each qualification and the implications of various positions about them is impossible here. Let us be satisfied to see that elders are commanded and greatly needed for things to be "in order" (verse 5). Perhaps if more brethren saw the value in God's organizational plan for the church and wanted elders there would be less fussing over every nuance of these qualifications. Verse 5 tells us Titus was on the island of Crete. This is a large island 160 miles long by 35 miles wide in the Mediterranean. Its citizens did not have a good reputation by any means (verse 12). The troubles there seem to contain some elements of Judaism (verse 14). These false teachers may be binding Jewish dietary restrictions (with its regulations about impure foods) on people. Jesus dealt with this (see Matt 15:11-20) but Paul and Titus must deal with it again. Paul has little use for these who undermine the Kingdom of God (verse 16).

2 - Titus' work will mainly consist of teaching "sound doctrine" (verse 1). The emphasis on teaching is made clear when we see how many times it is mentioned: "teach" or "speak" in 2:1, "teachers of good things" in 2:3; "train" in 2:4, "urge" or "exhort" in 2:6, 15, "show yourself" in and "your teaching" in 2:7, "teaching us" or "training us" (2:12), and "rebuke" (2:15). The center of all of this teaching is God's grace (verses 11-12) which changes our roles in society and what we do even as we grow older.

3 - Verses 5-6 speak of the Holy Spirit's work. This verse reminds us of Jesus' saying about "born of water and the Spirit" in John 3:5. It is simply a reference to how, when we have heard the Word that the Spirit inspired, we obey it and are born again by being baptized. Verse 6 says the Spirit is poured out on "us," a reference to the outpouring of the Spirit on Pentecost in Acts 2. Where is Nicapolis (verse 12)? There were seven cities named Nicapolis ("city of victory"). This is probably the Nicapolis on the western coast of Greece two hundred miles northwest of Athens.

Philemon - This is a very personal epistle. Onesimus was Philemon's slave. He ran away (perhaps even stealing Philemon's money), somehow met up with Paul and was converted. Paul now returns him with this letter that pleads for Philemon to treat Onesimus kindly. At first we might dismiss this epistle as having little value to modern times. However, it is a marvelous "postcard" that puts teachings on forgiveness, warmth, and care for others into action for us to see. Christianity is to change how we live and how we treat others! Apphia (verse 2) might be Philemon's wife. Note the importance of voluntarily doing the right thing, instead of being made to do so (verses 14, 20).

Jude - Jude is a short book full of questions! The author is probably the Lord's half-brother (Mark 6:3). His theme is evident. He wanted to write something positive but the faith must be defended (verse 3) from false teaching and teachers (verse 4). Jude cites examples of the judgment of the ungodly, relying on the Old Testament for his illustrations. It is those examples that may puzzle us. Who are the angels in chains and what did they do (verse 6)? We don't know and must simply accept the verse to mean what it says without engaging in speculation. Some angels sinned and were judged. That is all we can say. What of Michael and the body of Moses (verse 9)? Again, we don't have all the details but we can get Jude's point: these false teachers talk about what they don't know (verse 10) when even a mighty angel didn't talk that way. What are love feasts (verse 12)? This is probably just a reference to hospitality practiced in homes by individual Christians. The key to Jude is to see his emphasis on standing fast in the truth and not allowing false teachers and teaching to take hold and destroy souls.

Applications from This Week's Readings

What is your attitude toward the truth? In our "whatever" society it is easy to decide doctrinal correctness isn't all that important. Titus and Jude both help us rethink our attitude toward false teaching and false teachers. Philemon stresses the right relationships that come when we obey truth. Will you pursue truth this week or dismiss it as something for elders and preachers to worry with? Pray this week that you will put more emphasis on understanding and even defending truth. Back to Table of Contents.

ntroduction to Matthew - Matthew's gospel is the most Jewish of the Gospels. Repeatedly Matthew ties Jesus to the Old Testament and demonstrates He is the prophesied Messiah. While Matthew, Mark and Luke share similarities Matthew preserves large blocks of Jesus' teaching like the Sermon on the Mount), uses titles for Jesus like Son of David and Son of God, and tells of Jesus' birth. Matthew's portrait of Jesus is enormously important for understanding Jesus the Christ.

1 - The first verse of Matthew sets the tone for the entire Gospel. Matthew is showing that Jesus of Nazareth is the Messiah promised to the house of David and to Abraham. He is the fulfillment of every Old Testament promise and prophecy. To show that to Jews a genealogy is in order, and that follows (verses 2-17). This genealogy shows Jesus to be of the kingly line of David. There are some surprising people in it (Tamar, verse 3; Bathsheba, verse 6; Manasseh, verse 10). It also shortens the lineages up in places by skipping a generation so as to maintain the symmetry of 14 generations to each marker in Jewish history (verse 17). Why the number 14 is important to Matthew is uncertain. Verse 21 gives us Jesus' name and mission. His mission is unique, but His name is only the Greek form of "Joshua" and would not have been uncommon. It means "God saves."

2 - This chapter is very straightforward. Verse 1 mentions Herod the Great, the first of many Herods in the New Testament. He was cruel, paranoid, and perhaps even insane. Note how the wise men did not visit the stable (as is often seen in various depictions) but "the house" (verse 11). The emphasis in this chapter is on Jesus' fulfilling prophecy after prophecy, and God caring for the Child and His parents so that even as the devil tries to murder Jesus as an infant his every attempt is foiled. It is also possible that Matthew is answering the objection that Jesus came from Nazareth, when everyone knew the Messiah would come from Bethlehem. With this week's reading we turn again to watch Jesus. Matthew wants us to see King Jesus. Let's make sure in our reading that we are getting that, and most importantly, that we are submitting ourselves to the Lord of Lords and King of Kings!

3 - Verse 2 shows how John's message and Jesus' message dovetail perfectly. Both begin by proclaiming the coming Kingdom of heaven. John's demeanor, preaching style and even clothing and diet all fit the image of someone outside the religious establishment who was very much in the tradition of Old Testament prophets like Elijah (verse 4). John's baptism (verses 5-6) must have been a bitter pill for some to swallow, as Gentiles who converted to Judaism were required to do such! Being Jewish by birth wasn't good enough, John said (verse 9). It was time for a radical change of mind and heart if you were really going to be part of God's people. Of course, Jesus has not sin to repent of but He still desires John's baptism (verse 15) that He might fulfill every command of God.

4 - Jesus has been declared to be God's Son (3:17) but now the devil tempts Him to misuse His position and status. Jesus answers every temptation from Deuteronomy 6-8, a section of Scripture that discusses the testing of Israel and what they should have learned in the desert. Israel didn't learn to trust and obey God, but Jesus certainly will and does. Verse 8's temptation is exceptionally devious, as it offers Jesus a shortcut to the kingship and kingdom He came to claim. Verse 12 speaks of the danger for Jesus of being in Judea (where John was arrested) so He moved north. Again, Matthew ties Jesus to prophecy (verse 14). What is this "kingdom of heaven" Jesus preaches (verse 17)? Some want to substitute in "church" everywhere they see

"kingdom" and end up with some sort of institution. The kingdom is, first and foremost, the rule and reign of God in people's hearts. People who submit to God's rule and reign, of course, make up the church but we need to guard against institutionalizing what is an intensely personal concept. It is a mistake to read verses 18-22 as if Peter, Andrew, James and John had never met Jesus, He simply walked by and they dropped everything to follow a complete stranger. John 1:35ff shows us they knew and followed Jesus at some level prior to this call. This is, therefore, a request for them to permanently come and remain with Jesus from now on to be trained as apostles. They are willing to do so immediately (verse 22).

5-6 - The Sermon on the Mount is easily the greatest sermon ever preached. Trying to cover it in a few paragraphs here is simply a travesty, and we are surely only touching the "hem of the garment." A key theme to watch for is "more than the scribes and Pharisees." Traditional religion, with its desire to curry men's favor, just didn't work for Jesus. The citizens of His kingdom would have to do better. They would have to sincerely seek God with attitudes well captured in the Beatitudes (verses 1-12). Verse 18's "jot and tittle" references the two smallest strokes of a Hebrew letter. Jesus cared deeply about Scripture, didn't He? Verse 29 is not to be taken literally but instead to show how important cutting off anything that would pull down our spirituality really is. Make the sacrifices necessary to be pure and serve God! Verse 39 puzzles, but Jesus is simply saying that we must show in our actions that we love all, as mandated in verse 43.

Applications from This Week's Readings

The personal applications from the Sermon on the Mount just pour forth. Jesus stresses character, heart and pure devotion in every line. The serious disciple would do well to find the section of the Sermon that wounds him or her the deepest and then pray over and study that section repeatedly. This is, in a very real way, the constitution of the Kingdom. If we want to be part of Jesus' kingdom this is who we must be. Ask yourself again and again: am I what Jesus requires? Does my heart reflect the values of His Kingdom? Back to Table of Contents.

Week 30 - Matthew 6-10

Chapter 6 makes plain that righteousness to be seen of men is valueless before God (verses 1-8). Some ask about fasting today (verse 16) but Jesus isn't binding fasting. He is only regulating a very common custom. It is not wrong to fast, but it must not be done to gain the accolades of others. Verse 21 stands as a huge key to the whole Sermon: it is the heart that matters most. Again, we need to be careful with verse 33. This means I need to seek God's reign in my life first, that I need to let God rule me first, over any other concern of life.

7:1 may be the most misused verse in all of Scripture. Everyone is more than ready to quote "Don't judge me!" but isn't even saying "Don't judge me" a judgement that you have been judged by another? Jesus' words prohibit hypocritical judging, not all judging of every kind (see John 7:24). Indeed, verse 6 requires some judging! Verses 21-22 tells of those who are polite, orthodox, fervent and spectacular in their religion, but they are wrong. We do well to think about that.

8 - Matthew begins a section here of nine miracle stories, arranged in groups of three. In between there are some short sayings of Jesus focusing on discipleship's demands. These miracles are also in Mark but they are shorter here, really putting Jesus "front and center" so we see His power and authority. He has absolutely irresistible authority. Verse 4's call for silence is explained when we realize that Jesus' fame spread quickly enough without any help. Further, Jesus wanted people to listen to His message, not just seek His miracles. Note how Jesus is uncompromising in verses 18-22. Following Jesus must not take a backseat to anything. Mark and Luke mention only one demoniac while Matthew has two (verse 28). Matthew may make mention of them both because Jesus law required two witnesses and this is a Gospel to Jews. This well illustrates how the Gospels do not contradict but rather complement each other. Mark and Luke focus on one man because they want to give more detail about him (but speaking of one doesn't mean there wasn't another) while Matthew identifies two because that fits the purposes of his gospel.

9 - Jesus quotes Hosea in verse 13, urging the Pharisees to stop dead ritualism and really live as God's people. The teachings of verses 14-17 discuss what is appropriate to do. Some things just don't "fit," they "aren't done" because it isn't the right time for them. Verses 18-26 have the marvelous "miracle within a miracle" story, and show Jesus' power over even death. Verse 34 and verse 36 stand together to show the failure of the religious leadership of the day. Verse 38 urges prayer but we will see that those who are praying become those who are sent in chapter 10.

10 - This is the Limited Commission. Jesus' work cannot be done by Him alone so He commissions other to assist Him. Many of these verses are very famous and are often read in isolation. Read together they form a powerful set of teachings about how disciples will never be popular, but should instead expect persecution (verses 15-28, 34-39). In that persecution they should be certain God will care for them (verses 29-30, 40-42) and be determined to never give up or recant. Verses 32-33 are the keynotes of this chapter. Notice how any act of service, even a very small one, matters to Jesus if our motivation is right in doing it (verse 42).

Applications from This Week's Readings

One of the themes in this section of Matthew is rejecting Jesus. Look over the reason and list reasons why people refused and rejected Jesus. How do people refuse Jesus today? Why do they reject Him? Are you with those who receive Jesus and His teachings or do preconceived ideas, a love for tradition, or other problems hinder you from accepting Him? Back to Table of Contents.

Week 31 - Matthew 11-15

11 - Why John has doubts has long been a cause of speculation (verse 3). Perhaps Jesus wasn't acting like John the Messiah would. Jesus' answer is clear: I am doing what the Messiah was prophesied to do (verse 5). Verse 12 is difficult. It may mean the kingdom has always been attacked by violent men, but others translate it "pressing forward vigorously" meaning men like John the Baptist and their hard work push the kingdom forward. Do not mistake verses 28-30 to mean Christianity is easier than Judaism. Jesus contrasts the ways of Pharisees and all they had added to the Law with knowing Him and being in relation with Him. Obeying Jesus is a delight when we truly trust Him. We serve gladly and His burden is light when we want to serve because we know Jesus! It's not about less demanding law but about a relationship with Christ.

12 - Verses 1-8 have been mistakenly used to prop up situation ethics but such cannot work. First, the apostles are not starving to death, they are just hungry. Secondly, Jesus says David did wrong. All this section shows is that Jesus' opponents attack Him for violating their traditions when they are unwilling to speak against David who violated God's law. Verse 15 shows Matthew tying miracles to the Suffering Servant of Isaiah, quoting Isaiah in verses 17-21. This speaks of the gentle spirit of the Messiah. People are always concerned they may have done what verse 32 says can never be forgiven, but in context it is easy to understand what is meant. Jesus casts out a demon, and His enemies acknowledge He did so (verses 22-23) but then ascribe it to the devil's power (verse 24). Such is ridiculous, Jesus says (verses 25-30). Then Jesus says the heart that refuses to see what such miracles mean is a hardened heart that will never turn to God to ask forgiveness, and so cannot be forgiven. This means that one who is concerned about having committed the sin of verse 32 is showing the very opposite quality of heart and therefore cannot have so sinned! Jesus statements about demons (verses 43-45) raise many questions, but this isn't Demonology 101. Jesus wants the Jews to see they must turn fully to God or things will only get worse. John prepared the way, Jesus taught, but many were not really receiving God's work. Refusing God only leads to more hardness of heart and a person who is worse off than before.

13 - This great chapter has eight parables in it as well as the explanation for why Jesus told parables. In verses 11-12 it may seem Jesus doesn't want people to understand His teaching but that is, of course, not the case. The point is some don't want to understand. Their hearts are not right (verse 15) so they just don't get it. The parable of the sower becomes then the model for all how all parables work. As Jesus' words fall on different kinds of hearts different results must be expected from each kind of hearer. The parable of the tares (verses 24-30, 36-43) warns us about fake disciples. The parables of the mustard seed and leaven (verses 31-35) show how from small beginnings great things can happen. The hidden treasure and pearl of great price parables (verses 44-46) speak of the value of the kingdom. The chapter concludes with the parable of the dragnet (verses 47-50) which is similar to the parables of the tares. Finally Jesus tells how a scribe that knew the Old Law would find new things in it as he saw it now through the lens of the Messiah (verses 51-52). This is a strong contrast to verses 14-15. Finally, watch how Jesus, when explaining parables, didn't make every detail mean something. Parables illustrate one or two truths. Trying to make them an allegory in which everything stands for something twists them out of shape.

14 - Verse 1 tells of Herod Antipas, the son of the Herod that tried to kill baby Jesus. These verses about John (verses 3-12) show how controversy over divorce and remarriage has been a constant in human history. John lost his life because he would not compromise the truth. The

feeding of the 5000 comes about because of Jesus' compassion for people (verse 14). Verse 25's "fourth watch" would be between 3 AM and 6 AM. What a desperate situation the disciples were in! Verse 33 reminds us how powerful Jesus' miraculous control of wave, water and wind really was.

15 - Jesus is now drawing attention from important leaders, who travel all the way from Jerusalem to "check Him out" (verse 1). They duel over Jesus' unwillingness to bind their man-made rules about hand washing (verse 2). The bigger issue, Jesus says, is how their rules form convenient loopholes so people can evade the law of God and still justify themselves (verses 3-9). The example here is of a man dedicating his property to the temple (when he died), but since the law forbade breaking one's vows he then certainly couldn't use that property to support his parents, so ... tough luck, mom and dad, I can't help you! Jesus then goes to Gentile territory and meets a Gentile woman with a great need (verses 21-28). We gasp at Jesus' seeming harshness and unwillingness to help, but text cannot show us Jesus' tone of voice or the twinkle in His eye as He tested her faith. She knew Jesus would help her if she persisted and so she did and He did!

Applications from This Week's Readings

As we read Matthew the seed is being sown and our reaction to it will reveal what kind of soil our hearts are. Do we accept Jesus as the Messiah, the Son of God? If so, are we bearing fruit as we let that reality control everything about our walk of life? Am I good soil? Do I bear fruit for Jesus? Back to Table of Contents.

Week 32 - Matthew 16 - 20

16 - The theme of rejection and bad hearts continues. Such will receive no sign except the sign of Jesus' resurrection, called here the sign of Jonah (verse 4). That would be quite a sign for the Pharisees who plotted His death, and for the Sadducees who didn't believe in the resurrection of the dead! Jesus announces His plans to build "His church" in verses 18-19. He may mean here that He will build it using the leadership of Peter (something that certainly comes to pass in Acts) or that He will build the church on the confession Peter makes, i.e., the truth that He is the Son of God. Peter's insight didn't come from human wisdom ("flesh and blood") but from God revealing it to Him in the person of Jesus Christ (verse 17). Jesus did and said the things that ought to have convinced honest people who He was _ and it did convince Peter. We are quick to note Peter was not the first pope and that is certainly true. We should be as quick to see the church here is people who accept Jesus as God's Son, not a giant institution. The kingdom is of people! Peter's flash of brilliance earlier is replaced by complete misunderstanding in verse 22. Peter doesn't realize it but there can be no crown for the Christ without the cross. Jesus immediately links His church with His suffering (verse 21), something the disciples really struggle with.

17 - Jesus has told of His death but now the disciples see His glory. The Transfiguration is a glimpse of things to come. Peter blunders again, and is told Jesus has the preeminence over even great men like Elijah and Moses (verse 5). Then the disciples come off the mountain top to find trouble (verses 14-21). The demon possessed boy evidently intimidated the apostles into weakness and fear. Verse 20 shouldn't be taken literally, but clearly says that persistent faith that doesn't give up in the face of tough circumstances can accomplish much because it is linked to a great God who can do so much in His time and in His way.

18 - Jesus' call to be like a child (verse 3) has provoked every excursion into the good qualities of children, but His point is clear in verse 4. Jesus is talking about humility. Kids have little power, wealth, rank or authority. Does verse 10 teach that everyone has his own personal protector, i.e. a guardian angel? No, it simply says that angels are involved in watching out for our welfare, and while society dismisses children as unimportant God cares deeply for them. Every soul matters to God, which Jesus emphasizes in the parable of verses 10-14. Those that do run over and harm brethren are subject to specific disciplinary procedures, which God Himself says He will honor and attend (verses 18-20). Of course, a brother who repents must be forgiven, as verses 21-35 well shows.

19 - Verse 1 marks the final turning point, as Jesus sets Himself to go to Jerusalem. Watch His tone become more urgent as He warns the apostles what will happen there. Read verses 1-9 carefully and without preconceived notions and you may well be amazed that such a clear text has engendered so much controversy. The Lord avoids the squabbling of rabbis and goes back to God's original intention for the home (verses 4-6) to announce that God's plan was for one man and one woman to wed for a lifetime, with one and only one cause for divorce. Let us say (and live) what Jesus teaches here! In verse 16 we meet a good man who has done lots of good deeds but who has no place at the center of his heart for God. He is utterly unacceptable to the Lord in such a state. This bears much thought in our affluent world today.

20 - Verse 3's "third hour" would be 9:00 A.M. as the day began at 6:00 A.M. The parable of unexpected reward well illustrates Jesus' guarantee of rewards for His followers (19:28ff). Here we realize again how God doesn't do as humans do, and that should be a cause of much rejoicing. The parable of grace is interrupted by sober warnings in verses 17-19. Jesus is very

emphatic here. Coming right out of that James and John's mother show that the apostles don't have a clue what Jesus means (verses 20-28). They are still dreaming of earthly glory, palaces and thrones and wanted to be sure they got theirs. They will receive ample suffering, Jesus says, but the Kingdom won't be like they think. Matthew ends the chapter with two blind men. Mark and Luke only tell of one (Bartimaeus, Mark 10:46), but Jewish law requires two witnesses so Matthew tells of both men. Here are two who see Jesus as the Son of David and Messiah (verse 31).

Applications from This Week's Readings

18:10's reference to angels makes a good place for us to remember all God does for His children. We may not always understand what angels do or how they do their tasks, but they are for us and we should thank God for them. Read the following verses: Heb 1:14; Luke 15:10; Gal 3:19; 1 Peter 1:12. Angels, those incredible creatures of power and might, are interested in us and serve us! Let us not react to the wrong ideas about angels all around us by discounting them or deciding they have no place to play. God cares for us and He uses even the power of angels to execute His commands on our behalf! Thank God _ for angels. <u>Back to Table of Contents.</u>

Week 33 - Matthew 21-25

21 - This is one of Jesus' most deliberate actions. He clearly wants people to see Him as the Messiah of Zechariah 9:9-10. The crowd recognizes the statement Jesus is making (verse 9), but they don't seem to realize that if Jesus were coming to start a war with Rome He would ride a war horse, not a donkey. Jesus is a king, but not the kind they expect or want. The religious leaders continue to show their disdain for the common people (verse 16), the very ones who "get it." The withered fig tree (verses 18-22) doesn't represent Jesus throwing a fit of anger, but instead the nation of Israel that promised fruit but didn't deliver (note the connection at verse 43). We see more bad hearts in the dishonesty of verse 27, and in Jesus' pointed parables that close the chapter.

22 - The parables of Jesus are increasingly dark and violent, aren't they? The parable of the wedding feast (verses 1-14) is crystal clear in its meaning and application, but it speaks of a happy time that is marred by foolish and ungrateful citizens. The opposition to Jesus is becoming so pronounced that the Pharisees and Herodians join forces to attack Jesus in verses 15-22. Since the Pharisees were so concerned about law keeping and the Herodians were a political group these are strange allies! The Sadducees fail equally to trap Jesus (verses 23-33). Notice how Jesus makes His entire argument about the validity of the resurrection off the tense of one word in verses 32. God doesn't say "I was the God of Abraham, Isaac and Jacob" but "I am" meaning they are still alive. Being careful with Scripture and trusting that even the very tenses of verbs are inspired is to treat the Scripture like Jesus did. The chapter concludes with Jesus asking the questions. How can David's son be greater than David (verse 43)? Such couldn't be, unless of course, the Son of David, the Messiah, was Deity as Jesus was and is. Jesus is the explanation for Psalm 110, a passage that puzzled the rabbis but is now crystal clear.

23 - Verse 5's phylacteries were small cases or boxes that held a small piece of paper with scripture written on it. They were fastened to the wrist and forehead. The Pharisees were making these large so all would see them. Verses 9-10 do not condemn all titles but rather the seeking of titles, and undue emphasis on them. Jesus forbids tricky wording to get out of our promises in verses 16-22. Verse 23 tells us the Pharisees' problem: not law-keeping, but law keeping without putting first things first.

24 - The disciples are impressed with the Temple (verse 1). Herod's remodeling of Ezra's temple was impressive. Some stones were used that were as large as 20 to 40 feet in length and weighed more than 100 tons! The disciples wondered how such a structure, especially since it was God's Temple, could ever be desolated as Jesus said in 23:38? The chapter has provoked much speculation but if we kept the time frame Jesus gave in verse 34 before us, along with an understanding that Jesus is using Old Testament language the Olivet Discourse is not nearly so difficult. Remember as well that the disciples didn't understand Jesus would leave so they are surely not asking about the Second Coming! We must be content to see this chapter speaking of the destruction of Jerusalem by the Romans in AD 70. Verse 15 has "abomination of desolation" (from Daniel 12:11), but the parallel account in Luke 21:20 has "armies of Rome," making the term clear. Verses 27-30 throw many off because they aren't familiar with Old Testament judgement language. Read Isaiah 13:10, 13; 19:1; Ezekiel 32:7-8 and Amos 8:1-2 to see these metaphors of doom used of other cities and nations. Jesus concludes His warnings with strong words to be constantly ready (verses 36-51).

25 - Part of every Jewish wedding was the delay when the groom went to get the bride. It was

considered rude to be unprepared when they finally came. We may wonder why they didn't open the door in verse 11 but night was the hour of thieves, and these had insulted the groom by not being ready. This parable is often connected to Jesus' Second Coming but in context more directly relates to the destruction of Jerusalem. However its principles well apply to the coming that we should be ready for, Jesus' return. Verse 15 gives us a measure of money, not skills and abilities. The key in the parable is verse 26. The one talent man is rebuked for laziness. Jesus doesn't want His followers doing nothing while they await the Roman armies, or His Second Coming. They should be active in kingdom business. The third parable here does seem to be about the Second Coming. Notice how all nations are gathered (verse 32), and Jesus speaks of everlasting fire (verse 41), everlasting punishment and eternal life (verses 46).

Applications from This Week's Readings

Much of our reading has been about the judgment of God - either on the city of Jerusalem in AD 70 or even the final Judgment Day. Look carefully at what Jesus says about judgement in chapter 25. On that great Day will you be with the sheep or goats? Back to Table of Contents.

Week 34 - Matthew 26-28

26 - Matthew stresses how Jesus is in control of everything and will not be taken by surprise by His enemies (verse 1). Verses 6-12 record a simple act of kindness by Mary (see John 12:3) that cannot be measured in terms of dollars and cents. Verse 18 shows Jesus making secret preparations for the Last Supper. Judas will not know in advance where the Passover will be eaten, so he cannot betray Jesus there. The verses instituting the Lord's Supper (verses 26-29) set it squarely in the Passover. Jesus is doing nothing less than replacing the feast that memorialized when Israel became the covenant people of God with a "feast" that memorializes the act that gives everyone a chance to be an "Israelite." For so long, the Passover and its sacrificial lamb had pointed to Jesus and now that fulfillment was at hand. Watch the close ties between blood, covenant and forgiveness of sins as well. Verse 30's hymn would be from Psalms 115-118. Notice in verses 53-56 that Jesus is not held by the arresting soldiers, but by His determination to complete His mission. In verses 69-75 Peter fails spectacularly. If the Bible were only a tale made up by humans would one of its heroes act like this?

27 - After already suffering through mock trials before the Sanhedrin, Jesus is now dragged over to Pilate because the Jews did not have the right to execute lawbreakers (verse 1). Isn't it interesting that the Sanhedrin is worried about unlawful money in the treasury when they aren't concerned about lying and murder (verse 5)? Jesus' quiet dignity and courage impresses Pilate (verse 14), even while it is clear that nothing Jesus can say will stop the proceedings. Barabbas was a rebel (John 18:40), so it may not be surprising that the crowd would prefer a "freedom fighter" over Jesus. Verse 27's Praetorium would be in the Fortress Antonio, built in the corner of the Temple. Verse 45 tells us it was noon. The veil in the temple was some sixty feet tall, and was torn from the top down, not from the bottom up as humans would (verse 51). Access to God and forgiveness of sins has been obtained at Calvary! Verse 52 seems strange, and we are unsure of all it means, but clearly Jesus' death was momentous.

28 - Matthew's gospel ends with a bang. Even though Jesus had consistently been saying He would rise again no one seems to have taken Him seriously. So Matthew highlights everyone's unexpected joy and elation (verses 8-9). He also answers a vicious lie that was circulating about the resurrection (verse 15) and then records the Great Commission (verses 18-20). The story of Jesus ends, but what Jesus began goes on.

Introduction to 1 Corinthians - Paul founded this church in Acts 18:1-7, on the third missionary journey. He stayed 18 months. After leaving Corinth he received word of troubles and of questions about his teaching. This epistle is a virtual Q & A session, with Paul trying to help this church get things righted. It was probably written in the late 50's AD.

1 - Isn't it interesting that with all the problems Corinth had Paul begins with unity (verse 10)? Some try to use verse 17 to negate baptism's importance, but in the context it is clear Paul did baptize (verses 14, 16) and that his concern is party-ism and division. Paul then begins speaking to the issue of human thought and wisdom, pointing out that no man can know God's will by human reasoning (verses 18-31). God does differently than humans would expect!

2 - As Paul continues working with the idea of God's wisdom versus man's wisdom you can still hear accusations against his apostolic authority (verse 1). Verse 7's "mystery" means something that cannot be known without God revealing it. How does God reveal His will, the mystery? Through the words the Holy Spirit gave inspired men (verse 13). Notice that it is not just the concepts of the Bible that are inspired, but the very words. Unfortunately, the "natural man"

(verse 14) will not hear God's revelation. This verse does not mean the Spirit must directly aid us to understand the Bible, but that we must be willing to listen to God's Word.

Applications from This Week's Readings

What simple acts do we fail to do because we are concerned about what others will say of us or the cost of the sacrifice? Mary didn't miss her chance (26:6-13). Pray and ask God for an opportunity to serve someone this week _ and then seize upon it! Back to Table of Contents.

Week 35 - 1 Corinthians 3-7

3 - Verse 1 ties to chapter 2 with the key idea of "spiritual." The Corinthians were not listening to God's revelation but were instead carnally minded. Verse 4 picks up the troubles mentioned in 1:12. Paul is still working with the problem of division, although he has expanded on that to include being spiritually immature (the root of Corinth's division). Verses 14-15 reinforce verses 6-7. If those we teach go astray that is a loss, but the teacher doesn't lose his/her salvation for it!

4 - Again we hear the undertones of an attack on Paul's apostleship (verse 1). Verse 4 stands as a crucial point for all disciples. There is such concern today about what everyone else thinks of us, but that doesn't really matter, does it? Instead we need to listen to the Lord's revelation, the Bible (verse 6). We can't hear Paul's voice in verses 8-10 but it is clear that he is being sarcastic. The Corinthians boasted of so much yet needed help from the very ones they deemed themselves superior to: the apostles, especially Paul. Of course, Paul doesn't want them to just feel badly (verse 14) but to change. Notice the "not-but" construction in verse 14. The "not" phrase doesn't mean "absolutely none of this" or "not at all" but "this is not as important, don't emphasize this." The "but" phrase is where the writer's emphasis lies. Watch for this construction as it is common in the New Testament (note John 6:27 where Jesus is not saying "don't work" but emphasizing spiritual priorities).

5 - This chapter and chapter six deal with Corinth's refusal to get involved in its own troubles and sort them out. Here a man is in scandalous sexual sin, perhaps with his step-mother (verse 1) and the congregation is doing nothing about it. Verse 5 is difficult. It may be like the idea in Romans 1 that "God gave them up." Paul makes a play on the Passover and unleavened bread as he urges Corinth to purge out the attitude of tolerance toward sin (verses 6-8).

6 - We naturally wonder how Christians will judge the world (verse 2). In some sense we reign with Christ and will, evidently, participate in judging with Him. We should just accept it and wait to see how it works out! Verse 12 begins a little tangent on several linked matters: sexual immorality, idolatry and eating meat that had been sacrificed to idols. Paul will address all of these matters in the chapters to follow, so perhaps this is a kind of introduction and summary.

7 - This chapter contains some of the longest and most fully developed teachings on marriage in the New Testament. Understanding it in light of the "present distress" (verse 26) is essential. History tells us these were uncertain times in the world, with famine and shortages rampant. Further, persecution was breaking out against the church. This would not be a good time to pursue marriage, but Paul wants to be clear that marriage is not sinful or "less holy." Some have decided that we can ignore Paul's recommendations (verse 12) because they are not from Jesus, but Paul is an inspired apostle! He goes on to develop that Christianity does not change our outward relations in life (verses 17-24). Verses 36-38 are difficult because we are not sure if this is speaking of an engaged person or the father who gives his daughter in marriage. Whoever Paul is speaking of, it is still clear that Paul's main point is carried through: marriage may be difficult just now, but it is not sinful.

Applications from This Week's Readings

This week's readings highlight the value of God's revelation, the Bible. We simply cannot know the mind of God without Him revealing it to us (2:11-12). Thus, we should be very thankful for the Word. Second, we should be very determined to read this revelation and find out about God! Make certain as you read that you count the Bible as inspired, and as the source for the information we need of our Creator. Make a list of what you have learned of God just from 1 Corinthians. Back to Table of Contents.

Week 36 - 1 Corinthians 8-12

8 - Chapters 8-10 discuss the idea of Christian liberty using the example of meat that was offered to idols. Much of the meat available in the New Testament world would have been from idol temples. Could a Christian eat such? What if he/she had formerly been an idol worshiper? Do Christians have the liberty to eat such meat? Paul says Christians do, but they need to be careful how they use that right so as to not cause others to sin (verse 9). "Cause to offend" doesn't mean hurt feelings here. It means "tempted into sin." Christians must not help the devil do his evil work!

9 - If anyone at Corinth wonders if Paul will practice what he preaches (8:13), he now details how he has done exactly what he urges on them: give up liberty for others. Paul has given up the right to be supported by Corinth so that money wouldn't be an issue between them (verse 15). Paul will give up anything to "win the more" (verse 22). He disciplines himself as he is asking the Corinthians to do to win the prize of heaven (verses 25-27).

10 - Paul is sure that while eating idol-sacrificed meat isn't wrong, some at Corinth need to be careful about this liberty lest they fall back into idolatry (verses 14ff). The Israelites had great blessings and were God's people but idolatry was a huge stumbling block for even them (verses 1-5). So don't be proud and arrogant, but watch out (verses 6-13). Paul closes the chapter with very direct answers to questions that would arise in day to day living in an idolatrous culture. Verse 23 doesn't mean there is no such thing as sin, but in the area of liberty where all is lawful, not everything is helpful. Meat from idol temples was lawful to eat, but that didn't mean everyone should eat it.

11 - The first sixteen verses of this chapter are famous for their perplexity. Yet it is not that hard to understand what Paul is saying here. Some women in Corinth needed to be covered when they prayed and prophesied. Men should not be covered when praying. The difficulty is knowing exactly what the covering for women is, and how much of this chapter is applicable to today. Does Paul want women today to be covered? Is the covering an artificial veil, a woman's hair, or even more specifically, long hair on women? While these questions (and many others) cannot all be worked out in this brief format the reader needs to carefully study these matters. Verse 5 speaks of women praying and prophesying. Where is this going on? Paul will forbid women doing this in the common assembly in chapter 14, so where was this being done? Verse 6 seems to say something about the customs of that day, but there is uncertainty even about what those were. Verse 10 is extremely difficult. Paul then addresses another problem at Corinth: turning the Supper into a common meal that featured class distinctions based on income (verses 17-34)! Some are confused by verse 27. It does not refer to the worthiness of the participant, but instead references a taking which fails to give the respect to the Supper that it deserves. It is to take the Supper in an irreverent way. Those that do so just bring judgment upon themselves (verse 29), and become spiritually weak if not dead (verse 30).

12 - Discussing the Lord's Supper (11:18-34) leads Paul to another aspect of worship and questions from the brethren at Corinth: spiritual gifts. This will occupy his attention for the next three chapters. Obviously things are out of control, as some are saying "Jesus is accursed" and then that the Spirit made them say such (verse 3)! Early on Paul introduces the idea that all the differing spiritual gifts are needed (verse 7), an important point for a church infatuated with one gift, tongue speaking. The gift of faith in verse 9 cannot be the saving faith required of all Christians but must be an additional measure of faith, perhaps giving one a very tough faith.

Verse 13 is difficult to translate (baptized by the Spirit or in the Spirit?) and equally hard to understand. "By the Spirit" is used in verses 3 and 9 to mean "under the influence of" and that may be the sense here. "Drink the Spirit" is difficult, but Paul's point is clear: the Corinthians have all had the same experience, are all Christians, are all one body and so must act in a unified way. Verse 22's "weaker members" references our internal organs. They cannot survive outside the body, and are not as sturdy as fingers or hair, but are indispensable to the body.

Applications from This Week's Readings

Think again about matters of liberty and our example as discussed in chapters 8-10 of this week's reading. Can you think of matters that are not necessarily wrong but are not wise to engage in? How concerned are you about your influence, and what other (possibly weaker) Christians see in you? Do we imagine we are impervious to temptation and so are reckless, just ready to fall into sin like Israel of old? Back to Table of Contents.

Week 37 - 1 Corinthians 13-16; 2 Corinthians 1

13 - Paul now presses the Corinthians to pursue something greater than spiritual gifts: the way of love. Without love all is vain (verses 1-4), and love is permanent while spiritual gifts are passing away (verses 8-13). Verses 8-10 are key verses in understanding spiritual gift's duration. Paul speaks of the revelation gifts - prophecy, knowledge (not just any kind of knowledge but supernaturally given knowledge, see 12:8) and tongues - and says this means of revelation will cease when "the perfect comes" (verse 10). Logically "the perfect" can only refer to a full measure of whatever "the partial" is. So Paul says "we have partial revelation with these gifts. Someday we will have full revelation and not need them." That full revelation is the completed New Testament.

14 - Verse 2 tells us that when no interpreter was present only God could understand a tongue-speaker, so he speaks "to God." In verse 5 Paul begins to develop the theme that gifts are for edifying others, not getting attention for self, and must be used for edification. Verse 14 indicates that the mind and spirit must work together for prayer to be correct. Spoken words can have great power, as when one preaches (prophesying is speaking for God) and an unbeliever is convicted by the Word of God (verse 24). Paul's injunction against women speaking in church (verse 34) has been often misunderstood. It cannot mean a woman can never say anything in church, lest she be unable to sing. "Silent" is the same word as in verse 28, where a tongue speaker without an interpreter is told to be silent. That did not mean he was to say nothing, but to keep silent regarding his tongue speaking. Similarly, verse 34 doesn't mean a woman can never say a word in the assembly but that she be silent regarding the questions some were interrupting the assembly with (note verse 35).

15 - Paul changes gear here, now dealing with problems about the resurrection. Some in Corinth were saying there was no resurrection of the dead (verse 12), so Paul logically applies that to Jesus (verse 13), showing how that would undercut all of Christianity (verses 14-19). Paul likes the "through one" analogy (and will use it in Romans). Here he compares Adam's one act of sin that brought death to Christ's one act (the cross) that brings salvation and life (verses 21-22). Verse 29 is notoriously difficult. Paul's point, in the context of talking about the resurrection, seems to be "Why are we baptized if we just die and are no more? Are we just baptized to be numbered among the dead who never rise?" His wording is difficult however. The practice of baptism for dead unbelievers who are lost has arisen from this verse, but other verses clearly teach that no one can obey the Gospel for someone else (see 2 Corinthians 5:10).

16 - Verses 1-2 give authoritative information on how a church is to raise money. Some have tried to assert that the treasury can only be used for benevolence (its use here) but other passages supply more information about all the scriptural uses of the treasury (see Philippians 4:15). Paul closes with travel plans and the names of fellow workers. These verses put a very human face on the New Testament church, and on this grand apostle who had to concern himself not only with doctrine and revelations but also mundane matters like ship schedules and financial support (verse 6's "send" means financial support).

Introduction to 2 Corinthians - After reading 1 Corinthians we marvel at a church with so many problems, and we wonder if the first letter helped. 2 Corinthians tells the "rest of the story," letting us know that some things did improve, but in other areas the situation was worse. Key themes are the genuineness of Paul's apostleship, the collection for the poor Jewish saints in Jerusalem, and his deep love for the Corinthians.

1 - Verse 6 figures into Paul's "we suffer for you because we love you" theme. Paul's afflictions are the trials and persecutions he endures so he can bring the Gospel to people like the Corinthians. When he is comforted that is for them too _ they benefit from learning of his example. Verses 9-10 reference some terrible peril Acts doesn't record. Verse 12 gives the first hint that some are challenging Paul's apostleship and conduct. Verse 15 alerts us that some of the attack was based on Paul changing travel plans. Verse 22 is famous for spawning all kinds of wild ideas about the Holy Spirit. The emphasis, however, is on ownership and certainty. "Sealed" speaks to ownership, while "deposit" speaks of an escrow or guarantee of full payment in the future. The sealing may be miraculous gifts (a very public sign that one was a Christian, owned by God) or might even refer to baptism, the act by which God takes one as His own. The deposit of the Spirit probably refers to being in relationship with Deity, a relationship that will be fully developed in heaven. Being in Christ, in the Father, and in the Spirit now is only a taste (a deposit) of what is to come, but none of these relationships are mystical or spooky. We have relationship with God when we are obey His word and abide in it (note John 15:7; 1 John 3:24).

Applications from This Week's Readings

This last section of Corinthians and the beginning of 2 Corinthians reminds us how far from what God desires the church can go. The Corinthians needed to return to the pattern, and obey the instruction of the Lord as given by this inspired apostle. Do we assume we "have it made" and fail to continually check our teaching and practice against the New Testament standard?
Back to Table of Contents.

Week 38 - 2 Corinthians 2-6

2 - It is very difficult to work out all the "when" of Paul's travels and writings. Verse 1's "sorrowful visit" does not seem to be mentioned in Acts. But we learn here that since that visit didn't go well he wrote 1 Corinthians (mentioned in verse 4) while at Ephesus (1 Cor 16:8) and sent it with Titus (2 Cor 7:6-8). Anxious to hear how they received that letter he set off over land to find Titus (verses 12-13). Chapter 7 will tell how he found Titus and heard good news about their reception of 1 Corinthians. However, before Paul gets to that he has a long digression that lasts from 2:14-7:4. In this material Paul talks about his work as an apostle, beginning it with the image of a victory parade (verse 14). Paul sees the Corinthians as proof of his work, and proof that he is not a "peddler" of the Gospel (verse 17).

3 - We need to be careful with verse 6. Many try to make out that carefulness in obedience is legalism and "kills," versus being "free and easy," as in "I just follow the spirit of the law." Paul has no such ideas under consideration here. The "letter" that "kills" is Moses' Law (note verse 7) not careful obedience, which is never condemned in Scripture. The Law of Moses had glory (verses 7-9) but it could not give eternal life and is not as glorious as the Gospel which transforms us into the likeness of Christ (verse 18). "Freedom" in verse 17 is not liberty to do as we please and ignore God's Word, but freedom from the bondage of sin (cf. Romans 6:18-23).

4 - Verse 2 contains an echo of charges against Paul, as does verse 5. Some are false apostles who are treacherous and who do preach themselves. The Corinthians are accepting them and rejecting Paul _ a serious crisis! Verse 7 is a beautiful metaphor. The Gospel is a great treasure placed in lowly containers (human preachers) to show God's power. Verse 10 seems to mean that Paul had physical scars that showed his willingness to suffer for Jesus' (and the Corinthians') sake. Again we hear a theme Paul keeps coming back to in verses 16-18: tough times don't discourage us. We won't quit, Paul says!

5 - How can Paul go on and endure so much? He keeps the goal of heaven before him (verse 1). The imagery here is of clothing, and wanting to be better clothed, i.e. to go to heaven. Again, Paul mentions the Spirit being a guarantee or earnest (verse 5). As in 1:22 this probably just means that the relationship we have with Deity now is a foretaste of the perfect fellowship we will have with the Father, Son and Spirit in that "building not made with hands." So we must remain confident (verse 6) because we have faith (verse 7). All of life must be lived in view of eternity (verses 9-10), which for Paul means he isn't like the false apostles who will do anything to please men. Paul knows it is the judgment of God that matters (verses 11-16). So he preaches the real Gospel, designed to reconcile sinful people with God through Christ (verses 17-21).

6 - As Paul continues his pleading for the Corinthians to accept him he now mentions the hardships he has endured (verses 4-10). Yet it is clear that some at Corinth are not interested in receiving the apostle (verses 11-13). There may be other applications of Paul's admonition of verse 14ff but the context indicates primarily he has in mind pagan worship. We do well to remember that not all attachments with unbelievers are forbidden (see 1 Cor 7:12-16; 10:27). Paul does not want Christians forming attachments that would cause them to compromise their standards or their influence. Again, in this context, he is speaking of going to pagan idol worship.

Applications from This Week's Readings

Two keys emerge from reading 2 Corinthians. First, Paul has an incredible love for his brethren. He will sacrifice almost anything and put up with much hardship to help them know the Lord. Do

I care for my brethren like that? Secondly, Paul is determined to do what is right and never quit doing it, no matter what happens to him. Do I let others or difficult circumstances discourage me? Paul says never, ever, give up

Back to Table of Contents.

Week 39 - 2 Corinthians 7-11

7 - After much pleading Paul rejoins the material he began in 2:13 when he spoke of sending Titus to them. Verse 4 says he found Titus and Titus told him the brethren had received 1 Corinthians very well, even repenting! Paul is overjoyed (verses 6-7)! Real repentance may require making one feel bad but godly sorrow is a good thing because it brings about the repentance that saves souls (verses 9-10).

8 - Having been refreshed to hear such good news Paul now talks about another area of concern: the collection for the poor saints in Jerusalem. The Macedonian brethren to the north were giving in an extremely generous way (verses 2-4), because they first gave themselves (verse 5). Corinth had started this collection vigorously and with great intentions but they hadn't persevered and continued like they should (verses 6, 10-15). Note the way Paul motivates better giving: by appealing to the example of Jesus Christ (verse 9). Paul is very concerned that they complete their giving as it is close to time to take the contribution on to Jerusalem. He is sending a famous brother (maybe Luke or Barnabas) who will accompany their gift (verse 18). Paul himself is doing everything necessary to make certain there is no possibility of anyone even thinking there has been "monkey business" with this important contribution (verse 21). Integrity was important to Paul!

9 - The theme of giving continues in this chapter, as Paul urges with the Corinthians to do as they promised so they won't be embarrassed (verse 4). Some of the New Testament's most important teachings about giving are here. Make certain you get the principles of verses 6-7. Don't be misled by the "health and wealth" gospel that preaches giving just to get. This is certainly not what Paul has in mind in verse 6. God does bless us materially but that is so we can share and help others (note verse 11), not hoard up blessings for self and live in luxury. Paul wants the Corinthians to trust that God will take care of them and give freely and liberally. Some have tried to make verse 13 mean the collection was for Christians and non-Christians but this cannot be. In verse 14 Paul says the recipients are praying for the Corinthians. Can non-Christians pray? Further, elsewhere Paul specifically says that Christians will receive these funds (see Romans 15:26). Did Paul lie?

10 - You will note quite a change of tone in this chapter. After hearing from Titus (7:4) Paul seems quite cordial and happy. His admonition about giving in chapters 8 and 9 is light and gentle. Suddenly, we read Paul roaring at the brethren, and his tone is intensely personal. What happened? We are not sure but perhaps more news from Corinth arrived. Clearly some were outright rejecting Paul and his apostleship (note verses 2b, 7, 10). For Paul, everything now seems to be at risk again. So Paul makes a spirited attack on his enemies, sometimes even saying all of this is against his better judgment. The crisis is severe and Paul does not mince words about the troubles there. His critics boost themselves by commending each other and comparing themselves to each other but such is foolish and ungodly (verses 12-18).

11 - There may not be a chapter like this one anywhere in the New Testament! Paul is almost beside himself with concern about the Corinthian situation. False apostles are there, teaching error and telling the Corinthians Paul isn't really an apostle (verse 3-5)! To respond to this Paul uses a considerable dose of sarcasm and some tough talk. Yes, it was true that he didn't take wages from Corinth when he was there (verse 7) but how could that be construed to mean he was

a fraud? He did that to help them (verse 9). The Corinthians seemed captivated by the boasting of the false apostles, but Paul (reluctantly) lists his own accomplishments (verses 16-33) and it is quite a list. Paul is the genuine article, a real apostle of Christ!

Applications from This Week's Readings

Although giving is a crucial part of Christianity we may give little attention to it. Our reading this week places giving front and center, asking us hard questions like "Have I given myself first?," "Do I give purposefully?" and "Am I giving sacrificially and joyfully?" Perhaps the most important question to ask is "Do I see giving as participating in God's work, something that I would beg to do?" The Macedonians are our example in giving, but too often we follow the haphazard ways of Corinth. Pray and consider your giving habits this week. Back to Table of Contents.

Week 40 - 2 Corinthians 12-13; James 1-3

12-13 - In 11:30 Paul mentions weakness. Here he furthers that line of thought as he talks about revelations from God. Did the false apostles claim some grand revelation? Well, Paul had seen some pretty spectacular visions (verses 1-6). Verse 7 makes it clear the "man" Paul knows (verse 2) is indeed Paul. Regrettably there is so much speculation about Paul's "thorn in the flesh" (verse 7) that often Paul's point is badly missed. We need to be content admitting the text doesn't say what the thorn was, and therefore, we cannot and do not know what it was. Therefore, something else must be more important to focus on. Paul's point in verse 10 is exactly where we need to give our attention instead of vain speculation about what we cannot know! Paul says he needs to be dependent upon Christ and that anything that keeps him dependent upon Jesus is welcome. What a lesson! Paul concludes the chapter warning that he is coming (verse 14) and that there need to be some changes there or his coming will be sorrowful for all involved (13:1). The Corinthians may think they have some charges for Paul to answer, but he says it is time for them to do some soul searching to see if they are really disciples or if they have been drawn off course (verse 5). Verse 10 may be the summary verse of the entire epistle: make some changes now!

Introduction to James - This epistle is often called the "Proverbs of the New Testament." It is full of practical teaching, often composed with terms and phrases that Jesus Himself used. There are several James mentioned in the New Testament, but 1:1 probably references the brother of the Lord (1 Cor 15:7; Acts 1:14; 15:13-21; 21:18). He wrote to Jewish Christians living outside of Palestine.

1 - Verses 9-11 show reversal of common thinking. We think of the poor as lowly and the wealthy as exalted, but James turns that around. The rich man in verse 10 is probably not a Christian. He thinks he has so much, but he will fade away (verse 11). Get the contrast from verses 16-17 to verse 13: God doesn't tempt but instead blesses. Verses 19-27 put emphasis on listening to God's Word and then doing it.

2 - Verse 5 sets up the contrast between the way the recipients were judging and how God judges. The Lord has always had an interest in the poor (Proverbs 19:17). It is just so that often the poor can humble themselves and trust God easier than the rich can. Too often the rich attack Christianity and its values (verses 6-7). Note how much of these verses come directly from Luke 6:20ff. Verse 13 is puzzling. The readers need to show mercy to the poor, and should know that those who have been merciful will receive mercy instead of judgement on the Last Day.

3 - The implication of verse 6's "set on fire by hell" is that the devil uses the tongue to do evil. James ends the paragraph on wisdom (verses 13-18) with a proverb about sowing in peace. This makes the contrast to 1:20. Human anger doesn't produce righteousness but peace making will. This sounds a great deal like Jesus in Matthew 5:9.

Applications from This Week's Readings

Think about our world's attitude toward riches and the wealthy. Contrast that with what we have read in James. What is your attitude toward riches? What can you do to move your attitude away from our culture's thinking and toward James' view?

Back to Table of Contents.

Week 41 - James 4-5; 1 Peter 1-3

4 - Verse 2 speaks figuratively of brethren who are quarreling so much it is like they want to kill each other (see Matt 5:21-22). Verse 5 is very difficult to translate and understand. It may mean God opposes arguing and warring and has given us His Spirit (who reveals the Word) to oppose such activity, or that God longs for His people to express love instead of enmity. Verse 12 reminds us that only God has the right to judge.

5 - Verses 1-2 remind us of an Old Testament prophet attacking the rich who enjoy God's blessings but have forgotten Him. Treasure will not save in the day of judgment (verse 3). What do we make of verses 8-9 that sound as if the return of Christ is very soon? We should remember that for the Christian the Lord is as close as our own death. Further, we are to live as if we believe the Lord might come even today. These verses teach that urgency in day to day living. Why should the elders anoint the sick with oil (verse 14)? This famous verse puzzles us, but the explanation may be as simple as oil being used as medicine (see Luke 10:34). Note the "Lord will raise him up" not the oil, so we do well not to put too much emphasis on the oil! Verse 20 should not be taken as a way to "merit" forgiveness but tells us God forgives the one who repents.

Introduction to 1 Peter - Peter's epistle helps Christians, Jewish and Gentile, who were suffering for their faith. Written in the early 60's, perhaps from Rome (see 5:13), the book has a warm and pastoral tone as it encourages Christians to stand fast in a hostile environment.

1 - The churches Peter addresses (verse 1) are mostly in the provinces in the northern part of Turkey. Paul evangelized southern Turkey. Peter appears to have gone north. In verse 5 we see the activity of God (protects) and Christians (through faith, continued belief) coming together to assure salvation. Verse 13 begins the response to God's work by urging us to think and reason with our minds. "Gird up your mind" would be like our expression "roll up your sleeves." Note the indestructible nature of God's word (verses 23-25). What a promise!

2 - Verse 2's reference to the Word as the agent of growth is impressive when we realize there are Gentiles in Peter's audience. These had not grown up with the Old Testament Scriptures but were now admonished to study them. Peter says the Bible counts! Verses 4-8 use stone imagery to describe our relationship to Jesus. This metaphor is common in Scripture (see Isaiah 8:14; 28:16; 51:1, Psalm 118:22; Daniel 2:34). The "cornerstone" is the most important stone in a building. Verse 16 reminds us we are free to choose to serve God. That freedom is expressed, paradoxically, in service, not in selfishness. How do we honor "all men" (verse 17)? Peter means for us to recognize that God made every person and thus every person has value and significance. The chapter closes by appealing to the example of Christ who suffered and served. Read verses 23-25 carefully as they ring with echoes of Isaiah 53.

3 - "Likewise" in verse 1 ties to 2:13, where Peter begins direct admonition about various roles in life. Verse 6 urges women to willingly show their husbands they accept their leadership. Verse 7 challenges men to treat their wives right. Peter ends the section on suffering for righteousness sake (verses 13-17) with one of the most puzzling verses in the NT. What is verse 19 talking about? "The spirits in prison" could be the disobedient of Noah's day but seeing them as disobedient angels better fits the use of the term "spirits" throughout the Bible. It seems that Peter is saying that after the cross Jesus made a proclamation of victory and condemnation to some who previously had rejected God. Even if we don't understand all the specifics the point is

plain: Jesus subjected and triumphed over a difficult "audience" and thus Christians can count on Him to help them win victory, and even to triumph over their foes, as they are persecuted.

Applications from This Week's Readings

1 Peter 1:10-12 tells us that prophets and angels longed to know what we know: how God would reconcile sinners through the Christ. They didn't understand how the Messiah could suffer and be glorified. We do. We are "insiders" while prophets and angels were "outsiders!" The completed Word of God gives us such insight into who God is and how He operates and works. Be thankful for it! Back to Table of Contents.

Week 42 - 1 Peter 4-5; 2 Peter 1-3

4 - Verse 1 connects to 3:18. What are we to do with this information about Christ's suffering? We arm ourselves with the same attitude He had and we die to sin. The thought here is strikingly similar to Romans 6:7. The thought is that we are done with sin. Verse 6 speaks of preaching to the "dead," which probably references people who are spiritually dead. Verse 7's "end of all things is at hand" means the second coming is to be viewed as always impending (see Luke 7:26-27). Therefore we need to control our minds, a common refrain in 1 Peter (see 1:13). Verse 12 revisits the key theme of suffering.

5 - What can Christians look to for support in times of trial? Peter discusses elders and their responsibilities here (verses 1-4), as well as humble mutual support for each other (verse 5). The letter ends by naming Silas (Silvanus, verse 12) as the messenger (not the secretary) for Peter who is carrying the epistle. Verse 13 intrigues us. Was Peter really in Babylon or somewhere else? Because there is some evidence Peter was in Rome many think this is a reference to that city. Mark in verse 13 is John Mark, and is probably Peter's son in the faith.

Introduction to 2 Peter - 2 Peter is a special kind of letter (3:1), called a testament. This kind of literature was common in NT times. Testaments have two kinds of content. They contain admonitions the author wishes to give before dying, and then have some sort of revelation of the future. 2 Peter fits the pattern, with ethical instruction (1:3-11), and then in 2:1-3a; 3:1-4 Peter predicts the future: false teachers will arise. 1:12-15 has typical testament kind of language. Reading this as Peter's "last words" before death makes it powerful and moving. He is deeply concerned about false teachers and so puts inspired pen to paper one last time.

1 - Verse 4 tells of partaking of the divine nature. This may mean we become one with God by being united in purpose, action, sharing in His holiness, etc. Verse 10 contains a tremendous promise to spur our spiritual growth. There are hints of troubles in verse 16. In verse 19 Peter cites the Old Testament record as proof of what is right and true about Jesus. "Morning star" is a reference to Jesus (see Num. 24:17, which was taken as messianic in NT times, also Luke 1:17; Rev. 22:16). Verse 20 follows this by teaching prophecy doesn't originate with the prophet. Since it is a message from God it cannot be molded or interpreted as one desires.

2 - The trouble with false teachers is clearly detailed here. Verses 4-9 show that God can judge evildoers, having even judged angels (verse 4). We do not know anything about these erring angels so speculation is vain (some try to tie this to Genesis 6 but such is mistaken). Angels appear again in verse 11, where Peter says even angelic beings don't try some of the things these false teachers are so confident in. Balaam is the consummate example of a "prophet for hire" and is used that way repeatedly in the NT (verse 15). Read his story in Numbers 22.

3 - Verse 4 finds false teachers reasoning that because Jesus hasn't come yet He isn't coming at all! Peter responds by reminding his readers that God has destroyed the world before (verses 6-7) and will do so again (verses 7-10). How can we hasten the Lord's coming (verse 12)? In this context Peter must mean the preaching that causes repentance! Prayer, of course, would also play a part. The "new heavens and earth" (verse 13) is an expression from Isaiah 65:17-25 (see Rev. 21:1,8,27). It is not meant to be a source of speculation but consolation and motivation to right living (verses 11-12, 14)! Note that Paul's works were considered Scripture in NT times (verses 15-16).

Applications from This Week's Readings

Focus carefully on 2 Peter 3:11. The Lord will come again. Are you living in light of that truth or just holding it as an intellectual doctrine that does not transform you? Pray that you may more clearly understand the priorities that the eventual end of this world dictates. Back to Table of Contents.

Introduction to John - John's gospel is absolutely unique. It begins with a stunning prologue, omits much of the Galilean ministry material found in Matthew, Mark and Luke, and never mentions the church or Lord's Supper. It does have Nicodemus, the Samaritan women, six miracles and tremendous teaching not found in the other Gospels. John's work is carefully crafted to bring us to one conclusion: Jesus is God's Son (John 20:30-31). Hence, his main topic is Jesus as the Messiah.

. - Where to begin talking of Jesus? How about at the beginning? So John affirms Jesus' deity and power, even in creation (verses 1-4). The prologue turns dark when it says people didn't receive Jesus (verse 5) or the witness the Baptist bore to Him (verses 6-11). The whole question of the book is framed in verse 12: will we, the readers, believe? Verse 14 picks up the key Bible theme of God's glory filling the Tabernacle as it says Jesus literally "became flesh and tented among us." Jesus' mission was to "explain" or "make the Father known" to us (verse 18). After this dazzling beginning, John (who never names himself in his gospel) presents the testimony of John the Baptist (verses 19-36). John says his baptism is part of all of his work: to prepare for the coming of the king (verses 26-27). The dawn of the Messianic Age was upon them. The way to get ready was to repent, and baptism was a sign of that repentance. Verse 29 clearly picks up the imagery of Isaiah 53 and applies it to Jesus. We may wonder how John can say he didn't know Jesus (verse 33) but he means as the Messiah. The sign of the dove certified Jesus for John. We don't know what Jesus saw Nathaniel doing (verse 48) but Nathaniel is brought to faith.

2 - Many questions about the miracle at Cana (verses 1-11) detract from its purpose. This is not the place to argue social drinking (note that unfermented grape juice was considered a real delicacy in the NT world), or why Mary was so sure Jesus would do this miracle. The point is found in verse 11: it is a sign. Verse 4's "woman" sounds harsh but the term is not impolite in the original (see 19:26). Verse 13 records Jesus going to the Passover. John has three of these feasts (cf. 6:4; 11:55). Jesus finds banking and business going on in the Temple, obstructing the ability of worshipers to prayer. Note his anger as He drives them out (verses 15-16). The Jews make a crass literal application of Jesus' words in verse 20, missing His point entirely. We must be careful when we listen to Jesus so we can truly hear what He says.

3 - Jesus' interview with Nicodemus is famous (verses 1-15). Nicodemus sort of "gets it" about Jesus (verse 2) but when Jesus challenges him to the radical change necessary to be in the kingdom of God, a change that can only be described as a "new birth" (verse 5) he gets lost. Is that because as a Jew he was quite sure he was already in the kingdom? Verse 5 describes not two baptisms, but one: a "water-Spirit" birth. Jesus is speaking of water baptism. Verse 8 is a mini-parable: just because you can't see it doesn't mean it isn't there. Jesus brings us the information about the kingdom and entrance into it that no one else can because He is from heaven (verse 13). "Lifted up" is a key term in John (verse 14; see also 8:28; 12:32, 34). The language changes in verse 16 indicating that this is probably John's comments (despite the red ink in most Bibles). Note the past tenses and the reference to "God" instead of "My Father." Note the present reality of judgment in verse 18. Judgement and eternal life or death aren't something strictly future for John. Verse 31 refers to Jesus ("from above") and John ("from the earth"). Verse 33 has "seal" in some translations. It means the one who accepts John's testimony agrees with God's testimony.

4 - The story of the woman at the well is just a textbook study in how to patiently bring people

along to faith. A key in the story is Jesus' emphasis on the value of both sowing and reaping (verses 36-38). The person who plants the seed is one with the person reaping in God's eyes. Watch the emphasis on Jesus as the giver of life in verses 50, 51 and 53. Three times we are told the boy was "lives" instead of "was healed." This sets up Jesus' teaching on being able to give life in chapter 5 (note verse 26).

5 - Textual questions about verse 4 abound, as some high quality manuscripts do not contain this verse and it sounds like little more than a local superstition. I do not believe this kind of random healing is consistent with how God heals throughout Scripture. It was believed an angel troubled the water, but that doesn't mean one did so. Verse 11 amazes . Instead of asking about the healing they are totally focused on the violation of their own rules about the Sabbath! Verse 14 does not mean the man was paralyzed due to sin. It means being lost is worse than being a cripple! Jesus' explanation for working on the Sabbath is that God works on the Sabbath (holding all things together, for example) and so He does what His Father does (verse 17). He develops this unity of purpose and work through to the end of the chapter.

Applications from This Week's Readings

Trace out the rejection of the Jews in chapter five. Why won't they believe? How do those barriers prevent faith today? Are you with the Pharisees or do you truly believe in Jesus? Back to Table of Contents.

6 - Verse 4 gives us the time frame: it is about one year to Jesus death. Jesus' sign has some unintended results (verse 15), leading to Jesus' withdrawal (verses 16-25). Notice that signs didn't always work (verse 26). We are foolish to believe that the power to do miracles would result in more conversions today. Jesus challenges His audience to see that Moses didn't feed them, God did and that manna only fed their bodies not their spiritual needs as only He could (verses 32-33). How does the Father draw? See verse 45: "all be taught." What does Jesus mean by "eating His flesh and drinking His blood" (verses 51, 53-56)? Note the exact parallelism in "eat/drink and have eternal life" in verse 54 and verses 35, 40 and 47. Those verses say "believe and have eternal life." Eating and drinking are just figures of speech for believing in Jesus. They don't reference the Lord's Supper. They refer to believing completely and fully on the Lord. That is what brings life. How do we come to believe in Jesus? Verse 63 and 68 tell us: through the Words of life.

7 - Verse 2's feast means it is fall. Many translations have the word "yet" in the margin of verse 8 ("I am not yet going") to explain why Jesus does go to the feast in verse 10. Verse 13 contains the key idea in this section of John: people not believing in Jesus. Verse 23 connects back to the events of 5:1-16 and the charge of breaking Sabbath. Verse 31 shows how signs ought to work. Verses 37-39 are centered in a water ritual that was done on the last day of the Feast of Tabernacles to commemorate God giving Israel water in the wilderness. From Jesus comes living water, which becomes a blessing even for others (verse 38) around the disciple who believes. Verse 42 demonstrates John's command of irony.

8 - The dominant question here is the authenticity of 7:53-8:11. Many scholars argue against it, and it is true that it is not in some very high quality manuscripts. Yet we wonder how such a story could float around for so long and then worm its way into the Bible! There are some evidences for its authenticity and one early writer speaks of its removal for fear of encouraging adultery. We believe it to be part of Scripture. Verse 12 ties again to the Feast of Tabernacles as lights were used in its celebration. Jesus does not just bear witness to Himself (verse 14) but incorporates the testimony of the Father through the signs He does (verse 18). Verse 33 is about spiritual bondage, not political liberty. Jesus' answer to the question of verse 53 is "I don't make myself out to be anything. It is the Father who honors Me!" (verse 54). Verse 58 is a strong claim to deity.

9 - Verse 5 connects to 8:12. We do not know why Jesus anointed the man's eyes with mud (verse 6). Again John confronts us with the evidence of signs (note verses 16, 33).

10 - This chapter continues the controversy and discussion of chapter 9 (note especially verse 21). Jesus is the Good Shepherd in contrast to the wicked Jewish leadership accusing Him. Verse 7 makes it clear Jesus is the way, the only way to gain access to God. Read Ezekiel 36:10-15; 23-24 in connection with verses 11-14. Verse 16 speaks of the Gentiles. The Feast of Dedication (verse 22) celebrates the cleansing of the Temple by the Maccabees in 164 BC. It would be cold so Jesus seeks the shelter of the porches (verse 23). Verse 27 does not prove we hear the literal voice of Jesus today guiding us. "Sheep" is not literal in the verse, why should "voice" be? Further, the Jews heard His voice directly. It is not about hearing but responding and obeying! Jesus' argument from Psalm 82:6 in verse 34 is difficult. The key is to see the charge: "you make yourself God" (verse 33b). Jesus replies (again) that He doesn't make Himself anything, the Father does. Note "to whom the word of God came" (verse 35). This is Israel at Sinai. The rabbis

of Jesus' day understood the 82nd Psalm to mean Israel was given life (power over death) through the Law at Sinai. Israel was believed to have become deathless (beyond death's power) and holy by receiving the Law. If they obeyed its precepts they would live. Israel was called "god" because they were beyond death through Law. Understanding this we can see how Psalm 82 is a perfect defense against the charge that Jesus is making Himself equal with God. Jesus argues if God consecrated Israel and made them holy and deathless so that they may be called "god" then the One whom God consecrated and sent to earth can be called "God." In verse 40 Jesus leaves Jerusalem. He will not return until the final Passover.

Applications from This Week's Readings

John shows stubborn resistance to Jesus all through these chapters. Yet each of us must decide: do I believe in Jesus? Will I "eat His flesh and drink blood," i.e. fully believe in Him or will I turn away from Him? Examine your faith in Christ. How robust is it? What is it based on? How can you strengthen it? Back to Table of Contents.

Week 45 - John 11-15

1 - Verses 9-10 are a puzzling answer to the disciples' objection. They seem to relate to the idea of Jesus having a fixed time ("the day") to do His work. Jesus may even mean that as He walks in the light (doing God's will) He won't stumble but the Jews that attack Him are destined to tumble around in darkness. Again John shows the disciples responding stupidly as they again don't grasp Jesus' full meaning (verse 12). Verse 37 shows Jesus' signs working at least partially. John shows eye-witness knowledge in verse 49, as Caiphas was the high priest then (from AD 18-36). The chapter ends with things at a fever pitch (verses 55-57). Something dramatic is about to happen!

2 - Don't confuse this anointing story (verses 1-8) with Luke 7's story. They are not the same. In verse 7 Jesus' statement may infer that Mary knew Jesus would die and had planned to use this ointment for His burial. Deciding that the enemies of Jesus might prevent her from caring for His body she decided it was now or never, and did this great act of kindness. Verse 10 records incredible unbelief. Verses 12-19 record the Triumphal Entry. This is Sunday of Jesus' last week. What Jesus does is based on Zechariah 9 and is His most obvious and clear claim to be the Messiah. He is, however, not the Messiah they expect. He doesn't ride a war horse but a donkey. He is the King of Peace. Don't miss verse 23. The hour has come! Verses 31-32 tell us four things happen when Jesus dies. He judges the world (condemning sin), casts out the devil (defeating Satan), is exalted ("lifted up"), and draws all men to Himself. How did God blind them (verse 40)? By sending the Light of the world that gave them the chance to believe and live! God does not overrule free will.

3 - Verse 2 mentions Judas to show that Jesus washed even the betrayer's feet. The reference to the devil simply means Judas was tempted to do wrong. He is responsible for his treachery. Note Jesus' certainty in the midst of such a crisis (verse 3). Sadly, some have turned Jesus' acted-out teaching into religious ritual, but the rest of the NT records no such foot-washing ordinances. The lesson is to serve others' real needs, not wash the feet of people who don't even need such a washing today! Verse 18's quotation from Psalms is about Ahithophel, David's trusted counselor who helped Absalom in his rebellion. Verse 19 underlines John's purpose in writing this gospel. Verse 23 speaks of John. He is the "beloved disciple."

14 - Verse 2 is terribly rendered in the KJV and NKJV, causing many to think everyone will have their own mansion in heaven. Yet this is not what Jesus says by any means. The ESV has "in my Father's house are many rooms." Jesus makes it possible for us to live with God, not up the street from Him! The sign/belief theme is found in verse 11. Other verses modify and help our understanding of prayer in verses 13-14. Jesus will speak further of this in chapter 15. Wanting to do God's will modifies what we will ask for (see 15:7). Look at the relationship language of verses 23-24! Note that verse 26 is not a promise to you and I but the apostles. This is often misused today.

15 - Note how the branches are disciples (verse 5), not churches in a denominational structure. That also means that fruit here is not converting people (that would be making more branches) but the results of the Christian life in a disciple. All of this material is set against the backdrop of Jesus saying the apostles are His friends (verse 15). They are elevated beyond slave status to "friends of God," an electrifying thought. Jesus again promises the Holy Spirit to the apostles in verse 26.

Applications from This Week's Readings

15:7 is one of the most important texts on prayer in all of Scripture. Do you let your relationship with Jesus and the Word of God shape your prayer requests? Back to Table of Contents.

16 - Verse 4 reinforces the book's purpose to create faith. Verse 5 does not contradict 13:36 and 14:5 because the emphasis here is on the present. Jesus says "You are not asking now." Verses 9-11 reveal much of the Spirit's work. He "convicts" people of sin, of righteousness (the right way to live), and of judgment to come. This work is done, of course, through the Word the Spirit reveals. Is there any other way a person can learn what is wrong, what is right, or what the standard of judgment will be? Verses 16-22 reveal the confusion and uncertainty still in the disciples' minds. Verse 24 shows how we can pray in Christ's name, i.e. by His authority and based on what He has accomplished for us. Remember, verses appearing to give "carte blanche" to ask for anything in prayer must be understood in concert with other verses like John 15:7.

17 - In verses 1-5 Jesus prays for Himself. He gave up His glory to come here and now prays that it be restored. Verse 3 says "only true God" but certainly doesn't mean Jesus is deity! Once again, we must not camp on one isolated scripture! Jesus is simply emphasizing their relationship in redemption and setting monotheism over against the pagan idea of polytheism so prevalent in the NT world (see 1 Thess. 1:9). In verses 6-19 Jesus prays for His disciples. Verse 6 mentions the "name" of God, which is God's character and who He is. Jesus is praying God will keep His disciples firm and faithful. In verses 20-26 Jesus prays for us! Verse 22 references glory given to us. In John glory commonly refers to the manifestation of God's character or person, especially in this prayer. Jesus has given us that glory by explaining God to us.

18 - As we would expect, John's account of the Crucifixion contains material not in the other Gospels. The Romans play a much greater role, and Gethsemane is not mentioned. New material includes the trial with Annas, answer to the High Priest and slap, conversation with Pilate, Jesus carrying the cross, John and Jesus' mother and the cry from the cross. Please note: John and the other accounts can all be harmonized but such is beyond the scope of this material. Verse 6 reveals Jesus' powerful personality. He has astounded them before (7:45-46) and here they are awed by His courage and authority. Verse 13 shows how many Jews resented Pilate's predecessor deposing Annas in 15 AD. Some still regarded him as the true High Priest. Verse 36 is a crucial statement about the Kingdom.

19 - Pilate's problem is he is a coward (see verses 8, 12). Verse 14's time frame is helpful. "Preparation" here refers to preparing the Sabbath (see Mark 15:42). John means this was the "Passover week's day of preparation" which would be Friday. Pilate must have grinned at the admission he wrung out of the Jews (verse 15). They were willing to do or say anything to accomplish their dark ends. Verses 26-27 are tender moments. It must have been terribly hard on Jesus to die in front of His mother. The "disciple Jesus loved" is John, the writer of this Gospel. Verse 28 is probably citing Psalm 69:21. There is much discussion about what medical phenomenon accounts for verse 34 but John's purpose is much simpler: He just wants the reader to know Jesus is actually dead.

20 - Why doesn't Mary know Jesus in verse 14? Perhaps her tears and the unexpectedness of seeing Jesus account for her slowness to recognize Him. Verse 17's "don't cling" is difficult to translate. Many opinions are ventured as to what Jesus meant. Probably best is the idea of "Don't cling to me as if I'm going to disappear, I am real. Stop clinging to me and go share this good news." Verse 22 is a kind of symbolic action or acted out parable of what they would receive in Acts 2. Verse 23 references the power that comes with preaching the Gospel. Sins are forgiven by preaching of the Gospel.

Applications from This Week's Readings

Chapter 20 shows how everything changes because Jesus is risen. How much thought do you give to the Resurrection? Have you considered where we would be if He had not risen? Think about it! What is the impact on you personally that Jesus arose? Read Paul's sermon in Acts 17:22-31 and 1 Corinthians 15 if you need more to think about in this connection. Back to Table of Contents.

Week 47 - John 21; 1 John 1-4

1 - Verse 3 shows how the apostles were not sure what the resurrection meant. They went to Galilee to wait for Jesus (Mark 14:28) and while waiting, went back to work. Characteristically John has the insight while Peter is quick to do (verse 7). In verses 15-19 there is the famous "feed my sheep" conversation. Much is made of the differing terms for "love"in this text but I do not believe there is a "deeper" meaning to be discerned by defining "phileo" and "agape." Both verbs are used interchangeably in John (for the love of the Father for the Son, for example, in 3:35 and 5:20). The real key here is that Peter denied three times and now affirms three times. He is affirmed by Jesus and commissioned anew. Verses 23-25 conclude John by making it clear John is the beloved disciple and he wrote this gospel.

Introduction to 1 John - Reading John's epistles after reading his gospel is a delight because these letters are so tightly linked to the truths we just read. The language, style and emphasis are all the same. While John's audience knows the truth about Jesus, they are under attack by false teachers (see 4:1; 2:18, 2:29-3:10). Some of the problems are theological, with a denial that Jesus came in the flesh (4:2; 2 John 7; 2:22). Other problems center on taking sin lightly, teaching that it is of no real concern (2:1). This may mean that we are encountering Gnosticism's ugly teachings. Gnosticism was a big melting pot of philosophies and ideas, both Greek, pagan and even Jewish. It was not systematized but its many variants generally held two main tenets: matter was bad, and knowledge was supreme. So, if matter is bad how could God put on a material body? How important is sin if it is just something we do in our physical body anyway? John's answers help every disciple better know and follow Jesus.

1 - Verse 1 refers to Jesus Christ. Verse 3 features a wonderfully illustrative use of "fellowship." Remember, in the NT "fellowship" is sharing in spiritual benefits (1 Cor. 9:23; 2 Cor. 13:13), and that is how John uses it here. Verses 5-10 make it clear that God and sin are mutually exclusive. This means sin matters to disciples and must be taken seriously!

2 - John does not want any to consider sin "normal" or "natural" (verse 1). The Christian life opposes sin (see 3:8). The commandments John writes are not new (verses 7-8), because loving God and neighbor was part of the Old Law (Deut. 6:5). They are new in the Kingdom however. Verses 12-14 contain words of encouragement, though why there is repetition and who precisely is meant here is difficult. Verse 18 reminds Christians that it is always the "last hour" because Jesus could come at any time. John then speaks of "antichrists." Here this isn't some apocalyptic, end of the world figure, but simply those who teach error about Jesus (verses 22-23). Sometimes John uses the term without even "the" in front of it. The anointing of verse 20 seems to refer to Holy Spirit given gifts, like the gift of knowledge. They had those gifts and needed to use them (see also verses 26-28).

3 - This chapter emphasizes sin's incompatibility with Christianity and loving our brethren. Verses 6 and 9 can confuse as some translations make it sound as if Christians don't sin. However, both verses refer to the practice of sin, or remaining in sin. John has already said we can sin (1:7-8, 10; 2:1) so knows that Christians do sin. But Christians won't remain in sin. The ESV has "no one born of God makes a practice of sinning" for verse 9. John then gets very practical with the concept of loving others (verses 11-18), including frank discussion of providing for others' needs (verses 17-18). Note the tie in relationship ("abides") and obedience in verse 24.

4 - Verse 2 isn't giving the only test, but the first or beginning test. Just ask if they believe Jesus

came in the flesh. Notice here that just because someone says they are led by God doesn't make it so! Testing such "messengers" is not just a good idea but required. John now revisits the theme of loving others, adding the motivation of God's love for us (verse 7). Love isn't something God just does, but is an integral part of His character (verse 8). the train of thought from v. 16 is finished. God is love, the person who lives in love remains in God, and God in him, in this mutual indwelling love is completed and is not afraid. Verse 18 completes the thought of verse 16. We abide in God, and thus our fear dies. Sin leads to fear, but love to confidence. John is probably referencing here fear of final punishment.

Applications from This Week's Readings

Over and over, John makes practical our love for God. God is invisible making our relationship with Him hard to test, but the relationship we have with our brethren is visible and immediate. Nearly everyone claims to love God. Do you? Then what have you done for your brethren that shows it? Back to Table of Contents.

Week 48 - 1 John 5; 2 John; 3 John; Rev 1-2

John 5 - We shouldn't take the statement of verse 1a as an absolute, just as verse 1b isn't always true, so this is a general test. What does verse 6's "water and blood" reference? Probably Jesus' entire ministry, from His baptism to His death. The meaning here is that the true identity of Jesus can only be seen by looking at His whole life. Note that verse 7 in the KJV and NKJV is not well done. Verse 8 seems to reference the Spirit (speaking through the Word), baptism, and the Lord's Supper as three witnesses to Jesus' authenticity. Verse 10 speaks of believing (internalizing) the witness of God. Don't let verse 14 be the only passage consulted on the matter of prayer. Focus on "asking according to His will." Verses 16-17 are famous, but simply mean that a brother who won't ask for forgiveness (the sin that will lead to death) can't be forgiven by someone else's prayers. He needs to repent and ask God for forgiveness! The NKJV for verse 18 has "does not sin" but better is the ESV's "does not keep on sinning."

Introduction to 2 and 3rd John - These two "postcard" epistles contain both doctrine and practical admonitions. 2 John seems to be addressed to a community while 3 John is clearly addressed to an individual. The purpose of both letters is to urge the disciples to continue in love toward real brethren, but turn away from false teachers.

2 John - Verse 1's "elect lady" might be a certain woman John knew, or could be a figure for the church. The letter does seem to be addressed to a group with its many plural nouns. Verse 7 shows the purpose of the epistle. Not "confessing Jesus coming in the flesh" would cover all the different errors taught about Jesus' incarnation. Verses 10-11 doesn't mean you cannot say 'hello' to a false teacher but you can't give him a greeting, or show him hospitality, that would imply an official endorsement of him and his teaching. He is to be given no chance to propagate his evil doctrine.

3 John - Verse 6 means Gaius is supplying these brothers with their physical needs. In verses 9-10 we see that living in the time of the apostles didn't solve every problem. Apparently John wrote something and Diotrephes suppressed it! Instead of imitating Diotrophes be like Demetrius (verse 12).

Introduction to Revelation - How we approach Revelation bears much thought. Error has been taught because people arrived in Revelation with preconceived notions and ideas. However, if we look at 1:1 and 1:3 we see John telling us the events in this book will happen soon (note also 3:11; 16:15; 22:7; 22:12; 22:20). Further, the book was written to encourage NT Christian under the heavy duress of persecution. If we can keep our eye on these two facts, the book's stated time frame and purpose, we will not go far astray, and speculative ideas will be easily dismissed. We will say more about understanding the signs and symbols of this grand book when we arrive at chapter 4.

1 - Verse 7 sets forth the theme of Revelation from the start. Jesus is coming to judge evildoers. Note that not every "coming" of the Lord is literal, but that this can be a figure of speech referring to a coming in judgment (see Isaiah 19:1 for an example of this kind of language). Beginning verse 13 we are treated to an awesome sight, as John sees Jesus. We should resist trying to find some symbolic meaning in these colors and clothes. Instead of dissecting it let the picture of power and majesty stand intact and let it do its work: inspire and thrill and awe us. This is Jesus Christ, King of Kings and Lord of Lords! He rules and reigns!

2 - The Nicolaitans of verse 6 are a group that taught error but we do not know much about them.

Verse 14 reminds us of Balaam (see Numbers 22-25). Clearly someone is teaching that loose sexual standards are okay. Verse 17's speaks of manna, a white stone, and a new name. What these mean specifically eludes us, but it is clear this is a blessing to he who overcomes. Jezebel, the wicked wife of Ahab, is named in verse 20, as again troubles with sexual immorality are plaguing the church. How does Jesus give the "morning star" (verse 28)? Since Jesus is the morning star (22:16) this probably refers to being in relationship with Him.

Applications from This Week's Readings

All of the churches we have read about this week had good qualities and also problems. What can we learn from this as we look at our own local congregation? What would Jesus say to your local church if He were writing to it? Try to see both positives and areas that might need improvement. Pray you will be a help to church to grow in a positive way and eliminate troubles and problems. Back to Table of Contents.

3 - Verse 7 ties Jesus to the Messianic promises made to David (see 2 Sam 7, cf. Isaiah 22:22). One of the chief troubles the NT church faced was Jewish persecution. Verse 9 brings that to the forefront, mentioning how they are not really the Israel of God. Notice Jesus' great willingness to forgive and receive penitent saints back into fellowship in verse 20.

Thoughts on Revelation 4-21 - Signs, Symbols, and Puzzles

Chapter 4 begins the Revelation in earnest, plunging us into a world of visions and signs. A few guidelines here may help us keep our bearings as we read along. First, don't forget the book's purpose and time frame from chapter 1. However we interpret these signs the material must relate to encouraging to persecuted first-century saints (see 2:10). Secondly, we need to treat this material as its nature demands. Too many find a meaning in every detail, interpeting every color, every stone, and "every paw on every claw" to mean something. In contrast watch how rarely Revelation assigns detailed specific meanings to its figures (see 4:5b). This is because apocalyptic literature (a kind of material common in the first century) was meant to deal in big ideas by presenting bold images full of action and fury. Dissecting it destroys it, as surely as trying to figure out what the hero's hat band stands for would ruin a good Western movie! We have to be content with its broad brush and big picture, and not look at the giant mural of God's fight with Satan through a magnifying glass. Finally, a word about the historical realities Revelation deals with. Clearly wild speculation about ICBM's and war with the Soviet Union is not what John was shown. How would that help persecuted Christians in the first century? Generally, a more careful view of Revelation has argued that it deals with the fall of Rome or the destruction of Jerusalem. I believe the data in the book should points to it being primarily about God's vengeance on Jerusalem. A full discussion of this is not possible here but note how the great city in Rev 11:8 and 17-18 is obviously Jerusalem. Further, the vision is dated during the reign of the sixth king (17:9-11), which would be during Nero's time, well before Jerusalem's fall. Perhaps the best argument against the book dealing with Rome is that Rome doesn't fall for hundreds of years, defying the book's promise of "shortly come to pass." Dogmatism and Revelation don't go well together, but eventually one has to make some kind of decision as to what this book is about. Thus, this material will follow the early date/destruction of Jerusalem emphasis.

4 - Verses 2-3 identify God. We need not make every color symbolize something here. The picture stands as powerful and awesome. The creatures of verses 6-7 remind us of Ezekiel's creatures who bear God's throne (see Ezek 1:4-28; 10:1ff). They are amazing and incredible beings. We are privy to God's throne room here and the worship that goes on in it. What a scene!

5 - Verse 1's scroll represents the plan of God and the ability to execute it. Only Jesus can do that (verses 5-6). Note the obvious tie in "Lamb of God" to Isaiah 53. Jesus is worshiped just as God the Father was in chapter 4, a mighty statement of His deity.

6 - The seals are opened and amazing things happen. The first seal (verse 2) has been identified as Christ, the Roman Empire or even the spirit of conquest. It is hard to be certain. Verse 4 is clearly war, perhaps the war begun in AD 67 when the Jews revolted against Rome. Verse 5 shows the pain of war, as famine follows and prices for even a little bit of food get outrageously high. Of course, death (verses 7-8) follow war. We then see persecuted saints crying for justice, a major theme in Revelation (verses 9-11). Then there are great scenes of judgment that are notably similar to what Joel 2 and Matthew 24 use to talk of Jerusalem's judgment and

destruction.

7 - The action in this chapter isn't hard to understand. A group of people are sealed for protection from all the trouble and tribulation that is occurring (verse 3). The difficulty is "Who are these sealed people?" This seems to be the faithful disciples. In verse 9 the 144,000 (a symbolic number not to be taken literally) are seen in heaven, and are now a huge multitude. Perhaps this is the same group as in verses 5-8, now seen in heaven rejoicing.

Applications from This Week's Readings

Revelation often leaves people more than a little confused and feeling like they should see "more" here. But if you got that God is in control, that He is vitally concerned about the welfare of His people and He will judge the evildoers who hurt His church, then you got the message Jesus wanted the seven churches to have. Think carefully about the calls for perseverance and faithfulness under pressure Revelation contains. What are the implications for us today? What can you do to build more endurance? Back to Table of Contents.

8 - Some have commented that Revelation is like a grand symphony, with variations to a theme being played, added, and recombined as the movements go along. That is a fitting thought as chapter 8 sounds judgments that remind us of the seal judgments. Note the value of prayer (verse 8). Prayer causes God to act! Those actions are terrifying and terrible. The trumpets probably relate to the horrors of the Judean War. The first trumpet (verse 7) may be the warfare that occurred in Galilee, the second trumpet (verses 8-9) perhaps the battles in the Mediterranean, the third trumpet (verses 10-11) sounds like an important leader defecting (compare Isa 14:12ff), and the final trumpet (verses 12-13) seem to indicate conditions in Judea as the Roman armies swung south after Galilee.

9 - The fifth angel sounds and horrible locusts arrive, wreaking havoc (verses 1-12). There is much discussion and just as much uncertainty about their identity. They may represent the Jewish Zealots who took over the rebellion and killed many of their fellow Jews. Josephus describes the fierce infighting among the Jews even as the Romans marched against them! Perhaps the locusts and the huge army of the sixth trumpet just represent evil demonic forces at work. The sixth trumpet (verses 13-21) does summon a gargantuan army. The Roman general Titus brought armies from across the Euphrates to help his war efforts. The real emphasis is verses 20-21. Despite God bringing judgment people didn't repent. How sad!

10 - This chapter represents a pause in the judgments. A mighty angel (verse 1) appears and gives John a book (verse 2). The little book may be the rest of the message of Revelation (see verse 11). This is all very similar to Ezekiel 2:6-3:4 and probably means the same thing: John is commissioned to speak for God. Part of that speaking will be to warn that the time of delay is over (verse 7). Note the parallel in this verse and Luke 21:22, which certainly speaks of Jerusalem's destruction. Judgement is coming!

11 - John measures the temple (verse 1), which may be the literal temple, the church, or have a figurative meaning. Verse 2 gives the exact amount of time it took the Romans to end the rebellion: 42 months, from February AD 67 to August of AD 70. The two witnesses (verse 3) are prophets (verse 10) and appear to represent the Old Law. Moses and Elijah often sum up the Old Testament as the Law and the Prophets (see Matt 17). They die when the Temple is destroyed because the Old Covenant was based in that Temple and its rites (verses 7-8). The world rejoices because it hated the Jews and their peculiar laws and customs (verse 10). Following their resurrection the woes finish and Jerusalem is utterly judged (verses 14-19). Verse 19 shows that what was lost on earth is gained in heaven, as the literal temple is not needed and is now gone.

12 - The action here is not hard to follow. Jesus is born and the devil tries to kill Him before He can even begin His mission. Some of the specifics may be tougher. The woman of (verse 1) is not the church as Christ built the church not the other way around. This is probably the faithful remnant of Israel who kept the Messianic promises alive down through the centuries. There is no question the child is Jesus (verse 5), and that the remnant goes to the wilderness during the Jewish War for the 42 months it lasted, as Matt 24:16-18 instructed. The war in heaven (verse 7) is symbolic. The devil is defeated by Jesus' redemptive work (verse 11). The devil continues to attack the church (verses 13-14) but as verse 6 described she flees into the desert where God providentially protects her (verse 16).

Applications from This Week's Readings

One of the purposes of apocalyptic literature is to interpret the events happening on earth in light of the spiritual struggle going on between God and the devil. The destruction of Jerusalem looked like a military operation but was actually God's work, John says. We cannot always know how and where God is working today but let Revelation strengthen your belief that God is working and that there is still a battle going on between good and evil. Pray and ask God to help you find your part in this conflict and to fight very courageously. Back to Table of Contents.

Week 51 - Revelation 13-17

13 - The key question here is who or what is this beast (verse 1)? The best identification seems he obvious choice: the Roman Empire. The ten horns would be the tributary kingdoms that served the emperor. Rather than "symbolizing" the description of the beast (verse 2) we should just see a terrifying and strong foe. Verse 3 may reference how many thought Rome would die when Julius Caesar was assassinated but it did not. Others see the myth that Nero would revive and rule again, but why would John mention a legend? Some see the beast as Satan, instead of the Empire that Satan used, and thus this could refer to the defeat of Satan at the cross. Verse 10 echoes Jeremiah 15:2. The text is difficult to translate, and harder to be certain of its meaning. It may be a call for patience and perseverance. A second beast then appears (verses 11-18) who personifies false religion. He can do signs and sorcery, like Pharaoh's magicians (Exo 7-8). The key is he is a deceiver (verse 14). This is probably the religion of emperor worship, which was Empire-wide in Nero's time. The marks of verse 16 are not necessarily literal (we have a speaking beast calling fire out of heaven here - clearly literal - but then many make this mark absolutely literal!) but instead indicate submission and service to the Emperor. Those who refuse will suffer financial and social recriminations. Verse 18 is heavily debated. Every six-letter name possible has been fitted to this scheme where a number equals a letter, but Nero Caesar seems to be the best fit when the purposes of the book are considered.

14 - This chapter shows that not all succumb to the beast and his pressures. A huge throng, as seen in chapter 7, worship God still (verses 1-5). Three angels make announcements warning not to fall in with the beast (verses 6-13). Then there are two reapings. Perhaps the first is the saints who were martyred (verses 14-16), while the second seems to be an image of judgment (verses 17-20). That judgment picture will be seen again and amplified in chapters to come.

15 - God's people are seen victorious. They have overcome and will now see a just and powerful God answer their cries for justice!

16 - The winepress scene in chapter 14 gives way to bowls of judgment poured out. These judgements represent terrible affliction and horror of every kind. It is not necessary for us to find exact correspondence to historical events. In the Jewish War there was every kind of misery and death imaginable, including starvation, famine, civil war, and slaughter at the hands of Roman troops. Verse 6 is key. The punishment fits the crime, and the crime here is killing God's people and His prophets. Jesus said of Jerusalem "O Jerusalem, Jerusalem, the city that kills the prophets and stones those who are sent to it!" (Matt 23:37). Much has been made of the three frogs (verse 13) but these seem to be demonic forces that join in the misery and havoc of war. All of Satan's forces gather at Armageddon (verse 16) but notice there is no battle. Judgment is simply announced and then it is all over (verse 17). Such is God's power!

17 - The key identification here is the harlot (verse 1). Many see her as Rome, but Rome was not guilty of spiritual harlotry, as Israel was accused of by the O.T. prophets (Jeremiah 3:1ff; Hosea 2). Further, the beast is Rome. The Empire carried the harlot, the city of Jerusalem (and the Jews) by allowing them special privileges and prerogatives no one else in the Empire enjoyed. Verse 10 helps us date the book. The first six emperors were Julius, Augustus, Tiberius, Caligula, Claudius and then the sixth "which now is" would be Nero. Vespasian would be next, and his son Titus would be the eighth, hence being "of him" (verse 11). The ten kings of verse 12 are the puppet kings or subservient kings who served Rome. Jerusalem did sit upon many people (verse 2), as Jews came from all over the world to worship there. Further, tithes from the Jews

made her enormously wealthy city. This harlot or "great city" (verse 18) is positively identified in 11:8 as Jerusalem. She did rule, in a sense, by her authority over Jews scattered throughout the Empire.

Applications from This Week's Readings

We are very comfortable with civil liberties and Constitutional guarantees of the right to assemble and worship as we please. Do we take these freedoms for granted? What would you do if there was an outbreak of persecution today? Offer a prayer of thanksgiving that we have not had to live through such terrible times, and then ask God for more courage to be what He would have us to be in our (comparatively) easier day and times. Back to Table of Contents.

Week 52 - Revelation 18-22

18 - Verses 1-8 announce the doom of the city, and warn God's people to flee (see Matt 24:15-18). Verse 3 says Jerusalem is judged for her fornication (religious unfaithfulness to God). Think of how the rulers conspired to kill Jesus because they saw Him as a threat to their standing with Rome (see John 11:48ff). The world laments Jerusalem's fall because of the economic consequences (verses 9-19). But while the world laments the righteous rejoice in God's vengeance (verses 20-24). Again note the emphasis on "prophets" and the close parallels to Matt 23:34-37 and Luke 11:49-51.

19 - God is praised for His victory (verses 1-6), and the victorious are invited to a great feast called the marriage supper of the Lamb (verses 7-10). Verses 11-21 portray Christ going out to conquer and demolish His enemies. This may refer to the battle between the church and the Roman Empire. After Jerusalem was destroyed the Roman Empire did persecute the church (verses 19). But such efforts cannot possibly succeed, for they are fighting against God! The chapter ends again in triumph. The harlot has been judged and now the beast who supported her is judged and destroyed (verses 20-21). Is there a reference to the Word of God and Gospel preaching in the sword from Jesus' mouth (verse 15, 21)?

20 - This chapter is the premillenial position's mainstay. The teaching that Jesus failed in His first attempt to set up a physical kingdom and so will return to set up that literal kingdom and reign in physical Jerusalem for 1000 years is somehow pulled from these verses. Such contradicts other plain verses (like John 18:36; Mark 9:1; Col 1:13) and badly misuses Revelation itself. Note how the chapter says nothing about the second coming of Christ, a bodily resurrection, a reign of Christ on earth, the literal throne of David, or literal Jerusalem! Read carefully and we see that verses 1-3 tell us Satan will be bound for a long period of time (the thousand years of verse 3). Remember, the book has been promising "shortly come to pass" but now leaps far ahead with a time frame of a thousand years. The binding of Satan during this time probably represents the power of the Gospel limiting Satan during the Gospel age (see Matt 12:29; John 12:31-32). We shouldn't make the 1000 years a literal time frame any more than we would make the souls of verse 4 literally be headless (see Deut 7:9 and Ps 50:10 for use of 1000 to simply mean "lots"). Verse 4 means that the faithful, the overcomers, participate in Christ's victory. "The rest" (verse 5) are those of 19:21: the unfaithful. The "first resurrection" (verses 5-6) is when one dies to go and be with Christ. The "second death" is eternal condemnation (see 20:14-15; 21:8). Thus, the second resurrection will be when our bodies are raised, making the first death be when we die physically. Verses 7-9 tell us that after a while the Gospel will not have the binding effect it once did. Does this mean more and more people will turn from God's word and not listen to it? So Satan rallies and persecution breaks out again (verse 7). "Gog and Magog" (verse 8) are from Ezekiel 38, where they appear as enemies of God's people. They may attempt to attack the church but Jesus suddenly destroys them (verses 9-10). This may be Jesus' second coming (see 2 Thess 1:7-9), which leads directly into a scene of judgment (verses 11-15). This may well be the Final Judgement of all humanity.

21 - Many see this as a description of the church, not heaven. However, key parts of the description just don't fit the church on earth (note verses 3-4, also 21:3-4). After the judgment of chapter 20 eternity begins and heaven welcomes the saints! Note that the destroyed city is replaced with the New Jerusalem (verses 2, 10). The measurements of the city (verses 16-17) are enormous and the foundation stones, gates and streets are incredibly expensive and beautiful (verses 18-21). We don't have to make each gate or mineral mean something. It all describes

heaven as a place of magnificence, splendor and wonder. The literal temple has been destroyed but there is no need for such in this city (verse 22).

22 - This is God's home (22:1), and someday we will live there with Him! The book concludes with its refrain that its main events will happen soon (verses 6-7, 10-12, 20). Verse 11 probably just means there would be no time for last minute repentance. Note the repeated calls to remain faithful and not give up. Trust that Jesus will be victorious and stand with Him!

Applications from This Week's Readings

Chapter 21-22's pictures of heaven call to our hearts. Don't focus overly on the wealth of golden streets or make heaven into some sort of grand retirement center. John focuses on being in God's presence (21:3-4, 22; 22:1-5). Think about being with the Lord and pray that these grand scenes will move your heart to greater steadfastness and endurance. Back to Table of Contents.

Congratulations on completing the reading of the New Testament this year!

www.BibleClassMaterial.com
Lower Lights Publications
3808 Horizon Drive
Bedford, Texas 76021
817-267-8296

Made in the USA
Columbia, SC
02 January 2020